P9-DNB-673

WITHDRAWN

WITHDRAWN

Taking SIDES

Clashing Views on Controversial American History, Volume I, The Colonial Period to Reconstruction

Eighth Edition

Edited, Selected, and with Introductions by

Larry Madaras
Howard Community College

and
James M. SoRelle
Baylor University

Dushkin/McGraw-Hill
A Division of The McGraw-Hill Companies

To Maggie and Cindy

Photo Acknowledgments

Cover image: © 2000 by PhotoDisc, Inc.

Cover Art Acknowledgment

Charles Vitelli

Manufactured in the United States of America

Eighth Edition

123456789BAHBAH3210

Library of Congress Cataloging-in-Publication Data

Main entry under title:
    Taking sides: clashing views on controversial American history, volume I, the colonial period to reconstruction/edited, selected, and with introductions by Larry Madaras and James M. SoRelle.—8th ed.
    Includes bibliographical references and index.
    1. United States—History. I. Madaras, Larry, *comp.* II. SoRelle, James M., *comp.*
                                                                              973
    0-07-303188-7   ISSN: 1091-8833

Printed on Recycled Paper

PREFACE

The success of the past seven editions of *Taking Sides: Clashing Views on Controversial Issues in American History* has encouraged us to remain faithful to its original objectives, methods, and format. Our aim has been to create an effective instrument to enhance classroom learning and to foster critical thinking. Historical facts presented in a vacuum are of little value to the educational process. For students, whose search for historical truth often concentrates on *when* something happened rather than on *why*, and on specific events rather than on the *significance* of those events, *Taking Sides* is designed to offer an interesting and valuable departure. The understanding that the reader arrives at based on the evidence that emerges from the clash of views encourages the reader to view history as an *interpretive* discipline, not one of rote memorization.

As in previous editions, the issues are arranged in chronological order and can be easily incorporated into any American history survey course. Each issue has an issue *introduction*, which sets the stage for the debate that follows in the pro and con selections and provides historical and methodological background to the problem that the issue examines. Each issue concludes with a *postscript*, which ties the readings together, briefly mentions alternative interpretations, and supplies detailed *suggestions for further reading* for the student who wishes to pursue the topics raised in the issue. Also, Internet site addresses (URLs) have been provided on the *On the Internet* page that accompanies each part opener, which should prove useful as starting points for further research.

Changes to this edition   In this edition we have continued our efforts to maintain a balance between the traditional political, diplomatic, and cultural issues and the new social history, which depicts a society that benefited from the presence of African Americans, women, and workers of various racial and ethnic backgrounds. With this in mind, we present eight entirely new issues: *Was Columbus an Imperialist?* (Issue 2); *Did Thomas Jefferson Abandon His Political Ideals in Purchasing the Louisiana Territory?* (Issue 7); *Was Andrew Jackson's Indian Removal Policy Motivated by Humanitarian Impulses?* (Issue 8); *Were the Abolitionists "Unrestrained Fanatics"?* (Issue 9); *Did the Westward Movement Transform the Traditional Roles of Women in the Mid-Nineteenth Century?* (Issue 12); *Was the North's Victory Over the South Inevitable?* (Issue 14); *Did Abraham Lincoln Free the Slaves?* (Issue 15); and *Was It Wrong to Impeach Andrew Johnson?* (Issue 16). In addition, for Issue 3, *Was the Colonial Period a "Golden Age" for Women in America?* the NO side has been replaced to bring a fresh perspective to the debate. In all, there are 17 new selections.

i

A word to the instructor An *Instructor's Manual With Test Questions* (multiple-choice and essay) is available through the publisher for the instructor using *Taking Sides* in the classroom. A general guidebook, *Using Taking Sides in the Classroom*, which discusses methods and techniques for integrating the pro-con approach into any classroom setting, is also available. An online version of *Using Taking Sides in the Classroom* and a correspondence service for Taking Sides adopters can be found at http://www.dushkin.com/usingts/. For students, we offer a field guide to analyzing argumentative essays, *Analyzing Controversy: An Introductory Guide,* with exercises and techniques to help them to decipher genuine controversies.

    Taking Sides: Clashing Views on Controversial Issues in American History, Volume I is only one title in the Taking Sides series. If you are interested in seeing the table of contents for any of the other titles, please visit the Taking Sides Web site at http://www.dushkin.com/takingsides/.

Acknowledgments Many individuals have contributed to the successful completion of this edition. We appreciate the evaluations submitted to Dushkin/McGraw-Hill by those who have used *Taking Sides* in the classroom. Special thanks to those who responded with specific suggestions for this edition:

Gary Best
University of Hawaii at Hilo

James D. Bolton
Coastline Community
  College

Mary Borg
University of Northern
  Colorado

John Whitney Evans
College of St. Scholastica

Gordon Lam
Sierra College

Andrew O'Shaugnessy
University of
  Wisconsin–Oshkosh

Elliot Pasternack
Middlesex County College

Robert M. Paterson
Armstrong State College

Ethan S. Rafuse
University of Missouri at
  Kansas City

John Reid
Ohio State University–Lima

Murray Rubinstein
CUNY Baruch College

Neil Sapper
Amarillo College

Preston Shea
Plymouth State College

We are particularly indebted to Maggie Cullen, Cindy SoRelle, Barry A. Crouch, Virginia Kirk, Joseph and Helen Mitchell, and Jean Soto, who shared their ideas for changes, pointed us toward potentially useful historical works, and provided significant editorial assistance. Megan Arnold and Anne Marku-lis (Howard Community College) performed indispensable typing duties connected with this project. Susan E. Myers in the library at Howard Com-munity College provided essential help in acquiring books and articles on interlibrary loan. Finally, we are sincerely grateful for the commitment, en-couragement, and patience provided over the years by David Dean, former list manager for the Taking Sides series, David Brackley, senior developmen-tal editor, and the entire staff of Dushkin/McGraw-Hill.

Larry Madaras
Howard Community College

James M. SoRelle
Baylor University

CONTENTS IN BRIEF

CONTENTS

Professor of public policy Seymour Martin Lipset describes the United States
as an "outlier" because of its revolutionary origins and because statistically
it is more religious, optimistic, patriotic, rights-oriented, and individualistic
than other nations in the world. Professor of history Ian Tyrrell criticizes the
national focus of the concept of American exceptionalism and advocates the
development of a "transnational" history.

Kirkpatrick Sale, a contributing editor of *The Nation*, characterizes Christopher Columbus as an imperialist who was determined to conquer both the
land and the people he encountered. Robert Royal, vice president for research
at the Ethics and Public Policy Center, objects to Columbus's modern-day
critics and insists that Columbus should be admired for his courage, his willingness to take a risk, and his success in advancing knowledge about other
parts of the world.

Adjunct professor Lois Green Carr and historian Lorena S. Walsh identify
several factors that coalesced to afford women in seventeenth-century Maryland a higher status with fewer restraints on their social conduct than those
experienced by women in England. Professor Mary Beth Norton challenges
the "golden age" theory by insisting that women in colonial America typically
occupied a domestic sphere that was lacking in status, physically debilitating
over time, and a barrier to educational opportunity and political power.

Professor emeritus of American history Carl N. Degler argues that the status
of Africans in the English colonies developed within a framework of discrimination against peoples of African descent that predated the establishment of
a permanent status of slavery. Professor of history Oscar Handlin and author
Mary F. Handlin insist that black slavery developed out of severe labor demands in the colonies rather than as a response to any unique qualities of or
attitudes toward Africans.

Professor of history Patricia U. Bonomi defines the Great Awakening as a
period of intense revivalistic fervor that spawned an age of contentiousness
in the British mainland colonies. Professor of American history Jon Butler
argues that the colonial revivalistic activities of the eighteenth century had a
limited impact on pre-Revolutionary American society.

Political scientist John P. Roche asserts that the Founding Fathers were superb democratic politicians who created a Constitution that supported the needs of the nation and at the same time was acceptable to the people. Historian Alfred F. Young argues that the Founding Fathers were an elite group of college-educated lawyers, merchants, slaveholding planters, and "monied men" who were forced to make some democratic accommodations in writing the Constitution in order to ensure its acceptance.

David A. Carson, associate professor of history and social studies education, states that Thomas Jefferson initially abandoned his ideological commitment to states' rights and strict constructionism by his decision to support the acquisition of the Louisiana Territory. Barry J. Balleck, assistant professor of political science, concludes that Jefferson agreed to purchase the Louisiana Territory in support of his most deeply held political principle—the protection of republican government.

Professor Robert V. Remini argues that Andrew Jackson sincerely believed that the Indian Removal Act of 1830 was the only way to protect Native Americans from annihilation at the hands of white settlers. Historian and anthropologist Anthony F. C. Wallace counters that Andrew Jackson oversaw a harsh policy with regard to Native Americans. This policy resulted in the usurpation of land, attempts to destroy tribal culture, and the forcible removal of Native Americans from the southeastern United States.

Historian Avery Craven asserts that the fanaticism of the abolitionist crusade created an atmosphere of crisis that resulted in the outbreak of the Civil War. Irving Bartlett, retired professor of American civilization, differentiates between agitation and fanaticism and states that abolitionists like Wendell Phillips were deeply committed to improving the quality of life for all Americans.

Professor of history Albert J. Raboteau argues that the religious activities of American slaves were characterized by institutional and personal independence. Professor of history John B. Boles asserts that the primary religious experience of Southern slaves occurred within a biracial setting in churches dominated by whites.

Professor of history Rodolfo Acuña argues that Euroamericans waged unjust and aggressive wars against the Mexican government in the 1830s and 1840s. Professor of diplomatic history Norman A. Graebner argues that President James Polk pursued an aggressive policy that he believed would work without starting a war.

Professor of history Sandra L. Myres (1933–1991) argues that first- and second-generation American women often worked outside the home as teachers, missionaries, doctors, lawyers, ranchers, miners, and business people. According to professor John Mack Faragher, women were reluctant pioneers because they were unwilling to break away from their close network of female relatives and friends. However, nineteenth century marital laws gave their husbands the sole authority to make the decision to move west.

Professor of history Joel H. Silbey argues that historians have overemphasized the sectional conflict over slavery as the primary event leading to the Civil War. Professor of history Michael F. Holt maintains that both northern Republicans and southern Democrats seized the slavery issue to reinvigorate the loyalty of party voters.

Professor Richard N. Current maintains that it was the South's lack of man-power and economic resources and not the North's military superiority that doomed the Confederacy. Professor Albert Castel argues that the North's victory over the South was due to luck. Also, Northern military successes in the fall of 1864 helped to reelect President Abraham Lincoln, destroying the chance for a negotiated settlement rather than a defeat for the South.

Historian James M. McPherson maintains that Abraham Lincoln was the indispensable agent in emancipating the slaves through his condemnation of slavery as a moral evil, his refusal to compromise on the question of slavery's expansion, his skillful political leadership, and his implementation and direction of Union troops as an army of liberation. Professor Vincent Harding credits slaves themselves for engaging in a dramatic movement of self-liberation. Abraham Lincoln initially refused to declare the destruction of slavery as a war aim and then issued the Emancipation Proclamation, which failed to free any slaves in areas over which he had any authority.

Historian Irving Brant argues that President Andrew Johnson was the victim of partisan Republican politics and that the articles of impeachment passed by the House of Representatives violated the U.S. Constitution. Professor of history Harold M. Hyman contends that Congress's decision to impeach President Johnson was wholly justifiable on constitutional grounds in light of Johnson's repeated defiance of national law.

INTRODUCTION

The Study of History

Larry Madaras
James M. SoRelle

In a pluralistic society such as ours, the study of history is bound to be a complex process. How an event is interpreted depends not only on the existing evidence but also on the perspective of the interpreter. Consequently, understanding history presupposes the evaluation of information, a task that often leads to conflicting conclusions. An understanding of history, then, requires the acceptance of the idea of historical relativism. Relativism means that redefinition of our past is always possible and desirable. History shifts, changes, and grows with new and different evidence and interpretations. As is the case with the law and even with medicine, beliefs that were unquestioned 100 or 200 years ago have been discredited or discarded since.

Relativism, then, encourages revisionism. There is a maxim that "the past must remain useful to the present." Historian Carl Becker argued that every generation should examine history for itself, thus ensuring constant scrutiny of our collective experience through new perspectives. History, consequently, does not remain static, in part because historians cannot avoid being influenced by the times in which they live. Almost all historians commit themselves to revising the views of other historians, synthesizing theories into macrointerpretations, or revising the revisionists.

SCHOOLS OF THOUGHT

Three predominant schools of thought have emerged in American history since the first graduate seminars in history were given at the Johns Hopkins University in Baltimore in the 1870s. The *progressive* school dominated the professional field in the first half of the twentieth century. Influenced by the reform currents of Populism, progressivism, and the New Deal, these historians explored the social and economic forces that energized America. The progressive scholars tended to view the past in terms of conflicts between groups, and they sympathized with the underdog.

The post–World War II period witnessed the emergence of a new group of historians who viewed the conflict thesis as overly simplistic. Writing against the backdrop of the cold war, these *neoconservative* or *consensus* historians argued that Americans possess a shared set of values and that the areas of agreement within the nation's basic democratic and capitalistic framework were more important than the areas of disagreement.

In the 1960s, however, the civil rights movement, women's liberation, and the student rebellion (with its condemnation of the war in Vietnam) fragmented the consensus of values upon which historians and social scientists of the 1950s had centered their interpretations. This turmoil set the stage for the emergence of another group of scholars. *New Left* historians began to reinterpret the past once again. They emphasized the significance of conflict in American history, and they resurrected interest in those groups ignored by the consensus school. In addition, New Left historians critiqued the expansionist policies of the United States and emphasized the difficulties confronted by Native Americans, African Americans, women, and urban workers in gaining full citizenship status.

Progressive, consensus, and New Left history is still being written. The most recent generation of scholars, however, focuses upon social history. Their primary concern is to discover what the lives of "ordinary Americans" were really like. These new social historians employ previously overlooked court and church documents, house deeds and tax records, letters and diaries, photographs, and census data to reconstruct the everyday lives of average Americans. Some employ new methodologies, such as quantification (enhanced by advancing computer technology) and oral history, while others borrow from the disciplines of political science, economics, sociology, anthropology, and psychology for their historical investigations.

The proliferation of historical approaches, which are reflected in the issues debated in this book, has had mixed results. On the one hand, historians have become so specialized in their respective time periods and methodological styles that it is difficult to synthesize the recent scholarship into a comprehensive text for the general reader. On the other hand, historians know more about the American past than at any other time in history. They dare to ask new questions or ones that previously were considered to be germane only to scholars in other social sciences. Although there is little agreement about the answers to these questions, the methods employed and issues explored make the "new history" a very exciting field to study.

The topics that follow represent a variety of perspectives and approaches. Each of these controversial issues can be studied for its individual importance to our nation's history. Taken as a group, they interact with one another to illustrate larger historical themes. When grouped thematically, the issues reveal continuing motifs in the development of American history.

COMPARATIVE HISTORY: AMERICA IN A GLOBAL PERSPECTIVE

Issue 1, on American exceptionalism, examines the historical development of the United States from a global perspective. Seymour Martin Lipset presents the United States as the only nation that defines itself on the basis of an ideology of liberty, egalitarianism, individualism, populism, and laissez-faire. His viewpoint is countered by Ian Tyrrell, who emphasizes that the themes of U.S. historical development are variations of those that are common to other nations. He encourages a global view.

The role of American history within the larger framework of world history is central to the discussion presented in Issue 2, as well. Kirkpatrick Sale places the "discovery" of America by Christopher Columbus within the context of European imperialism of the late fifteenth century. Robert Royal takes Sale and other Columbus denigrators to task for failing to recognize Columbus's courage and the many benefits derived from his and other European explorer's voyages to the New World.

A discussion of early nineteenth century foreign policy in Issue 11 concerns both United States diplomatic relations with the rest of the world and our self-perception within the world of nations. Did the United States government conceive of its power as continental, hemispheric, or worldwide? And what were the consequences of these attitudes? Rodolfo Acuña argues that the United States waged a racist and imperialistic war against Mexico for the purpose of conquering what became the American Southwest. Norman A. Graebner contends that President James K, Polk pursued an aggressive (but not imperialistic) policy that would force Mexico to recognize the U.S. annexation of Texas and to sell New Mexico and California to its northern neighbor without starting a war.

NEW SOCIAL HISTORY

Some of the most innovative historical research over the last 30 years reflects the interests of the new social historians. The work of several representatives of this group who treat the issues of gender and race appears in this volume.

Two issues explore the field of women's history. One question frequently asked is whether or not the colonial period was a "golden age" for women in America. In Issue 3, Lois Green Carr and Lorena S. Walsh argue that "immigrant predominance, early death, late marriage and sexual imbalance" gave women in early Maryland power in the household that English women did not enjoy. Mary Beth Norton, however, challenges the "golden age" theory by emphasizing the subordinate status occupied by colonial women in virtually every aspect of their daily lives.

Issue 12 examines women as participants in the westward movement of the mid-nineteenth century. Sandra L. Myers portrays the frontier as a liberating environment for both men and women. Westering women did not just stay at home and raise a family; they often worked as teachers and nurses as well as in nontraditional occupations as physicians, lawyers, ranchers, shopkeepers, and salespersons. John Mack Faragher reminds us that men were largely responsible for the decision to move their families west even when the women in those families preferred to maintain their existing female networks.

Within the past three decades, our perception of blacks in American history has changed dramatically. More consideration has been given to African Americans as active participants in the development of America, not simply as "victims" or "problems." In Issue 4, Carl N. Degler concludes that the presence of racial prejudice created a favorable environment for the establishment of a system of race-based slavery. Oscar Handlin and Mary F. Handlin, however, believe that colonial labor shortages, not racism, provided the justification for the enslavement of peoples of African descent.

Many scholars have considered the impact of the slave system on the black community, including religious institutions. In Issue 10, Albert J. Raboteau argues that slaves were able to maintain their own systems of religious worship without interference from their masters. John B. Boles, on the other hand, insists that the primary religious activities in which slaves engaged operated in a biracial setting in the churches of their masters.

RELIGION, REFORM, AND WAR

Beyond suggesting that much of the colonizing experiment in British North America was motivated by a search for religious freedom, many textbooks avoid extended discussions of religion as a force in history. In the last half-century, however, professional historians have assumed that the religious revivals of the mid-eighteenth century, known as the "Great Awakening," sparked intercolonial unity, and some have described this event as a direct precursor to the political upheaval of the American Revolution. In Issue 5, Patricia U. Bonomi offers a traditional view of the Great Awakening as a series of revivals occurring throughout the American colonies from 1739 to 1745, which generated a divisiveness that affected a number of religious, social, and political institutions. Jon Butler denies that any great unified revival movement emerged in the eighteenth century, and he suggests that historians should abandon altogether the label "Great Awakening."

During the 1830s and 1840s, a wave of reformism swept across the United States. Various individuals and groups sought to strengthen the democratic experiment in the nation by ridding the society of its imperfections. Issue 8 is framed within the context of the role of humanitarianism in the formulation of public policy with regard to Native Americans. Robert V. Remini insists that President Andrew Jackson's support for the Indian Removal Act of 1830 was predicated on Jackson's desire to protect Native Americans from almost certain annihilation at the hands of white settlers in the southeastern United States. Anthony F. C. Wallace depicts Jackson as a key initiator of the brutal program of forced removal of several tribes from their long-time homeland.

The major and most controversial reform effort in the pre–Civil War period was the movement to abolish slavery. Issue 9 deals with the motivations of those who became abolitionists. Avery Craven states that the Civil War was caused unnecessarily by extremists in both the North and the South. In particular, Craven denounces the abolitionists as irresponsible fanatics who filled their propagandistic literature and speeches with lies about lazy, aristocratic plantation owners who constantly brutalized their slaves. Irving H. Bartlett's sympathetic portrayal of Wendell Phillips reflects a revisionist approach to the abolitionists.

The Civil War is one of the most frequently studied episodes in American history. An enormous volume of literature has emerged that addresses the military decisions and battlefield engagements that comprised the war. In Issue 14, Richard N. Current attributes the Union victory to diminishing manpower and economic resources in the Confederacy rather than to Northern military superiority. While Current concludes that this result was inevitable, Albert Castel argues that it was more a product of luck.

POLITICS IN AMERICA

The American people gave legitimacy to their revolution through the establishment of a republican form of government. The United States has existed under two constitutions: The first established the short-lived confederation from 1781 to 1789; the second was written in 1787 and remains in effect over 200 years later. In Issue 6, John P. Roche contends that the drafters of the Constitution of the United States were democratic reformers. Alfred F. Young argues that the Founding Fathers were an elitist group who made some democratic accommodations in framing the Constitution to make sure it was acceptable to the democratically controlled ratifying conventions.

No discussion of American politics is complete without an examination of the lives of some of the key presidents. Two of the greatest (according to historians) were Thomas Jefferson and Abraham Lincoln. Issue 7 examines Jefferson's political idealogy and seeks to determine the degree to which he remained committed to his beliefs once he entered the White House. With respect to the decision to purchase the Louisiana Territory from the French in 1803, David A. Carson argues that Jefferson betrayed a philosophical commitment to strict constructionism and states' rights. Barry J. Balleck maintains that President Jefferson's decision with regard to Louisiana was consistent with his most deeply held political goals—the protection and expansion of republican government.

Abraham Lincoln's image as "the Great Emancipator" is the focus of the essays in Issue 15. James M. McPherson supports the view that Lincoln's leadership was essential to ending slavery. Vincent Harding, however, defends the position that slaves were the agents of their own freedom, while Lincoln was reluctant to make emancipation a war issue.

Most historians have argued that Lincoln became president in 1860 because sectional conflicts over the slavery issue divided the nation and destroyed the second political party system, which was comprised of Whigs and Democrats, in the late 1850s. Political historians, employing a statistical analysis of election issues, voter behavior, and legislative patterns on the local, state, and national levels, however, have rejected or significantly modified the traditional emphasis on sectionalism in the 1850s. In Issue 13, Joel H. Silbey argues that historians have paid too much attentions to the sectional conflict over slavery and have neglected to analyze local ethnocultural issues as keys to the Civil War. Michael F. Holt maintains that both Northern Republicans and Southern Democrats seized the slavery issue to highlight the sharp differences existing between them and thus to reinvigorate the loyalty of their traditional partisans.

One of the political and constitutional crises of the era of Reconstruction was the impeachment and trial of President Andrew Johnson. In Issue 16, Irving Brant condemns the partisan process by which Johnson was threatened with removal from office. Harold M. Hyman, however, concludes that Johnson's repeated defiance of the Congress and national law provided clear justification for the impeachment efforts against him.

CONCLUSION

The process of historical study should rely more on thinking than on memorizing data. Once the basics of who, what, when, and where are determined, historical thinking shifts to a higher gear. Analysis, comparison and contrast, evaluation, and explanation take command. These skills not only increase our knowledge of the past but they also provide general tools for the comprehension of all the topics about which human beings think.

The diversity of a pluralistic society, however, creates some obstacles to comprehending the past. The spectrum of differing opinions on any particular subject eliminates the possibility of quick and easy answers. In the final analysis, conclusions are often built through a synthesis of several different interpretations, but, even then, they may be partial and tentative.

The study of history in a pluralistic society allows each citizen the opportunity to reach independent conclusions about the past. Since most, if not all, historical issues affect the present and future, understanding the past becomes essential to social progress. Many of today's problems have a direct connection with the past. Additionally, other contemporary issues may lack obvious direct antecedents, but historical investigation can provide illuminating analogies. At first, it may appear confusing to read and to think about opposing historical views, but the survival of our democratic society depends on such critical thinking by acute and discerning minds.

On the Internet . . .

http://www.dushkin.com

Institute for the Study of Civic Values

The Institute for the Study of Civic Values is a nonprofit organization established in Philadelphia in 1973 to promote the fulfillment of America's historic civic ideals. At a time when millions of Americans are struggling to identify the values that we share, the institute believes that it is our civic values—the principles embodied in the Declaration of Independence, the Constitution, and the Bill of Rights—that bring us together as a people.
http://www.libertynet.org/edcivic/iscvhome.html

The Columbus Navigation Homepage

This noted site by Keith A. Pickering examines the history, navigation, and landfall of Christopher Columbus. Click on "Links to other sites about Columbus and his times" to find dozens of sites on Columbus, including scholarly papers on Columbus's treatment of the American Indians.
http://www1.minn.net/~keithp/

Excerpts from Slave Narratives

Steven Mintz, from the University of Houston, has edited and presents here dozens of excerpts from slave narratives. The excerpts are organized by category, including conditions of slave life, religion, resistance, and emancipation.
http://vi.uh.edu/pages/mintz/primary.htm

Spiritual Leaders During the Great Awakening

This site is devoted to some spiritual leaders of the Great Awakening.
http://dylee.keel.econ.ship.edu/ubf/leaders/leaders.htm

PART 1

Colonial Society

Colonial settlement took place in the context of conditions that were unique to that time and place. The ethnic identity of the colonists affected their relations with Native Americans and Africans, as well as with each other. Many of the attitudes, ideals, and institutions that emerged from the colonial experience served the early settlers well and are still emulated today. Others, such as slavery and racism, have left a less positive legacy.

■ Is America Exceptional?

■ Was Columbus an Imperialist?

■ Was the Colonial Period a "Golden Age" for Women in America?

■ Did Racism Cause the Enslavement of Africans in America?

■ Was There a Great Awakening in Mid-Eighteenth-Century America?

ISSUE 1

Is America Exceptional?

YES: Seymour Martin Lipset, from *American Exceptionalism: A Double-Edged Sword* (W. W. Norton, 1996)

NO: Ian Tyrrell, from "American Exceptionalism in an Age of International History," *American Historical Review* (October 1991)

ISSUE SUMMARY

YES: Professor of public policy Seymour Martin Lipset describes the United States as an "outlier" because of its revolutionary origins and because statistically it is more religious, optimistic, patriotic, rights-oriented, and individualistic than other nations in the world.

NO: Professor of history Ian Tyrrell criticizes the national focus of the concept of American exceptionalism and advocates the development of a "transnational" history, which focuses upon themes of historical development common to the United States and other countries.

In 1994 House Speaker Newt Gingrich told members of the Heritage Foundation that it was time to "reassert American exceptionalism." The message was clear: the United States had lost those qualities that distinguished it from other nations around the world. Indeed, Gingrich was merely recognizing what a number of social scientists and historians had been saying for the past 20 years—that the concept of American exceptionalism had diminished as U.S. claims to preeminence in global affairs had dwindled. It seemed that publisher Henry Luce's 1941 prophecy that the twentieth century would be "the American century" was in jeopardy.

While Alexis de Tocqueville is frequently credited with originating the concept of American exceptionalism in his classic *Democracy in America* (1835), the idea predates the French aristocrat's arrival in the United States by two centuries. John Winthrop's lay sermon, "A Modell of Christian Charity," delivered to the Puritan passengers aboard the *Arbella* bound for Massachusetts Bay Colony in 1630, was probably the earliest reference to America (or a small portion thereof) having a distinctive, special mission to play on the world stage. Drawing upon the Sermon on the Mount, Winthrop explained the importance of establishing a pure Christian commonwealth in the New World. "For we must consider that we shall be as a city upon a hill," he intoned. "The eyes of all people are upon us." A secularized version of this mission was presented in 1776 with the publication of Thomas Paine's famous Revolutionary-era pamphlet *Common Sense*. Following the creation of the United States, Thomas Jefferson, Noah Webster, and other prominent citizens of the new nation voiced the belief that the country possessed a number of characteristics that set it apart from corrupt and decaying Europe. While Tocqueville identified the twin components of democracy and equality as the basis for American distinctiveness, it was an American historian, Frederick Jackson Turner, who captured the attention of scholars and students by associating the unique qualities of national character in the United States with the frontier experience. The Turner thesis remained a hot topic of historical discussion for three-quarters of a century as Turnerians and anti-Turnerians debated the details of the impact of the frontier on American life. Is the United States different in fundamental ways from other nations? Has its historical development produced distinctive institutions and citizens? Is it legitimate to focus upon certain characteristics that may appear to separate the United States from other nations at a time when more emphasis is being placed upon global integration? These are some of the questions generated by the following selections.

In the first selection, Seymour Martin Lipset reaffirms the notion of American exceptionalism by insisting that the United States is the only nation that defines itself on the basis of an ideology—the American Creed—whose component parts include liberty, egalitarianism, individualism, populism, and laissez-faire. Drawing from the statistical evidence of the social scientist's polling and survey techniques, Lipset concludes that the United States is different from, though not necessarily superior to, other nations. Specifically, he argues that Americans tend to be the most religious, optimistic, patriotic, rights-oriented, and individualistic citizens on the planet. At the same time, when compared to other nations (especially in Western Europe) the United States has the highest crime rates, the most people incarcerated in the country's penal institutions, and the lowest percentage of the eligible electorate who vote. All of these conditions, he claims, are products of the same ideological attachment, thereby proving that American exceptionalism is a double-edged sword.

Ian Tyrrell argues that American exceptionalism is an artificial construct that is largely anachronistic in the modern world of internationalism and global connections. American historians, he insists, should be more closely attuned to the potential for a historiography that transcends national boundaries. Tyrrell advocates the implementation of a "transnational" paradigm in which the history of the United States appears less unique. At most, he believes, the story of American historical development is a variation on themes that are common to other nations.

YES

Seymour Martin Lipset

AMERICAN EXCEPTIONALISM: A DOUBLE-EDGED SWORD

The American difference, the ways in which the United States varies from the rest of the world, is a constant topic of discussion and in recent years, of concern. Is the country in decline economically and morally? Is Japan about to replace it as the leading economic power? Why does the United States have the highest crime rate, the most persons per capita in prison? Does the growth in the proportion of illegitimate births of single-mother families reflect basic changes in our moral order? Why is our electoral turnout rate so low?

Americans once proudly emphasized their uniqueness, their differences from the rest of the world, the vitality of their democracy, the growth potential of their economy. Some now worry that our best years as a nation are behind us. Americans distrust their leaders and institutions. The public opinion indicators of confidence in institutions are the lowest since polling on the subject began in the early sixties. These concerns suggest the need to look again at the country in comparative perspective, at the ways it differs from other economically developed nations. As I have frequently argued, it is impossible to understand a country without seeing how it varies from others. Those who know only one country know no country.

The idea of American exceptionalism has interested many outside the United States. One of the most important bodies of writing dealing with this country is referred to as the "foreign traveler" literature. These are articles and books written by visitors, largely European, dealing with the way in which America works as compared with their home country or area. Perhaps the best known and still most influential is Alexis de Tocqueville's *Democracy in America*. The French aristocrat came here in the 1830s to find out why the efforts at establishing democracy in his native country, starting with the French Revolution, had failed while the American Revolution had produced a stable democratic republic. The comparison, of course, was broader than just with France; no other European country with the partial exception of Great Britain was then a democracy. In his great book, Tocqueville is the first to refer to the United States as exceptional—that is, qualitatively different from all other countries. He is, therefore, the initiator of the writings on American exceptionalism.

The concept could only have arisen by comparing this country with other societies. Tocqueville looked at the United States through the eyes of someone who knew other cultures well, particularly that of his native country, but also to some considerable degree Great Britain. *Democracy in America* deals only with the United States and has almost no references to France or any other country, but Tocqueville emphasized in his notes that he never wrote a word about America without thinking about France. A book based on his research notes, George Pierson's *Tocqueville and Beaumont in America*, makes clear the ways in which Tocqueville systematically compared the United States and France. At one point, he became sensitive to the fact that America was a very decentralized country, while France was reputed to be the opposite. Tocqueville commented that he had never given much thought to what centralization in France meant since as a Frenchman, he did what came naturally. He then wrote to his father, a prefect of one of the regional administrative districts, and asked him to describe the concentration of political power in France. His father apparently sat down and wrote a lengthy memorandum dealing with the subject.

When Tocqueville or other "foreign traveler" writers or social scientists have used the term "exceptional" to describe the United States, they have not meant, as some critics of the concept assume, that America is better than other countries or has a superior culture. Rather, they have simply been suggesting that it is qualitatively different, that it is an outlier. Exceptionalism is a double-edged

concept. As I shall elaborate, we are the worst as well as the best, depending on which quality is being addressed.

The United States is exceptional in starting from a revolutionary event, in being "the first new nation," the first colony, other than Iceland, to become independent. It has defined its *raison d'être* ideologically. As historian Richard Hofstadter has noted, "It has been our fate as a nation not to have ideologies, but to be one." In saying this, Hofstadter reiterated Ralph Waldo Emerson and Abraham Lincoln's emphases on the country's "political religion," alluding in effect to the former's statement that becoming American was a religious, that is, ideological act. The ex-Soviet Union apart, other countries define themselves by a common history as birthright communities, not by ideology.

The American Creed can be described in five terms: liberty, egalitarianism, individualism, populism, and laissez-faire. Egalitarianism, in its American meaning, as Tocqueville emphasized, involves equality of opportunity and respect, not of result or condition. These values reflect the absence of feudal structures, monarchies and aristocracies. As a new society, the country lacked the emphasis on social hierarchy and status differences characteristic of postfeudal and monarchical cultures. Postfeudal societies have resulted in systems in which awareness of class divisions and respect for the state have remained important, or at least much more important than in the United States. European countries, Canada, and Japan have placed greater emphasis on obedience to political authority and on deference to superiors.

Tocqueville noted, and contemporary survey data document quantitatively, that the United States has been the most religious country in Christendom. It has exhibited greater acceptance of biblical beliefs and higher levels of church attendance than elsewhere, with the possible exception of a few Catholic countries, such as Poland and Ireland, where nationalism and religion have been interwoven. The American religious pattern, as Tocqueville emphasized in seeking to account for American individualism, is voluntary, in other words, not state-supported. All denominations must raise their own funds, engaging in a constant struggle to retain or expand the number of their adherents if they are to survive and grow. This task is not incumbent upon state-financed denominations.

The United States ... is the only country where most churchgoers adhere to *sects*, mainly the Methodists and Baptists, but also hundreds of others. Elsewhere in Christendom the Anglican, Catholic, Lutheran, and Orthodox *churches* dominate. The churches are hierarchical in structure and membership is secured by birthright. Parishioners are expected to follow the lead of their priests and bishops. Sects, by contrast, are predominantly congregational; each local unit adheres voluntarily, while the youth are asked to make a religious commitment only upon reaching the age of decision. Churches outside of the United States historically have been linked to the state; their clergy are paid by public authorities, their hierarchy is formally appointed or confirmed by the government, and their schools are subsidized by taxes.

American Protestant sectarianism has both reinforced and been strengthened by social and political individualism. The sectarian is expected to follow a moral code, as determined by his/her own sense of rectitude, reflecting a personal relationship with God, and in many cases an interpretation of biblical truth, one not mediated by bishops or determined by the state. The American sects assume the perfectibility of human nature and have produced a moralistic people. Countries dominated by churches which view human institutions as corrupt are much less moralistic. The churches stress inherent sinfulness, human weakness, and do not hold individuals or nations up to the same standards as do the sectarians who are more bitter about code violations.

The strength of sectarian values and their implications for the political process may be seen in reactions to the supreme test of citizenship and adherence to the national will, war. State churches have not only legitimated government, for example, the divine role of kings; they have invariably approved of the wars their nations have engaged in, and have called on people to serve and obey. And the citizens have done so, unless and until it becomes clear their country is being defeated. Americans, however, have been different. A major anti-war movement sprang up in every conflict in which the United States has been involved, with the notable exception of World War II, which for the country began with an attack. Americans have put primacy not to "my country right or wrong," but rather to "obedience to my conscience." Hence, those who opposed going to war before it was declared continued to be against it after Congress voted for war.

Protestant-inspired moralism not only has affected opposition to wars, it has determined the American style in foreign relations generally, including the ways we go to war. Support for a war is as moralistic as resistance to it. To endorse a war and call on people to kill others and die for the country, Americans must define their role in a conflict as being on God's side against Satan—for morality, against evil. The United States primarily goes to war against evil, not, in its self-perception, to defend material interests. And comparative public opinion data reveal that Americans are more patriotic ("proud to be an American") and more willing to fight if their country goes to war than citizens of the thirty or so other countries polled by Gallup.

The emphasis in the American value system, in the American Creed, has been on the individual. Citizens have been expected to demand and protect their rights on a personal basis. The exceptional focus on law here as compared to Europe, derived from the Constitution and Bill of Rights, has stressed rights against the state and other powers. America began and continues as the most anti-statist, legalistic, and rights-oriented nation.

The American Constitution intensifies the commitment to individualism and concern for the protection of rights through legal actions. The American Bill of Rights, designed to protect the citizenry against the abuse of power by government, has produced excessive litigiousness. It has fostered the propensity of Americans to go to court not only against the government, but against each other. The rights of minorities, blacks and others, women, even of animals and plants, have grown extensively since World War II through legal action.

The American disdain of authority, for conforming to the rules laid down by the state, has been related by some observers to other unique American traits, such as the highest crime rate, as well as the lowest level of voting participation, in the developed world. Basically, the American revolutionary libertarian tradition does not encourage obedience to the state and the law. This point may be illustrated by examining the results when the American and Canadian governments tried to change the system of measurements and weights to metric from the ancient and less logical system of miles and inches, pounds and ounces. A quarter century ago, both countries told their citizens that in fifteen years, they must use only metric measurements, but that both systems could be used until a given date. The Canadians, whose Tory-monarchical history and structures have made for much greater respect for and reliance on the state, and who have lower per capita crime, deviance, and litigiousness rates than Americans, conformed to the decision of their leaders and now follow the metric system, as anyone who has driven in Canada is aware. Americans ignored the new policy, and their highway signs still refer to miles, weights are in pounds and ounces, and temperature readings are in Fahrenheit.

An emphasis on group characteristics, the perception of status in collectivity terms, necessarily encourages group solutions.... In Europe, the emphasis on explicit social classes in postfeudal societies promoted class-consciousness on the part of the lower strata and to some extent *noblesse oblige* by the privileged. The politics of these countries, some led by Tories such as Disraeli and Bismarck, and later by the lower-class-based, social democratic left, favored policies designed to help the less affluent by means of state solutions such as welfare, public housing, public employment, and medical care. Americans, on the other hand, have placed greater stress on opening the door to individual mobility and personal achievement through heavy investment in mass education.

The cross-national differences are striking. This country has led the world by far in the proportion of people completing different levels of mass education from early in the nineteenth century, first for elementary and high schools, later for colleges and graduate institutions. While America has long predominated in the ratio of those of college and university age attending or completing tertiary education, the numbers and proportions involved have been massive since World War II. A report on the proportion of 20- to 24-year-olds in higher education, as of 1994, indicates that it is almost double, 59 percent, in the United States to that in most affluent European countries and Japan: the Netherlands (33%), Belgium (32%), France (30%), Germany (30%), Japan (30%), and Austria (29%). And America spends a greater proportion of its gross domestic product (GDP) on education, 7.0 percent, than does the European Union, 5.3 percent, or Japan, 5.0 percent.

Conversely, European countries have devoted a much larger share of their GNP, of their public funds, to bettering the living conditions of their working classes and the less privileged generally. The European social democrats have had frequent opportunities to hold office since the 1930s. To transform the situation of the working class, they have emphasized group improvement policies, such as public housing, family allowances and state medicine. Until recently, however, they preserved a class-segregated educational system with elite high schools and failed to focus on the expansion of university education.

American values were modified sharply by forces stemming from the Great Depression and World War II. These led to a much greater reliance on the state and acceptance of welfare and planning policies, the growth of trade unions and of class divisions in voting. While these changes continue to differentiate the contemporary United States from the pre-Depression era, the prosperous conditions which characterized most of the postwar period led the population to revert in some part to the values of the founders, especially distrust of a strong state. Support for diverse welfare entitlement policies has declined; trade union membership has dropped considerably, from a third to a sixth of the employed labor force; and class-linked electoral patterns have fallen off. Americans remain much more individualistic, meritocratic-oriented, and anti-statist than peoples elsewhere. Hence, the values which form the context for public policy are quite different from those in other developed countries, as the results of the 1994 congressional elections demonstrated.

These differences can be elaborated by considering the variations between the American Constitution and those of "most other liberal democracies... [which contain] language establishing affirmative welfare rights or obligations." Some writers explain the difference by the fact that except for the American, almost all other constitutions were drawn up since World War II and, therefore, reflect a commitment to the welfare state, to upgrading the bottom level. But as Mary Ann Glendon has emphasized,

> The differences long predate the postwar era. They are legal manifestations of divergent, and deeply rooted, cultural attitudes toward the state and its functions. Historically, even eighteenth- and nineteenth-century continental European constitutions and codes acknowledged state obligations to provide food, work, and financial aid to persons in

need. And continental Europeans today, whether of the right or the left, are much more likely than Americans to assume that governments have affirmative duties.... By contrast, it is almost obligatory for American politicians of both the right and the left to profess mistrust of government.

In much of the writing on the subject, American exceptionalism is defined by the absence of a significant socialist movement in the United States. This again is a comparative generalization, emphasizing that socialist parties and movements have been weaker in the United States than anywhere else in the industrialized world, and also that the membership of trade unions has been proportionately smaller than in other countries. Analysts have linked those facts to the nature of the class system as well as to attitudes toward the state. Where workers are led by the social structure to think in fixed class terms, as they are in postfeudal societies, they have been more likely to support socialist or labor parties or join unions. But class has been a theoretical construct in America. The weakness of socialism is undoubtedly also related to the lower legitimacy Americans grant to state intervention and state authority....

* * *

Some who criticize an emphasis on American exceptionalism as a way of understanding current and future events have questioned the insistence that historical factors linked to the settlement of the colonies and the ideology of the founders continue to influence American behavior and values. Max Weber dealt with this topic in an interesting and insightful way, which I have relied on in earlier work. He suggested that history operates to determine the future of a nation the way a game in which the dice become loaded does. According to Weber, by conceiving of a nations's history starting as a game in which the dice are not loaded at the beginning, but then becomes biased in the direction of each past outcome, one has an analogue of the way in which culture is formed. Each time the dice come up with a given number, the probability of rolling that number again increases.

Frank Underhill, a Canadian historian, suggested processes similar to Weber's in comparing the United States and Canada. He noted that, in the United States in the late eighteenth and nineteenth centuries, the left-disposed forces favoring populism, egalitarianism, and the like tended to win the major conflicts, starting with the Revolution, moving to the war hawks of 1812, the Jacksonian period, and the Civil War. The more conservative groups, the Federalists, the pro-British peace forces in 1812, the Whigs and defenders of slavery, lost out. Underhill believes that each outcome gave the egalitarian side an advantage in the next major domestic conflict. Conversely, he argues that in his native country, Canada, the conservative forces were dominant in each important struggle from the American Revolution on, through the War of 1812, the Mackenzie-Papineau Rebellion of the middle 1830s, and the founding of the Dominion of Canada in 1867 under the aegis of conservatives. Those who respected authority won in Canada, while those who were more populist triumphed in the United States. Since Canadian conservatives have been Tories, believers in what a British Tory Harold Macmillan called "paternalistic socialism," statism is more acceptable north of the border than south of it. Ironically, as a result of losing the Revolution, Canadian public policy has been closer to that of social democratic countries, while the more libertarian ideology of revolutionary America has made the country the most resistant to welfare state policies and the social democratic and communitarian ethoses.

Other dissenters from the exceptionalism thesis contend that the concept is too imprecise, too unmeasurable, to be useful in explaining continuity or change in behavior on the national or group level. It may be argued that survey or polling data, available since the 1930s, provide quantitative indicators of attitudes and values which can be compared longitudinally or cross-nationally. It is important to distinguish between attitudes and values. Attitudes are much more malleable; they vary with events and contexts. They may change to reflect current social developments, recessions, corruption scandals, or violent periods, and therefore may counter assumptions about deep-rooted variations among nations. At given times, Americans may show up as more supportive than others of certain government welfare policies, less hostile to trade unions, less patriotic, or more willing to spend money to deal with a given problem.

Values are well-entrenched, culturally determined sentiments produced by institutions or major historical events, for example, a new settler society, a Bill of Rights, Protestant sectarianism, wars, and the like. They result in deep beliefs, such as deference or antagonism to authority, individualism or group-centeredness, and egalitarianism or elitism, which form the organizing principles of societies. Value-based explanations may relate to institutional differences to other countries, for example, constitutional constraints on state power, divided or united authority structures, religious systems. They also bear on behavioral outcomes, such as litigiousness or propensity to use government to deal with social problems—welfare, health, unemployment. Opinion surveys may also provide indicators of values. For example, degrees of egalitarianism may be reflected in the responses to questions in the World Values Survey conducted in 1980 and 1990 concerning equal or differentiated pay to persons of varying qualifications doing the same job. Americans are the most likely to approve of merit-based difference in reward, much more so than Japanese, Europeans, or Israelis. And indicators of basic beliefs derived from data in surveys may be used to test or elaborate hypotheses about sources of cross-national variations in behavior, such as social policy or crime rates.

Comprehensive surveys of the attitudes of 15,000 managers from many countries around the world taken from 1986 to 1993 find that American executives emphasize individualism much more than their counterparts elsewhere, and together with the Japanese are outliers with respect to different indicators of values. . . . Charles Hampden-Turner and Alfons Trompenaars conclude that

American managers are by far the strongest individualists in our national samples. This means that they regard the individual as the basic unit and building block of the enterprise and the origin of all its success. They are also more inner-directed, i.e., they locate the source of the organization's purpose and direction in the inner convictions of its employees. No culture is as dedicated to making each individual's dream come true. Americans believe you should "make up your own mind" and "do your own thing" rather than allow yourself to be influenced too much by other people and the external flow of events. Taken together, these are the prime attributes of entrepreneurship: the self-determined individual tenaciously pursuing a personal dream.

Some critics of the concept of American exceptionalism ascribe to its exponents the belief that America had a consensual history, that its past is less marked by conflict than other countries. Nothing could be further from the truth. I have analyzed the interrelationship between consensus and conflict in social science and historical analysis in my book *Consensus and Conflict* and will not repeat the discussion here. I would only note that as Sacvan Bercovitch, Richard Hofstadter, Samuel Huntington, and Gunnar Myrdal, among many, have stressed the United States is distinguished by an emphasis on adversarial relations among groups, and by intense, morally based conflicts about public policy, precisely because its people quarrel sharply about how to apply the basic principles of Americanism they purport to agree about. Conflicts which are defined in moral terms are more intense, as in America, than those which are seen primarily as reflecting interests, as in Europe.

America continues to be qualitatively different. To reiterate, exceptionalism is a two-edged phenomenon; it does not mean better. This country is an outlier. It is the most religious, optimistic, patriotic, rights-oriented, and individualistic. With respect to crime, it still has the highest rates; with respect to incarceration, it has the most people locked up in jail; with respect to litigiousness, it has the most lawyers per capita of any country in the world, with high tort and malpractice rates. It also has close to the lowest percentage of the eligible electorate voting, but the highest rate of participation in voluntary organizations. The country remains the wealthiest in real income terms, the most productive as reflected in worker output, the highest in proportions of people who graduate from or enroll in higher education (post-grade 12) and in postgraduate work (post-grade 16). It is the leader in upward mobility into professional and other high-status and elite occupations, close to the top in terms of commitment to work rather than leisure, but the least egalitarian among developed nations with respect to income distribution, at the bottom as a provider of welfare benefits, the lowest in savings, and the least taxed....

I would ... like to note that those who emphasize social morbidity, who focus on moral decline, for example, or on the high crime or divorce rates, ignore the evidence that much of what they deplore is closely linked to American values which presumably they approve of, those which make for achievement and independence. As Robert Merton points out, the stress on success, on getting ahead, presses the unsuccessful or those without the means to win out legitimately —the poor and the oppressed minorities—to violate the rules of the game. Individualism as a value leads not only to self-reliance and a reluctance to be dependent on others, but also to independence in family relationships, including a greater propensity to leave a mate if the marital relationship becomes troubled. America is the most moralistic country in the developed world. That moralism flows in large part from the country's unique Protestant sectarian and ideological commitments. Given this background, it is not surprising that Americans are also very critical of their society's institutions and leaders. Europeans, who take their national identity from common historical traditions, not ideologies, and are reared in a church tradition, have been unable to understand the American response to Watergate or the sexual peccadilloes of politicians. . . .

The United States and other developed countries have obviously changed considerably over the past two centuries as they have industrialized, urbanized, and become democratized. But I would argue that the relative differences among them have remained. Thus, while statism has grown considerably in the United States, particularly since the Depression of the 1930s and the New Deal, and the country clearly can no longer be described as laissez-faire, it is still less welfare-oriented, less statist, and more laissez-faire than almost all the European nations, and more moralistic. Alone in the developed world, the country has not moved toward comprehensive health care under the sponsorship of the government. In general, we have hung back behind other nations with respect to state industrial policies. In November 1994, the electorate gave control of Congress to the most ardently anti-statist major political party in the world, thereby rejecting the moderate (by international standards) welfare-oriented policies of Bill Clinton and the Democrats. The Republican campaign's "Contract with America" promised to drastically cut back on taxation and the scope of government in a country which has been at the bottom among industrialized nations in terms of the proportion of national income raised in taxes, extent of public ownership, and expenditures for entitlements and welfare. The major divisive, religion-linked social controversies in America, abortion and gay rights, are non-issues in all the industrialized European countries, including the Catholic ones (non-industrialized Ireland and Poland excepted). No one burns down abortion clinics in Europe, Australasia, or Japan. But given the emphasis on moralism, American politicians define interest issues as well as value conflicts in ethical terms. Commenting on the Republican tactics in the 1994 elections, Suzanne Garment notes that the author of the GOP contract, House Speaker Newt Gingrich, "thought the 'secular religion' he saw on the left could be successfully opposed only by equally moralistic rhetoric." To understand why Americans act as they do, as distinct from the Europeans and the Japanese, it is necessary to see the ways in which the country has been exceptional all through its history.

NO

Ian Tyrrell

AMERICAN EXCEPTIONALISM IN AN AGE OF INTERNATIONAL HISTORY

In an era of unprecedented internationalization in historiography, the legacies of nationalism and exceptionalism still haunt the study of American history. History conceived as the origins and growth of the nation-state on the German model took root in many countries, yet nowhere has a nation-centered historical tradition been more resilient than in the United States. There, modern historicism, with its emphasis on the uniqueness of all national traditions, was grafted onto an existing tradition of exceptionalism. The pre-historicist idea of the United States as a special case "outside" the normal patterns and laws of history runs deep in American experience. Its origins, Dorothy Ross shows, lay in the merger of the republican and millennial traditions that formed an ideology of exceptionalism prominent in American historical writing. In this liberal world view, the United States avoided the class conflicts, revolutionary upheaval, and authoritarian governments of "Europe" and presented to the world an example of liberty for others to emulate. This exceptionalist ideology persisted into the twentieth century, influenced such luminaries as Frederick Jackson Turner, and surfaced again in "consensus" historiography in the 1950s.

The rise of historical specialization has shattered these confident assumptions but put nothing convincing in their place. Even though many American historians today eschew exceptionalism, in the absence of an alternative organizing framework the vast bulk of U.S. history is still written in terms that accept the primacy of the national focus. More important, the exceptionalism of the liberal tradition has undergone a modest revival. In popular culture, exceptionalism remains strong, and in intellectual discourse, the debate over Paul Kennedy's *Rise and Fall of the Great Powers* (1987) shows how deeply ingrained are traditions of America as radically unique. In new work by Daniel Bell and Seymour Martin Lipset, the principles of exceptionalism are "reaffirmed." Postmodernist European observer Jean Baudrillard has followed in the tracks of earlier foreign critics to wonder at American uniqueness. In the fields of labor history, women's history, socialism, and foreign policy, important books have returned to the classic theme of Alexis de Tocqueville

From Ian Tyrrell, "American Exceptionalism in an Age of International History," *American Historical Review*, vol. 96 (October 1991). Copyright © 1991 by Ian Tyrrell. Reprinted by permission. Notes omitted.

to emphasize once more American difference from Europe. Other historians avoid the language of exceptionalism assiduously but posit national difference as so central to American historiography that notions of exceptionalism are bound to be encouraged. All this despite the new social history, with its emphasis on the themes of gender, class, race, and ethnicity, themes that appear to cut across the central tenets of the faith in the United States of America as an exception.

At the heart of this resilience of American exceptionalism is a paradox. To some critics, American historiography seems too narrow in its concentration on American uniqueness, yet in no other national historical tradition has comparative history received more rhetorical support. Alongside the belief in American exceptionalism, there has been in American historiography a marked impulse to relate American history to that of the rest of the world. To take one prominent example, much of Arthur Schlesinger, Sr.'s voluminous writing was concerned with what he called "national traits." In *Paths to the Present* (1949), he addressed the question raised in the eighteenth century by J. Hector St. John Crèvecoeur, "What Then Is the American, This New Man?" Alongside work unmistakably influenced by the exceptionalist tradition, however, Schlesinger wrote essays stressing America's global relationships. His warning is instructive: "History as conventionally written stresses national differences—even when not genuinely such —to the neglect of national similarities. This emphasis," Schlesinger noted, glossed "over the fundamental interdependence of peoples."

Schlesinger's essay was first published in 1941 under the title "World Currents in American Civilization." Even then, as a glance at his bibliography shows, a substantial literature on American connections with "world history" existed. The presence of this strand of historical writing suggests that American exceptionalism has not gone unchallenged. A subordinate tradition of international analysis requires recognition in any account of American exceptionalism. This tradition offers instructive themes for the reconceptualization of national historiography in the United States and in other countries as well. American historians have been prominent in the drive to establish comparative history as a genre, for example, and have heralded such efforts as evidence of greater cosmopolitanism in American historical analysis. Technically, they are correct. The critical absence has not been comparative and international perspectives themselves but rather the failure of comparative history to transcend the boundaries of nationalist historiography. As an alternative, the possibilities of a transnational history must be considered. This does not mean that nationalism and the history of the nation-state can be ignored. It does mean that these national perspectives must be historicized and relativized by developing a new historiographical project organized in terms of a simultaneous consideration of differing geographical scales—the local, the national, and the transnational— in American historical thought.

The national focus I am criticizing here may seem merely to reflect a rock-bottom historical "reality." No one doubts the importance of both nationalism and nation-state in the modern world. Yet, all too often, the primacy of these concepts is assumed by historians. This penchant for national frameworks reflects not merely the historian's common-sense observation of the contemporary world but also the way historical knowledge has been produced. History is not a set of data to be deposited into tidy boxes, of which the national box is the most obvious and sensible. History is, much more than most historians are willing to accept, a constructed body of knowledge. The role of the nation-state framework in the production of that history must be acknowledged, if alternative views of American history are to be advanced. Other disciplines have been much more open to transnational analysis than history has been, and even American historians, when they turn to the subject of European history, have made contributions to comparative and international history that demonstrate just how artificial the dominance of the national framework in American historiography can be. But these innovative achievements have not been fully appreciated by other national contingents of historians. This suggests that the problem lies less in the facts of American history or American perversity than in the nature of historical training. A focus on national difference is an occupational hazard among all historians, not just those of the United States. American exceptionalism presents a special case of the more general problem of history written from a national point of view.

* * *

None of this would be worth discussing if American history were truly exceptional, but exceptionalism has always contained an insuperable logical difficulty. The history of the United States cannot be exceptional unless contrasted with other histories that conform to fixed patterns of historical development. In the twentieth century, American advocates of exceptionalism have, paradoxically, been hostile to the very idea of laws of histori-

cal development represented in, for example, Marxism, and have argued that these schematic accounts do not apply to American history. Yet such schemes of history underpin the explanations exceptionalist advocates give for American difference from other countries. The logical difficulty has been compounded by changes in the Marxist tradition itself. Marxists no longer hold to a rigid stages theory of historical development, and the fragmentation of the Marxist tradition has removed the contrast on which modern interpretations of exceptionalism have been constructed. Added to this, the exceptionalist tradition assumed an essentialist dichotomy between "America" and "Europe" that denies the complexity and variation European historians—Marxist and non-Marxist—have found in their own histories.

Many American historians have accepted these logical difficulties and argue instead either for national uniqueness or national difference. Since all national histories are unique, there is nothing objectionable about this maneuver, at least in principle. Yet "uniqueness" does have overtones of national superiority, and the concept has been used, for example by David Potter, in a sense that clearly implies exceptionalism. In his *People of Plenty* (1954), Potter reworked the familiar frontier thesis and explained differences between "Europe" and "America" in terms of American abundance. "Europe cannot think of altering the relationship between the various levels of society without assuming a class struggle; but America has altered and can alter these relationships without necessarily treating one class as the victim or even, in an ultimate sense, the antagonist of another." This polarized and ahistorical treatment of two worlds defined by the presence or absence of class conflict echoed the preoccupations of earlier writers like Turner and the nineteenth-century originators of exceptionalism.

Even the historians who have emphasized national difference in more neutral fashion have helped perpetuate the concern with exceptionalism. To understand this, it helps to put individual historical works in the context of inherited historiography and keep in mind that far more history is written about the United States than any other country. If the United States is said to be different, the sum total of that research produces more evidence of specifically American difference. All histories may be distinctive, but American history becomes, through the sheer volume produced, "more distinctive" than others. Further, the focus on American difference cannot be divorced from the context of exceptionalism as an inherited ideology. The historian may deny the notion of exceptionalism, but his or her analysis reinforces the existing, deeply ingrained assumption that the history of the United States has been endowed with special features until the contrary is proven. For these reasons, exceptionalism is in practice inseparable from the concept of national distinctiveness in American historiography, and the two notions have become linked through comparative history. Although comparative history is by no means an American monopoly, the search to define, explore, and test the uniqueness of the American past has produced an impressive body of comparative history by world standards. For many years, this link was merely implicit. Advocates of exceptionalism such as Turner assumed American uniqueness rather than investigated it. More recently, the growth of comparative history, in part a product of the consensus historians' preoccupation with American uniqueness, has allowed systematic testing of exceptionalist ideas. Comparative history is for this reason not necessarily antagonistic to exceptionalism.

These connections are not always made clear by practitioners, and comparative history may sometimes be seen simply as a way of making the discipline in the United States more cosmopolitan. But even the supporters of comparative history acknowledge that the genre has its defects. The most obvious problem is the tendency to compare whole countries and to take for granted the primacy of the national unit of analysis. Thus slavery in the United States is compared to slavery in Brazil or to serfdom in Russia. Neither regional variations nor transnational influences are necessarily excluded in such accounts. Nevertheless, the historian is forced to subordinate variations in both time and space to the elaboration and explanation of larger national differences.

Carried to an extreme, this type of comparative analysis reifies national characteristics. The classic case is the work of Louis Hartz, in *The Liberal Tradition in America* (1955) and *The Founding of New Societies* (1964). Here the liberal "fragment" derived from Europe's more complex social structure determines the nature of political debate. The fragment becomes frozen and loses its dialectical relationship with other fragments to produce a self-perpetuating "tradition." All major political and ideological developments can be explained in terms of such a national pathology.

It is not necessary to deal with an entire national tradition in order to fall into this error. Some local case studies do likewise. A well-crafted and informative comparison by Norbert MacDonald of the divergent histories of Vancouver and Seattle illustrates the point. Here are two similarly situated cities. Geographical influences are relatively constant, therefore a comparison may reveal something significant about the national scene. Such a comparison suggested to this author striking differences "in local characteristics and processes" that reflected "the distinctive histories, roles and values of two separate nations." Urban history, in this account, is national history writ small. At least one reviewer understood the message to be that such a comparison showed up the distinctive national features of American history identified with exceptionalism. But how different would the perspective be if Vancouver were contrasted with other Canadian cities or port cities elsewhere in the world? We cannot know at present, because the research design in comparative history is narrowly conceived to test purely national differences rather than convey a more varied sense of the elements that make up the diversity of historical experience. The focus on national factors as an explanation of urban trends ignores the very real uncertainty among Canadians about their national culture and their frank recognition of regional differences. It also fails to take into account the degree of American cultural penetration that makes a sense of "Canadian" difference impossible to measure in terms of a two-way national comparative framework.

Most comparative history involves just two countries, but the choice of countries for comparison is as important as the number of countries studied. Take the recent example of Donald Meyer's learned foray into feminist history, *Sex and Power* (1987). Meyer synthesized recent women's history to ask, in effect, if the American women's movement has been exceptional. Comparing the case of the United States with those of Sweden, the Soviet Union, and Italy, Meyer answered this question in the affirmative, but he did not make comparisons with Britain or its colonies, where similar movements for women's emancipation flourished. In this respect, Meyer's analysis can be contrasted with the older but still useful survey by Richard Evans in *The Feminists* (1977). A British historian of German history, Evans was not preoccupied with American national distinctiveness. He acknowledged important differences between the United States and some other key countries in the timing and scope of women's reform and feminist agitation but also stressed regional comparisons between, for example, the American West and some of the Australian colonies. More important, he grouped sets of countries together to produce a typology of movements for women's emancipation. Although his particular typology had the disadvantage of overemphasizing the "liberal" and "bourgeois" character of feminism in the Anglo-American world, his approach did enable him to set the question of American feminism in a broader international context that emphasized the American case as a variation on a theme.

Seymour Martin Lipset acknowledged the complication that the choice of countries introduces into comparative history. "Generalizations may invert when the unit of comparison changes. For example, Canada looks different when compared to the U.S. than when contrasted to Britain." Yet Lipset has not fully overcome the problem, as his own illustration shows. "Figuratively, on a scale of zero to one hundred, with the U.S. close to zero on a given trait and Britain at one hundred, Canada would fall around thirty. Thus, when Canada is evaluated by reference to the United States, it appears as more elitist, law-abiding, and statist, but when considering the variations between Canada and Britain, Canada looks more anti-statist, violent, and egalitarian." But Lipset's own standard of comparison is revealed in his deployment of the numerical grid. Almost invariably in American scholarship, the benchmark is the United States. Comparisons between the other countries are either ignored or played down. This procedure cannot test notions of American exceptionalism adequately, and the outcome of the piling up of differences between the United States and a variety of other cases in a range of miscellaneous matters is to ensure that American exceptionalism is "reaffirmed."

This penchant for stressing national difference has some practical roots. Modern archives are organized nationally, and historians making comparisons have to rely to a large extent on these, as well as on the national historical traditions in each country that are in part a product of such mundane matters. Dependence on the existing monographic scholarship is particularly noticeable in comparative work done by historical sociologists and political scientists. By relying on national historiographies for the basic building blocks of comparative history, scholars do not validate exceptionalism but rather reflect the disciplinary traditions of the academic world they have inherited.

For Americanists, this means making the problematic of American exceptionalist historiography central to comparative analysis. Much comparative history is written from the perspective of key issues in U.S. history. As Raymond Grew has perceptively noted, comparisons have "typically . . . dealt with issues that rise from within American historiography—frontiers, slavery, and immigrant groups . . . But rarely . . . has the exploration moved from the other direction, beginning with issues identified more fully in some other historical tradition to reveal something previously overlooked about American society . . . [E]ven the most successful systematic, transnational comparisons have led American historians back to the familiar mines rather than out toward new horizons." Among those familiar mines, none is more prominent than the topic of American uniqueness.

It should be clear by now that the critics of exceptionalism cannot defeat the notion by exposing its illogicalities or by using the methodology of comparative history. The legacy of exceptionalism can only be laid to rest in two ways: by confronting the national focus of exceptionalist analysis, and by dealing with the special conditions of historical production that have shaped and sustained exceptionalism through the organization of historical knowledge in national units. This is why exceptionalism must be linked to national history and why the paradigm of national history must be rigorously scrutinized from the perspective of alternative transnational approaches. I do not mean to suggest that American history must be homogenized as part of some amorphous international history. The alternatives to national history I propose would contextualize nationalism and depict U.S. history as a variation on transnational themes. . . .

* * *

However transnationalism is approached in American history, the question of its relationship to the history of the nation cannot be avoided. This is a problem for all historiographies, because of the importance of the nation-state in the modern world, but, for much of American history, it is a crucial point. The United States may be enmeshed in a global interdependence, but the relationship of U.S. history to transnational themes is different from that of many—though not all—other countries. A great power does not have the same relation to systems of international law, organizations, or movements that a small power does. Transnational analysis must therefore confront the problem of hegemony on the international level. This is not the same as saying that the United States is exceptional, since power is transitory and has shifted markedly over the course of the five hundred years of European exploration and settlement of the Americas. Nationalism and the state must still be historicized, and in so doing exceptionalism may be put in its proper place.

How can the nation-state be incorporated in this project? American historians interested in developing a transnational approach must specify the relations of three phenomena: first, the international context of national action in all of its manifestations. This would include not only international economic relations but also transnational connections in religion, culture, and social life; second, the development of the nation-state constrained by these international contexts; third, the groups and classes that operate both within the nation-state and at the international level. A key example would be the way certain American women reformers at the turn of the century, dispirited in some measure by the failure to achieve the vote in the United States, established international feminist connections and proposed that feminism be the basis of a new internationalism. The failure of the American nation-state

to give equal citizenship rights made some feminists hostile to nationalism. Said Ellen Sargent, a California suffragist, in 1910: "who that realizes the situation can be patriotic? ... Our own *United States* have the *home* made *material* of which anarchists are made." In her study of *Feminism in Germany and Scandinavia* (1915), Katharine Anthony expanded on the point: "The disenfranchisement of a whole sex, a condition which has existed throughout the civilized world until a comparatively recent date, has bred in half the population an unconscious internationalism. The man without a country was a tragic exception; the woman without a country was the accepted rule." The result? "The enfranchisement of women now under way" had in Anthony's view "come too late to inculcate in them the narrow views of citizenship which were once supposed to accompany the gift of the vote. Its effect" would, she predicted, "rather be to make the unconscious internationalism of the past the conscious internationalism of the future."

Anthony's predictions went astray, but that does not make her sentiments unimportant. The goals of feminists were diverse; their aims to bolster international solidarity between women and to provide compensation for losses at home were salient ones. Yet international ideology and organization also served to achieve goals at the national level. American women stepped in this case outside the boundaries of the state in order to put pressure on it by manipulating international opinion.

The choice was not necessarily a clear one between international and national action. Both planes of activity could be pursued simultaneously; what on one level is an internationalist strategy could also have force in building a social movement in the United States. Take the case of Pan-Africanism as practiced by Marcus Garvey's Universal Negro Improvement Association (UNIA). This ideology could be interpreted as much as an attempt to create a racial solidarity that could aid upward social mobility as a concrete endeavor to leave the United States. The Garvey movement was rooted in a long tradition of African-American emigrationist sentiment. Migration was not necessarily out of the country; it is arguable that such migration had its psychological and ideological dimension and that its spatial dimensions depended on particular circumstances. Thus southern black "exodusters" of the 1870s went to Kansas; a later generation of ghetto migrants continued to reject racism and socioeconomic deprivation in different ways through the "Back-to-Africa" movement. Local social conditions proved fertile for the development of Pan-African ideology as a response to an intellectual climate of European colonialism and racism. In this way, the local history of social movements can be linked to international contexts.

This three-tiered model of social action can illuminate the relationship between transnational patterns on the one hand and the development of the state and modern nationalism on the other. Such an approach would tie in with the concern of political scientists and sociologists such as Theda Skocpol to examine the relationship between class forces and the growth of state power in comparative perspective. What needs to be added to their reconceptualization of the role of the state is a stronger sense of the interplay between domestic and international forces in the shaping of state power. Transnational factors do not simply define the possibilities for social action within the state in the way that Skocpol has indi-

cated; classes and groups have on occasion moved beyond state boundaries to contribute to the international forces shaping and limiting state power. This perspective helps contextualize American exceptionalism. The particular constellation of international and domestic class and group forces gives the state its specific character. In this way, American national power can be historicized by relating it to the changing balance of these forces. The growth of the American nation-state can thereby be depicted not as an exception to patterns of national power in a world of nations but as a particular, and constantly changing, expression of complex forces.

All this is a formidable task for any group of historians yet not an impossible one. The chief obstacles are practical and are connected to the resilience of historiography written from the national point of view. The detailed strategy of execution would demand a separate essay, since changes in historians' ways of producing knowledge are required, but the main points can be swiftly indicated. The growing strength of international connections in the contemporary world will surely make historians reconsider these relationships in past times. The internationalization of scholarship itself is steadily eroding the boundaries that at the turn of the century created strong national historiographical traditions, including American exceptionalism. In part, historians could achieve much along the lines suggested were they simply to build on work already done by the Americanists on international history, comparative history, and regional history discussed in this essay. A new focus on the interplay of global connections and local variations would bring much of this older work into a more helpful relation to current political and economic concerns in ways that would by-pass the temptation to revive exceptionalism. But other strategies are required as well. More could be done by scholarly associations and universities to create institutional frameworks in which these issues could be addressed. Certainly, such tasks cannot be accomplished through individual action alone. Pooling the talents of historians to explore transnational themes is needed. More than at any time since the turn of the century, American historians are alive to the potential for a historiography that transcends national boundaries. Yet only with institutional support can the momentous changes occurring today in global relations be matched in American historical writing by a new "age of international history."

POSTSCRIPT

Is America Exceptional?

The selection by Lipset represents his most recent defense of the concept of American exceptionalism. The most important of his previous works on this topic include *Agrarian Socialism* (University of California Press, 1950; rev. and exp. ed., 1971) and *The First New Nation: The United States in Historical and Comparative Perspective* (Basic Books, 1963). Support for Lipset's interpretation can be found in Daniel Boorstin, *The Genius of American Politics* (University of Chicago Press, 1953); Louis Hartz, *The Liberal Tradition in America* (Harcourt Brace Jovanovich, 1991); and the essays in Byron Shafer, ed., *Is America Different? A New Look Back at American Exceptionalism* (Oxford University Press, 1991). Critics of exceptionalism are represented in Daniel Bell's "The End of American Exceptionalism," *Public Interest* (Fall 1975); Laurence Veysey, "The Autonomy of American History Reconsidered," *American Quarterly* (Fall 1979); and William C. Spengemann, *A Mirror for Americanists: Reflections on the Idea of American Literature* (University Press of New England, 1989). Michael Kammen's "The Problem of American Exceptionalism: A Reconsideration," *American Quarterly* (March 1993) presents a valuable summary of both sides of the debate.

The issue of exceptionalism is also at the heart of discussions of the nature of American culture carried on by historians interested in the Old World and New World roots of the American people and the society they created beginning in the seventeenth century. Just how new and different was that early American culture? How much did it depart from the cultural heritage of those tens of thousands of immigrants who arrived in England's North American colonies prior to the American Revolution? Opposing historical perspectives such as those emphasized in Tyrrell's selection can be found in Gary Nash's *Red, White, and Black: The Peoples of Early America*, 2d ed. (Prentice Hall, 1974), which emphasizes the need to appreciate the numerous non-English and non-European elements of American culture, and David Hackett Fischer's *Albion's Seed: Four British Folkways in America* (Oxford University Press, 1989), which suggests that there is a distinctly British tone in American culture and society.

Frederick Jackson Turner's famous frontier thesis and its influence in creating a distinct American character was presented originally as "The Significance of the Frontier in American History," a paper read at the annual meeting of the American Historical Association in 1893. The staunchest disciple of Turner was Ray Allen Billington, whose *The Far Western Frontier, 1830–1860* (Harper & Row, 1956), *The Frontier Heritage* (Holt, Rinehart & Winston, 1966), and *Frederick Jackson Turner* (Oxford University Press, 1973) deserve attention. An important extension of the Turner thesis is offered in David M. Potter, *People of Plenty: Economic Abundance and the American Character* (University of Chicago Press, 1954), which identifies another factor contributing to the distinctive American character. Michael Kammen, in *People of Paradox: An Inquiry Concerning the Origins of American Civilization* (Alfred A. Knopf, 1972), argues that American distinctiveness is derived from the contradiction produced by a culture created from an interaction of Old and New World patterns. Students interested in pursuing these questions of culture and character should examine Michael McGiffert, ed., *The Character of Americans: A Book of Readings*, rev. ed. (Dorsey Press, 1970) and David Stannard, "American Historians and the Idea of a National Character," *American Quarterly* (May 1971).

ISSUE 2

Was Columbus an Imperialist?

YES: Kirkpatrick Sale, from *The Conquest of Paradise: Christopher Columbus and the Columbian Legacy* (Alfred A. Knopf, 1990)

NO: Robert Royal, from *1492 and All That: Political Manipulations of History* (Ethics and Public Policy Center, 1992)

ISSUE SUMMARY

YES: Kirkpatrick Sale, a contributing editor of *The Nation*, characterizes Christopher Columbus as an imperialist who was determined to conquer both the land and the people he encountered during his first voyage to the Americas in 1492.

NO: Robert Royal, vice president for research at the Ethics and Public Policy Center, objects to Columbus's modern-day critics and insists that Columbus should be admired for his courage, his willingness to take a risk, and his success in advancing knowledge about other parts of the world.

On October 12, 1492 Christopher Columbus, a Genoese mariner sailing under the flag and patronage of the Spanish monarchy, made landfall on a tropical Caribbean island, which he subsequently named San Salvador. This action established for Columbus the fame of having discovered the New World and, by extension, America. Of course, this "discovery" was ironic since Columbus and his crew members were not looking for a new world but, instead, a very old one—the much-fabled Orient. By sailing westward instead of eastward, Columbus was certain that he would find a shorter route to China. He did not anticipate that the land mass of the Americas would prevent him from reaching this goal or that his "failure" would guarantee his fame for centuries thereafter.

Columbus's encounter with indigenous peoples, whom he named "Indians" (los indios), presented further proof that Europeans had not discovered America. These "Indians" were descendants of the first people who migrated from Asia at least thirty thousand years earlier and fanned out in a southeasterly direction until they populated much of North and South America. By the time Columbus arrived, Native Americans numbered approximately forty million, three million of whom resided in the continental region north of Mexico.

None of this, however, should dilute the significance of Columbus's explorations, which were representative of a wave of Atlantic voyages emanating from Europe in the fifteenth, sixteenth, and seventeenth centuries. Spawned by the intellectual ferment of the Renaissance in combination with the rise of the European nation-state, these voyages of exploration were made possible by advances in shipbuilding, improved navigational instruments and cartography, the desirability of long-distance commerce, support from ruling monarchs, and the courage and ambition of the explorers themselves.

Columbus's arrival (and return on three separate occasions between 1494 and 1502) possessed enormous implications not only for the future development of the United States, but for the Western Hemisphere as a whole, as well as for Europe and Africa. These consequences attracted a significant amount of scholarly and media attention in 1992 in connection with the quincentennial celebration of Columbus's first arrival on American shores and sparked often acrimonious debate over the true meaning of Columbus's legacy. Many wished to use the occasion to emphasize the positive accomplishments of Europe's contact with the New World. Others sought to clarify some of the negative results of Columbus's voyages, particularly as they related to European confrontations with Native Americans.

This debate provides the context for the essays that follow. To what extent should we applaud Columbus's exploits? Are there reasons that we should question the purity of Columbus's motivations? Did the European "discovery" of America do more harm than good?

Kirkpatrick Sale treats Columbus's arrival as an invasion of the land and the indigenous peoples that he encountered. By assigning European names to virtually everything he observed, Columbus, according to Sale, was taking possession on behalf of the Spanish monarchy. Similarly, one of Columbus's major goals was to build and arm a fortress by which he could carry out the subjugation and enslavement of the native population. Columbus's policies of conquest, religious conversion, settlement, and exploitation of natural resources were an example of European imperialism.

Robert Royal rejects the argument that Columbus was motivated by European arrogance and avarice. He also disputes the notion that Columbus was driven by a desire for gold or by racist assumptions of Native American inferiority. Royal asserts that Columbus exhibited genuine concern for justice in his contacts with the Native Americans and concludes that Columbus, though not without his faults, merits the admiration traditionally accorded his accomplishments.

YES

Kirkpatrick Sale

1492–93

Admiral [Cristóbal] Colón [Christopher Columbus] spent a total of ninety-six days exploring the lands he encountered on the far side of the Ocean Sea—four rather small coralline islands in the Bahamian chain and two substantial coastlines of what he finally acknowledged were larger islands—every one of which he "took possession of" in the name of his Sovereigns.

The first he named San Salvador, no doubt as much in thanksgiving for its welcome presence after more than a month at sea as for the Son of God whom it honored; the second he called Santa María de la Concepcíon, after the Virgin whose name his flagship bore; and the third and fourth he called Fernandina and Isabela, for his patrons, honoring Aragon before Castile for reasons never explained (possibly protocol, possibly in recognition of the chief sources of backing for the voyage). The first of the two large and very fertile islands he called Juana, which Fernando says was done in honor of Prince Juan, heir to the Castilian throne, but just as plausibly might have done in recognition of Princess Juana, the unstable child who eventually carried on the line; the second he named la Ysla Española, the "Spanish Island," because it resembled (though he felt it surpassed in beauty) the lands of Castile.

It was not that the islands were in need of names, mind you, nor indeed that Colón was ignorant of the names the native peoples had already given them, for he frequently used those original names before endowing them with his own. Rather, the process of bestowing new names went along with "taking possession of" those parts of the world he deemed suitable for Spanish ownership, showing the royal banners, erecting various crosses and pronouncing certain oaths and pledges. If this was presumption, it had an honored heritage: it was Adam who was charged by his Creator with the task of naming "every living creature," including the product of his own rib, in the course of establishing "dominion over" them.

Colón went on to assign no fewer than sixty-two other names on the geography of the islands—capes, points, mountains, ports—with a blithe assurance suggesting that in his (and Europe's) perception the act of name-giving was in some sense a talisman of conquest, a rite that changed raw neutral stretches of far-off earth into extensions of Europe. The process began slowly, even haltingly—he forgot to record, for example, until four days afterward that he named the landfall island San Salvador —but by the time he came to Española at the end he went on a naming spree, using more than two-thirds of all the titles he concocted on that one coastline. On certain days it became almost a frenzy: on December 6 he named six places, on the nineteenth six more, and on January 11 no fewer than ten—eight capes, a point, and a mountain. It is almost as if, as he sailed along the last of the islands, he was determined to leave his mark on it the only way he knew how, and thus to establish his authority—and by extension Spain's—even, as with baptism, to make it thus sanctified, and real, and official. (One should note that it was only his *own* naming that conveyed legitimacy: when Colón thought Martín Alonso Pinzón had named a river after himself, he immediately renamed it Río de Gracia instead.)

This business of naming and "possessing" foreign islands was by no means casual. The Admiral took it very seriously, pointing out that "it was my wish to bypass no island without taking possession" (October 15) and that "in all regions [I] always left a cross standing" (November 16) as a mark of Christian dominance. There even seem to have been certain prescriptions for it (the instructions from the Sovereigns speak of "the administering of the oath and the performing of the rites prescribed in such cases"), and Rodrigo de Escobedo was sent along as secretary of the fleet explicitly to witness and record these events in detail.

But consider the implications of this act and the questions it raises again about what was in the Sovereigns' minds, what in Colón's. Why would the Admiral assume that these territories were in some way *un*possessed—even by those clearly inhabiting them—and thus available for Spain to claim? Why would he not think twice about the possibility that some considerable potentate—the Grand Khan of China, for example, whom he later acknowledged (November 6) "must be" the ruler of Española—might descend upon him at any moment with a greater military force than his three vessels commanded and punish him for his territorial presumption? Why would he make the ceremony of possession his very first act on shore, even before meeting the inhabitants or exploring the environs, or finding out if anybody there objected to being thus possessed—particularly if they actually owned the great treasures he hoped would be there? No European would have imagined that anyone— three small boatloads of Indians, say— could come up to a European shore or island and "take possession" of it, nor would a European imagine marching up to some part of North Africa or the Middle East and claiming sovereignty there with impunity. Why were these lands thought to be different?

Could there be any reason for the Admiral to assume he had reached "unclaimed" shores, new lands that lay far from the domains of any of the potentates of the East? Can that really have been in his mind—or can it all be explained as simple Eurocentrism, or Eurosuperiority, mixed with cupidity and naiveté?

In any case, it is quite curious how casually and calmly the Admiral took to this task of possession, so much so that he gave only the most meager description of the initial ceremony on San Salvador, despite its having been a signal event in his career. He recorded merely that he went ashore in his longboat, armed, followed by the captains of the two caravels, accompanied by royal standards and banners and two representatives of the court to "witness how he before them all was taking, as in fact he took, possession of the said island for the King and Queen." He added that he made "the declarations that are required, as is contained at greater length in the testimonies which were there taken down in writing," but he unfortunately didn't specify what these were and no such documents survive; we are left only with the image of a party of fully dressed and armored Europeans standing there on the white sand in the blazing morning heat while Escobedo, with his parchment and inkpot and quill, painstakingly writes down the Admiral's oaths.

Fernando Colón did enlarge on this scene, presumably on the authority of his imagination alone, describing how the little party then "rendered thanks to Our Lord, kneeling on the ground and kissing it with tears of joy for His great favor to them," after which the crew members "swore obedience" to the Admiral "with such a show of pleasure and joy" and "begged his pardon for the injuries that through fear and little faith they had done him." He added that these goings-on were performed in the presence of the "many natives assembled there," whose reactions are not described and whose opinions are not recorded. . . .

Once safely "possessed," San Salvador was open for inspection. Now the Admiral turned his attention for the first time to the "naked people" staring at him on the beach—he did not automatically give them a name, interestingly enough, and it would be another six days before he decided what he might call them—and tried to win their favor with his trinkets.

They all go around as naked as their mothers bore them; and also the women, although I didn't see more than one really young girl. All that I saw were young people [mancebos], none of them more than 30 years old. They are very well built, with very handsome bodies and very good faces; their hair [is] coarse, almost like the silk of a horse's tail, and short. They wear their hair over their eyebrows, except for a little in the back that they wear long and never cut. Some of them paint themselves black (and they are of the color of the Canary Islanders, neither black nor white), and some paint themselves white, and some red, and some with what they find. And some paint their faces, and some of them the whole body, and some the eyes only, and some of them only the nose.

It may fairly be called the birth of American anthropology.

A crude anthropology, of course, as superficial as Colón's descriptions always were when his interest was limited, but simple and straightforward enough, with none of the fable and fantasy that characterized many earlier (and even some later) accounts of new-found peoples. There was no pretense to objectivity, or any sense that these people might be representatives of a culture equal to, or in any way a model for, Europe's. Colón immediately presumed the inferiority of the natives, not merely because (a sure enough sign) they were naked, but because (his society could have no surer measure) they seemed so technologically backward. "It appeared to me that these people were very poor in everything," he wrote on that first day, and, worse still, "they have no iron." And they went on to prove their inferiority to the Admiral by being ignorant of even such a basic artifact of European life as a sword: "They bear no arms, nor are they acquainted with them," he wrote, "for I showed them swords and they grasped them by the blade and cut themselves through ignorance." Thus did European arms spill the first drops of native blood on the sands of the New World, accompanied not with a gasp of compassion but with a smirk of superiority.

Then, just six sentences further on, Colón clarified what this inferiority meant in his eyes:

> They ought to be good servants and of good intelligence [*ingenio*].... I believe that they would easily be made Christians, because it seemed to me that they had no religion. Our Lord pleasing, I will carry off six of them at my departure to Your Highnesses, in order that they may learn to speak.

No clothes, no arms, no possessions, no iron, and now no religion—not even speech: hence they were fit to be servants, and captives. It may fairly be called the birth of American slavery.

Whether or not the idea of slavery was in Colón's mind all along is uncertain, although he did suggest he had had experience as a slave trader in Africa (November 12) and he certainly knew of Portuguese plantation slavery in the Madeiras and Spanish slavery of Guanches in the Canaries. But it seems to have taken shape early and grown ever firmer as the weeks went on and as he captured more and more of the helpless natives. At one point he even sent his crew ashore to kidnap "seven head of women, young ones and adults, and three small children"; the expression of such callousness led the Spanish historian Salvador de Madariaga to remark, "It would be difficult to find a starker utterance of utilitarian subjection of man by man than this passage [whose] form is

no less devoid of human feeling than its substance."

To be sure, Colón knew nothing about these people he encountered and considered enslaving, and he was hardly trained to find out very much, even if he was moved to care. But they were in fact members of an extensive, populous, and successful people whom Europe, using its own peculiar taxonomy, subsequently called "Taino" (or "Taíno"), their own word for "good" or "noble," and their response when asked who they were. They were related distantly by both language and culture to the Arawak people of the South American mainland, but it is misleading (and needlessly imprecise) to call them Arawaks, as historians are wont to do, when the term "Taino" better establishes their ethnic and historical distinctiveness. They had migrated to the islands from the mainland at about the time of the birth of Christ, occupying the three large islands we now call the Greater Antilles and arriving at Guanahani (Colón's San Salvador) and the end of the Bahamian chain probably sometime around A.D. 900. There they displaced an earlier people, the Guanahacabibes (sometimes called Guanahatabeys), who by the time of the European discovery occupied only the western third of Cuba and possibly remote corners of Española; and there, probably in the early fifteenth century, they eventually confronted another people moving up the islands from the mainland, the Caribs, whose culture eventually occupied a dozen small islands of what are called the Lesser Antilles.

The Tainos were not nearly so backward as Colón assumed from their lack of dress. (It might be said that it was the Europeans, who generally kept clothed head to foot during the day despite temperatures regularly in the eighties, who were the more unsophisticated in garmenture—especially since the Tainos, as Colón later noted, also used their body paint to prevent sunburn.) Indeed, they had achieved a means of living in a balanced and fruitful harmony with their natural surroundings that any society might well have envied. They had, to begin with, a not unsophisticated technology that made exact use of their available resources, two parts of which were so impressive that they were picked up and adopted by the European invaders: *canoa* (canoes) that were carved and fire-burned from large silk-cotton trees, "all in one piece, and wonderfully made" (October 13), some of which were capable of carrying up to 150 passengers; and *hamaca* (hammocks) that were "like nets of cotton" (October 17) and may have been a staple item of trade with Indian tribes as far away as the Florida mainland. Their houses were not only spacious and clean —as the Europeans noted with surprise and appreciation, used as they were to the generally crowded and slovenly hovels and huts of south European peasantry—but more apropos, remarkably resistant to hurricanes; the circular walls were made of strong cane poles set deep and close together ("as close as the fingers of a hand," Colón noted), the conical roofs of branches and vines tightly interwoven on a frame of smaller poles and covered with heavy palm leaves. Their artifacts and jewelry, with the exception of a few gold trinkets and ornaments, were based largely on renewable materials, including bracelets and necklaces of coral, shells, bone, and stone, embroidered cotton belts, woven baskets, carved statues and chairs, wooden and shell utensils, and pottery of variously intricate decoration depending on period and place.

Perhaps the most sophisticated, and most carefully integrated, part of their technology was their agricultural system, extraordinarily productive and perfectly adapted to the conditions of the island environment. It was based primarily on fields of knee-high mounds, called *conucos*, planted with *yuca* (sometimes called manioc), *batata* (sweet potato), and various squashes and beans grown all together in multicrop harmony: the root crops were excellent in resisting erosion and producing minerals and potash, the leaf crops effective in providing shade and moisture, and the mound configurations largely resistant to erosion and flooding and adaptable to almost all topographic conditions including steep hillsides. Not only was the *conuco* system environmentally appropriate—"conuco agriculture seems to have provided an exceptionally ecologically well-balanced and protective form of land use," according to David Watts's recent and authoritative *West Indies*—but it was also highly productive, surpassing in yields anything known in Europe at the time, with labor that amounted to hardly more than two or three hours a week, and in continuous yearlong harvest. The pioneering American geographical scholar Carl Sauer calls Taino agriculture "productive as few parts of the world," giving the "highest returns of food in continuous supply by the simplest methods and modest labor," and adds, with a touch of regret, "The white man never fully appreciated the excellent combination of plants that were grown in conucos."

In their arts of government the Tainos seem to have achieved a parallel sort of harmony. Most villages were small (ten to fifteen families) and autonomous, although many apparently recognized loose allegiances with neighboring villages, and they were governed by a hereditary official called a *kaseke* (*cacique*, in the Spanish form), something of a cross between an arbiter and a prolocutor, supported by advisers and elders. So little a part did violence play in their system that they seem, remarkably, to have been a society without war (at least we know of no war music or signals or artifacts, and no evidence of intertribal combats) and even without overt conflict (Las Casas reports that no Spaniard ever saw two Tainos fighting). And here we come to what was obviously the Tainos' outstanding cultural achievement, a proficiency in the social arts that led those who first met them to comment unfailingly on their friendliness, their warmth, their openness, and above all—so striking to those of an acquisitive culture—their generosity.

"They are the best people in the world and above all the gentlest," Colón recorded in his *Journal* (December 16), and from first to last he was astonished at their kindness:

They became so much our friends that it was a marvel.... They traded and gave everything they had, with good will [October 12].

I sent the ship's boat ashore for water, and they very willingly showed my people where the water was, and they themselves carried the full barrels to the boat, and took great delight in pleasing us [October 16].

They are very gentle and without knowledge of what is evil; nor do they murder or steal [November 12].

Your Highnesses may believe that in all the world there can be no better or gentler people... for neither better people nor land can there be.... All the people show the most singular loving behavior and they speak pleasantly [December 24].

I assure Your Highnesses that I believe that in all the world there is no better people nor better country. They love their neighbors as themselves, and they have the sweetest talk in the world, and are gentle and always laughing [December 25].

Even if one allows for some exaggeration—Colón was clearly trying to convince Ferdinand and Isabella that his Indians could be easily conquered and converted, should that be the Sovereigns' wish—it is obvious that the Tainos exhibited a manner of social discourse that quite impressed the rough Europeans. But that was not high among the traits of "civilized" nations, as Colón and Europe understood it, and it counted for little in the Admiral's assessment of these people. However struck he was with such behavior, he would not have thought that it was the mark of a benign and harmonious society, or that from it another culture might learn. For him it was something like the wondrous behavior of children, the naive guilelessness of prelapsarian creatures who knew no better how to bargain and chaffer and cheat than they did to dress themselves: "For a lace-point they gave good pieces of gold the size of two fingers" (January 6), and "They even took pieces of the broken hoops of the wine casks and, like beasts [*como besti*], gave what they had" (Santangel Letter). Like beasts; such innocence was not human.

It is to be regretted that the Admiral, unable to see past their nakedness, as it were, knew not the real virtues of the people he confronted. For the Tainos' lives were in many ways as idyllic as their surroundings, into which they fit with such skill and comfort. They were well fed and well housed, without poverty or serious disease. They enjoyed considerable leisure, given over to dancing, singing, ballgames, and sex, and expressed themselves artistically in basketry, woodworking, pottery, and jewelry. They lived in general harmony and peace, without greed or covetousness or theft. In short, as Sauer says, "the tropical idyll of the accounts of Columbus and Peter Martyr was largely true." . . .

One of the alternative possibilities for future Spanish glory in these none too promising islands suggested itself to Colón almost from the first. On his third day of exploration—a Sunday at that —he had set out to see "where there might be a fortress [built]" and in no time at all found a spit of land on which "there might be a fortress"—and from which "with fifty men they [the Tainos] could all be subjected and made to do all that one might wish" (October 14). Now, during the second leg of exploration along the north coast of Cuba, this grew into a full-blown fantasy of a colonial outpost, complete with a rich trade and merchants. And so Colón went on, rather like a young boy playing soldiers, turning various pieces of landscape into military sites: Puerto de Mares on November 5, a harbor for "a store and a fortress" on November 12, another harbor where "a fortress could be erected" on November 16, a placed where "a town or city and fortress" could be built on November 27 —until finally, as we shall see, misfortune enabled him to translate his fancy into reality.

Now there was no particular reason to go about constructing fortresses—"I don't see that it would be necessary, because these people are very unskilled in arms" (October 14)—but that was the way his architectural imagination, suffused with his vision of colonial destiny, seemed to work: a spit of land, a promontory, a protected harbor, and right away he saw a fort. Such was the deeply ingrained militarism of fifteenth-century Europe, in which fortresses represent edifices more essential to civilization even than churches or castles.

It may have been that Colón began his explorations with nothing more than an idea of establishing some sort of entrepôt in these islands, a fortress-protected trading post rather like the one the Portuguese had established, and Colón had perhaps visited, on the Gold Coast of Africa, at El Mina. But as he sailed along the coast of Cuba he seems to have contrived something even grander, not just a trading port but an outright colonial settlement, an outpost of empire where Spaniards would settle and prosper, living off the labor of the natives ("Command them to do what you will," December 16) and the trade of the Europeans.

On November 27, toward the end of his sojourn along Cuba, Colón put into a large "very singular harbor" which he named Puerto Santo (today known as Puerto Baracoa, about a hundred miles from the eastern tip of the island) and was nearly speechless at its tropical splendor: "Truly, I was so astounded at the sight of so much beauty that I know not how to express myself." The vision of conquest, however, loosened his tongue, and at great length, too:

And Your Highnesses will command a city and fortress to be built in these parts, and these lands converted; and I assure Your Highnesses that it seems to me that there could never be under the sun [lands] superior in fertility, in mildness of cold and heat, in abundance of good and healthy water. . . . So may it please God that Your Highnesses will send here, or that there will come, learned men and they will see the truth of all. And although before I have spoken of the site of a town and fortress on the Rio de Mares... yet there is no comparing that place with this here or with the Mar de Nuestra Señora; for inland here must be great settlements and innumerable people and things of great profit; for here, and in all else that I have discovered and have hopes of discovering before I return to Castile, I say that all Christendom will do business [dad negociaçion] with them, but most of all Spain, to which all this should be subject. And I say that Your Highnesses ought not to consent that any foreigner trade or set foot here except Catholic Christians, since this was the end and the beginning of the enterprise [proposito], that it was for the enhancement and glory of the Christian religion, nor should anyone who is not a good Christian come to these parts.

It may fairly be called the birth of European colonialism.

Here, for the first time that we know, are the outlines of the policy that not only Spain but other European countries would indeed adopt in the years to come, complete with conquest, religious conversion, city settlements, fortresses, exploitation, international trade, and exclusive domain. And that colonial policy would be very largely responsible for endowing those countries with the pelf, power, patronage, and prestige that allowed them to become the nation-states they did.

Again, one is at a loss to explain quite why Colón would so casually assume a right to the conquest and colonialization, even the displacement and enslavement, of these peaceful and inoffensive people 3,000 miles across the ocean. Except, of course, insofar as might, in European eyes, made that right, and after all "they bear no arms, and are all naked and of no skill in arms, and so very cowardly that a thousand would not stand against [aguardariá] three" (December 16). But assume it he did, and even Morison suggests that "every man in the fleet from servant boy to Admiral was convinced that no Christian need do a hand's turn of work in the Indies; and before them opened the delightful vision of growing rich by exploiting the labor of docile natives." The Admiral at least had no difficulty in seeing the Tainos in this light: "They are fit to be ordered about and made to work, to sow and do everything else that may be needed" (December 16); "nothing was lacking but to know the language and to give them orders, because all that they are ordered to do they will do without opposition" (December 21).

Missed in the dynamics of the assumed right of colonialism was an extraordinary opportunity, had it only been possible for the Christian intruders to know it, an opportunity for a dispirited and melancholy Europe to have learned something about fecundity and regeneration, about social comeliness and amity, about harmony with the natural world. The appropriate architecture for Colón to have envisioned along these shores might have been a forum, or an amphitheater, or an academy, perhaps an auditorium or a tabernacle; instead, a fortress....

Originally, so he tells us (October 19), Colón had planned to return to Castile sometime in April, when, he presumably knew from his earlier travels, the North Atlantic would be past its winter storm season. But now, after the wreck of the Santa María and with news that the Pinta was not far away, he apparently decided to sail back immediately. It was a risky decision and most unseamanlike—as he would soon discover, when he was blown off course and almost capsized by two fierce storms in February and March—that leads one to assume that the Admiral's need was dire. Yet all he ever said, a few days later, was that he intended to head back home "without detaining himself further," because "he had found that which he was seeking" (January 9) and intended "to come at full speed to carry the news" (January 8)....

Whatever the reasons for his haste, the Admiral certainly made his way along the remainder of the island's coast with great alacrity, and little more than a week after he met up with Pinzón, the two caravels were off on the homeward leg. Only one notable stop was made, at a narrow bay some 200 miles east of La Navidad, where a party Colón sent ashore discovered, for the first time, some Indians with bows and arrows.

The Admiral having given standing orders that his men should buy or barter away the weaponry of the Indians—they had done so on at least two previous occasions, presumably without causing enmity—these men in the longboat began to dicker with the bowmen with the plumes. After just two bows were sold, the Indians turned and ran back to the cover of the trees where they kept their remaining weapons and, so the sailors assumed, "prepared... to attack the Christians and capture them." When they came toward the Spaniards again brandishing ropes—almost certainly meaning to trade these rather than give up their precious bows—the sailors panicked and, "being prepared as always the Admiral advised them to be," attacked the Indians with swords and halberds, gave one "a great slash on the buttocks" and shot another in the breast with a crossbow. The Tainos grabbed their fallen comrades and fled in fright, and the sailors would have chased them and "killed many of them" but for the pilot in charge of the party, who somehow "prevented it." It may fairly be called the first pitched battle between Europeans and Indians in the New World— the first display of the armed power, and the will to use it, of the white invaders.

And did the Admiral object to this, transgressing as it did his previous idea of trying to maintain good relations with the natives so as to make them willing trading partners, if not docile servants? Hardly at all: now, he said, "they would have fear of the Christians," and he celebrated the skirmish by naming the cape and the harbor de las Flechas—of the Arrows.

It was not the first time (or the last) that Colón was able to delude himself— it may indeed have been a European assumption—that violence can buy obedience. Twice before, he had used a display of European arms to frighten the Tainos, to no purpose other than instilling more fear and awe than they already felt: once on December 26, when he had a Turkish longbow, a gun [*espingarda*], and a lombard demonstrated, at which occasion the people "all fell to earth" in terror and the *kaseke* "was astonished"; then again on the eve of his departure from La Navidad, when he ordered a lombard fired from the new fortress out at the remains of the *Santa María* so that Guacanagarí, when he saw "how it pierced the side of the ship and how the ball went far out to sea," would then "hold the Christians whom [Colón] left behind as friends" and be so scared "that he might fear them." Strange behavior at any time; toward this softhearted *kaseke* and his kindly people, almost inexplicable.

NO

Robert Royal

EL ALMIRANTE

Let us hear what their comments are now—those who are so ready with accusations and quick to find fault, saying from their safe berths there in Spain, "Why didn't you do this or that when you were over there." I'd like to see their sort on this adventure. Verily I believe, there's another journey, of quite a different order, for them to make, or all our faith is vain.

— Columbus
Lettera Rarissima

After centuries of controversies, the life of Columbus lies beneath mountains of interpretation and misinterpretation. Sharp criticism of *El Almirante* (the admiral)—and sharp reaction to it—go back to the very beginnings of his explorations, as the passage cited above, written at a particularly threatening moment during Columbus's fourth and final voyage to the New World, graphically shows. Then, as now, it was easy for people who had never dared comparable feats to suggest how the whole business might have been done better. And in truth, Columbus's manifest errors and downright incapacities as a leader of men, anywhere but on the sea, played into the hands of his critics and properly made him the target of protests. His failures in leadership provoked atrocities against the Caribbean natives and harsh punishment, including executions, of Spaniards as well. Stubbornness, obsessiveness, and paranoia often dominated his psyche. Even many of his closest allies in the initial ventures clashed with him over one thing or another. In the wake of the titanic passions his epochal voyages unleashed, it is no wonder that almost every individual and event connected with his story has been praised or damned by someone during the past five hundred years....

FACT AND IMAGINATION

The temptation to project modern categories back upon earlier historical periods is always strong. Reviewing these first late-fifteenth-century contacts now, with knowledge of what befell indigenous peoples later, we are particularly inclined to read large-scale portents into small events. If Columbus mentions how easy it would be to subdue the natives, or expresses impatience

From Robert Royal, *1492 and All That: Political Manipulations of History* (Ethics and Public Policy Center, 1992). Copyright © 1992 by Ethics and Public Policy Center, Washington, D.C. Reprinted by permission. Notes omitted.

with his failure to find the high and rich civilization of Asia, many historians readily fall into the error of seeing his attitudes as a combination of careless imperialism and greed, or even as a symbol of all that was to follow. We would do well to recall, however, that the Spanish record after Columbus is complex and not wholly bad, particularly in its gradual elaboration of native rights.

In Columbus the man, several conflicting currents existed side by side. [Bartolomé de] Las Casas is an important witness here because of both his passionate commitment to justice for Indians and his personal association with Columbus for several years. In a telling remark, Las Casas notes that while Christopher's brother, Bartolomé, was a resolute leader, he lacked the "sweetness and benignity" of the admiral. Columbus's noble bearing and gentle manners are confirmed in many other sources. Nevertheless, Las Casas can be harsh in his criticism. Chapter 119 of *History of the Indies* concludes with the judgment that both brothers mistakenly began to occupy land and exact tribute owing to "the most culpable ignorance, which has no excuse, of natural and divine law."

After five hundred years it may seem impossible to reconcile the contradictory traits Las Casas mentions. He attempted an explanation of his own:

> Truly, I would not dare blame the admiral's intentions, for I knew him well and I know his intentions were good. But ... the road he paved and the things he did of his own free will, as well as sometimes under constraint, stemmed from his ignorance of the law. There is much to ponder here and one can see the guiding principle of this whole Indian enterprise, namely, as is clear from the previous chapters, that the

admiral and his Christians, as well as all those who followed after him in this land, worked on the assumption that the way to achieve their desires was first and foremost to instill fear in these people, to the extent of making the name Christian synonymous with terror. And to do this, they performed outstanding feats never before invented or dreamed of, as, God willing, I will show later. And this is contrary and inimical to the way that those who profess Christian benignity, gentleness and peace ought to negotiate the conversion of infidels.

As this excerpt shows, Las Casas's style of writing and mode of reasoning do not always yield great clarity, and his assessment here begs several questions. Columbus's policies, and official Spanish policy generally, were much more given to gentleness and kindness in the beginning than Las Casas, who only witnessed later troubled times, allows to appear. There is no question that conflicts with natives and factional infighting among Spaniards drove the admiral to more onerous measures, including enslavement of Indians captured in military actions.

While Las Casas's condemnation is cast in terms of absolute justice and as such has permanent relevance to evaluating Columbus's role in the New World, we should remember that Columbus was placed in unprecedented circumstances and should not be judged in the same way as we would a modern trained anthropologist. Paolo Emilio Taviani, an admiring but not uncritical recent biographer of Columbus, demonstrates the difficulty attending every particular of the first contact:

> The European scale of values was different from that of the natives. "They give everything for a trifle"; obviously what was a trifle on the European scale

was not so for the natives. For them "a potsherd or a broken glass cup" was worth "sixteen skeins of cotton." Columbus warned that would never do, because from unrestricted trade between the two mentalities, the two conceptions of value, grave injustices would result, and so he immediately prohibited the cotton trade, allowing no one to take any and reserving the acquisition entirely for the king of Spain. A just prohibition, not easy to impose on ninety men—what strength could it have when nine hundred, nine thousand, or ninety thousand Europeans would arrive? Such were the first troubles in an encounter between two worlds that did not understand one another.

If we wish to task Columbus for all the asymmetries that ensued, we should credit him as well for this initial attempt, later repeated by many Spanish governors and theologians, to find some just route through the thicket of massive cultural difference. He failed and permitted far more wicked practices than unequal trade, but we should not let subsequent events blind us to his authentic concern for justice in the first contacts.

SOME BRIGHTER MOMENTS

In spite of the cultural gulf, mutual affections and understanding did, at times, appear. After over two months of exploration in the Caribbean, Columbus's ship, the *Santa Maria*, went aground on Christmas 1492 in what is now Haiti. There Columbus encountered a people and a chief so helpful that his log entries for the following days view the entire episode as providential. He would never have chosen, as he admits, to come ashore or build the settlement of La Navidad (Christmas)

there. He did not like the harbor at all. Yet he concluded that his relations with the Taínos and their chief Guacanagarí must be part of a divine plan in light of the friendship that sprung up between the two peoples.

Some Columbus scholars, perhaps a bit jaded from staring overlong at the historical lacunae and inconsistencies of the man, see in these log entries only an attempt to cover up the disastrous loss of the ship or a propaganda ploy to make the Spanish monarchs think well of the discoveries. Robert H. Fuson, a modern translator of the log, is a marine historian rather than a Columbus specialist. He is sometimes rightly criticized for his rather naive historical interpretations. But it is precisely because he is not predisposed to suspicion that he notices something overlooked by scholars occupied with weighing too many contradictory theories about the Haiti episode:

Affection for the young chief in Haiti, and vice versa, is one of the most touching stories of love, trust, and understanding between men of different races and cultures to come out of this period in history. His [Columbus's] instructions to the men he left behind at La Navidad, for January 2, clearly illustrate his sincere fondness and respect for the Indians.

The January 2 entry, as we shall see below, indicates that Columbus had some ulterior motives in placating the natives. But that does not negate his genuine good feeling toward them or his gratitude for their generosity. Even if we assume that Columbus is putting the best interpretation on events for Ferdinand and Isabella, some sort of fellow feeling undeniably had arisen, at least temporarily, across the vast cultural divide separating the Taínos and the

Europeans. Despite the great evils that would come later, this altruism was not without its own modest legacies.

An extreme but common form of the over-simple charges often leveled against the Europeans in general and Columbus in particular has come from the pen of the novelist Hans Koning. Writing in the *Washington Post* to influence public sentiments about the quincentenary, Koning insisted that from 1492 to 1500,

> there is not one recorded moment of awe, of joy, of love, of a smile. There is only anger, cruelty, greed, terror, and death. That is the record. Nothing else, I hold, is relevant when we discuss our commemoration of its 500th anniversary.

Riding the wave of revisionism about American history now sweeping over education, Koning made these claims under the title "Teach the Truth About Columbus."

The only problem with his assessment is that every particular in his catalog of what constitutes the truth is false. To take them in order: Columbus certainly records awe at his discoveries throughout his four voyages. His praise of the land's beauty was partly meant, of course, to convince the king and queen of the value of the properties Columbus had discovered for them. But some of it is simply awe; Columbus's enthusiasm for many of the new lands reaches a climax when he describes the sheer loveliness of the Venezuelan coast, which he believed to be the site of the original Garden of Eden, the earthly paradise. If that is not a record of awe, it is difficult to imagine what would be.

The relations between natives and Spaniards before 1500 are not, *pace* Koning, unrelieved darkness either. If anything, they are a frustrating reminder of a road not taken. Smiles there were—recorded smiles—at least on the native Taíno side: "They love their neighbors as themselves, and they have the softest and gentlest voices in the world and are always smiling" (*Log*, Tuesday, 25 December 1492). Columbus had reason to appreciate these people since they had just helped him salvage what was salvageable from the wreck of the *Santa Maria*. In the feast natives and Spaniards held after the rescue, the cacique Guacanagarí placed a crown on Columbus's head. The admiral reciprocated by giving him a scarlet cloak and a pair of colored boots, "and I placed upon his finger a large silver ring. I had been told that he had seen a silver ring on one of my sailors and desired it very much. The King was joyful and overwhelmed." Guacanagarí grew so close to Columbus that he asked if he and his brother might return with him to Castile.

When it came time to leave for Spain, Columbus placed thirty-nine men "under the command of three officers, all of whom are very friendly to King Guacanagarí," and furthermore ordered that "they should avoid *as they would death* annoying or tormenting the Indians, bearing in mind how much they owe these people." The emphasis added to this last quotation has a double purpose. Clearly, Columbus recognized the temptations his men would have; just as clearly he was determined, to the best of his ability, to anticipate and block those temptations. This is the entry of January 2 that Fuson reads as expressing sincere kindness and affection. That reading may be a little too simple, but it is not entirely mistaken.

What this incident and the founding of the settlement definitely are *not*, however, are instances of simple European arrogance and imperialism, or what John Noble Wilford, a recent biographer of Columbus, has called "a personal transition from discoverer to imperialist." Even when full-scale war between some Indians and Spaniards broke out during Columbus's second voyage, Guacanagarí remained loyal to Columbus in spite of— or perhaps in opposition to—commands from another local chief, Caonabó, for a cacique alliance. No source denies this loyalty between the Taíno and the admiral, even under trying cultural tensions and warfare. Though we are right to abhor many far-less-happy subsequent events between the inhabitants of the two worlds, the record of the early interaction is richer and more diverse than most people, blinded by contemporary polemics, think. Hans Koning might do well to calm down and read some of these passages.

THE LIST OF CHARGES

The principal moral questions about Columbus arise essentially from three of his actions:

1. He immediately kidnapped some Taínos during his first voyage for questioning and use as interpreters. In that act he showed not only his contempt for Indian life but his belief that Spanish language, culture, and religion were superior and rightly to be imposed on native peoples.

2. After the destruction of La Navidad and the turmoil that ensued during the second voyage, Columbus foolishly ordered exploratory missions without adequate safeguards to restrain outrageously violent men like Mosen Pedro Margarit and Alonso de Ojeda. He then punished the natives who objected to Spaniards living off the land or who resisted their commands. In addition to setting this evil precedent, he shipped home some natives to become slaves with a very poor excuse:

> Since of all the islands those of the cannibals are much the largest and much more fully populated, it is thought here that to take some of the men and women and to send them home to Castile would not be anything but well, for they may one day be led to abandon that inhuman custom that they have of eating men, and there in Castile, learning the language, they will much more readily receive baptism and secure the welfare of their souls.

3. Columbus instituted a system of gold tribute from the natives that was heavy—nearly impossible, in fact, given the small quantity of gold on the island of Hispaniola—and that was harshly enforced.

Each of these charges is true and no amount of admiration for Christopher Columbus can excuse what is simply inexcusable. Even the argument by Felipe Fernández-Armesto, one of the fairest Columbus historians, that "Columbus and his successors were guilty only of applying the best standards of their time" makes two false assumptions. First, that such behavior represents the best contemporary standards.... Second, that individuals should not be criticized for acting like the majority of their contemporaries because they are bound by culture and history. The latter argument draws strength from current philosophical schools that hold there are no privileged or absolute positions outside of historically conditioned views. But if we think we should condemn Aztec human sacrifice as wrong—not simply a different cultural form, but wrong—then we must admit there are universal principles that also allow us to criticize improper

European use of force, enslavement, and exploitation.

Yet just as we try to understand the reasons behind Aztec human sacrifice or Carib cannibalism, and both tribes' imperialism toward other native peoples, we should also try to see what led to Columbus's behavior. Columbus, as Las Casas testified above, was not by nature a brutal man like Ojeda or Cortés. The first sign of harshness by him, in fact, seems to have been his acquiescence, during the second voyage, in a death sentence against some Indians on Hispaniola who had been caught stealing. Significantly, the pleading of another Indian moved him to remit the sentence in that case (the wavering too is characteristic of the uncertainty in handling questions of governance). Though he apparently regarded the Indians as inferior and always approached them with much the same assumption of superiority that Spaniards approached the Guanches of the Canary Islands and African tribes, he seemed at least partly—and when circumstances allowed—aware that good treatment was both morally called for and favorable to Spanish interests.

A fairer reading of the record reveals some mitigating factors, though these by no means add up to an exoneration.

1. Though Columbus did kidnap some Indians, two interpreters among them, he set one of them free immediately upon returning to Hispaniola during the second voyage. He hoped that the Indian set at liberty would tell others of Spain's wonders and of Columbus's good intentions. This was naive, crude, and manipulative on his part, but shows some perspicacity and good will.

2. Slavery was always a bone of contention between Columbus and the Spanish monarchs—they vehemently opposed this way of "civilizing" their subjects in the Indies. Columbus was not clear in his own mind about the issue. As late as the third voyage, the last in which he would be permitted to visit the growing colony on Hispaniola, Columbus ordered that slaves could only be taken during just war. His thinking was muddled, as was the thinking of the world for at least another half century until several crucial questions about Indian rights and just claims were sorted out.

3. The imposition of gold tribute for Spanish services stemmed from the belief that much gold existed on Hispaniola. And Indian failures to meet what seemed to the Spaniards modest levies were mistakenly attributed to laziness. Indians loved the tiny hawk's bells that the Spaniards brought as trinkets; asking them to fill a bell with gold every two months seemed a reasonable request. Since all governments tax in some fashion, Spain was doing only what caciques and Carib conquerors had been doing for time immemorial. The Spanish system did not "introduce" a new evil to an idyllic people without politics, but it proved peculiarly burdensome because it was imposed from the outside and in ignorance of the realities on Hispaniola. Furthermore, contrary to many wild charges, the Spaniards never intended to commit "genocide." A ready supply of native workers served Spanish self-interest. European and African diseases, however, soon laid waste whole tribes.

Fernández-Armesto argues that Columbus's recourse to violence on Hispaniola resulted mostly from his basic inability to rule well, from "misjudgment rather than wickedness." Gonzalo Fernandez de Oviedo, who became the official Spanish historian of the New World, said that to govern the Hispaniola colony correctly a person would have to be "angelic indeed superhuman." Columbus was far from either; in fact, he was far from possessing even normal political acumen. During his second and third voyages he clearly tried to avoid facing political difficulties on Hispaniola by exploring further. The problem was not merely lack of political skill. As a foreigner, he felt that he could trust only family members and close personal friends. (In fact, recent research has revealed that the Columbus family belonged to an anti-Spanish faction in Genoa, a political embarrassment that may help account for some of Columbus's reticence about his early life.) The resentments arising from difficult conditions, moreover, served to reinforce his tendencies toward paranoia. His rule of both Indians and Spanish oscillated between being too indecisive and too harsh.

We should also understand the kinds of Indians and colonists he had to govern. Columbus had trouble enough with the natives and complained:

> At home they judge me as a governor sent to Sicily or to a city or two under settled government and where the laws can be fully maintained, without fear of all being lost.... I ought to be judged as a captain who went from Spain to the Indies to conquer a people, warlike and numerous, and with customs and beliefs very different from ours.

Even the Taínos were probably far less gentle than Columbus earlier reported and "not so innocent as Las Casas tried to show." The Caribs, their fierce, cannibalistic enemies, seem to have been as terrified of the supposedly pacific Taínos as vice versa. And recent archeological investigations suggest that the Taínos, contrary to Columbus's impression of them

as being without religion, had a complex system of belief and ritual akin to those in Central America and Mexico. They appear to have played a ritual ball game re-enacting the cosmic struggle between light and darkness and ending with the religious sacrifice of one or more human victims. An early Spanish conquistador estimated that twenty thousand people were sacrificed yearly on Hispaniola alone, though that figure may be wildly exaggerated. In any event, native tribes were profoundly *other* to the unsophisticated sailors and explorers in Columbus's day—and remain profoundly other to us today.

The Spaniards with whom Columbus had to deal were not much better. After the second voyage he asked the monarchs to think carefully about whom they were sending on the voyages and to choose "such persons that there be no suspicion of them and that they consider the purpose for which they have been sent rather than their personal interests." Not only were some of the colonists unusually violent, but many Spanish gentlemen who had come expecting easy wealth resented Columbus, the need to work, and the unhealthy conditions on the island. In dealing with these settlers, as Las Casas observed, "The Admiral had to use violence, threats, and constraint to have the work done at all." ...

BAD IN ANY CASE

... In Kirkpatrick Sale [*The Conquest of Paradise: Christopher Columbus and the Columbian Legacy*], Columbus is uniquely and doubly condemned for being medieval *and* for being of the Renaissance. His medieval side reflects superstitions, and his Renaissance side shows the destructive force of naked instrumental and mathematical reason, which Sale largely identifies with Renaissance Europe. Nevertheless, Sale also feels free to castigate Columbus for his lack of interest in numbers, that is, for not giving us the exact mathematical coordinates of the island where he made first landfall. Poor Columbus is merely the product of various opposing evil traditions that define Europe and Europeans—of which we are all the heirs, save, of course, the Kirkpatrick Sales who transcend cultural determinism.

All these attempts at neat categorizations assume that we can define a man, as well as a historical period, with far sharper boundaries than is ever the case. The mixture of human weakness and human greatness in even a key figure is never easy to calculate. The novelist Anthony Burgess has recently created a Mozart who says, "My desire and my hope is to gain honor, fame, and money." That sentence plausibly formulates a great deal of truth about Mozart's life. Yet few music lovers would deduce from this that Mozart's work is, therefore, solely the product of ambition and cupidity, or try to explain the man and his music by sociological analysis of the late eighteenth century. Columbus similarly spoke of "God, gold, and glory," and many of the Europeans who followed him were driven by multiple motives, not all of which were, by any means, merely self-serving.

Kirkpatrick Sale, as usual, well formulates the ultimate issue behind much of the public controversy over 1992:

> In the final analysis, it is not so important whether Columbus was a good man. What matters is that he brought over a culture centered on its own superiority. The failings of the man were and remain the failures of the culture.

This is a strained argument. It certainly does matter, if only for the sake of historical justice, that we try to discern the mix of good and evil in Columbus *per se.* Furthermore, no one can simply be identified with a whole culture. Every individual both draws on and opposes elements in his surroundings. If the preceding pages show anything, they show that Columbus, like the rest of us, was not simply good or bad. As a great human spirit, both his virtues and faults appear larger and more vivid than they do in most people. And his historical influence reflects the dimensions of what he was. The argument about the European sense of superiority, however, can be engaged quite well without dragging in Columbus, as if he were a mere conduit for European culture.

One reason that freedom arose in the West is the traditional Western separation of the City of Man from the City of God.... [M]any of the early missionaries and theologians showed, in the very face of state power and financial interests, that Christian principles pointed toward other paths than those most often taken by settlers in the New World. Columbus and Las Casas were sometimes at odds over specifics, but were not fundamentally opposed on these matters. Las Casas is the greater figure for his moral passion and courage, but Columbus, in spite of his faults, deserves no little admiration. Emblematic, perhaps, of their relationship is the suggestion of Simón Bolívar in 1819 that a newly liberated area of South America be named Colombia and its capital Las Casas: "Thus will we prove to the world that we not only have the right to be free, but we will demonstrate that we know how to honor the friends and benefactors of mankind."

POSTSCRIPT

Was Columbus an Imperialist?

Whether or not we view Christopher Columbus's actions in the Americas as the work of an imperialist, there is no doubt that the impact of his arrival in the Western Hemisphere carried with it enormous consequences, not the least of which was the so-called "Columbian Exchange," which involved a reciprocal trade in plants and animals, human beings, diseases, and ideas. For example, the introduction of destructive microorganisms produced epidemic outbreaks of smallpox, tuberculosis, measles, typhoid, and syphilis that decimated human populations on both sides of the Atlantic. On a more positive note, Europeans brought food items such as wheat and potatoes to the New World and brought home maize, beans, and manioc. Native Americans benefited from horses and other farm animals introduced from Europe, but these benefits were offset by the efforts of the Europeans to enslave and kill the indigenous peoples whom they encountered. The best study of these various by-products of European exploration is Alfred W. Crosby, *The Columbian Exchange: Biological and Cultural Consequences of 1492* (Greenwood Press, 1973).

The effects of the encounters between Europeans and Native Americans is explored in Gary B. Nash, *Red, White & Black: The Peoples of Early North America*, 3rd ed. (Prentice Hall, 1992) and two works by James Axtell, *The European and the Indian: Essays in the Ethnohistory of Colonial North America* (Oxford University Press, 1981) and *The Invasion Within: The Contest of Cultures in Colonial North America* (Oxford University Press, 1985). Alvin M. Josephy, Jr., examines the pre-Columbian Native Americans in *1492: The World of the Indian Peoples Before the Arrival of Columbus* (Alfred A. Knopf, 1992).

Samuel Eliot Morison, *The European Discovery of America: The Northern Voyages* (Oxford University Press, 1971); David Beers Quinn, *England and the Discovery of America, 1481–1620* (Harper & Row, 1974); Wallace Notestein, *The English People on the Eve of Colonization, 1603–1630* (Harper & Brothers, 1954); Charles Gibson, *Spain in America* (Harper & Row, 1966); and W. J. Eccles, *France in America* (Harper & Row, 1972), discuss European contacts in North America.

Perhaps the best biographical treatment of Columbus is Samuel Eliot Morison's generally sympathetic *Admiral of the Ocean Sea: A Life of Christopher Columbus*, 2 vols. (Little, Brown, 1942). For a more recent objective and scholarly study, see Felipe Fernandez-Armesto, *Columbus* (Oxford University Press, 1991).

ISSUE 3

Was the Colonial Period a "Golden Age" for Women in America?

YES: Lois Green Carr and Lorena S. Walsh, from "The Planter's Wife: The Experience of White Women in Seventeenth-Century Maryland," *William and Mary Quarterly* (January 1977)

NO: Mary Beth Norton, from "The Myth of the Golden Age," in Carol Ruth Berkin and Mary Beth Norton, eds., *Women of America: A History* (Houghton Mifflin, 1979)

ISSUE SUMMARY

YES: Adjunct professor Lois Green Carr and historian Lorena S. Walsh identify several factors that coalesced to afford women in seventeenth-century Maryland a higher status with fewer restraints on their social conduct than those experienced by women in England.

NO: Professor Mary Beth Norton challenges the "golden age" theory by insisting that women in colonial America, whether white, black, or Native American, typically occupied a domestic sphere that was lacking in status, physically debilitating over time, and a barrier to educational opportunity and political power.

For generations students in American history classes have read of the founding of the colonies in British North America, their political and economic development, and the colonists' struggles for independence, without ever being confronted by a female protagonist in this magnificent historical drama. The terms *Sons of Liberty* and *Founding Fathers* reflect the end result of a long tradition of gender-specific myopia. In fact, only in the last generation have discussions of the role of women in the development of American society made their appearance in standard textbooks. Consequently, it is useful to explore the status of women in colonial America.

The topic is quite complex. The status of colonial women was determined by cultural attitudes that were exported to the New World from Europe, by the specific conditions confronting successive waves of settlers—male and female—in terms of labor requirements, and by changes produced by colonial maturation over time. It would be impossible to pinpoint a single, static condition in which *all* colonial women existed.

What was the status of women in the British North American colonies? To what degree did the legal status of women differ from their *de facto* status?

A half-century of scholarship has produced the notion that colonial women enjoyed a more privileged status than either their European contemporaries or their nineteenth-century descendants. This view, developed in the writings of Richard B. Morris, Elizabeth Dexter, and Mary Beard, was reinforced in the 1970s by John Demos and Roger Thompson. For example, Demos contends that despite the fact that Plymouth Colony was based on a patriarchal model in which women were expected to subordinate themselves to men, women still shared certain responsibilities with their husbands in some business activities and in matters relating to their children. They not only performed all household duties but also assisted the men with agricultural duties outside the home when the necessity arose. However, women were closed off from any formal public power in the colony even when they performed essential economic functions within the community. Society as a whole viewed them as "weaker vessels," physically, intellectually, and morally.

The following essays explore the status of women in seventeenth-century America. Lois Green Carr and Lorena S. Walsh assess this issue against the backdrop of four factors in colonial Maryland: the predominance of an immigrant population; the early death of male inhabitants; the late marriages of women due to their indentured servitude; and the sexual imbalance in which men greatly outnumbered women. As a result of these conditions, Maryland women experienced fewer restraints on their social conduct and enjoyed more power than did their English counterparts. Most became planter's wives, enjoyed considerable freedom in choosing their husbands, and benefited from a substantial right to inherit property.

Mary Beth Norton's essay is broader in scope, giving consideration to women's status in both the sixteenth and seventeenth centuries and including women of various socioeconomic backgrounds. While noting that more research needs to be done on the conditions of African American and Native American women in the colonies, she includes evidence suggesting that, regardless of race, women shared a subordinate status in colonial America. Women's lives were circumscribed, according to Norton, by their general confinement to domestic responsibilities, social isolation from other women, and the absence of significant educational and political opportunities.

YES

Lois Green Carr and
Lorena S. Walsh

THE PLANTER'S WIFE: THE EXPERIENCE OF WHITE WOMEN IN SEVENTEENTH-CENTURY MARYLAND

Four facts were basic to all human experience in seventeenth-century Maryland. First, for most of the period the great majority of inhabitants had been born in what we now call Britain. Population increase in Maryland did not result primarily from births in the colony before the late 1680s and did not produce a predominantly native population of adults before the first decade of the eighteenth century. Second, immigrant men could not expect to live beyond age forty-three, and 70 percent would die before age fifty. Women may have had even shorter lives. Third, perhaps 85 percent of the immigrants, and practically all the unmarried immigrant women, arrived as indentured servants and consequently married late. Family groups were never predominant in the immigration to Maryland and were a significant part for only a brief time at mid-century. Fourth, many more men than women immigrated during the whole period. These facts—immigrant predominance, early death, late marriage, and sexual imbalance—created circumstances of social and demographic disruption that deeply affected family and community life.

We need to assess the effects of this disruption on the experience of women in seventeenth-century Maryland. Were women degraded by the hazards of servitude in a society in which everyone had left community and kin behind and in which women were in short supply? Were traditional restraints on social conduct weakened? If so, were women more exploited or more independent and powerful than women who remained in England? Did any differences from English experience which we can observe in the experience of Maryland women survive the transformation from an immigrant to a predominantly native-born society with its own kinship networks and community traditions? The tentative argument put forward here is that the answer to all these questions is Yes. There were degrading aspects of servitude, although these probably did not characterize the lot of most women; there were fewer restraints on social conduct, especially in courtship, than in England; women were less protected but also more powerful than those who remained at home; and at least some of these changes survived the appearance in Maryland of New World creole communities....

Maryland was settled in 1634, but in 1650 there were probably no more than six hundred persons and fewer than two hundred adult women in the province. After that time population growth was steady; in 1704 a census listed 30,437 white persons, of whom 7,163 were adult women. Thus in discussing the experience of white women in seventeenth-century Maryland we are dealing basically with the second half of the century....

Whatever their status, one fact about immigrant women is certain: many fewer came than men. Immigrant lists, head-right lists, and itemizations of servants in inventories show severe imbalance. On a London immigrant list of 1634–1635 men outnumbered women six to one. From the 1650s at least until the 1680s most sources show a ratio of three to one. From then on, all sources show some, but not great, improvement. Among immigrants from Liverpool over the years 1697–1707 the ratio was just under two and one half to one.

Why did not more women come? Presumably, fewer wished to leave family and community and venture into a wilderness. But perhaps more important, women were not as desirable as men to merchants and planters who were making fortunes raising and marketing tobacco, a crop that requires large amounts of labor. The gradual improvement in the sex ratio among servants toward the end of the century may have been the result of a change in recruiting the needed labor. In the late 1660s the supply of young men willing to emigrate stopped increasing sufficiently to meet the labor demands of a growing Chesapeake population. Merchants who recruited servants for planters turned to other sources, and among these sources were women. They did not crowd the ships arriving in the Chesapeake, but their numbers did increase.

To ask the question another way, why did women come? Doubtless, most came to get a husband, an objective virtually certain of success in a land where women were so far outnumbered. The promotional literature, furthermore, painted bright pictures of the life that awaited men and women once out of their time; and various studies suggest that for a while, at least, the promoters were not being entirely fanciful. Until the 1660s, and to a less degree the 1680s, the expanding economy of Maryland and Virginia offered opportunities well beyond those available in England to men without capital and to the women who became their wives.

Nevertheless, the hazards were also great, and the greatest was untimely death. Newcomers promptly became ill, probably with malaria, and many died. What proportion survived is unclear; so far no one has devised a way of measuring it. Recurrent malaria made the woman who survived seasoning less able to withstand other diseases, especially dysentery and influenza. She was especially vulnerable when pregnant. Expectation of life for everyone was low in the Chesapeake, but especially so for women. A woman who had immigrated to Maryland took an extra risk, though perhaps a risk not greater than she might have suffered by moving from her village to London instead.

The majority of women who survived seasoning paid their transportation costs by working for a four- or five-year term of service. The kind of work depended on the status of the family they served. A female servant of a small planter—who through about the 1670s might have had a servant—probably worked at the hoe. Such a man could not afford to buy labor that would not help with the cash crop. In wealthy families women probably were household servants, although some are occasionally listed in inventories of well to-do planters as living on the quarters—that is, on plantations other than the dwelling plantation. Such women saved men the jobs of preparing food and washing linen but doubtless also worked in the fields. In middling households experience must have varied. Where the number of people to feed and wash for was large, female servants would have had little time to tend the crops.

Tracts that promoted immigration to the Chesapeake region asserted that female servants did not labor in the fields, except "nasty" wenches not fit for other tasks. This implies that most immigrant women expected, or at least hoped, to avoid heavy field work, which English women—at least those above the cottager's status—did not do. What proportion of female servants in Maryland found themselves demeaned by this unaccustomed labor is impossible to say, but this must have been the fate of some....

The woman who immigrated to Maryland, survived seasoning and service, and gained her freedom became a planter's wife. She had considerable liberty in making her choice. There were men aplenty and no fathers or brothers were hovering to monitor her behavior or disapprove her preference. This is the modern way of looking at her situation, of course. Perhaps she missed the protection of a father, a guardian, or kinfolk, and the participation in her decision of a community to which she felt ties. There is some evidence that the absence of kin and the pressures of the sex ratio created conditions of sexual freedom in courtship that were not customary in England. A register of marriages and births for seventeenth-century Somerset County shows that about one-third of the immigrant women whose marriages are recorded were pregnant at the time of the ceremony—nearly twice the rate in English parishes. There is no indication of community objection to this freedom so long as marriage took place. No presentments for bridal pregnancy were made in any of the Maryland courts.

The planter's wife was likely to be in her mid-twenties at marriage. An estimate of minimum age at marriage for servant women can be made from lists of indentured servants who left London over the years 1683–1684 and from age judgments in Maryland county court records. If we assume that the 112 female indentured servants going to Maryland and Virginia whose ages are given in the London lists served full four-year terms, then only 1.8 percent married before age twenty but 68 percent after age twenty-four. Similarly, if the 141 women whose ages were judged in Charles County between 1666 and 1705 served out their terms according to the custom of the country, none married before age twenty-two, and half were twenty-five or over. When adjustments are made for the ages at which wives may have been purchased, the figures drop, but even so the majority of women waited until at least age twenty-four to marry. Actual age at marriage in Maryland can be found for few seventeenth-century female immigrants, but observations for Charles and Somerset counties place the mean age at about twenty-five.

Because of the age at which an immigrant woman married, the number of children she would bear her husband was small. She had lost up to ten years of her childbearing life—the possibility of perhaps four or five children, given the usual rhythm of childbearing. At the same time, high mortality would reduce both the number of children she would bear over the rest of her life and the number who would live. One partner to a marriage was likely to die within seven years, and the chances were only one in three that a marriage would last ten years. In these circumstances, most women would not bear more than three or four children—not counting those stillborn—to any one husband, plus a posthumous child were she the survivor. The best estimates suggest that nearly a quarter, perhaps more, of the children born alive died during their first year and that 40 to 55 percent would not live to see age twenty. Consequently, one of her children would probably die in infancy, and another one or two would fail to reach adulthood. Wills left in St. Mary's County during the seventeenth century show the results. In 105 families over the years 1660 to 1680 only twelve parents left more than three children behind them, including those conceived but not yet born. The average number was 2.3, nearly always minors, some of whom might die before reaching adulthood.

For the immigrant woman, then, one of the major facts of life was that although she might bear a child about every two years, nearly half would not reach maturity. The social implications of this fact are far-reaching. Because she

married late in her childbearing years and because so many of her children would die young, the number who would reach marriageable age might not replace, or might only barely replace, her and her husband or husbands as child-producing members of the society. Consequently, so long as immigrants were heavily predominant in the adult female population, Maryland could not grow much by natural increase. It remained a land of newcomers....

A hazard of marriage for seventeenth-century women everywhere was death in childbirth, but this hazard may have been greater than usual in the Chesapeake. Whereas in most societies women tend to outlive men, in this malaria-ridden area it is probable that men outlived women. Hazards of childbirth provide the likely reason that Chesapeake women died so young. Once a woman in the Chesapeake reached forty-five, she tended to outlive men who reached the same age....

However long they lived, immigrant women in Maryland tended to outlive their husbands—in Charles County, for example, by a ratio of two to one. This was possible, despite the fact that women were younger than men at death, because women were also younger than men at marriage. Some women were widowed with no living children, but most were left responsible for two or three. These were often tiny, and nearly always not yet sixteen.

This fact had drastic consequences, given the physical circumstances of life. People lived at a distance from one another, not even in villages, must less towns. The widow had left her kin 3,000 miles across an ocean, and her husband's family was also there. She would have to feed her children and make her own tobacco crop. Though neighbors might help, heavy labor would be required of her if she had no servants, until—what admittedly was usually not difficult—she acquired a new husband.

In this situation dying husbands were understandably anxious about the welfare of their families. Their wills reflected their feelings and tell something of how they regarded their wives. In St. Mary's and Charles counties during the seventeenth century, little more than one-quarter of the men left their widows with no more than the dower the law required —one-third of his land for her life, plus outright ownership of one-third of his personal property. If there were no children, a man almost always left his widow his whole estate. Otherwise there were a variety of arrangements.

During the 1660s, when testators begin to appear in quantity, nearly a fifth of the men who had children left all to their wives, trusting them to see that the children received fair portions. Thus in 1663 John Shircliffe willed his whole estate to his wife "towards the maintenance of herself and my children into whose tender care I do Commend them Desireing to see them brought up in the fear of God and the Catholick Religion and Chargeing them to be Dutiful and obedient to her." As the century progressed, husbands tended instead to give the wife all or a major part of the estate for her life, and to designate how it should be distributed after her death. Either way, the husband put great trust in his widow, considering that he knew she was bound to remarry. Only a handful of men left estates to their wives only for their term of widowhood or until the children came of age. When a man did not leave his wife a life estate, he often gave her land outright or more than her dower third of his movable property.

Such bequests were at the expense of his children and showed his concern that his widow should have a maintenance which young children could not supply.

A husband usually made his wife his executor and thus responsible for paying his debts and preserving the estate. Only 11 percent deprived their wives of such powers. In many instances, however, men also appointed overseers to assist their wives and to see that their children were not abused or their property embezzled. Danger lay in the fact that a second husband acquired control of all his wife's property, including her life estate in the property of his predecessor. Over half of the husbands who died in the 1650s and 1660s appointed overseers to ensure that their wills were followed. Some trusted to the overseers' "Care and good Conscience for the good of my widow and fatherless children." Others more explicit made overseers responsible for seeing that "my said child ... and the other [expected child] (when pleases God to send it) may have their right Proportion of my Said Estate and that the said Children may be bred up Chiefly in the fear of God." A few men —but remarkably few—authorized overseers to remove children from households of stepfathers who abused them or wasted their property. On the whole, the absence of such provisions for the protection of the children points to the husband's overriding concern for the welfare of his widow and to his confidence in her management, regardless of the certainty of her remarriage. Evidently, in the politics of family life women enjoyed great respect.

We have implied that this respect was a product of the experience of immigrants in the Chesapeake. Might it have been instead a reflection of the English culture? Little work is yet in print that allows comparison of the provisions for Maryland widows with those made for the widows of English farmers. Possibly Maryland husbands were making traditional wills which could have been written in the communities they left behind. However, Margaret Spufford's recent study of three Cambridgeshire villages in the late sixteenth century and early seventeenth century suggests a different pattern. In one of these villages, Chippenham, women usually did receive a life interest in the property but in the other two they did not. If the children were all minors, the widow controlled the property until the oldest son came of age, and then only if she did not remarry. In the majority of cases adult sons were given control of the property with instructions for the support of their mothers. Spufford suggests that the pattern found in Chippenham must have been very exceptional. On the basis of village censuses in six other counties, dating from 1624 to 1724, which show only 3 percent of widowed people heading households that included a married child, she argues that if widows commonly controlled the farm, a higher proportion should have headed such households. However, she also argues that widows with an interest in land would not long remain unmarried. If so, the low percentage may be deceptive.…

Remarriage was the usual and often the immediate solution for a woman who had lost her husband. The shortage of women made any woman eligible to marry again, and the difficulties of raising a family while running a plantation must have made remarriage necessary for widows who had no son old enough to make tobacco. One indication of the high incidence of remarriage is the fact that there were only sixty women, almost all of them widows, among the 1,735 people who left probate inventories in four southern Maryland counties over the second half of the century. Most other women must have died while married and therefore legally without property to put through probate.

One result of remarriage was the development of complex family structures. Men found themselves responsible for stepchildren as well as their own offspring, and children acquired half-sisters and half-brothers. Sometimes a woman married a second husband who himself had been previously married, and both brought children of former spouses to the new marriage. They then produced children of their own. The possibilities for conflict over the upbringing of children are evident, and crowded living conditions, found even in the households of the wealthy, must have added to family tensions. Luckily, the children of the family very often had the same mother. In Charles County at least, widows took new husbands three times more often than widowers took new wives. The role of the mother in managing the relationships of half-brothers and half-sisters or stepfathers and stepchildren must have been critical to family harmony.

Early death in this immigrant population thus had broad effects on Maryland society in the seventeenth century. It produced what we might call a pattern of serial polyandry, which enabled more men to marry and to father families than the sex ratios otherwise would have permitted. It produced thousands of orphaned children who had no kin to maintain them or preserve their property, and thus gave rise to an institution almost unknown in England, the orphans' court, which was charged with their protection. And early death, by creating families in which the mother was the unifying element, may have increased her authority within the household.

When the immigrant woman married her first husband, there was usually no property settlement involved, since she was unlikely to have any dowry. But her remarriage was another matter. At the very least, she owned or had a life interest in a third of her former husband's estate. She needed also to think of her children's interests. If she remarried, she would lose control of the property. Consequently, property settlements occasionally appear in the seventeenth-century court records between widows and their future husbands. Sometimes she and her intended signed an agreement whereby he relinquished his rights to the use of her children's portions. Sometimes he deeded to her property which she could dispose of at her pleasure. Whether any of these agreements or gifts would have survived a test in court is unknown. We have not yet found any challenged. Generally speaking, the formal marriage settlements of English law, which bypassed the legal difficulties of the married woman's inability to make a contract with her husband, were not adopted by immigrants, most of whom probably came from levels of English society that did not use these legal formalities.

The wife's dower rights in her husband's estate were a recognition of her role in contributing to his prosperity, whether by the property she had brought to the marriage or by the labor she performed in his household. A woman newly freed from servitude would not bring property, but the benefits of her labor would be great. A man not yet prosperous enough to own a servant might need his wife's help in the fields as well as in the house, especially if he were pay-

ing rent or still paying for land. Moreover, food preparation was so time-consuming that even if she worked only at household duties, she saved him time he needed for making tobacco and corn. The corn, for example, had to be pounded in the mortar or ground in a handmill before it could be used to make bread, for there were very few water mills in seventeenth-century Maryland. The wife probably raised vegetables in a kitchen garden; she also milked the cows and made butter and cheese, which might produce a salable surplus. She washed the clothes and made them if she had the skill. When there were servants to do field work, the wife undoubtedly spent her time entirely in such household tasks. A contract of 1681 expressed such a division of labor. Nicholas Maniere agreed to live on a plantation with his wife and child and a servant. Nicholas and the servant were to work the land; his wife was to "Dresse the Vitualls milk the Cowes wash for the servants and Doe allthings necessary for a woman to doe upon the s[ai]d plantation." ...

Historians have only recently begun to explore the consequences of the shift from an immigrant to a predominantly native population. We would like to suggest some changes in the position of women that may have resulted from this transition. It is already known that as sexual imbalance disappeared, age at first marriage rose, but it remained lower than it had been for immigrants over the second half of the seventeenth century. At the same time, life expectancy improved, at least for men. The results were longer marriages and more children who reached maturity. In St. Mary's County after 1700, dying men far more often than earlier left children of age to maintain their widows, and widows may have felt less inclination and had less opportunity to remarry.

We may speculate on the social consequences of such changes. More fathers were still alive when their daughters married, and hence would have been able to exercise control over the selection of their sons-in-law. What in the seventeenth century may have been a period of comparative independence for women, both immigrant and native, may have given way to a return to more traditional European social controls over the creation of new families. ...

We may also find the wife losing ground in the household polity, although her economic importance probably remained unimpaired. Indeed, she must have been far more likely than a seventeenth-century immigrant woman to bring property to her marriage. But several changes may have caused women to play a smaller role than before in household decision-making. Women became proportionately more numerous and may have lost bargaining power. Furthermore, as marriages lasted longer, the proportion of households full of stepchildren and half-brothers and half-sisters united primarily by the mother must have dimished. Finally, when husbands died, more widows would have had children old enough to maintain them and any minor brothers and sisters. There would be less need for women to play a controlling role, as well as less incentive for their husbands to grant it. The provincial marriage of the eighteenth century may have more closely resembled that of England than did the immigrant marriage of the seventeenth century.

If this change occurred, we should find symptoms to measure. There should be fewer gifts from husbands to wives of property put at the wife's disposal. Husbands should less frequently make bequests to wives that provided them with property beyond their dower. A wife might even be restricted to less than her dower, although the law allowed her to choose her dower instead of a bequest. At the same time, children should be commanded to maintain their mothers.

St. Mary's County wills show some of these symptoms. Wives occasionally were willed less than their dower, an arrangement that was rare in the wills examined for the period before 1710. More important, there was some decrease in bequests to wives of property beyond their dower, and a tendency to confine the wife's interest to the term of her widowhood or the minority of the oldest son. On the other hand, children were not exhorted to help their mothers or give them living space. Widows evidently received at least enough property to maintain themselves, and husbands saw no need to ensure the help of children in managing it. Still, St. Mary's County women lost some ground, within the family polity. Evidently, as demographic conditions became more normal, St. Mary's County widows began to lose ground to their children, a phenomenon that deserves further study.

NO

Mary Beth Norton

THE MYTH OF THE GOLDEN AGE

HOUSEHOLD PATTERNS

When discussing colonial women, we must focus on the household, for that was where most of their lives were spent. As daughters as well as wives and mothers, white women were expected to devote their chief energies to house-keeping and to the care of children, just as their husbands were expected to support them by raising crops or working for wages. Household tasks were not easily or lightly accomplished, although their exact nature varied accord-ing to the wealth and size of the family and its place of residence. In addition to the common chores still done today—cooking, cleaning, and washing—colonial women had the primary responsibility for food preservation and cloth production.

On farms women raised chickens, tended vegetable gardens, and ran the dairy, making cheese and butter for family use. When hogs and cattle were butchered in the fall, women supervised the salting and smoking of the meat so that the family would have an adequate supply for the winter. They also gathered and dried fruits, vegetables, and berries and occasionally oversaw the making of hard cider, the standard drink in the colonies. In towns and cities women also performed many of these chores, though on a lesser scale: They raised a few chickens and a cow or two, cultivated a kitchen garden, and preserved the beef and pork purchased at the local market. Only the wealth-iest women with numerous servants could escape tiring physical labor, and as mistresses of the household they too had to understand the processes in-volved, for otherwise they could not ensure that the jobs were done correctly.

The task of making cloth by hand was tedious and time consuming. If women lived in towns and could afford to do so, they would usually purchase English cloth rather than manufacture their own. On remote farms or in poorer households, however, females had no choice: If the family was to have clothes, they had to spin the wool or flax threads, then weave those threads into material that could be used for dresses, shirts, and trousers. Usually girls were taught to spin at the early age of 7 or 8 so that they could relieve their mothers of that chore. Weaving demanded more technical skill, not to mention a large, bulky loom, and so not all women in an area would learn to weave. Instead neighbors would cooperate, "changing work," and the woman who wove the cloth for her friends would be paid in cash or by barter.

Native American women had similar work roles. They did not spin or weave, but they did make clothing for the family by tanning and processing the hides of animals killed by their husbands and fathers. They had greater responsibilities for the cultivation of plants than did their white counterparts; the men of many tribes devoted most of their time to hunting, leaving their wives with the major share of the burden of raising the corn, squash, and beans that formed the staples of their diet. But like the whites, Native American cultures drew a division between the domestic labors of women and the public realm of men. Only in rare instances—as when the older women of the matrilineal Iroquois society named the chief of the tribe—did Indian women intrude upon that male realm.

The patterns for African women were somewhat more complex, but their lives too were largely determined by the type of household in which they lived. A female slave in a northern urban home —and there were many such by the mid-eighteenth century—would probably have been a cook or a maid. On small farms slave women would have been expected to work in both field and house. On large southern tobacco or rice plantations, however, black women might specialize in certain tasks, devoting themselves exclusively to spinning, cooking, childcare, dairy work, or poultry keeping, or they might be assigned to the fields. Black women were therefore more likely than whites to engage in labor out of doors. Significantly, the household in

which they lived was not theirs: Their interests and wishes, and those of their husbands and children, always had to be subordinated to the interests of their white masters and mistresses. White women's lives, we might say, were governed by the whims of men, legally and in reality; but black women's lives were governed by white men and white women, and perhaps even by white children.

WOMEN'S LIVES OUTSIDE THE HOME

For female whites or blacks living on isolated farms or plantations, opportunities for contacts with persons outside their immediate families were extremely rare. Thus, farm and plantation women took advantage of every excuse they could to see friends and neighbors: Quilting bees and spinning frolics were common in the North, barbecues were prevalent in the South. Church attendance provided a rural woman not only with the solace of religion, but also with a chance to greet acquaintances and exchange news. Literate women kept in touch with each other by writing letters, many of them carried not by the rudimentary colonial mail service but by passing travelers, usually men.

Because there were few colonial newspapers, and those were published exclusively in cities like Boston or Philadelphia, most farm areas were a part of what has been termed an *oral culture*. Much of the important information about local and regional developments was passed on by person-to-person contact, which generally occurred at the local tavern or the county courthouse, both of which were male bastions. As a result, white farm women tended to be excluded from men's communication networks and to rely for news on exchanges with each other or with their husbands.

Urban women were not nearly so isolated. Close to their friends, they could visit every day. Their attendance at church was not limited to infrequent occasions, and so they could become more active in religious affairs than their rural sisters. They had greater opportunities to receive an education, since the few girls' schools were located in or near colonial cities. For the most part their education consisted of elementary reading, writing, and arithmetic, with perhaps some needlework or musical training thrown in for good measure. Once women knew how to read, they had newspapers and books at their disposal. Moreover, because their household tasks were less demanding than those of their rural counterparts, they had more time to take advantage of all these amenities of the urban setting.

If this account makes it seem as though colonial women's lives lacked variety, that impression is correct. Their environment was both limited and limiting: limited, because of the small sphere of activity open to them; limiting, because they could not realistically aspire to leave that sphere. Faced with a paucity of alternatives, colonial women made the best of their situation. What evidence is available suggests that both white and black women often married for love, and that they cared a great deal for their children. Their female friends provided support in moments of crisis—such as childbirth or the death of a family member—and women could take some satisfaction from knowing that they were active contributors to their families' well-being.

THE MYTH ANALYZED

Historians of American women have traditionally regarded the seventeenth and eighteenth centuries as a "golden age" in which women were better off than their English female contemporaries or their descendants of the succeeding Victorian era. Elisabeth Anthony Dexter explicitly asserted as much; other authors have accepted the same argument implicitly by contending that female Americans "lost status" in the nineteenth century. But even leaving aside the troublesome (and infrequently addressed) issue of how status is measured, there are a number of difficulties with the standard interpretation. Evaluation of women's position depends on what aspects of their experience are relevant to an understanding of their social and economic position, for no one would claim that colonial females exerted much political power.

Three basic assertions support the traditional interpretation. First, historians have noted the imbalanced sex ratio in all the colonies before 1700 and in some parts thereof during later years. Hypothesizing that the absence of sufficient numbers of women to provide wives for all male colonists would lead men to compete vigorously for mates, they have concluded that women would wield a good deal of power through their choice of a spouse. Second, scholars have commonly pointed to the economic contributions women made to the colonial household through their work in food processing and cloth production. They have correctly noted that it was practically impossible for a man to run a colonial household properly without a wife, for a woman's labor was essential to the survival of the family. They presume, then, that husbands recognized their wives' vital contributions to the household by according them a voice in decision making, and that a woman's economic role translated itself into a position of power within the home. Third and finally, historians argue that sex roles in early America were far more fluid and less well defined than they were in the nineteenth and twentieth centuries. They quote both foreign travelers' accounts and newspaper advertisements to show that in many instances women labored at tasks later considered masculine and frequently ran their own businesses.

In assessing these common contentions, we must look closely at their component parts in light of recent scholarship. When we do so, all are rendered suspect. The first argument asserts that a scarcity of women works to their advantage in the marriage market and assumes that the choice of a husband was entirely within a seventeenth-century colonial woman's discretion. Yet demographic studies have clearly demonstrated that, when women are scarce, the average female age at first marriage drops, sometimes precipitously. Even in New England, where the sex ratio was closer to being balanced than anywhere else in the early settlements, the average marriage age for women seems to have fallen into the high teens during the first years of colonization, in sharp contrast to England, where the nuptial age for women remained near the mid- 20s.

These figures have several implications. Initially, they suggest that first marriages were not long delayed by women's searches for spouses who met exacting criteria. Furthermore, since seventeenth-century brides were often teenagers, even more frequently so in the Chesapeake Bay area than in New England, one wonders just how much power they could have

wielded. Immature themselves, legally the wards of their parents, it is highly unlikely that they had much to say about the choice of a spouse.

A possible counter-argument might assert that the advantages of the imbalanced sex ratio are more applicable to a woman's second or third marriage than to her first, because then she would be older and in addition would have control of her first husband's property. Although studies of remarriage patterns in the early years of the colonies are not completely satisfactory, they nevertheless appear to challenge even this claim. In New England, life expectancy in the seventeenth century was sufficiently great that few marriages seem to have been broken early by death. Therefore, relatively few persons married more than once. In the Chesapeake area, where mortality was much higher, the frequency of remarriage was similarly high, but analyses of wills demonstrate that widows were rarely given much control over their dead husbands' estates. The property was usually held in trust for the decedent's minor children, with the widow receiving only a life interest in part of it. Sometimes even that income was to cease upon her remarriage.

Taken as a whole, then, the evidence indicates that seventeenth-century English women transplanted to American shores might not find the imbalanced sex ratio to be beneficial. After all, a scarce resource can be as easily exploited as it is cherished. . . . Also, by approximately 1720 the sex ratio had evened out in the Chesapeake, having already reached that point to the northward, so that whatever advantages women may have derived from the situation were negated and cannot be used to characterize the entire colonial period.

Turning next to the assertion that women's economic role gave them a powerful position in the household, we can discern problems with both the evidence and the reasoning that support it. Historians have not systematically examined the conditions under which women wield familial power, assuming instead that an essential economic contribution would almost automatically lead to such a result. Anthropologists who have investigated the question, however, have discovered that the mere fact that a woman's economic contribution to the household is significant is not sufficient to give her a voice in matters that might otherwise be deemed to fall within the masculine sphere. Rather, what is important is a woman's ability to control the distribution of familial resources. Thus, African women who not only cultivate crops but also sell that produce to others are more likely to wield power in their households than are their counterparts in other tribes whose husbands take on the trading role, or who live in a subsistence economy that does not allow for the sale of surplus goods.

That this analogy is indeed appropriate, despite the wide difference in time and space between twentieth-century Africa and colonial America, is suggested by a recent study of female Loyalist exiles in England after the American Revolution. In order to win compensation from the British government for the losses their families suffered as a result of their political sympathies, the women had to submit descriptions of the property confiscated from them by the rebels. In the process, they revealed their basic ignorance of family landholdings and income, in turn demonstrating that their husbands had not regularly discussed financial affairs with them. If the Loyalist women refugees, who were drawn from all ranks of society, had actively participated in economic decision making, then they would have been far better able to estimate their losses than they proved to be. Thus, the second foundation of the traditional interpretations is shown to be questionable.

The third standard contention, that colonial sex roles were relatively fluid, is rendered at least partially doubtful by other aspects of the same study of Loyalist exiles. The wide variations in the contents of men's and women's Loyalist claims, and the inability or the unwillingness of men to describe household furnishings in the same detail adopted by women, appear to indicate that a fairly rigid line separated masculine and feminine spheres in the colonies. Indeed, the fact that men did not talk about finances with their wives suggests that both sexes had a strong sense of the proper roles of women and men; women did not meddle with politics or economics, which were their husbands' provinces, and men did not interfere with their wives' overseeing of domestic affairs, excluding child rearing, where they did take an active role. Moreover, even though the claims show that some women did engage in business activities, their number was relatively small (fewer than 10 percent of the claimants), and most of them worked in their husbands' enterprises rather than running their own.

That the number of Loyalist women working in masculine areas was not uniquely limited has been suggested by a recent study of Baltimore women in the 1790s, which concludes that only about 5 percent of the female urban population worked outside the home. Thus, it seems likely that eighteenth-century Americans made quite distinct divisions between male and female roles, as reflected in the small numbers of women engaging in masculine occupations and in the fact that men did not normally interfere in the female sphere.

NEW ISSUES

Recent scholarship has considered a number of issues not even raised by earlier authors. Interest in these different areas of inquiry owes a great deal to current trends in the study of the history of the American family, of minority groups, and of ordinary people. Although this work has just begun, it is nevertheless already casting innovative light on the subject of colonial women's role in society.

In the first place, it is important to point out that published studies of the lives of colonial women have, with but one or two exceptions, centered wholly on whites. Even though at the time of the Revolution blacks constituted almost 20 percent of the American population, a higher percentage than at any time thereafter, historians have completely neglected the study of female slaves in the colonial era. Therefore, all the statements that women had a relatively good position in the colonies must be immediately qualified to exclude blacks. No one could seriously argue that enslavement was preferable to freedom, especially since female slaves were highly vulnerable to sexual as well as economic exploitation by their masters. Intriguingly, recent work has shown that the sexual imbalance among the earliest African slaves in the South was just as pronounced as that among whites, so that female blacks probably found themselves in a demographic situation comparable to that of their white mistresses. The sex-role definitions applied to whites, though, were never used with respect to blacks. The labor of slave women was too valuable for their masters to pay attention to the niceties of sex; thus, many of them spent their lives laboring in tobacco fields or on sugar plantations alongside their husbands, although others were indeed used as house servants performing typically feminine tasks.

The one concession wise colonial masters made to the sex of female slaves was a recognition of their importance as child-bearers. Since under the law any child of a slave woman was also a slave, masters could greatly increase their human property simply by encouraging their female slaves' fertility. For example, Thomas Jefferson, whose solvency for some years depended on the discreet sale of young blacks, ordered his overseers to allow pregnant and nursing women special privileges, including lighter work loads and separate houses. Since colonial slave women normally bore their first children at the age of 17 or 18, they would experience perhaps 10 or 11 pregnancies (not all of which would result in live births) during their fertile years, which may be contrasted to the standard pattern among white eighteenth-century women, who married perhaps 4 to 6 years later and thus bore fewer children (the average being 6 offspring who lived).

This attention to childbearing patterns has led to a major challenge to the "golden age" theory.... [C]olonial women were either pregnant or nursing during most of their mature years. Such a pattern of constant childbearing was debilitating, even if it was not fatal to as many women as we once thought; the diaries of white female colonists are filled with references to their continued poor health, and the records of planters show similar consequences among female slaves. Furthermore, the care of so many children must have been exhausting, especially when combined with the extraordinary household demands made on women: production of clothing and time-consuming attention to food preservation and preparation, not to mention candle- and soap-making and doing laundry in heavy iron pots over open fires, with all the water carried by hand from the nearest well or stream. It is questionable how much household power could have been wielded by a woman constantly occupied with such work, even if she was in good health.

It is instructive to stress once again the lack of options in colonial women's lives. Until late in the eighteenth century, marriage was a near-universal experience for women; in an overwhelmingly agricultural society, most female whites ended up as farm wives and most female blacks were farm laborers. For black women burdened with small children, running away was not even the remote chance it was for young unattached male slaves. (In any case, until the Revolution there was no safe place to go, except Spanish Florida, because all the colonies, north and south, allowed slaveholding.)

It might be contended that since most white men were farmers, white women's lack of opportunities was not unique to them. But boys like John Adams, Richard Cranch, and John Shaw had opportunities to gain an education that were closed to their wives, the sisters Abigail, Mary, and Elizabeth Smith. All were exceptionally intelligent and well-informed women, but none received other than a rudimentary formal education, despite the fact that their father was a minister. Since the ability to write a good letter—defined as one that was neat, intelligently constructed, properly grammatical, and carefully spelled—was the mark of a person of substance and standing in colonial America, it is easy to discern the source of the distress Abigail Adams constantly expressed about her inability to write and spell well.

If a white woman did not want to be a farm wife, assuming she had a choice in the matter, then she had only a narrow range of alternatives. In order to take advantage of those alternatives she had to be located in an urban area, where she could support herself in one of three ways: by running a small school in her home; by opening a shop, usually but not always one that sold dry goods; or by in some manner using the household skills she had learned from her mother as a means of making money. This might involve hiring out as a servant, doing sewing, spinning, or weaving for wealthy families, or, if she had some capital, setting up a boardinghouse or inn. There were no other choices, and women who selected one of these occupations—or were compelled by adverse economic circumstances to do so—were frequently regarded as anomalous by their contemporaries.

A major component of the traditional view of American women's history is the assertion that the 40-year period centering on 1800 was a time of retrogression. Joan Hoff Wilson, the most recent proponent of this interpretation, links the setbacks she discerns in women's position explicitly to consequences of the American Revolution. But other work published in the last few years points to an exactly opposite conclusion: It has been suggested (if not yet fully proved) by a number of scholars that the late eighteenth century witnessed a series of advances for women, in some respects at least.

An examination of all extant Massachusetts divorce records seems to indicate, for example, that at the end of the century women seeking divorces were more likely to have their complaints judged fairly and were less likely to be oppressed by application of a sexual double standard than their predecessors had been. In a different area, it has been noted that women's educational opportunities improved dramatically after the mid-1780s.... Finally, extensive research into the patterns of first marriage in one New England town has uncovered changes in marital alliances that can be interpreted as evidence of a greater exercise of independent judgment by girls. Analysis of the records of Hingham, Massachusetts, has shown that in the latter years of the century more daughters married out of birth order and chose spouses whose economic status differed from that of their own parents than had previously been the case. If we assume that both sorts of actions would be contrary to parents' wishes, and couple that assumption with the knowledge that in the same town the premarital conception rate (judged by a comparison of wedding dates with the timing of births of first children) simultaneously jumped to more than 30 percent, we receive the clear impression that parental control of sons and daughters was at a low ebb.

Paradoxically, that last piece of evidence can also be read as suggesting a greater exploitation of women by men. The rise in premarital conception rates, which stretched over the entire eighteenth century and peaked in its last two decades, does not necessarily mean that all the women involved were willing participants seeking what would today be termed sexual fulfillment. On this issue, as on others discussed in this [selection], a great deal more research is needed in order to allow historians to gain a fuller picture of the female experience in colonial America.

POSTSCRIPT

Was the Colonial Period a "Golden Age" for Women in America?

Surveys of American women's history that address the colonial period include June Sochen, *Herstory: A Woman's View of American History* (Alfred A. Knopf, 1974); Mary P. Ryan, *Womenhood in America: From Colonial Times to the Present* (New Viewpoints, 1975); and Nancy Woloch, *Women and the American Experience* (Alfred A. Knopf, 1984). Support for the "golden age" theory can be found in Richard B. Morris, *Studies in the History of American Law*, 2d ed. (Octagon Books, 1964); Elizabeth Anthony Dexter, *Colonial Women of Affairs*, 2d ed. (Houghton Mifflin, 1931); Mary Ritter Beard, *Woman as Force in History* (Macmillan, 1946); Eleanor Flexner, *Century of Struggle* (Belknap Press, 1959); Roger Thompson, *Women in Stuart England and America: A Comparative Study* (Routledge & Kegan, 1974); and Page Smith, *Daughters of the Promised Land: Women in American History* (Little, Brown, 1977).

Many of the scholarly monographs that include discussions of colonial women focus disproportionately on New England. For example, Edmund S. Morgan, *The Puritan Family: Religion and Domestic Relations in Seventeenth-Century New England* (Boston Public Library, 1944) and John Demos, *A Little Commonwealth: Family Life in Plymouth Colony* (Oxford University Press, 1970) both discuss the status of women within the context of the New England family. N. E. H. Hull, *Female Felons: Women and Serious Crime in Colonial Massachusetts* (University of Illinois Press, 1987) and Cornelia Hughes Dayton, *Women Before the Bar: Gender, Law, and Society in Connecticut, 1639–1789* (University of North Carolina Press, 1995) treat the legal status of female New Englanders. Also of interest are Lyle Koehler, *A Search for Power: The Weaker Sex in Seventeenth Century New England* (University of Illinois Press, 1980) and Laurel Thatcher Ulrich, *Good Wives: Image and Reality in the Lives of Women in Northern New England, 1650–1750* (Alfred A. Knopf, 1980).

Women in colonial Virginia are discussed in Darrett B. Rutman and Anita H. Rutman, *A Place in Time: Middlesex County, Virginia, 1650–1750* (W. W. Norton, 1984) and Kathleen M. Brown, *Good Wives, Nasty Wenches, and Anxious Patriarchs: Gender, Race, and Power in Colonial Virginia* (University of North Carolina Press, 1996).

Women in the age of the American Revolution are the focus of Carol Ruth Berkin, *Within the Conjurer's Circle: Women in Colonial America* (General Learning Press, 1974); Linda Grant DePauw and Conover Hunt, *"Remember the Ladies": Women in America, 1750–1815* (Viking Press, 1976); Mary Beth Norton, *Liberty's Daughters: The Revolutionary Experience of American Women, 1750–1800* (Little, Brown 1980); Linda Kerber, *Women of the Republic: Intellect and*

Ideology in Revolutionary America (University of North Carolina Press, 1980); Charles W. Akers, *Abigail Adams: An American Woman* (Little, Brown, 1980); and Joy Day Buel and Richard Buel, Jr., *The Way of Duty: A Woman and Her Family in Revolutionary America* (W. W. Norton, 1984). For the conclusion that the American Revolution failed to advance women's status, see Joan Hoff Wilson, "The Illusion of Change: Women and the American Revolution" in Alfred F. Young, ed., *The American Revolution: Explorations in the History of American Radicalism* (Northern Illinois University Press, 1976).

ISSUE 4

Did Racism Cause the Enslavement of Africans in America?

YES: Carl N. Degler, from "Slavery and the Genesis of American Race Prejudice," *Comparative Studies in Society and History: An International Quarterly* (October 1959)

NO: Oscar Handlin and Mary F. Handlin, from "Origins of the Southern Labor System," *William and Mary Quarterly* (3rd. ser., vol. 7, 1950)

ISSUE SUMMARY

YES: Professor emeritus of American history Carl N. Degler offers a revisionist interpretation of the relationship between slavery and racism, concluding that the status of Africans in the English colonies developed within a framework of discrimination against peoples of African descent that predated the establishment of a permanent status of slavery.

NO: Professor of history Oscar Handlin and author Mary F. Handlin insist that black slavery developed out of severe labor demands in the colonies rather than as a response to any unique qualities of or attitudes toward Africans, and that racism developed in the British North American colonies only after the statutory creation of chattel slavery in the 1660s.

The arrival at Jamestown, Virginia, of a Dutch frigate carrying 20 Africans in 1619 marked a momentous event for the future development of England's North American colonies. The introduction of a new racial component generated political, economic, and social repercussions that are still felt in modern America. With the development of black slavery, American colonists set the stage for a long-term moral dilemma that ultimately produced the bloodshed and destruction of civil war.

In the last 40 years, historians have given considerable attention to colonial American slavery. Their research, however, has left unresolved a question regarding those first Africans in Jamestown: Were the first blacks in England's North American colonies immediately bound out as slaves? Although the evidence is inconclusive, there is strong reason to believe that those initial Africans became indentured servants and were freed after fulfilling their contracts to their masters. These individuals formed the basis for the nation's free black population, which by 1860 numbered approximately 500,000.

If slavery did not originate with those first Africans, when did the institution appear? The process was remarkably gradual in the Chesapeake where the first slave codes were not enacted by the Virginia and Maryland legislatures until the 1660s. Some extant records, however, suggest that the status of "slave" was being given to black servants at least 20 years prior to the appearance of a *de jure* system. In 1640 John Punch, a black servant, was arrested with two white fellow servants and charged with the crime of running away. All were found guilty, and the two white men were whipped and given additional time to serve on their indentures. Punch, however, was only whipped. The court record revealed that since he was already serving his master for life, no time could be added to his labor obligation. In other words, John Punch was a slave.

By 1750 the institution of slavery had emerged in all the British colonies in North America. The preponderance of male bondsmen, however, prevented American slave populations from expanding naturally. Masters, therefore, depended upon shipments from Africa for new slaves until the sex ratio achieved greater parity. In addition, heavy concentrations of slaves did not appear until the rise of large plantations. In New England, such plantations were limited to Rhode Island's Narragansett Valley; in the Mid-Atlantic colonies, New Yorkers and Pennsylvanians acquired some extensive lands worked by slaves; and in the South, large plantations cultivating tobacco and rice appeared in the eighteenth century.

The following essays examine the origins of this colonial slave system and address the role of racial prejudice as an explanation for the particular form that chattel slavery in the Americas took. Did racism cause slavery? Or did the presence of an enforced labor system in which the workers were always peoples of African descent create an environment that bred racist attitudes among whites? Carl N. Degler takes issue with Alexis de Tocqueville's observation that the institution of slavery was the source of prejudice against African Americans. Prior to the development of slave statutes in any of the North American colonies, says Degler, Africans, whether servant or free, were treated as inferior to whites. Degler concludes, "Long before black labor was as economically important as unfree white labor, the Negro had been consigned to a special discriminatory status which mirrored the social discrimination Englishmen practiced against him."

According to Oscar Handlin and Mary F. Handlin, however, slavery was not a response to any unique qualities of peoples of African descent. Rather, it emerged from an adjustment to American conditions of traditional European institutions. Africans did not endure a lack of freedom because of their race; in fact, they shared the misfortune of servitude not only with Native Americans but also with migrants from England, Scotland, and Ireland. The Handlins state that not until the 1660s were race and slavery definitely linked in colonial statutes, and from this point the gap in treatment of whites and blacks began to widen.

YES

Carl N. Degler

SLAVERY AND THE GENESIS OF AMERICAN RACE PREJUDICE

Over a century ago, [the French statesman Alexis de] Tocqueville named slavery as the source of the American prejudice against the Negro. Contrary to the situation in antiquity, he remarked: "Among the moderns the abstract and transient fact of slavery is fatally united with the physical and permanent fact of color." Furthermore, he wrote, though "slavery recedes" in some portions of the United States, "the prejudice to which it has given birth is immovable". More modern observers of the American past have also stressed this causal connection between the institution of slavery and the color prejudice of Americans. Moreover, it is patent to anyone conversant with the nature of American slavery, particularly as it functioned in the nineteenth century, that the impress of bondage upon the character and future of the Negro in the United States has been both deep and enduring.

But if one examines other societies which the Negro entered as a slave, it is apparent that the consequences of slavery have not always been those attributed to the American form. Ten years ago, for example, Frank Tannenbaum demonstrated that in the Spanish and Portuguese colonies in South America, slavery did not leave upon the freed Negro anything like the prejudicial mark which it did in the United States. He and others have shown that once the status of slavery was left behind, the Negro in the lands south of the Rio Grande was accorded a remarkable degree of social equality with the whites. In the light of such differing consequences, the role of slavery in the development of the American prejudice against the Negro needs to be re-examined, with particular attention paid to the historical details of origins. . . .

* * *

It has long been recognized that the appearance of legal slavery in the laws of the English colonies was remarkably slow. The first mention does not occur until after 1660—some forty years after the arrival of the first Negroes. Lest we think that slavery existed in fact before it did in law, two historians have assured us recently that such was not the case. "The status of Negroes was that of servants", Oscar and Mary Handlin have written, "and so they

From Carl N. Degler, "Slavery and the Genesis of American Race Prejudice," *Comparative Studies in Society and History: An International Quarterly*, vol. 2, no. 1 (October 1959). Copyright © 1959 by Cambridge University Press. Reprinted by permission. Notes omitted.

were identified and treated down to the 1660's". This late, or at least, slow development of slavery complicates our problem. For if there was no slavery in the beginning, then we must account for its coming into being some forty years after the introduction of the Negro. There was no such problem in the history of slavery in the Iberian colonies, where the legal institution of slavery came in the ships with the first settlers.

The Handlins' attempt to answer the question as to why slavery was slow in appearing in the statutes is, to me, not convincing. Essentially their explanation is that by the 1660's, for a number of reasons which do not have to be discussed here, the position of the white servant was improving, while that of the Negroes was sinking to slavery. In this manner, the Handlins contend, Negro and white servants, heretofore treated alike, attained different status. There are at least two major objections to this argument. First of all, their explanation, by depending upon the improving position of white servants as it does, cannot apply to New England, where servants were of minor importance. Yet the New England colonies, like the Southern, developed a system of slavery for the Negro that fixed him in a position of permanent inferiority. The greatest weakness of the Handlins' case is the difficulty in showing that the white servant's position was improving during and immediately after the 1660's.

Without attempting to go into any detail on the matter, several acts of the Maryland and Virginia legislatures during the 1660's and 1670's can be cited to indicate that an improving status for white servants was at best doubtful. In 1662, Maryland restricted a servant's travel without a pass to two miles beyond his master's house; in 1671 the same colony lengthened the time of servants who arrived without indenture from four to five years. Virginia in 1668 provided that a runaway could be corporally punished and also have additional time exacted from him. If, as these instances suggest, the white servant's status was not improving, then we are left without an explanation for the differing status accorded white and Negro servants after 1660.

Actually, by asking why slavery developed late in the English colonies we are setting ourselves a problem which obscures rather than clarifies the primary question of why slavery in North America seemed to leave a different mark on the Negro than it did in South America. To ask why slavery in the English colonies produced discrimination against Negroes after 1660 is to make the tacit assumption that prior to the establishment of slavery there was none. If, instead, the question is put, "Which appeared first, slavery or discrimination?" then no prejudgment is made. Indeed, it now opens a possibility for answering the question as to why the slavery in the English colonies, unlike that in the Spanish and Portuguese, led to a caste position for Negroes, whether free or slave. In short, the recent work of the Handlins and the fact that slavery first appeared in the statutes of the English colonies forty years after the Negro's arrival, have tended to obscure the real possibility that the Negro was actually *never* treated as an equal of the white man, servant or free.

It is true that when Negroes were first imported into the English colonies there was no law of slavery and therefore whatever status they were to have would be the work of the future. This absence of a status for black men, which, it will be remembered was not true for the Spanish and Portuguese colonies, made it possible for almost any kind of status to be worked out. It was conceivable that they would be accorded the same status as white servants, as the Handlins have argued; it was also possible that they would not. It all depended upon the reactions of the people who received the Negroes.

It is the argument of this paper that the status of the Negro in the English colonies was worked out within a framework of discrimination; that from the outset, as far as the available evidence tells us, the Negro was treated as an inferior to the white man, servant or free. If this be true, then it would follow that as slavery evolved as a legal status, it reflected and included as a part of its essence, this same discrimination which white men had practised against the Negro all along and before any statutes decreed it. It was in its evolution, then, that American colonial slavery differed from Iberian, since in the colonies of Spain and Portugal, the legal status of the slave was fixed before the Negro came to the Americas. Moreover, in South America there were at least three major traditional safeguards which tended to protect the free Negro against being treated as an inferior. In summary, the peculiar character of slavery in the English colonies as compared with that in the Iberian, was the result of two circumstances. One, that there was no law of slavery at all in the beginning, and two, that discrimination against the Negro antedated the legal status of slavery. As a result, slavery, when it developed in the English colonies, could not help but be infused with the social attitude which had prevailed from the beginning, namely, that Negroes were inferior.

* * *

It is indeed true as the Handlins in their article have emphasized that before the seventeenth century the Negro was rarely called a slave. But this fact should not overshadow the historical evidence which points to the institution without employing the name. Because no discriminatory title is placed upon the Negro we must not think that he was being treated like a white servant; for there is too much evidence to the contrary. Although the growth of a fully developed slave law was slow, unsteady and often unarticulated in surviving records, this is what one would expect when an institution is first being worked out. It is not the same, however, as saying that no slavery or discrimination against the Negro existed in the first decades of the Negro's history in America.

As will appear from the evidence which follows, the kinds of discrimination visited upon Negroes varied immensely. In the early 1640's it sometimes stopped short of lifetime servitude or inheritable status—the two attributes of true slavery—in other instances it included both. But regardless of the form of discrimination, the important point is that from the 1630's up until slavery clearly appeared in the statutes in the 1660's, the Negroes were being set apart and discriminated against as compared with the treatment accorded Englishmen, whether servants or free.

The colonists of the early seventeenth century were well aware of a distinction between indentured servitude and slavery. This is quite clear from the evidence in the very early years of the century. The most obvious means the English colonists had for learning of a different treatment for Negroes from that for white servants was the slave trade and the slave systems of the Spanish and Portuguese colonies. As early as 1623, a voyager's book published in London indicated that Englishmen knew of the Negro as a slave in the South American colonies of Spain. The book told of the trade in "blacke people" who were "sold unto the Spaniard for him to carry into the West Indies, to remaine as slaves, either in their Mines or in any other servile uses, they in those countries put them to". In the phrase "remaine as slaves" is the element of unlimited service.

The Englishmen's treatment of another dark-skinned, non-Christian people—the Indians—further supports the argument that a special and inferior status was accorded the Negro virtually from the first arrival. Indian slavery was practised in all of the English settlements almost from the beginning and, though it received its impetus from the perennial wars between the races, the fact that an inferior and onerous service was established for the Indian makes it plausible to suppose that a similar status would be reserved for the equally different and pagan Negro....

* * *

From the evidence available it would seem that the Englishmen in Virginia and Maryland learned their lesson well. This is true even though the sources available on the Negro's position in these colonies in the early years are not as abundant as we would like. It seems quite evident that the black man was set apart from the white on the continent just as he was being set apart in the island colonies. For example, in Virginia in 1630, one Hugh Davis was "soundly whipped before an Assembly of Negroes and others for abusing himself to the dishonor

of God and the shame of Christians, by defiling his body in lying with a negro." The unChristian-like character of such behavior was emphasized ten years later when Robert Sweet was ordered to do penance in Church for "getting a negro woman with child". An act passed in the Maryland legislature in 1639 indicated that at that early date the word "slave" was being applied to non-Englishmen. The act was an enumeration of the rights of "all Christian inhabitants (slaves excepted)". The slaves referred to could have been only Indians or Negroes, since all white servants were Christians. It is also significant of the differing treatment of the two races that though Maryland and Virginia very early in their history enacted laws fixing limits to the terms for servants who entered without written contracts, Negroes were never included in such protective provisions. The first of such laws were placed upon the books in 1639 in Maryland and 1643 in Virginia; in the Maryland statute, it was explicitly stated: "Slaves excepted".

In yet another way, Negroes and slaves were singled out for special status in the years before 1650. A Virginia law of 1640 provided that "all masters" should try to furnish arms to themselves and "all those of their families which shall be capable of arms"—which would include servants —"(excepting negros)". Not until 1648 did Maryland get around to such a prohibition, when it was provided that no guns should be given to "any Pagan for killing meate or to any other use", upon pain of a heavy fine. At no time were white servants denied the right to bear arms; indeed, as these statutes inform us, they were enjoined to possess weapons.

One other class of discriminatory acts against Negroes in Virginia and Maryland before 1660 also deserves to be noticed. Three different times before 1660 —in 1643, 1644 and 1658—the Virginia assembly (and in 1654, the Maryland legislature) included Negro and Indian women among the "tithables". But white servant women were never placed in such a category, inasmuch as they were not expected to work in the fields. From the beginning, it would seem, Negro women, whether free or bond, were treated by the law differently from white women servants.

It is not until the 1640's that evidence of a status for Negroes akin to slavery, and, therefore, something more than mere discrimination begins to appear in the sources. Two cases of punishment for runaway servants in 1640 throw some light on the working out of a differentiated status for Negroes. The first case concerned three runaways, of whom two were white men and the third a Negro. All three were given thirty lashes, with the white men having the terms owed their masters extended a year, at the completion of which they were to work for the colony for three more years. The other, "being a Negro named John Punch shall serve his said master or his assigns for the time of his natural Life here or elsewhere". Not only was the Negro's punishment the most severe, and for no apparent reason, but he was, in effect, reduced to slavery. It is also clear, however, that up until the issuing of the sentence, he must have had the status of a servant.

The second case, also of 1640, suggests that by that date some Negroes were already slaves. Six white men and a Negro were implicated in a plot to run away. The punishments meted out varied, but Christopher Miller "a dutchman" (a prime agent in the business) was given the harshest treatment of all:

thirty stripes, burning with an "R" on the cheek, a shackle placed on his leg for a year "and longer if said master shall see cause" and seven years of service for the colony upon completion of this time due his master. The only other one of the seven plotters to receive the stripes, the shackle and the "R" was the Negro Emanuel, but, significantly, he did not receive any sentence of work for the colony. Presumably he was already serving his master for a life-time—i.e., he was a slave. About this time in Maryland it does not seem to have been unusual to speak of Negroes as slaves, for in 1642 one "John Skinner mariner" agreed "to deliver unto... Leonard Calvert, fourteen negro-men-slaves and three women-slaves".

From a proceeding before the House of Burgesses in 1666 it appears that as early as 1644 that body was being called upon to determine who was a slave. The Journal of the House for 1666 reports that in 1644 a certain "mulata" bought "as a slave for Ever" was adjudged by the Assembly "no slave and but to serve as other Christian servants do and was freed in September 1665". Though no reason was given for the verdict, from the words "other Christian servants" it is possible that he was a Christian, for it was believed in the early years of the English colonies that baptism rendered a slave free. In any case, the Assembly uttered no prohibition of slavery as such and the owner was sufficiently surprised and aggrieved by the decision to appeal for recompense from the Assembly, even though the Negro's service was twenty-one years, an unheard of term for a "Christian servant".

In early seventeenth century inventories of estates, there are two distinctions which appear in the reckoning of the value of servants and Negroes. Uniformly, the Negroes were more valuable, even as children, than any white servant. Secondly, the naming of a servant is usually followed by the number of years yet remaining to his service; for the Negroes no such notation appears. Thus in an inventory in Virginia in 1643, a 22-year old white servant, with eight years still to serve, was valued at 1,000 pounds of tobacco, while a "negro boy" was rated at 3,000 pounds and a white boy with seven years to serve was listed as worth 700 pounds. An eight-year old Negro girl was calculated to be worth 2,000 pounds. On another inventory in 1655, two good men servants with four years to serve were rated at 1,300 pounds of tobacco, and a woman servant with only two years to go was valued at 800 pounds. Two Negro boys, however, who had no limit set to their terms, were evaluated at 4,100 pounds apiece, and a Negro girl was said to be worth 5,500 pounds.

These great differences in valuation of Negro and white "servants" strongly suggest, as does the failure to indicate term of service for the Negroes, that the latter were slaves at least in regard to lifetime service. Beyond a question, there was some service which these blacks were rendering which enhanced their value—a service, moreover, which was not or could not be exacted from the whites. Furthermore, a Maryland deed of 1649 adumbrated slave status not only of life-time term, but of inheritance of status. Three Negroes "and all their issue both male and female" were deeded.

Russell and Ames culled from the Virginia court records of the 1640's and 1650's several instances of Negroes held in a status that can be called true slavery. For example, in 1646 a Negro woman and a Negro boy were sold to Stephen Charlton to be of use to him and his "heyers etc. for ever". A Negro girl was sold in 1652 "with her Issue and produce... and their services forever". Two years later a Negro girl was sold to one Armsteadinger "and his heyers... forever with all her increase both male and female". For March 12, 1655 the minutes of the Council and General Court of Virginia contain the entry, "Mulatto held to be a slave and appeal taken". Yet this is five years before Negro slavery is even implied in the statutes and fifteen before it is declared. An early case of what appears to be true slavery was found by Miss Ames on the Virginia eastern shore. In 1635 two Negroes were brought to the area; over twenty years later, in 1657, the widow of the master was bequeathing the child of one of the original Negroes and the other Negro and her children. This was much more than mere servitude—the term was longer than twenty years and apparently the status was inheritable.

Wesley Frank Craven, in his study of the seventeenth-century Southern colonies, has concluded that in the treatment of the Negro "the trend from the first was toward a sharp distinction between him and the white servant". In view of the evidence presented here, this seems a reasonable conclusion.

Concurrently with these examples of onerous service or actual slavery of Negroes, there were of course other members of the race who did gain their freedom. But the presence of Negroes rising out of servitude to freedom does not destroy the evidence that others were sinking into slavery; it merely underscores the unsteady evolution of a slave status. The supposition that the practice of slavery long antedated the law is strengthened by the tangential manner in which recognition of Negro slavery first appeared in the Virginia statutes. It occurred in 1660 in a law dealing with punishments for runaway servants, where casual reference was made to those "negroes who are incapable of making satisfaction by addition of time", since they were already serving for life.

Soon thereafter, as various legal questions regarding the status of Negroes came to the fore, the institution was further defined by statute law. In 1662 Virginia provided that the status of the offspring of a white man and a Negro would follow that of the mother—an interesting and unexplained departure from the common law and a reversion to Roman law. The same law stated that "any christian" fornicating "with a negro man or woman... shall pay double the fines imposed by the former act". Two years later Maryland prescribed service for Negroes "durante vita" and provided for hereditary status to descend through the father. Any free white woman who married a slave was to serve her husband's master for the duration of the slave's life, and her children would serve the master until they were thirty years of age. Presumably, no penalty was to be exacted of a free white man who married a Negro slave.

As early as 1669 the Virginia law virtually washed its hands of protecting the Negro held as a slave. It allowed punishment of refractory slaves up to and including accidental death, relieving the master, explicitly, of any fear of prosecution, on the assumption that no man would "destroy his owne estate".

In fact by 1680 the law of Virginia had erected a high wall around the Negro. One discerns in the phrase "any negro or other slave" how the word "negro" had taken on the meaning of slave. Moreover, in the act of 1680 one begins to see the

lineaments of the later slave codes. No Negro may carry any weapon of any kind, nor leave his master's grounds without a pass, nor shall "any negro or other slave... presume to lift his hand in opposition against any christian", and if a Negro runs away and resists recapture it "shalbe lawful for such person or persons to kill said negroe or slave...".

Yet it would be a quarter of a century before Negroes would comprise even a fifth of the population of Virginia. Thus long before slavery or black labor became an important part of the Southern economy, a special and inferior status had been worked out for the Negroes who came to the English colonies. Unquestionably it was a demand for labor which dragged the Negro to American shores, but the status which he acquired here cannot be explained by reference to that economic motive. Long before black labor was as economically important as unfree white labor, the Negro had been consigned to a special discriminatory status which mirrored the social discrimination Englishmen practised against him.

* * *

In the course of the seventeenth century New Englanders, like Southerners, developed a system of slavery which seemed permanently to fasten its stigma upon the Negro race. But because of the small number of Negroes in the northern provinces, the development of a form of slavery, which left a caste in its wake, cannot be attributed to pressure from increasing numbers of blacks, or even from an insistent demand for cheap labor. Rather it seems clearly to be the consequence of the general social discrimination against the Negro. For in the northern region, as in the southern, discrimination against the

Negro preceded the evolution of a slave status and by that fact helped to shape the form that institution would assume.

References to the status of the Negroes in New England in this period are scattered, but, as was true of the Southern provinces, those references which are available suggest that from the earliest years a lowly, differential status, if not slavery itself, was reserved and recognized for the Negro—and the Indian, it might be added. The earliest date asserted in the sources for the existence of Negro slavery in Massachusetts is that of 1639. John Josselyn tells of a Negro woman held on Noddles Island in Boston harbor. Her master sought to mate her with another Negro, Josselyn says, but she kicked her prospective lover out of the bed, saying that such behavior was "beyond her slavery . . .". Though the first legal code of Massachusetts, the Body of Liberties of 1641, prohibited "bond-slavery" for the inhabitants, it clearly permitted enslavement of those who are "sold to us", which would include Negroes brought in by the international slave trade.

Such use of Negroes was neither unknown nor undesirable to the Puritans. Emanuel Downing wrote to John Winthrop in 1645 about the desirability of a war against the Indians so that captives might be taken who, in turn, could be exchanged

for Moores, which wilbe more gayneful pilladge for us then [sic] wee conceive, for I doe not see how wee can thrive until wee gett into a stock of slaves sufficient to doe all our busines, for our children's children will hardly see this great Continent filled with people, soe that our servants will still desire freedome for themselves, and not stay but for verie great wages. And I suppose

you know verie well how we shall maynteyne 20 Moores cheaper than one English servant.

The following year the Commissioners of the United Colonies recommended that in order to spare the colonies the cost of imprisoning contumacious Indians they should be given over to the Englishmen whom they had damaged or "be shipped out and exchanged for Negroes as the cause will justly serve". Negroes were here being equated with Indians who were being bound out as prisoners: this was treatment decidedly a cut lower than that visited upon white servants. That enslavement of Negroes was well known in New England by the middle of the century at the latest is revealed by the preamble to an act of Warwick and Providence colonies in 1652. It was said that it "is a common course practised amongst Englishmen to buy negers, to that end they may have them for service or slaves forever . . .".

By mid-century, Negroes were appearing in the inventories of estates and, significantly, the valuation placed upon them was very close to that found in Virginia inventories of the same period. Their worth is always much more than that of a white servant. Thus in 1650 "a neager Maide" was valued at £25; in 1657 the well-known merchant, Robert Keayne left "2 negros and a negro child" estimated to be worth £30. "A negro boy servant" was set at £20 in an estate of 1661. A further indication of the property character of Negroes was the attachment by the constable of Salem in 1670 of a Negro boy "Seasar" as the "proper goods of the said Powell".

Despite the small numbers of Negroes in New England in this early period, the colonies of that region followed the example of the Southern and insular provinces in denying arms to the blacks in their midst—a discrimination which was never visited upon the English servant. In 1652 Massachusetts provided that Indians and Negroes could train in the militia the same as whites, but this apparently caused friction. The law was countermanded in 1656 by the statement "henceforth no negroes or Indians, altho servants of the English, shalbe armed or permitted to trayne". Although as late as 1680 it was officially reported to London that there were no more than thirty "slaves" in Connecticut, that colony in 1660 excluded Indians and "negar servants" from the militia and "Watch and Ward".

Edward Randolph in 1676 reported that there were a few indentured servants in Massachusetts "and not above two hundred slaves", by which he meant Negroes, for he said "they were brought from Guinea and Madagascar". But it was not until 1698 that the phrase "Negro slave" actually appeared in the Massachusetts statutes. The practice of slavery was preceding the law in Massachusetts precisely as it had in the South. Though an official report to London in 1680 distinguished between Negro slaves and servants in Connecticut, the law of that colony did not bother to define the institution of slavery. Indeed, as late as 1704, the Governor gave it as his opinion that all children born of "negro bondwomen are themselves in like condition, i.e., born in servitude", though he admitted that there was no statute which said so. His contention was, however, that such legislation was "needless, because of the constant practice by which they are held as such...".

During the last years of the seventeenth century, laws of Connecticut and Mas-sachusetts continued to speak of Negroes as "servants", but it was very clear that the Negro's status was not being equated with that of the white servant. The General Court of Connecticut observed in 1690 that "many persons of this Colony doe... purchase negroe servants" and, since these servants run away, precautions have to be taken against such eventualities. It was therefore laid down that all "negro or negroes shall" be required to have a pass in order to be outside the town bounds. Any inhabitant could stop a Negroe, free or slave, and have him brought before a magistrate if the black man were found to be without such a pass. Moreover, all ferrymen, upon pain of fine, were to deny access to their ferries to all Negroes who could not produce a pass. Massachusetts in 1698 forbade trade with "any Indian, or negro servant or slave, or other known dissolute, lewd, and disorderly person, of whom there is just cause of suspicion".

By the early years of the eighteenth century, the laws of Connecticut and Massachusetts had pretty well defined the Negro's subordinate position in society. Massachusetts acted to restrict the manumission of slaves by providing in 1703 that "molatto or negro slaves" could be freed only if security was given that they would not be chargeable upon the community. Another law set a curfew upon Indians, mulattoes and Negroes for nine o'clock each night. In 1705 Massachusetts became the only New England province to prohibit sexual relations between Negroes and mulattoes and Englishmen or those of "any other Christian nation". Moreover, "any negro or mulatto" presuming to "smite or strike" an English person or any of another Christian nation would be "severely whipped". In 1717

Negroes were barred from holding land in Connecticut.

Thus, like the colonists to the South, the New Englanders enacted into law, in the absence of any prior English law of slavery, their recognition of the Negroes as different and inferior. This was the way of the seventeenth century; only with a later conception of the brotherhood of all men would such legal discrimination begin to recede; but by then, generations of close association between the degraded status of slavery and black color would leave the same prejudice against the Negro in the North that it did in the South.

It would seem, then, that instead of slavery being the root of the discrimination visited upon the Negro in America, slavery was itself molded by the early colonists' discrimination against the outlander. In the absence of any law of slavery or commandments of the Church to the contrary—as was true of Brazil and Spanish-America—the institution of slavery into which the African was placed in the English colonies inevitably mir-rored that discrimination and, in so doing, perpetuated it.

Once the English embodied their discrimination against the Negro in slave law, the logic of the law took over. Through the early eighteenth century, judges and legislatures in all the colonies elaborated the law along the discriminatory lines laid down in the amorphous beginnings. In doing so, of course, especially in the South, they had the added incentive of perpetuating and securing a labor system which by then had become indispensable to the economy. The cleavage between the races was in that manner deepened and hardened into the shape which became quite familiar by the nineteenth century. In due time, particularly in the South, the correspondence between the black man and slavery would appear so perfect that it would be difficult to believe that the Negro was fitted for anything other than the degraded status in which he was almost always found. It would also be forgotten that the discrimination had begun long before slavery had come upon the scene.

NO Oscar Handlin and Mary F. Handlin

ORIGINS OF THE SOUTHERN LABOR SYSTEM

In the bitter years before the Civil War, and after, men often turned to history for an explanation of the disastrous difference that divided the nation against itself. It seemed as if some fundamental fault must account for the tragedy that was impending or that had been realized; and it was tempting then to ascribe the troubles of the times to an original separateness between the sections that fought each other in 1861.

The last quarter century has banished from serious historical thinking the ancestral cavaliers and roundheads with whom the rebels and Yankees had peopled their past. But there is still an inclination to accept as present from the start a marked divergence in the character of the labor force, free whites in the North, Negro slaves in the South. Most commonly, the sources of that divergence are discovered in geography. In the temperate North, it is held, English ways were transposed intact. But the soil and climate of the South favored the production of staples, most efficiently raised under a regime of plantation slavery.

In this case, however, it is hardly proper to load nature with responsibility for human institutions. Tropical crops and climate persisted in the South after 1865 when its labor system changed, and they were there before it appeared. Negro slavery was not spontaneously produced by heat, humidity, and tobacco. An examination of the condition and status of seventeenth-century labor will show that slavery was not there from the start, that it was not simply imitated from elsewhere, and that it was not a response to any unique qualities in the Negro himself. It emerged rather from the adjustment to American conditions of traditional European institutions.

By the latter half of the eighteenth century, slavery was a clearly defined status. It was

> the condition of a natural person, in which, by the operation of law, the application of his physical and mental powers depends ... upon the will of another ... and in which he is incapable ... of ... holding property [or any other rights] ... except as the agent or instrument of another. In slavery, ... the state, in ignor-

ing the personality of the slave, . . . commits the control of his conduct . . . to the master, together with the power of transferring his authority to another.

Thinking of slavery in that sense, the Englishmen of 1772 could boast with Lord Mansfield that their country had never tolerated the institution; simply to touch the soil of England made men free. But the distinction between slave and free that had become important by the eighteenth century was not a significant distinction at the opening of the seventeenth century. In the earlier period, the antithesis of "free" was not "slave" but unfree; and, within the condition of unfreedom, law and practice recognized several gradations.

The status that involved the most complete lack of freedom was villeinage, a servile condition transmitted from father to son. The villein was limited in the right to hold property or make contracts; he could be bought and sold with the land he worked or without, and had "to do all that that the Lord will him command"; while the lord could "rob, beat, and chastise his Villain at his will." It was true that the condition had almost ceased to exist in England itself. But it persisted in Scotland well into the eighteenth century. In law the conception remained important enough to induce Coke in 1658/9 to give it a lengthy section; and the analogy with villeinage served frequently to define the terms of other forms of servitude.

For, law and practice in the seventeenth century comprehended other forms of involuntary bondage. The essential attributes of villeinage were fastened on many men not through heredity and ancient custom, as in the case of the villein, but through poverty, crime, or mischance. A debtor, in cases "where there is not sufficient distresse of goods" could be "sold at an outcry." Conviction for vagrancy and vagabondage, even the mere absence of a fixed occupation, exposed the free-born Englishman, at home or in the colonies, to the danger that he might be bound over to the highest bidder, his labor sold for a term. Miscreants who could not pay their fines for a wide range of offenses were punished by servitude on "publick works" or on the estates of individuals under conditions not far different from those of villeinage. Such sentences, in the case of the graver felonies, sometimes were for life.

The sale by the head of a household of members of his family entailed a similar kind of involuntary servitude. A husband could thus dispose of his wife, and a father of his children. Indeed, reluctance to part with idle youngsters could bring on the intercession of the public authorities. So, in 1646, Virginia county commissioners were authorized to send to work in the public flaxhouse two youngsters from each county, kept at home by the "fond indulgence or perverse obstinacy" of their parents. Orphans, bastards, and the offspring of servants were similarly subject to disposal at the will of officials.

Moreover servitude as an estate was not confined to those who fell into it against their wills. It also held many men who entered it by agreement or formal indenture, most commonly for a fixed span of years under conditions contracted for in advance, but occasionally for life, and frequently without definite statement of terms under the assumption that the custom of the country was definite enough.

Early modification in the laws regulating servitude did not, in England or the colonies, alter essentially the nature of the condition. Whether voluntary or involuntary, the status did not involve substantially more freedom in law than villeinage. It was not heritable; but servants could be bartered for a profit, sold to the highest bidder for the unpaid debts of their masters, and otherwise transferred like movable goods or chattels. Their capacity to hold property was narrowly limited as was their right to make contracts. Furthermore, the master had extensive powers of discipline, enforced by physical chastisement or by extension of the term of service. Offenses against the state also brought on punishments different from those meted out to free men; with no property to be fined, the servants were whipped. In every civic, social, and legal attribute, these victims of the turbulent displacements of the sixteenth and seventeenth centuries were set apart. Despised by every other order, without apparent means of rising to a more favored place, these men, and their children, and their children's children seemed mired in a hard, degraded life. That they formed a numerous element in society was nothing to lighten their lot.

The condition of the first Negroes in the continental English colonies must be viewed within the perspective of these conceptions and realities of servitude. As Europeans penetrated the dark continent in search of gold and ivory, they developed incidentally the international trade in Blacks. The Dutch in particular found this an attractive means of breaking into the business of the Spanish colonies, estopped by the policy of their own government from adding freely to their supply of African labor. In the course of this exchange through the West Indies, especially through Curacao, occasional small lots were left along the coast between Virginia and Massachusetts.

Through the first three-quarters of the seventeenth century, the Negroes, even in the South, were not numerous; nor were they particularly concentrated in any district. They came into a society in which a large part of the population was to some degree unfree; indeed in Virginia under the Company almost everyone, even tenants and laborers, bore some sort of servile obligation. The Negroes' lack of freedom was not unusual. These newcomers, like so many others, were accepted, bought and held, as kinds of servants. They were certainly not well off. But their ill-fortune was of a sort they shared with men from England, Scotland, and Ireland, and with the unlucky aborigenes held in captivity. Like the others, some Negroes became free, that is, terminated their period of service. Some became artisans; a few became landowners and the masters of other men. The status of Negroes was that of servants; and so they were identified and treated down to the 1660's.

The word, "slave" was, of course, used occasionally. It had no meaning in English law, but there was a significant colloquial usage. This was a general term of derogation. It served to express contempt; "O what a rogue and peasant slave am I," says Hamlet (Act II, Scene 2). It also described the low-born as contrasted with the gentry; of two hundred warriors, a sixteenth-century report said, eight were gentlemen, the rest slaves. The implication of degradation was also transferred to the low kinds of labor; "In this hal," wrote More (1551), "all vyle seruice, all slauerie ... is done by bondemen."

It was in this sense that Negro servants were sometimes called slaves. But the same appelation was, in England, given to other non-English servants,—to a Russian, for instance. In Europe and in the American colonies, the term was, at various times and places, applied indiscriminately to Indians, mulattoes, and mestizos, as well as to Negroes. For that matter, it applied also to white Englishmen. It thus commonly described the servitude of children; so, the poor planters complained, "Our children, the parents dieinge" are held as "slaues or drudges" for the discharge of their parents' debts. Penal servitude too was often referred to as slavery; and the phrase, "slavish servant" turns up from time to time. Slavery had no meaning in law; at most it was a popular description of a low form of service.

Yet in not much more than a half century after 1660 this term of derogation was transformed into a fixed legal position. In a society characterized by many degrees of unfreedom, the Negro fell into a status novel to English law, into an unknown condition toward which the colonists unsteadily moved, slavery in its eighteenth- and nineteenth-century form. The available accounts do not explain this development because they assume that this form of slavery was known from the start.

Can it be said, for instance, that the seventeenth-century Englishman might have discovered elsewhere an established institution, the archetype of slavery as it was ultimately defined, which seemed more advantageous than the defined English customs for use in the New World? The internationally recognized "slave trade" has been cited as such an institution. But when one notes that the Company of Royal Adventurers referred to their cargo as "Negers," "Negro-Servants," "Servants... from Africa," or "Negro person," but rarely as slaves, it is not so clear that it had in view some unique or different status. And when one remembers that the transportation of Irish servants was also known as the "slave-trade," then it is clear that those who sold and those who bought the Negro, if they troubled to consider legal status at all, still thought of him simply as a low servant.

Again, it has been assumed that Biblical and Roman law offered adequate precedent. But it did not seem so in the perspective of the contemporaries of the first planters who saw in both the Biblical and Roman institutions simply the equivalents of their own familiar forms of servitude. King James's translators rendered the word, "bond-servant"; "slave" does not appear in their version. And to Coke the Roman *servus* was no more than the villein ("and this is hee which the civilians call servus").

Nor did the practice of contemporary Europeans fall outside the English conceptions of servitude. Since early in the fifteenth century, the Portuguese had held Moors, white and black, in "slavery," at home, on the Atlantic islands, and in Brazil. Such servitude also existed in Spain and in Spanish America where Negroes were eagerly imported to supply the perennial shortage of labor in the Caribbean sugar islands and the Peruvian mines. But what was the status of such slaves? They had certain property rights, were capable of contracting marriages, and were assured of the integrity of their families. Once baptised it was almost a matter of course that they would become free; the right to manumission was practically a "contractual arrangement". And once free, they readily intermarried with their former masters. These were no chattels, devoid of personality. These were human beings whom chance had rendered unfree, a situation completely comprehensible within the degrees of unfreedom familiar to the English colonist. Indeed when Bodin wishes to illustrate the condition of such "slaves," he refers to servants and apprentices in England and Scotland.

Finally, there is no basis for the assertion that such a colony as South Carolina simply adopted slavery from the French or British West Indies. To begin with, the labor system of those places was not yet fully evolved. Travelers from the mainland may have noted the advantages of Negro labor there; but they hardly thought of chattel slavery. The Barbadian gentlemen who proposed to come to South Carolina in 1663 thought of bringing "Negros and other servants." They spoke of "slaves" as did other Englishmen, as a low form of servant; the "weaker" servants to whom the Concessions referred included "woemen children slaves." Clearly American slavery was no direct imitation from Biblical or Roman or Spanish or Portuguese or West Indian models. Whatever connections existed were established in the eighteenth and nineteenth centuries when those who justified the emerging institution cast about for possible precedents wherever they might be found.

If chattel slavery was not present from the start, nor adopted from elsewhere, it was also not a response to any inherent qualities that fitted the Negro for plantation labor. There has been a good deal of speculation as to the relative efficiency of free and slave, of Negro, white, and Indian, labor. Of necessity, estimates of which costs were higher, which risks—through mortality, escape, and rebellion—greater, are inconclusive. What is con-clusive is the fact that Virginia and Maryland planters did not think Negro labor more desirable. A preference for white servants persisted even on the islands. But when the Barbadians could not get those, repeated representations in London made known their desire for Negroes. No such demands came from the continental colonies. On the contrary the calls are for skilled white labor with the preference for those most like the first settlers and ranging down from Scots and Welsh to Irish, French, and Italians. Least desired were the unskilled, utterly strange Negroes.

It is quite clear in fact that as late as 1669 those who thought of large-scale agriculture assumed it would be manned not by Negroes but by white peasants under a condition of villeinage. John Locke's constitutions for South Carolina envisaged an hereditary group of servile "leetmen"; and Lord Shaftsbury's signory on Locke Island in 1674 actually attempted to put that scheme into practice. If the holders of large estates in the Chesapeake colonies expressed no wish for a Negro labor supply, they could hardly have planned to use black hands as a means of displacing white, whether as a concerted plot by restoration courtiers to set up a new social order in America, or as a program for lowering costs.

Yet the Negroes did cease to be servants and became slaves, ceased to be men in whom masters held a proprietary interest and became chattels, objects that were the property of their owners. In that transformation originated the southern labor system.

Although the colonists assumed at the start that all servants would "fare alike in the colony," the social realities of their situation early gave rise to differences of treatment. It is not necessary to resort to racialist assumptions to account for such measures; these were simply the reactions of immigrants lost to the stability and security of home and isolated in an immense wilderness in which threats from the unknown were all about them. Like the millions who would follow, these immigrants longed in the strangeness for the company of familiar men and singled out to be welcomed those who were most like themselves. So the measures regulating settlement spoke specifically in this period of differential treatment for various groups. From time to time, regulations applied only to "those of our own nation," or to the French, the Dutch, the Italians, the Swiss, the Palatines, the Welsh, the Irish, or to combinations of the diverse nationalities drawn to these shores.

In the same way the colonists became aware of the differences between themselves and the African immigrants. The rudeness of the Negroes' manners, the strangeness of their languages, the difficulty of communicating to them English notions of morality and proper behavior occasioned sporadic laws to regulate their conduct. So, Bermuda's law to restrain the insolencies of Negroes "who are servents" (that is, their inclination to run off with the pigs of others) was the same in kind as the legislation that the Irish should "straggle not night or dai, as is too common with them." Until the 1660's the statutes on the Negroes were not at all unique. Nor did they add up to a decided trend.

But in the decade after 1660 far more significant differentiations with regard to term of service, relationship to Christianity, and disposal of children, cut the Negro apart from all other servants and gave a new depth to his bondage.

In the early part of the century duration of service was of only slight importance. Certainly in England where labor was more plentiful than the demand, expiration of a term had little meaning; the servant was free only to enter upon another term, while the master had always the choice of taking on the old or a new servitor. That situation obtained even in America as long as starvation was a real possibility. In 1621, it was noted, "vittles being scarce in the country noe man will tacke servants." As late as 1643 Lord Baltimore thought it better if possible to hire labor than to risk the burden of supporting servants through a long period. Under such conditions the number of years specified in the indenture was not important, and if a servant had no indenture the question was certainly not likely to rise.

That accounts for the early references to unlimited service. Thus Sandys's plan for Virginia in 1618 spoke of tenants-at-half assigned to the treasurer's office, to "belong to said office for ever." Again, those at Berkeley's Hundred were perpetual "after the manner of estates in England." Since perpetual in seventeenth-century law meant that which had "not any set time expressly allotted for [its]... continuance," such provisions were not surprising. Nor was it surprising to find instances in the court records of Negroes who seemed to serve forever. These were quite compatible with the possibility of ultimate freedom. Thus a colored man bought in 1644 "as a Slave for Ever," nevertheless was held "to serve as other Christians servants do" and freed after a term.

The question of length of service became critical when the mounting value of labor eased the fear that servants would be a drain on "vittles" and raised the expectation of profit from their toil. Those eager to multiply the number of available hands by stimulating immigration had not only to overcome the reluctance of a prospective newcomer faced with the trials of a sea journey; they had also to counteract the widespread reports in England and Scotland that servants were harshly treated and bound in perpetual slavery.

To encourage immigration therefore, the colonies embarked upon a line of legislation designed to improve servants' conditions and to enlarge the prospect of a meaningful release, a release that was not the start of a new period of servitude, but of life as a freeman and landowner. Thus Virginia, in 1642, discharged "publick tenants from their servitudes, who, like one sort of villians anciently in England" were attached to the lands of the governor; and later laws provided that no person was to "be adjudged to serve the collonie hereafter." Most significant were the statutes which reassured prospective newcomers by setting limits to the terms of servants without indentures, in 1638/9 in Maryland, in 1642/3 in Virginia. These acts seem to have applied only to voluntary immigrants "of our own nation." The Irish and other aliens, less desirable, at first received longer terms. But the realization that such discrimination retarded "the peopling of the country" led to an extension of the identical privilege to all Christians.

But the Negro never profited from these enactments. Farthest removed from the English, least desired, he communicated with no friends who might be deterred from following. Since his coming was involuntary, nothing that happened to him would increase or decrease his numbers. To raise the status of Europeans by shortening their terms would ulti-mately increase the available hands by inducing their compatriots to emigrate; to reduce the Negro's term would produce an immediate loss and no ultimate gain. By midcentury the servitude of Negroes seems generally lengthier than that of whites; and thereafter the consciousness dawns that the Blacks will toil for the whole of their lives, not through any particular concern with their status but simply by contrast with those whose years of labor are limited by statute. The legal position of the Negro is, however, still uncertain; it takes legislative action to settle that.

The Maryland House, complaining of that ambiguity, provoked the decisive measure; "All Negroes and other slaues," it was enacted, "shall serve Durante Vita." Virginia reached the same end more tortuously. An act of 1661 had assumed, in imposing penalties on runaways, that *some* Negroes served for life. The law of 1670 went further; "all servants not being christians" brought in by sea were declared slaves for life.

But slavery for life was still tenuous as long as the slave could extricate himself by baptism. The fact that Negroes were heathens had formerly justified their bondage, since infidels were "perpetual" enemies of Christians. It had followed that conversion was a way to freedom. Governor Archdale thus released the Spanish Indians captured to be sold as slaves to Jamaica when he learned they were Christians. As labor rose in value this presumption dissipated the zeal of masters for proselytizing. So that they be "freed from this doubt" a series of laws between 1667 and 1671 laid down the rule that conversion alone did not lead to a release from servitude. Thereafter manumission, which other servants could demand by right at the end of their terms, in the case of Negroes lay entirely within the discretion of the master....

Meanwhile the condition of the Negro deteriorated. In these very years, a startling growth in numbers complicated the problem. The Royal African Company was, to some extent, responsible, though its operations in the mainland colonies formed only a very minor part of its business. But the opening of Africa to free trade in 1698 inundated Virginia, Maryland, and South Carolina with new slaves. Under the pressure of policing these newcomers the regulation of Negroes actually grew harsher.

The early laws against runaways, against drunkenness, against carrying arms or trading without permission had applied penalties as heavy as death to all servants, Negroes and whites. But these regulations grew steadily less stringent in the case of white servants. On the other hand fear of the growing number of slaves, uneasy suspicion of plots and conspiracies, led to more stringent control of Negroes and a broad view of the master's power of discipline. Furthermore the emerging difference in treatment was calculated to create a real division of interest between Negroes on the one hand and whites on the other. Servants who ran away in the company of slaves, for instance, were doubly punished, for the loss of their own time and for the time of the slaves, a provision that discouraged such joint ventures. Similarly Negroes, even when freed, retained some disciplinary links with their less fortunate fellows. The wardens continued to supervise their children, they were not capable of holding white servants, and serious restrictions limited the number of manumissions.

The growth of the Negro population also heightened the old concern over sexual immorality and the conditions of marriage. The law had always recognized the interest of the lord in the marriage of his villein or neife and had frowned on the mixed marriage of free and unfree. Similarly it was inclined to hold that the marriage of any servant was a loss to the master, an "Enormious offense" productive of much detriment "against the law of God," and therefore dependent on the consent of the master. Mixed marriages of free men and servants were particularly frowned upon as complicating status and therefore limited by law.

There was no departure from these principles in the early cases of Negro-white relationships. Even the complicated laws of Maryland in 1664 and the manner of their enactment revealed no change in attitude. The marriage of Blacks and whites was possible; what was important was the status of the partners and of their issue. It was to guard against the complications of status that the laws after 1691 forbade "spurious" or illegitimate mixed marriages of the slave and the free and punished violations with heavy penalties. Yet it was also significant that by then the prohibition was couched in terms, not simply of slave and free man, but of Negro and white. Here was evidence as in the policing regulations of an emerging demarkation.

The first settlers in Virginia had been concerned with the difficulty of preserving the solidarity of the group under the disruptive effects of migration. They had been enjoined to "keepe to themselves" not to "marry nor give in marriage to the heathen, that are uncircumcised." But such resolutions were difficult to maintain and had gradually relaxed until the colonists included among "themselves" such groups as the Irish, once the objects of very general contempt. A common lot drew them together; and it was the absence of a common lot that drew these apart from the Negro. At the opening of the eighteenth century, the Black was not only set off by economic and legal status; he was "abominable," another order of man.

Yet the ban on intermarriage did not rest on any principle of white racial purity, for many men contemplated with equanimity the prospect of amalgamation with the Indians. That did not happen, for the mass of Redmen were free to recede into the interior while those who remained sank into slavery as abject as that of the Blacks and intermarried with those whose fate they shared.

Color then emerged as the token of the slave status; the trace of color became the trace of slavery. It had not always been so; as late as the 1660's the law had not even a word to describe the children of mixed marriages. But two decades later, the term mulatto is used, and it serves, not as in Brazil, to whiten the Black, but to affiliate through the color tie the offspring of a spurious union with his inherited slavery. (The compiler of the Virginia laws then takes the liberty of altering the texts to bring earlier legislation into line with his own new notions.) Ultimately the complete judicial doctrine begins to show forth, a slave cannot be a white man, and every man of color was descendent of a slave.

The rising wall dividing the legal status of the slave from that of the servant was buttressed by other developments which derogated the qualities of the Negro as a human being to establish his inferiority and thus completed his separation from the white. The destruction of the black man's personality involved, for example, a peculiar style of designation. In the seventeenth century many immigrants in addition to the Africans—Swedes, Armenians, Jews—had brought no family names to America. By the eighteenth all but the Negroes had acquired them. In the seventeenth century, Indians and Negroes bore names that were either an approximation of their original ones or similar to those of their masters,—Diana, Jane, Frank, Juno, Anne, Maria, Jenny. In the eighteenth century slaves seem increasingly to receive classical or biblical appelations, by analogy with Roman and Hebrew bondsmen. Deprivation by statute and usage of other civic rights, to vote, to testify, to bring suit, even if free, completed the process. And after 1700 appear the full slave codes, formal recognition that the Negroes are not governed by the laws of other men.

The identical steps that made the slave less a man made him more a chattel. All servants had once been reckoned property of a sort; a runaway was guilty of "Stealth of ones self." Negroes were then no different from others. But every law that improved the condition of the white servant chipped away at the property element in his status. The growing emphasis upon the consent of the servant, upon the limits of his term, upon the obligations to him, and upon the conditional nature of his dependence, steadily converted the relationship from an ownership to a contractual basis. None of these considerations applied to the Negro; on the contrary considerations of consent and conditions disappeared from his life. What was left was his status as property,—in most cases a chattel though for special purposes real estate. . . .

The distinctive qualities of the southern labor system were then not the simple products of the plantation. They were rather the complex outcome of a process by which the American environment broke down the traditional European conceptions of servitude. In that process the weight of the plantation had pinned down on the Negro the clearly-defined status of a chattel, a status left him as other elements in the population achieved their liberation. When, therefore, Southerners in the eighteenth century came to think of the nature of the rights of many they found it inconceivable that Negroes should participate in those rights. It was more in accord with the whole social setting to argue that the slaves could not share those rights because they were not fully men, or at least different kinds of men. In fact, to the extent that Southerners ceased to think in terms of the seventeenth-century degrees of freedom, to the extent that they thought of liberty as whole, natural, and inalienable, they were forced to conclude that the slave was wholly unfree, wholly lacking in personality, wholly a chattel.

Only a few, like St. George Tucker and Thomas Jefferson, perceived that here were the roots of a horrible tragedy that would some day destroy them all.

POSTSCRIPT

Did Racism Cause the Enslavement of Africans in America?

Although the positions taken by Degler and the Handlins in the preceding essays appear to be mutually exclusive, some historians have noted that these views may not be as incompatible as they seem. Peter Kolchin, in *American Slavery, 1619–1877* (Hill & Wang, 1993), argues that, in fact, the existing evidence does not fully sustain either point of view. The more critical question is how slavery and racism interacted to create the pattern of race relations that developed in colonial America and carried over into the new United States. In this regard, the work of Winthrop Jordan is particularly significant. Jordan has demonstrated that long before slavery developed in British North America, the English possessed several deeply ingrained stereotypes concerning Africans. First, the English were startled by the blackness of the peoples they encountered on the West African coast, and embedded in their concept of blackness were a number of negative connotations. Second, from the perspective of English ethnocentricity, Africans were uncivilized; their ways of life were so different that the English had no inclination to regard African culture as valid. Third, the belief that Africans were heathens who practiced no legitimate religion also set them apart from European Christians in fundamental ways. See Winthrop Jordan, *White Over Black: American Attitudes Toward the Negro, 1550–1812* (University of North Carolina Press, 1968). Despite this evidence, which would seem to support Degler, Jordan surprisingly describes the European enslavement of Africans as an "unthinking decision." Moreover, it should be remembered that despite these prejudicial attitudes, the initial response of English colonists to the arrival of Africans in their midst was not to enslave them. Hence, Jordan is more comfortable with the conclusion that slavery and racism formed a vicious circle that basically reinforced one another. Professor Jordan's direct response to the Handlins-Degler debate can be reviewed in his essay "Modern Tensions and the Origins of American Slavery," *Journal of Southern History* (February 1962). For a more recent discussion of this debate, see Alden T. Vaughan, "The Origins Debate: Slavery and Racism in Seventeenth-Century Virginia," *Virginia Magazine of History and Biography* (July 1989).

Despite the fact that historians of slavery have generally focused upon the antebellum period, there is a growing body of literature pertaining to colonial British North America. The history of African Americans in colonial America is surveyed in Donald R. Wright, *African Americans in the Colonial Era: From African Origins Through the American Revolution* (Harlan Davidson, 1990). The details of the Atlantic slave trade are treated best in Basil Davidson, *Black*

Mother: The African Slave Trade: Precolonial History, 1450–1850 (Little, Brown, 1961); Daniel P. Mannix, *Black Cargoes: A History of the Atlantic Slave Trade, 1518–1865* (Viking Press, 1962); Philip D. Curtin, *The Atlantic Slave Trade: A Census* (University of Wisconsin, 1969); and Edward Reynolds, *Stand the Storm: A History of the Atlantic Slave Trade* (Allison & Busby, 1985). The development of slavery in various British mainland colonies is treated in Edmund S. Morgan, *American Slavery, American Freedom: The Ordeal of Colonial Virginia* (W. W. Norton, 1975); T. H. Breen and Stephen Innes, *'Myne Owne Ground': Race and Freedom on Virginia's Eastern Shore, 1640–1676* (Oxford University Press, 1980); Mechal Sobel, *The World They Made Together: Black and White Values in Eighteenth-Century Virginia* (Princeton University Press, 1987); Marvin L. Michael Kay and Lorin Lee Cary, *Slavery in North Carolina, 1748–1775* (University of North Carolina Press, 1995); Peter H. Wood, *Black Majority: Negroes in Colonial South Carolina from 1670 Through the Stono Rebellion* (Alfred A. Knopf, 1974); Daniel C. Littlefield, *Rice and Slaves: Ethnicity and the Slave Trade in Colonial South Carolina* (Louisiana State University Press, 1981); Betty Wood, *Slavery in Colonial Georgia, 1730–1775* (University of Georgia Press, 1985); and Edgar J. McManus, *A History of Negro Slavery in New York* (Syracuse University Press, 1966) and *Black Bondage in the North* (Syracuse University Press, 1973).

The question of African cultural survivals in America and the assimilation process by which Africans became African Americans is debated in Melville J. Herskovits, *The Myth of the Negro Past* (1941), which emphasizes the survival and adaptation of West African folkways, and E. Franklin Frazier, *The Negro Family in the United States* (1939), which denies the influence of African traditions in the American setting. Studies that support the idea of "survivals" include Sterling Stuckey, *Slave Culture: Nationalist Theory and the Foundations of Black America* (Oxford University Press, 1987); Margaret Washington Creel, *"A Peculiar People": Slave Religion and Community Culture Among the Gullahs* (New York University Press, 1988); and William D. Piersen, *Black Yankees: The Development of an Afro-American Subculture in Eighteenth-Century New England* (University of Massachusetts Press, 1988).

ISSUE 5

Was There a Great Awakening in Mid-Eighteenth-Century America?

YES: Patricia U. Bonomi, from *Under the Cope of Heaven: Religion, Society, and Politics in Colonial America* (Oxford University Press, 1986)

NO: Jon Butler, from "Enthusiasm Described and Decried: The Great Awakening as Interpretative Fiction," *Journal of American History* (September 1982)

ISSUE SUMMARY

YES: Professor of history Patricia U. Bonomi defines the Great Awakening as a period of intense revivalistic fervor that laid the foundation for socioreligious and political reform by spawning an age of contentiousness in the British mainland colonies.

NO: Professor of American history Jon Butler argues that to describe the colonial revivalistic activities of the eighteenth century as the "Great Awakening" is to seriously exaggerate their extent, nature, and impact on pre-Revolutionary American society and politics.

Although generations of American schoolchildren have been taught that the British colonies in North America were founded by persons fleeing religious persecution in England, the truth is that many of those early settlers were motivated by other factors, some of which had little to do with theological preferences. To be sure, the Pilgrims and Puritans of New England sought to escape the proscriptions established by the Church of England. Many New Englanders, however, did not adhere to the precepts of Calvinism and were therefore viewed as outsiders. The Quakers who populated Pennsylvania were mostly fugitives from New England, where they had been victims of religious persecution. But to apply religious motivations to the earliest settlers of Virginia, South Carolina, or Georgia is to engage in a serious misreading of the historical record. Even in New England the religious mission of (the first governor of Massachusetts Bay Colony) John Winthrop's "city upon a hill" began to erode as the colonial settlements matured and stabilized.

Although religion was a central element in the lives of the seventeenth- and eighteenth-century Europeans who migrated to the New World, proliferation of religious sects and denominations, emphasis upon material gain in all parts of the colonies, and the predominance of reason over emotion that is associated with the Deists of the Enlightenment period all contributed to a gradual but obvious movement of the colonists away from the church and clerical authority. William Bradford (the second governor of Plymouth Colony), for example, expressed grave concern that many Plymouth residents were following a path of perfidy, and William Penn (the founder of Pennsylvania) was certain that the "holy experiment" of the Quakers had failed. Colonial clergy, fearful that a fall from grace was in progress, issued calls for a revival of religious fervor. Therefore, the spirit of revivalism that spread through the colonies in the 1730s and 1740s was an answer to these clerical prayers.

The episode known as the First Great Awakening coincided with the Pietistic movement in Europe and England and was carried forward by dynamic preachers such as Gilbert Tennant, Theodore Frelinghuysen, and George Whitefield. They promoted a religion of the heart, not of the head, in order to produce a spiritual rebirth. These revivals, most historians agree, reinvigorated American Protestantism. Many new congregations were organized as a result of irremediable schisms between "Old Lights" and "New Lights." Skepticism about the desirability of an educated clergy sparked a strong strain of anti-intellectualism. Also, the emphasis on conversion was a message to which virtually everyone could respond, regardless of age, sex, or social status. For some historians, the implications of the Great Awakening extended beyond the religious sphere into the realm of politics and were incorporated into the American Revolution.

In the following selections, Patricia U. Bonomi writes from the traditional assumption that a powerful revivalistic force known as the Great Awakening occurred in the American colonies in the mid-eighteenth century. Following a survey of the converging forces that served as precursors to this revivalistic movement, she explains that the Great Awakening grew out of clerical disputes among Presbyterians and quickly spread to other denominations throughout the colonies, abetted by dynamic itinerant preachers such as George Whitefield. Before the enthusiasm subsided, she concludes, the Awakening had instilled a tradition of divisiveness that would affect a number of American social, political, and religious structures.

Jon Butler counters that closer scrutiny of the Great Awakening reveals that the revivals were regional episodes that did not affect all of the colonies equally and, hence, had only a modest impact on American colonial religion. Butler suggests that because the mid-eighteenth-century revivals did not produce the kinds of dramatic changes, religious or political, frequently ascribed to them, historians should abandon the concept of the Great Awakening altogether.

YES

Patricia U. Bonomi

"THE HOSANNAS OF THE MULTITUDE": THE GREAT AWAKENING IN AMERICA

The Great Awakening—that intense period of revivalist tumult from about 1739 to 1745—is one of the most arresting subjects of American history. The eighteenth century, and the latter part of the seventeenth, were of course punctuated with religious episodes that seemed to erupt without warning and draw entire communities into a vortex of religious conversions and agitations of soul. Yet those episodes tended not to spread beyond the individual churches or towns in which they originated. By the third decade of the eighteenth century, however, a number of currents were converging to prepare the way for an unprecedented burst of religious fervor and controversy.

The two major streams of thought shaping western religious belief in the eighteenth century—Enlightenment rationalism and Continental pietism—were by the 1720s reaching increasing numbers of Americans through the world of print, transatlantic learned societies, and such recently arrived spokesmen as the Anglican moderate George Berkeley, on the one side, and the Dutch Reformed pietist Theodore Frelinghuysen, on the other. By the 1730s, American clergymen influenced by the spiritual intensity and emotional warmth of Reformed pietism were vigorously asserting that religion was being corrupted by secular forces; in their view a conversion experience that touched the heart was the only road to salvation. The rationalists demurred, preferring a faith tempered by "an enlightened Mind ... not raised Affections." This contest between reason and innate grace was in one sense as old as Christianity itself. In New England, where it was often cast as a competition between Arminians and Antinomians, only the Calvinists' ability to hold the two elements in exquisite balance had averted a schism. Rationalist attitudes ... were sufficiently prevalent in the eighteenth-century South to obstruct the development of heart religion there until the later colonial years. In the Middle Colonies, every point of view was heard, though by the 1730s tension was rising between the entrenched ministers of more orthodox opinion and incoming clergymen who insisted on conversion as the *sine qua non* of vital religion.

Adding to currents of religious unease in the early eighteenth century were a number of other developments: an accelerating pace of commercial growth; land shortages as well as land opportunities; the unprecedented diversity of eighteenth-century immigration; and a rapid climb in total population. Population growth now created dense settlements in some rural as well as urban areas, facilitating mass public gatherings. Moreover, the proliferation of churches and sects, intensifying denominational rivalries, and smallpox and earthquake alarms that filled meetinghouses to overflowing all contributed to a sense of quickening in church life.

Into this volatile and expectant environment came some of the most charismatic and combative personalities of the age. And as the electricity of a Tennent crackled, and the thunder of a Whitefield rolled, a storm broke that, in the opinion of many, would forever alter American society. The Great Awakening created conditions uniquely favorable to social and political, as well as religious, reform by piercing the facade of civility and deference that governed provincial life to usher in a new age of contentiousness. By promoting church separations and urging their followers to make choices that had political as well as religious implications, the Awakeners wrought permanent changes in public practices and attitudes. Before it subsided, the revival had unsettled the lives of more Americans and disrupted more institutions than any other single event in colonial experience to that time. To see how a religious movement could overspill its boundaries to reshape cultural understanding and political expectations, we must take a closer look at some of the churches and people caught up in the revival.

PRESBYTERIAN BEGINNINGS

The Great Awakening began not as a popular uprising but as a contest between clerical factions. Thus only those churches with a "professional" clergy and organized governing structure—the Presbyterian, Congregational, Dutch Reformed, and eventually the Anglican— were split apart by the revival. The newer German churches and the sects, having little structure to overturn, remained largely outside the conflict. These events have usually been viewed from the perspective of New England Congregationalism, though the first denomination to be involved in the Awakening was the Presbyterian Church in the Middle Colonies. All of the strains and adjustments experienced by other colonial denominations over a longer time span were compressed, in the Presbyterian case, into the fifty years from the beginning of Ulster immigration around 1725 to the Revolution. Thus the Presbyterian example serves as a kind of paradigm of the experience of all churches from their initial formation through the Great Awakening and its aftermath. It reveals too how a dispute between ministers rapidly widened into a controversy that tested the limits of order and introduced new forms of popular leadership that challenged deferential traditions.

Presbyterians looked to the future with reasonably high hopes by the third decade of the eighteenth century. To all appearances they possessed a more stable and orderly church structure than any of their middle-colony competitors. Unlike the Anglicans, they required no bishop to perform the essential rites of ordination and confirmation; nor did they suffer quite the same shortage of ministers as the German churches. The supply of Presbyterian clergy, if never adequate, had at least been sufficient to support the formation of a rudimentary governing structure. Three presbyteries and the Synod of Philadelphia were in place before the first wave of immigration from Ulster reached the Delaware basin, enabling the twenty-five to thirty ministers active in the Middle Colonies to direct growth and protect professional standards in the period of expansion after 1725. Congregations were under the care of laymen ordained to the office of "elder" and, when available, ministers. Supervising presbyteries in each region maintained oversight of local congregations and ordained and disciplined the clergy. At the top was the synod, which provided a forum where clerical disputes over church doctrine and governing authority could be resolved *in camera* [secretly].

Yet the controls imposed by the Presbyterian hierarchy were hardly all that they appeared to be. Beneath orderly processes were tensions which had been expanding steadily before finally bursting forth in fratricidal strife and schism after 1739. Any reading of eighteenth-century Presbyterian records discloses at least three kinds of strains beneath the surface: between parishioners, between people and minister, and within the professional clergy itself.

The Presbyterian Church was the focal point and mediator of Scotch-Irish community life from the late 1720s on, when thousands of Ulster Scots began entering the colonies annually. As the westward-migrating settlers moved beyond the reach of government and law, the Presbyterian Church was the only institution that kept pace with settlement. By stretching resources to the limit, the synod, and especially the presbyter-

ies, kept in touch with their scattered brethren through itinerant preachers and presbyterial visitations. Ministers, invariably the best educated persons on the early frontier, were looked to for leadership in both religious and community affairs, and they often took up multiple roles as doctors, teachers, and even lawyers. So closely did the Scotch-Irish identify with the Kirk [Church] that it was often said they "could not live without it."

But if the church was a vital center it was also an agency of control. Presbyterian ministers—whom some regarded as a "stiff-necked... [and] pedantick crew"—expected to guide their parishioners' spiritual growth and moral safety in America as they had done in the Old Country, and at first, by and large, they succeeded. Congregations gathered spontaneously in Scotch-Irish settlements, much as they did in immigrant German communities. A major difference between the two societies was that from an early stage lay Presbyterians submitted themselves to clerical authority. As soon as a Presbyterian congregation was formed, it requested recognition and the supply of a minister from the local presbytery. Often the presbytery could provide only a probationer or itinerant preacher for the Sabbath, and many settlements were fortunate to hear a sermon one or two Sundays a month. The congregations nonetheless proceeded to elect elders, deacons to care for the poor and sick, and trustees to oversee the collection of tithes for the minister's salary. The governing "session," comprised of elders and minister, functioned as a kind of court, hearing charges and ruling on a variety of matters, including disputes between parishioners over land or debt, domestic difficulties, and church doctrine.

The main responsibility of the session was to enforce moral discipline. Its rulings could be appealed to the supervising presbytery. The presbytery minutes consequently have much to tell us about the quality of clerical authority. But they also disclose the growing undercurrent of resistance that such authority aroused among the freer spirits in the Scotch-Irish settlements....

NEW SIDES VS. OLD SIDES

The Great Awakening split the Presbyterian Church apart, and through the cracks long-suppressed steam hissed forth in clouds of acrimony and vituperation that would change the face of authority in Pennsylvania and elsewhere. As the passions of the Awakening reached their height in the early 1740s, evangelical "New Side" Presbyterians turned on the more orthodox "Old Sides" with the ferocity peculiar to zealots, charging them with extravagant doctrinal and moral enormities. The internecine spectacle that ensued, the loss of proportion and professional decorum, contributed to the demystification of the clergy, forced parishioners to choose between competing factions, and overset traditional attitudes about deference and leadership in colonial America.

The division that surfaced in 1740–1741 had been developing for more than a decade. Presbyterian ministers had no sooner organized their central association, the Synod of Philadelphia, in 1715 than the first lines of stress appeared, though it was not until a cohesive evangelical faction emerged in the 1730s that an open split was threatened. Most members of the synod hoped to model American Presbyterianism along orderly lines, and in 1729 an act requiring all ministers

and ministerial candidates to subscribe publicly to the Westminster Confession had been approved. In 1738 the synod had further ruled that no minister would be licensed unless he could display a degree from a British or European university, or from one of the New England colleges (Harvard or Yale). New candidates were to submit to an examination by a commission of the synod on the soundness of their theological training and spiritual condition. The emergent evangelical faction rightly saw these restrictions as an effort to control their own activities. They had reluctantly accepted subscription to the Westminster Confession, but synodical screening of new candidates struck them as an intolerable invasion of the local presbyteries' right of ordination.

The insurgents were led by the Scotsman William Tennent, Sr., and his sons, William, Jr., Charles, John, and Gilbert. William, Sr. had been educated at the University of Edinburgh, receiving a bachelor's degree in 1693 and an M.A. in 1695. He may have been exposed to European pietism at Edinburgh, where new ideas of every sort were brewing in the last quarter of the seventeenth century. Though ordained a minister of the Anglican church in 1706, Tennent did not gain a parish of his own, and in 1718 he departed the Old World for the New. When he applied for a license from the Synod of Philadelphia in 1718, Tennent was asked his reasons for leaving the Church of England. He responded that he had come to view government by bishops as anti-scriptural, that he opposed ecclesiastical courts and plural benefices, that the church was leaning toward Arminianism, and that he disapproved of "their ceremonial way of worship." All this seemed sound enough to the Presbyterians, and Tennent was licensed forthwith. Having a strong interest in scholarship and pedagogy, Tennent built a one-room schoolhouse in about 1730 in Neshaminy, Bucks County —the Log College, as it was later derisively called—where he set about training young men for the ministry. Exactly when Tennent began to pull away from the regular synod leadership is unclear, but by 1736 his church at Neshaminy was split down the middle and the anti-evangelical members were attempting to expel him as minister.

In 1739 the synod was confronted with a question on professional standards that brought the two factions closer to a complete break. When the previous year's synod had erected commissions to examine the education of all ministerial candidates not holding degrees from approved universities, Gilbert Tennent had charged that the qualification was designed "to prevent his father's school from training gracious men for the Ministry." Overriding the synod's rule in 1739, the radical New Brunswick Presbytery licensed one John Rowland without reference to any committee, though Rowland had received "a private education"—the synod's euphemism for the Log College. Sharply criticizing the presbytery for its disorderly and divisive action, the synod refused to approve Rowland until he agreed to submit himself for examination, which he in turn refused to do.

* * *

Since education was central to the dispute, it is unfortunate that no Log College records have survived to describe the training given the remarkable group of men that came under William Tennent, Sr.'s tutelage. We do know that they emerged to become leaders of the revivalist movement, and would in turn prepare

other religious and educational leaders of the middle and southern colonies. The little existing evidence casts doubt on the synod's charge that Tennent and his followers were "destroyers of good learning" who persisted in foisting unlettered Log College students upon an undiscriminating public. As Gilbert Tennent insisted, the insurgents "desired and designed a well-qualified Ministry as much as our Brethren." To be sure, their theological emphasis was at variance with that of the Old Side clergy, and there may have been parts of the traditional curriculum they did not value as highly, as had been true with the innovative dissenting academies in Britain. But as competition between the two factions intensified, restrained criticism gave way to enmity. Thus when the synod charged that Gilbert Tennent had called "Physicks, Ethicks, Metophysicks and Pnuematicks [the rubric under which Aristotelian philosophy was taught in medieval universities] meer Criticks, and consequently useless," its members could not resist adding that he did so "because his Father cannot or doth not teach them."

Yet there is much that attests to both William Tennent, Sr.'s learning and his pedagogical talents. That he was a polished scholar of the classics, spoke Latin and English with equal fluency, and was a master of Greek was confirmed by many who knew him. He also "had some acquaintance with the ... Sciences." A hint of the training Tennent offered comes from the licensing examination given his youngest son Charles in 1736 by the Philadelphia Presbytery, among whose members were several who would later emerge as chief critics of the Tennents. Young Charles was tested on his "ability in prayer [and] in the

Languages," in the delivery of a sermon and exegesis, and on his answers to "various suitable questions on the arts and sciences, especially Theology and out of Scripture." He was also examined on the state of his soul. Charles Tennent was apparently approved without question.

The strongest evidence of the quality of a Log College education comes, however, from the subsequent careers and accomplishments of its eighteen to twenty-one "alumni." Their deep commitment to formal education is demonstrated by the number of academies they themselves founded, including Samuel Blair's "classical school" at Faggs Manor in Pennsylvania, Samuel Finley's academy at Nottingham, and several others. Two early presidents of the College of New Jersey (Princeton) were Samuel Finley and Samuel Davies (the latter having been educated by Blair at Faggs Manor). Moreover, the published sermons and essays of Samuel Finley, Samuel Blair, and Gilbert Tennent not only pulse with evangelical passion but also display wide learning. In the opinion of a leading Presbyterian historian the intellectual accomplishments of the Log College revivalists far outshone those of the Old Side opposers, among whom only the scholarly Francis Alison produced significant writings. As George Whitefield observed when he visited Neshaminy in 1739 and saw the rough structure of logs that housed the school: "All that we can say of most universities is, that they are glorious without."

* * *

But the distinction that the Log College men would achieve was still unknown in 1739, when the New Brunswick Presbytery defied the synod by licensing John Rowland. It was at this juncture, more-over, that the twenty-six-year-old English evangelist, George Whitefield, made his sensational appearance. Whitefield's visits to New Jersey and Pennsylvania in the winter of 1739–1740 provided tremendous support for the Presbyterian insurgents, as thousands of provincials flocked to hear him and realized, perhaps for the first time, something of what the American evangelists had been up to. The public support that now flowed to Tennent and the New Side exhilarated its members, inciting them to ever bolder assaults on the synod.

The revivalists had to this point preached only in their own churches or in temporarily vacant pulpits, but that winter they began to invade the territory of the regular clergy. This action raised the issue of itinerant preaching, perhaps the thorniest of the entire conflict, for it brought the parties face to face on the question of who was better qualified to interpret the word of God. It was in this setting that Gilbert Tennent was moved on March 8, 1740 to deliver his celebrated sermon, *The Danger of an Unconverted Ministry*, to a Nottingham congregation engaged in choosing a new preacher. It was an audacious, not to say reckless, attack on the Old Side clergy, and Tennent would later qualify some of his strongest language. But the sermon starkly reveals the gulf that separated the two factions by 1740. It also demonstrates the revivalists' supreme disregard for the traditional limits on public discussion of what amounted to professional questions....

In this influential and widely disseminated sermon Tennent set forth the three principal issues over which Presbyterians would divide: the conversion experience, education of the clergy, and itinerant preaching. While his tone may have owed something to Whitefield's recent influence—humility was never a strong point with the evangelists—it also reflected the growing self-confidence of the insurgents, as a wave of public support lifted them to popular heights. During the synod of 1740 the anti-revivalist clergy, in a demonstration of their reasonableness, agreed to certain compromises on the issues of itinerancy and licensing, but when the revivalists continued to denounce them publicly as carnal and unconverted, their patience came to an end.

The break between Old Side and New Side Presbyterians came during the synod of 1741 when a protest signed by twelve ministers and eight elders demanded that the revivalists be expelled from the synod. In a preemptive move, the New Side clergy voluntarily withdrew from the Philadelphia Synod to their presbyteries, where their work continued with great zeal and met with success that would outshine that of their rivals. In 1745 the evangelical party, joined by other friends of the revival from the Middle Colonies, formed the Synod of New York, which would sustain a lively existence until 1758 when the Presbyterian schism was finally repaired.

* * *

Disagreements over theological emphasis, professional standards, and centralized authority were the most immediate causes of the Presbyterian schism, but other differences between Old and New Sides had the effect of making the conflict sharper. Disparities in education, age (and therefore career expectations), and cultural bias are of special interest.

The twelve Old Sides who moved to expel the revivalist radicals in 1741 have sometimes been labeled the "Scotch-Irish" party for good reason. Nine were born in Northern Ireland, and two in Scotland (the birthplace of the twelfth is unknown). All were educated abroad, mainly in Scotland, and especially at the University of Glasgow. Most came to the colonies between the ages of twenty-eight and thirty-two, after having completed their education. The typical Old Side clergyman was about forty-two at the time of the schism. The New Side ministers who formed the Synod of New York in 1745 numbered twenty-two. Of the twenty-one whose places of birth can be ascertained, ten were born in New England or on eastern Long Island, one in Newark, New Jersey, eight in Northern Ireland (including Gilbert, William, Jr., and Charles Tennent), one in Scotland, and one in England. Most of those born abroad emigrated to the colonies during their middle teens; Charles Tennent was but seven, and the oldest was William Robinson, the son of an English Quaker doctor, who emigrated at about twenty-eight after an ill-spent youth. The educational profile of the New Side preachers is in striking contrast to that of the Old. Of the twenty-two, nine received degrees from Yale College, two were Harvard men, and ten were educated at the Log College. One had probably gone to a Scottish university. The typical New Side minister was about thirty-two at the time of the schism, or a decade younger than his Old Side counterpart.

Several tendencies suggest themselves. The Old Sides, more mature than their adversaries, were also more settled in their professional careers; further, their Scottish education and early professional experiences in Ulster may have instilled a respect for discipline and ecclesiastical order that could not easily be cast aside. They knew it was difficult to keep up standards in provincial societies, especially the heterodox Middle Colonies where competition in religion, as in everything else, was a constant challenge to good order. Still, it was irritating to be treated as intruders by the resident notables, or by such as the Anglicans, who pretended to look down on the Presbyterians as "men of small talents and mean education." There was security in knowing that the first generation of Presbyterian leaders had been educated and licensed in accordance with the most exacting Old World criteria. But the tradition must be continued, for succeeding generations would gain respect only if the ministry were settled on a firm professional base. Though Harvard and Yale were not Edinburgh and Glasgow, they did pattern their curricula after the British universities and to that extent could serve until the Presbyterian Church was able to establish a college of its own. And only if Presbyterian leaders could control the education and admission of candidates to the ministry might they hold their heads high among rival religious groups. A professional ministry was thus crucial to the "Scotch-Irish" party's pride and sense of place.

The New Side party, on the other hand, cared less about professional niceties than about converting sinners. Its members were at the beginning of their careers, and most, being native-born or coming to the colonies in their youth, were not so likely to be imbued with an Old World sense of prerogative and order. They never doubted that an educated clergy was essential, but education had to be of the right sort. By the 1730s Harvard and Yale were being guided, in their view, by men of rationalist leanings who simply did not provide the type of training wanted by the revivalists. Thus

the New Sides chafed against the controls favored by their more conservative elders, controls that restricted their freedom of action, slowed their careers, and were in their opinion out of touch with New World ways.

The anti-institutionalism of the revivalists caused some critics to portray them as social levellers, though there were no significant distinctions in social outlook or family background between Old and New Sides. But as with any insurgent group that relies in part on public support for its momentum, the New Sides tended to clothe their appeals in popular dress. At every opportunity they pictured the opposers as "the Noble & Mighty" elders of the church, and identified themselves with the poor and "common People"— images reinforced by the Old Sides' references to the evangelists' followers as an ignorant and "wild Rabble."

The revivalists may not have been deliberate social levellers, but their words and actions had the effect of emphasizing individual values over hierarchical ones. Everything they did, from disrupting orderly processes and encouraging greater lay participation in church government, to promoting mass assemblies and the physical closeness that went with them, raised popular emotions. Most important, they insisted that there were choices, and that the individual himself was free to make them.

The people, it might be suspected, had been waiting for this. The long years of imposed consensus and oversight by the Kirk had taken their toll, and undercurrents of restlessness had strengthened as communities stabilized and Old World values receded. Still, the habit of deferring to the clergy was deeply rooted in Presbyterian culture, making inertia an accomplice of church authority. By 1740, however, with the clergy themselves, or a part of them, openly promoting rebellion, many Presbyterians "in imitation of their example," as it was said, joined the fray. The result was turbulence, shattered and divided congregations, and a rash of slanderous reports against Old Side clergymen. Most such charges were either proved false or are deeply suspect, owing to their connection with the factional conflict. But aspersions against the ministerial character had now become a subject of public debate, suggesting that the schisms of the Awakening were effectively challenging the old structures of authority....

* * *

So volatile had the revival become that it could no longer be contained within a single region. Thus when George Whitefield carried the crusade northward, the tumults and divisions that had seized the Presbyterian Church spread to the Congregational meetinghouses of New England.

THE "DIVINE FIRE" KINDLED IN NEW ENGLAND

Whitefield's initial visit to Boston in September 1740 was greeted with tremendous interest, for the "Grand Itinerant" was the first figure of international renown to tour the colonies. During an eleven-day period he preached at least nineteen times at a number of different churches and outdoor sites, including New South Church where the huge crowd was thrown into such a panic that five were killed and many more injured. Fifteen thousand persons supposedly heard Whitefield preach on Boston Common. Even allowing for an inflated count, these were surely the largest crowds ever assembled in Boston or any other colonial city. As Samuel Johnson once said, Whitefield would have been adored if he wore a nightcap and preached from a tree. Whitefield's tours outside of Boston, and then into western Massachusetts and Connecticut, were attended by similar public outpourings. No one, it seems, wanted to miss the show. In December Gilbert Tennent arrived in Boston, having been urged by Whitefield to add more fuel to the divine fires he had kindled there. Tennent's preaching, which lacked Whitefield's sweetness but none of his power, aroused a popular fervor that matched or exceeded that inspired by the Englishman.

Most Congregational ministers, including those at Boston, had welcomed Whitefield's tour as an opportunity to stimulate religious piety. Tennent's torrid preaching may have discomfited some, but it was not until 1742 that three events led to a polarization of the clergy into "New Light" supporters and "Old Light" opposers of the Great Awakening. First came the publication in Boston of Tennent's sermon, *The Danger of an Unconverted Ministry*, which one Old Light would later blame for having "sown the Seeds of all that Discord, Intrusion, Confusion, Separation, Hatred, Variance, Emulations, Wrath, Strife, Seditions, Heresies, &c. that have been springing up in so many of the Towns and Churches thro' the Province...." Another was the publication of Whitefield's 1740 *Journal*, in which he criticized "most" New England preachers for insufficient piety and observed of Harvard and Yale that "their Light is become Darkness." The final provocation was the arrival in Boston on June 25, 1742 of the Reverend James Davenport, a newly fledged evangelist who already had Connecticut in an uproar and would soon have all Boston by the ears.

Davenport had been expelled from Connecticut on June 3 after being adjudged "disturbed in the rational Faculties of his Mind." Now the twenty-six-year-old evangelist was determined to share his special insights with the people of Boston. Forewarned about Davenport's odd behavior, the ministers of Boston and Charlestown (the majority of whom favored the Awakening) requested that the intruder restrain his "assuming Behavior . . . especially in judging the spiritual State of Pastors and People," and decided not to offer him their pulpits. Davenport was undeterred. He preached on the Common and in the rain on Copp's Hill; he proclaimed first three and then nine more of Boston's ministers "by name" to be unconverted; and he announced that he was "ready to drop down dead for the salvation of but one soul." Davenport was followed, according to one critic, by a "giddy Audience . . . chiefly made up of idle or ignorant Persons" of low rank. To some of Boston's soberer citizens the crowd appeared "menacing," and one newspaper essayist found Davenport's followers "so red hot, that I verily believe they would make nothing to kill Opposers." Such was the anarchy threatened by religious enthusiasm. . . .

In the months that followed, New Englanders, like middle-colony Presbyterians before them, would witness and then be drawn into a fierce struggle between the two factions, as their once-decorous ministers impugned the intelligence and integrity of their rivals in public sermons and essays. The Old Light writers were especially bellicose, losing no opportunity to rebuke the "enthusias-tic, factious, censorious Spirit" of the revivalists. Schisms were threatened everywhere, and as early as 1742 some congregations had "divided into Parties, and openly and scandalously separated from one another." As the Connecticut Old Light, Isaac Stiles, warned, the subversion of all order was threatened when "Contempt is cast upon Authority both Civil and Ecclesiastical." Most distressing to those who believed that "Good Order is the Strength and Beauty of the World," was the Awakening's tendency to splinter New England society. "Formerly the People could bear with each other in Charity when they differ'd in Opinion," recalled one writer, "but they now break Fellowship and Communion with one another on that Account."

Indeed, awakened parishioners were repeatedly urged to withdraw from a "corrupt ministry." "O that the precious Seed might be preserved and *separated* from all gross Mixtures!" prayed the Connecticut New Light Jonathan Parsons. And spurred on by Parsons and other New Lights, withdraw they did. In Plymouth and Ipswich, from Maine to the Connecticut River Valley, the New England separatist movement gained momentum from 1743 onward. . . .

* * *

The Great Awakening, as Richard Hofstadter put it, was "the first major intercolonial crisis of the mind and spirit" in eighteenth-century America. No previous occurrence in colonial history compared with it in scale or consequences. True, the floodtide of evangelical fervor soon subsided, but nothing could quite restore the old cultural landscape. The unitary ideal of the seventeenth century continued to be eroded in the post-Awakening years by further church separations. Moreover, as the Reverend William Shurtleff noted in 1745, the "dividing Spirit is not confin'd to those that are Friends" of the revival. Nor was it confined to the religious sphere. That "dividing Spirit" would be manifested everywhere after mid-century in the proliferation of religious and political factions.

NO

Jon Butler

ENTHUSIASM DESCRIBED AND DECRIED: THE GREAT AWAKENING AS INTERPRETATIVE FICTION

In the last half century, the Great Awakening has assumed a major role in explaining the political and social evolution of prerevolutionary American society. Historians have argued, variously, that the Awakening severed intellectual and philosophical connections between America and Europe (Perry Miller), that it was a major vehicle of early lower-class protest (John C. Miller, Rhys Isaac, and Gary B. Nash), that it was a means by which New England Puritans became Yankees (Richard L. Bushman), that it was the first "intercolonial movement" to stir "the people of several colonies on a matter of common emotional concern" (Richard Hofstadter following William Warren Sweet), or that it involved "a rebirth of the localistic impulse" (Kenneth Lockridge).

American historians also have increasingly linked the Awakening directly to the Revolution. Alan Heimert has tagged it as the source of a Calvinist political ideology that irretrievably shaped eighteenth-century American society and the Revolution it produced. Harry S. Stout has argued that the Awakening stimulated a new system of mass communications that increased the colonists' political awareness and reduced their deference to elite groups prior to the Revolution. Isaac and Nash have described the Awakening as the source of a simpler, non-Calvinist protest rhetoric that reinforced revolutionary ideology in disparate places, among them Virginia and the northern port cities. William G. McLoughlin has even claimed that the Great Awakening was nothing less than "the Key to the American Revolution."

These claims for the significance of the Great Awakening come from more than specialists in the colonial period. They are a ubiquitous feature of American history survey texts, where the increased emphasis on social history has made these claims especially useful in interpreting early American society to twentieth-century students. Virtually all texts treat the Great Awakening as a major watershed in the maturation of prerevolutionary American society. *The Great Republic* terms the Awakening "the greatest event in the history of

From Jon Butler, "Enthusiasm Described and Decried: The Great Awakening as Interpretative Fiction," *Journal of American History*, vol. 69 (September 1982), pp. 305–314. Copyright © 1982 by *Journal of American History*. Reprinted by permission. Notes omitted.

religion in eighteenth-century America." *The National Experience* argues that the Awakening brought "religious experiences to thousands of people in every rank of society" and in every region. *The Essentials of American History* stresses how the Awakening "aroused a spirit of humanitarianism," "encouraged the notion of equal rights," and "stimulated feelings of democracy" even if its gains in church membership proved episodic. These texts and others describe the weakened position of the clergy produced by the Awakening as symptomatic of growing disrespect for all forms of authority in the colonies and as an important catalyst, even cause, of the American Revolution. The effect of these claims is astonishing. Buttressed by the standard lecture on the Awakening tucked into most survey courses, American undergraduates have been well trained to remember the Great Awakening because their instructors and texts have invested it with such significance.

Does the Great Awakening warrant such enthusiasm? Its puzzling historiography suggests one caution. The Awakening has received surprisingly little systematic study and lacks even one comprehensive general history. The two studies, by Heimert and Cedric B. Cowing, that might qualify as general histories actually are deeply centered in New England. They venture into the middle and southern colonies only occasionally and concentrate on intellectual themes to the exclusion of social history. The remaining studies are thoroughly regional, as in the case of books by Bushman, Edwin Scott Gaustad, Charles Hartshorn Maxson, Dietmar Rothermund, and Wesley M. Gewehr, or are local, as with the spate of articles on New England towns and Jonathan Edwards or Isaac's articles and book on Virginia. The result is that the general character of the Great Awakening lacks sustained, comprehensive study even while it benefits from thorough local examinations. The relationship between the Revolution and the Awakening is described in an equally peculiar manner. Heimert's seminal 1966 study, despite fair and unfair criticism, has become that kind of influential work whose awesome reputation apparently discourages further pursuit of its subject. Instead, historians frequently allude to the positive relationship between the Awakening and the Revolution without probing the matter in a fresh, systematic way.

The gap between the enthusiasm of historians for the social and political significance of the Great Awakening and its slim, peculiar historiography raises two important issues. First, contemporaries never homogenized the eighteenth-century colonial religious revivals by labeling them "the Great Awakening." Although such words appear in Edwards's *Faithful Narrative of the Surprising Work of God*, Edwards used them alternately with other phrases, such as "general awakening," "great alteration," and "flourishing of religion," only to describe the Northampton revivals of 1734–1735. He never capitalized them or gave them other special emphasis and never used the phrase "the Great Awakening" to evaluate all the prerevolutionary revivals. Rather, the first person to do so was the nineteenth-century historian and antiquarian Joseph Tracy, who used Edwards's otherwise unexceptional words as the title of his famous 1842 book, *The Great Awakening*. Tellingly, however, Tracy's creation did not find immediate favor among American historians. Charles Hodge discussed the Presbyterian revivals in his *Constitutional History of the Presbyterian Church* without describing them as part of a "Great Awakening," while the influential Robert Baird refused even to treat the eighteenth-century revivals as discrete and important events, much less label them "the Great Awakening." Baird all but ignored these revivals in the chronological segments of his *Religion in America* and mentioned them elsewhere only by way of explaining the intellectual origins of the Unitarian movement, whose early leaders opposed revivals. Thus, not until the last half of the nineteenth century did "the Great Awakening" become a familiar feature of the American historical landscape.

Second, this particular label ought to be viewed with suspicion, not because a historian created it—historians legitimately make sense of the minutiae of the past by utilizing such devices—but because the label itself does serious injustice to the minutiae it orders. The label "the Great Awakening" distorts the extent, nature, and cohesion of the revivals that did exist in the eighteenth-century colonies, encourages unwarranted claims for their effects on colonial society, and exaggerates their influence on the coming and character of the American Revolution. If "the Great Awakening" is not quite an American Donation of Constantine, its appeal to historians seeking to explain the shaping and character of prerevolutionary American society gives it a political and intellectual power whose very subtlety requires a close inspection of its claims to truth.

How do historians describe "the Great Awakening"? Three points seem especially common. First, all but a few describe it as a Calvinist religious revival in which converts acknowledged their sinfulness without expecting salvation. These colonial converts thereby distinguished themselves from Englishmen caught up in contemporary Methodist revivals and from Americans involved in the so-called Second Great Awakening of the early national period, both of which imbibed Arminian principles that allowed humans to believe they might effect their own salvation in ways that John Calvin discounted. Second, historians emphasize the breadth and suddenness of the Awakening and frequently employ hurricane metaphors to reinforce the point. Thus, many of them describe how in the 1740s the Awakening "swept" across the mainland colonies, leaving only England's Caribbean colonies untouched. Third, most historians argue that this spiritual hurricane affected all facets of prerevolutionary society. Here they adopt Edwards's description of the 1736 Northampton revival as one that touched "all sorts, sober and vicious, high and low, rich and poor, wise and unwise," but apply it to all the colonies. Indeed, some historians go farther and view the Great Awakening as a veritable social and political revolution itself. Writing in the late 1960s, Bushman could only wonder at its power: "We inevitably will underestimate the effect of the Awakening on eighteenth-century society if we compare it to revivals today. The Awakening was more like the civil rights demonstrations, the campus disturbances, and the urban riots of the 1960s combined. All together these may approach, though certainly not surpass, the Awakening in their impact on national life."

No one would seriously question the existence of "the Great Awakening" if historians only described it as a short-lived Calvinist revival in New England during the early 1740s. Whether stimulated by Edwards, James Davenport, or the British itinerant George Whitefield, the New England revivals between 1740 and 1745 obviously were Calvinist ones. Their sponsors vigorously criticized the soft-core Arminianism that had reputedly overtaken New England Congregationalism, and they stimulated the ritual renewal of a century-old society by reintroducing colonists to the theology of distinguished seventeenth-century Puritan clergymen, especially Thomas Shepard and Solomon Stoddard.

Yet, Calvinism never dominated the eighteenth-century religious revivals homogenized under the label "the Great Awakening." The revivals in the middle colonies flowed from especially disparate and international sources. John B. Frantz's recent traversal of the German revivals there demonstrates that they took root in Lutheranism, German Reformed Calvinism (different from the New England variety), and Pietism (however one wants to define it). Maxson stressed the mysticism, Pietism, Rosicrucianism, and Freemasonry rampant in these colonies among both German and English settlers. In an often overlooked observation, Maxson noted that the Tennents' backing for revivals was deeply linked to a mystical experience surrounding the near death of John Tennent and that both John Tennent and William Tennent, Jr., were mystics as well as Calvinists. The revivals among English colonists in Virginia also reveal eclectic roots. Presbyterians brought Calvinism into the colony for the first time since the 1650s, but Arminianism underwrote the powerful Methodist awakening in the colony and soon crept into the ranks of the colony's Baptists as well.

"The Great Awakening" also is difficult to date. Seldom has an "event" of such magnitude had such amorphous beginnings and endings. In New England, historians agree, the revivals flourished principally between 1740 and 1743 and largely ended by 1745, although a few scattered outbreaks of revivalism occurred there in the next decades. Establishing the beginning of the revivals has proved more difficult, however. Most historians settle for the year 1740 because it marks Whitefield's first appearance in New England. But everyone acknowledges that earlier revivals underwrote Whitefield's enthusiastic reception there and involved remarkable numbers of colonists. Edwards counted thirty-two towns caught up in revivals in 1734–1735 and noted that his own grandfather, Stoddard, had conducted no less than five "harvests" in Northampton before that, the earliest in the 1690s. Yet revivals in Virginia, the site of the most sustained such events in the southern colonies, did not emerge in significant numbers until the 1750s and did not peak until the 1760s. At the same time, they also continued into the revolutionary and early national periods in ways that make them difficult to separate from their predecessors.

Yet even if one were to argue that "the Great Awakening" persisted through most of the eighteenth century, it is obvious that revivals "swept" only some of the mainland colonies. They occurred in Massachusetts, Connecticut, Rhode Island, Pennsylvania, New Jersey, and Virginia with some frequency at least at some points between 1740 and 1770. But New Hampshire, Maryland, and Georgia witnessed few revivals in the same years, and revivals were only occasionally important in New York, Delaware, North Carolina, and South Carolina. The revivals also touched only certain segments of the population in the colonies where they occurred. The best example of the phenomenon is Pennsylvania. The revivals there had a sustained effect among English settlers only in Presbyterian churches where many of the laity and clergy also opposed them. The Baptists, who were so important to the New England revivals, paid little attention to them until the 1760s, and the colony's taciturn Quakers watched them in perplexed silence. Not even Germans imbibed them universally. At the same time that Benjamin Franklin was emptying his pockets in response to the preaching of Whitefield in Philadelphia—or at least claiming to do so—the residents of Germantown were steadily leaving their churches, and Stephanie Grauman Wolf reports that they remained steadfast in their indifference to Christianity at least until the 1780s.

Whitefield's revivals also exchanged notoriety for substance. Colonists responded to him as a charismatic performer, and he actually fell victim to the Billy Graham syndrome of modern times: his visits, however exciting, produced few permanent changes in local religious patterns. For example, his appearances in Charleston led to his well-known confrontation with Anglican Commissary Alexander Garden and to the suicide two years later of a distraught follower named Anne LeBrasseur. Yet they produced no new congregations in Charleston and had no documented effect on the general patterns of religious adherence elsewhere in the colony. The same was true in Philadelphia and New York City despite the fact that Whitefield preached to enormous crowds in both places. Only Bostonians responded differently. Supporters organized in the late 1740s a new "awakened" congregation that reputedly met with considerable initial success, and opponents adopted a defensive posture exemplified in the writings of Charles Chauncy that profoundly affected New England intellectual life for two decades.

Historians also exaggerate the cohesion of leadership in the revivals. They have accomplished this, in part, by overstressing the importance of Whitefield and Edwards. Whitefield's early charismatic influence later faded so that his appearances in the 1750s and 1760s had less impact even among evangelicals than they had in the 1740s. In addition, Whitefield's "leadership" was ethereal, at best, even before 1750. His principal early importance was to serve as a personal model of evangelical enterprise for ministers wishing to promote their own revivals of religion. Because he did little to organize and coordinate integrated colonial revivals, he also failed to exercise significant authority over the ministers he inspired.

The case against Edwards's leadership of the revivals is even clearer. Edwards defended the New England revivals from attack. But, like Whitefield, he never organized and coordinated revivals throughout the colonies or even throughout New England. Since most of his major works were not printed in his lifetime, even his intellectual leadership in American theology occurred in the century after his death. Whitefield's lack of knowledge about Edwards on his first tour of America in 1739–1740 is especially telling on this point. Edwards's name does not appear in Whitefield's journal prior to the latter's visit to Northampton in 1740, and Whitefield did not make the visit until Edwards had invited him to do so. Whitefield certainly knew of Edwards and the 1734–1735 Northampton revival but associated the town mainly with the pastorate of Edwards's grandfather Stoddard. As Whitefield described the visit in his journal: "After a little refreshment, we crossed the ferry to Northampton, where no less than three hundred souls were saved about five years ago. Their pastor's name is Edwards, successor and grandson to the great Stoddard, whose memory will be always precious to my soul, and whose books entitled 'A Guide to Christ,' and 'Safety of Appearing in Christ's Righteousness,' I would recommend to all."

What were the effects of the prerevolutionary revivals of religion? The claims for their religious and secular impact need pruning too. One area of concern involves the relationship between the revivals and the rise of the Dissenting denominations in the colonies. Denomination building was intimately linked to the revivals in New England. There, as C. C. Goen has demonstrated, the revivals of the 1740s stimulated formation of over two hundred new congregations and several new denominations. This was accomplished mainly through a negative process called "Separatism," which split existing Congregationalist and Baptist churches along prorevival and antirevival lines. But Separatism was of no special consequence in increasing the number of Dissenters farther south. Presbyterians, Baptists, and, later, Methodists gained strength from former Anglicans who left their state-supported churches, but they won far more recruits among colonists who claimed no previous congregational membership.

Still, two points are important in assessing the importance of revivals to the expansion of the Dissenting denominations in the colonies. First, revivalism never was the key to the expansion of the colonial churches. Presbyterianism expanded as rapidly in the middle colonies between 1710 and 1740 as between 1740 and 1770. Revivalism scarcely produced the remarkable growth that the Church of England experienced in the eighteenth century unless, of course, it won the favor of colonists who opposed revivals as fiercely as did its leaders. Gaustad estimates that between 1700 and 1780 Anglican congregations expanded from about one hundred to four hundred, and Bruce E. Steiner has outlined extraordinary Anglican growth in the Dissenting colony of Connecticut although most historians describe the colony as being thoroughly absorbed by the revivals and "Separatism."

Second, the expansion of the leading evangelical denominations, Presbyterians and Baptists, can be traced to many causes, not just revivalism or "the Great Awakening." The growth of the colonial population from fewer than three hundred thousand in 1700 to over two million in 1770 made the expansion of even the most modestly active denominations highly likely. This was especially true because so many new colonists did not settle in established communities but in new communities that lacked religious institutions. As Timothy L. Smith has written of seventeenth-century settlements, the new eighteenth-century settlements welcomed congregations as much for the social functions they performed as for their religious functions. Some of the denominations reaped the legacy of Old World religious ties among new colonists, and others benefited from local anti-Anglican sentiment, especially in the Virginia and Carolina backcountry. As a result, evangelical organizers formed many congregations in the middle and southern colonies without resorting to revivals at all. The first Presbyterian congregation in Hanover County, Virginia, organized by Samuel Blair and William Tennent, Jr., in 1746, rested on an indigenous lay critique of Anglican theology that had turned residents to the works of Martin

Luther, and after the campaign by Blair and Tennent, the congregation allied itself with the Presbyterian denomination rather than with simple revivalism.

The revivals democratized relations between ministers and the laity only in minimal ways. A significant number of New England ministers changed their preaching styles as a result of the 1740 revivals. Heimert quotes Isaac Backus on the willingness of evangelicals to use sermons to "insinuate themselves into the affections' of the people" and notes how opponents of the revivals like Chauncy nonetheless struggled to incorporate emotion and "sentiment" into their sermons after 1740. Yet revivalists and evangelicals continued to draw sharp distinctions between the rights of ministers and the duties of the laity. Edwards did so in a careful, sophisticated way in *Some Thoughts concerning the Present Revival of Religion in New England*. Although he noted that "disputing, jangling, and contention" surrounded "lay exhorting," he agreed that "some exhorting is a Christian duty." But he quickly moved to a strong defense of ministerial prerogatives, which he introduced with the proposition that "the Common people in exhorting one another ought not to clothe themselves with the like authority, with that which is proper for ministers." Gilbert Tennent was less cautious. In his 1740 sermon *The Danger of an Unconverted Ministry*, he bitterly attacked "Pharisee-shepherds" and "Pharisee-teachers" whose preaching was frequently as "unedifying" as their personal lives. But Gilbert Tennent never attacked the ministry itself. Rather, he argued for the necessity of a *converted* ministry precisely because he believed that only preaching brought men and women to Christ and that only ordained

ministers could preach. Thus, in both 1742 and 1757, he thundered against lay preachers. They were "of dreadful consequence to the Church's peace and soundness in principle. . . . [F]or Ignorant Young Converts to take upon them authoritatively to Instruct and Exhort publickly tends to introduce the greatest Errors and the greatest anarchy and confusion."

The 1740 revival among Presbyterians in New Londonderry, Pennsylvania, demonstrates well how ministers shepherded the laity into a revival and how the laity followed rather than led. It was Blair, the congregation's minister, who first criticized "dead Formality in Religion" and brought the congregation's members under "deep convictions" of their "natural unregenerate state." Blair stimulated "soul exercises" in the laity that included crying and shaking, but he also set limits for these exercises. He exhorted them to "moderate and bound their passions" so that the revival would not be destroyed by its own methods. Above this din, Blair remained a commanding, judgmental figure who stimulated the laity's hopes for salvation but remained "very cautious of expressing to People my Judgment of the Goodness of their States, excepting where I had pretty clear Evidences from them, of their being savingly changed." . . .

Nor did the revivals change the structure of authority within the denominations. New England Congregationalists retained the right of individual congregations to fire ministers, as when Northampton dismissed Edwards in 1750. But in both the seventeenth and eighteenth centuries, these congregations seldom acted alone. Instead, they nearly always consulted extensively with committees of ordained ministers when firing as well as when hiring ministers. In the middle colonies, however, neither the prorevival Synod of New York nor the antirevival Synod of Philadelphia tolerated such independence in congregations whether in theory or in practice. In both synods, unhappy congregations had to convince special committees appointed by the synods and composed exclusively of ministers that the performance of a fellow cleric was sufficiently dismal to warrant his dismissal. Congregations that acted independently in such matters quickly found themselves censured, and they usually lost the aid of both synods in finding and installing new ministers.

Did the revivals stir lower-class discontent, increase participation in politics, and promote democracy in society generally if not in the congregations? Even in New England the answer is, at best, equivocal. Historians have laid to rest John C. Miller's powerfully stated argument of the 1930s that the revivals were, in good part, lower-class protests against dominant town elites. The revivals indeed complicated local politics because they introduced new sources of potential and real conflict into the towns. New England towns accustomed to containing tensions inside a single congregation before 1730 sometimes had to deal with tensions within and between as many as three or four congregations after 1730. Of course, not all of these religious groups were produced by the revivals, and, as Michael Zuckerman has pointed out, some towns never tolerated the new dissidents and used the "warning out" system to eject them. Still, even where it existed, tumult should not be confused with democracy. Social class, education, and wealth remained as important after 1730 in choosing town and church officers as they had been before 1730, and Edward M. Cook, Jr., notes that after 1730 most new re-

vival congregations blended into the old order: "dissenters [took] their place in town affairs once they stopped threatening the community and symbolically became loyal members of it." ...

What, then, ought we to say about the revivals of religion in prerevolutionary America? The most important suggestion is the most drastic. Historians should abandon the term "the Great Awakening" because it distorts the character of eighteenth-century American religious life and misinterprets its relationship to prerevolutionary American society and politics. In religion it is a deus ex machina that falsely homogenizes the heterogeneous; in politics it falsely unites the colonies in slick preparation for the Revolution. Instead, a four-part model of the eighteenth-century colonial revivals will highlight their common features, underscore important differences, and help us assess their real significance.

First, with one exception, the prerevolutionary revivals should be understood primarily as regional events that occurred in only half the colonies. Revivals occurred intermittently in New England between 1690 and 1745 but became especially common between 1735 and 1745. They were uniformly Calvinist and produced more significant local political ramifications—even if they did not democratize New England—than other colonial revivals except those in Virginia. Revivals in the middle colonies occurred primarily between 1740 and 1760. They had remarkably eclectic theological origins, bypassed large numbers of settlers, were especially weak in New York, and produced few demonstrable political and social changes. Revivals in the southern colonies did not occur in significant numbers until the 1750s, when they were limited largely to Virginia, missed Maryland almost entirely, and did not occur with any regularity in the Carolinas until well after 1760. Virginia's Baptist revivalists stimulated major political and social changes in the colony, but the secular importance of the other revivals has been exaggerated. A fourth set of revivals, and the exception to the regional pattern outlined here, accompanied the preaching tours of the Anglican itinerant Whitefield. These tours frequently intersected with the regional revivals in progress at different times in New England, the middle colonies, and some parts of the southern colonies, but even then the fit was imperfect. Whitefield's tours produced some changes in ministerial speaking styles but few permanent alterations in institutional patterns of religion, although his personal charisma supported no less than seven tours of the colonies between 1740 and his death in Newburyport, Massachusetts, in 1770.

Second, the prerevolutionary revivals occurred in the colonial backwaters of Western society where they were part of a long-term pattern of erratic movements for spiritual renewal and revival that had long characterized Western Christianity and Protestantism since its birth two centuries earlier. Thus, their theological origins were international and diverse rather than narrowly Calvinist and uniquely American. Calvinism was important in some revivals, but Arminianism and Pietism supported others. This theological heterogeneity also makes it impossible to isolate a single overwhelmingly important cause of the revivals. Instead, they appear to have arisen when three circumstances were present—internal demands for renewal in different international Christian communities, charismatic preachers, and special, often unique, local circumstances

that made communities receptive to elevated religious rhetoric.

Third, the revivals had modest effects on colonial religion. This is not to say that they were "conservative" because they did not always uphold the traditional religious order. But they were never radical, whatever their critics claimed. For example, the revivals reinforced ministerial rather than lay authority even as they altered some clergymen's perceptions of their tasks and methods. They also stimulated the demand for organization, order, and authority in the evangelical denominations. Presbyterian "New Lights" repudiated the conservative Synod of Philadelphia because its discipline was too weak, not too strong, and demanded tougher standards for ordination and subsequent service. After 1760, when Presbyterians and Baptists utilized revivalism as part of their campaigns for denominational expansion, they only increased their stress on central denominational organization and authority.

Indeed, the best test of the benign character of the revivals is to take up the challenge of contemporaries who linked them to "outbreaks of enthusiasm" in Europe. In making these charges, the two leading antirevivalists in the colonies, Garden of Charleston and Chauncy of Boston, specifically compared the colonial revivals with those of the infamous "French Prophets" of London, exiled Huguenots who were active in the city between 1706 and about 1730. The French Prophets predicted the downfall of English politicians, raised followers from the dead, and used women extensively as leaders to prophesy and preach. By comparison, the American revivalists were indeed "conservative." They prophesied only about the millennium, not about local politicians, and described only the necessity, not the certainty, of salvation. What is most important is that they eschewed radical change in the position of women in the churches. True, women experienced dramatic conversions, some of the earliest being described vividly by Edwards. But, they preached only irregularly, rarely prophesied, and certainly never led congregations, denominations, or sects in a way that could remotely approach their status among the French Prophets.

Fourth, the link between the revivals and the American Revolution is virtually nonexistent. The relationship between prerevolutionary political change and the revivals is weak everywhere except in Virginia, where the Baptist revivals indeed shattered the exclusive, century-old Anglican hold on organized religious activity and politics in the colony. But, their importance to the Revolution is weakened by the fact that so many members of Virginia's Anglican aristocracy also led the Revolution. In other colonies the revivals furnished little revolutionary rhetoric, including even millennialist thought, that was not available from other sources and provided no unique organizational mechanisms for anti-British protest activity. They may have been of some importance in helping colonists make moral judgments about eighteenth-century English politics, though colonists unconnected to the revivals made these judgments as well.

In the main, then, the revivals of religion in eighteenth-century America emerge as nearly perfect mirrors of a regionalized, provincial society. They arose erratically in different times and places across a century from the 1690s down to the time of the Revolution. Calvinism underlay some of them, Pietism and Arminianism others. Their leadership was local and, at best, regional, and they helped reinforce—but were not the key to—the proliferation and expansion of still-regional Protestant denominations in the colonies. As such, they created no intercolonial religious institutions and fostered no significant experiential unity in the colonies. Their social and political effects were minimal and usually local, although they could traumatize communities in which they upset, if only temporarily, familiar patterns of worship and social behavior. But the congregations they occasionally produced usually blended into the traditional social system, and the revivals abated without shattering its structure. Thus, the revivals of religion in prerevolutionary America seldom became proto-revolutionary, and they failed to change the timing, causes, or effects of the Revolution in any significant way.

Of course, it is awkward to write about the eighteenth-century revivals of religion in America as erratic, heterogeneous, and politically benign. All of us have walked too long in the company of Tracy's "Great Awakening" to make our journey into the colonial past without it anything but frightening. But as Chauncy wrote of the Whitefield revivals, perhaps now it is time for historians "to see that Things have been carried too far, and that the Hazard is great ... lest we should be over-run with *Enthusiasm*."

POSTSCRIPT

Was There a Great Awakening in Mid-Eighteenth-Century America?

Butler's critique of efforts to link the Great Awakening with the American Revolution is part of a longstanding debate. He suggests that there is not enough evidence to support, for example, William McLoughlin's thesis that the revivals were a "key" that opened the door to the War for Independence. He emphasizes the regional element in revivalist activities, suggesting that they did not have a broad impact. If Butler is correct, however, there is still room to argue that the Revolution was not without its religious elements.

In his book *Religion in America: Past and Present* (Prentice Hall, 1961), Clifton E. Olmstead argues for a broader application of religious causes to the origins of the American Revolution. First, Olmstead contends that the Great Awakening did foster a sense of community among American colonists, thus providing the unity required for an organized assault on English control. Moreover, the Great Awakening further weakened existing ties between the colonies and England by drawing adherents of the Church of England into the evangelical denominations that expanded as a result of revivalistic Protestantism. Second, tensions were generated by the demand that an Anglican bishop be established in the colonies. Many evangelicals found in this plan evidence that the British government wanted further control over the colonies. Third, the Quebec Act, enacted by Parliament in 1774, not only angered American colonists by nullifying their claims to western lands, but it also heightened religious prejudice in the colonies by granting tolerance to Roman Catholics. Fourth, ministers played a significant role in encouraging their parishioners to support the independence movement. Finally, many of the revolutionaries, imbued with the American sense of mission, believed that God was ordaining their activities.

Further support for each of these views can be found in Rhys Isaac, *The Transformation of Virginia, 1740–1790* (University of North Carolina Press, 1982); Ruth H. Bloch, *Visionary Republic* (Cambridge University Press, 1985); and Harry S. Stout, *The New England Soul: Preaching and Religious Culture in Colonial New England* (Oxford University Press, 1986). Students interested in further analyses of the Great Awakening should consult Edwin Scott Gaustad, *The Great Awakening in New England* (Peter Smith, 1957); and Marilyn J. Westerkamp, *Triumph of the Laity: Scots-Irish Piety and the Great Awakening, 1625–1760* (Oxford University Press, 1987).

An Internet site devoted to some spiritual leaders of the Great Awakening can be found at http://dylee.keel.econ.ship.edu/ubf/leaders/leaders.htm.

On the Internet . . .

The Constitution of the United States

Sponsored by the National Archives and Records Administration, this site presents a wealth of information on the U.S. Constitution. From here you can link to the biographies of the 55 delegates to the Constitutional Convention, take an in-depth look at the convention and the ratification process, read a transcription of the complete text of the Constitution, and view high-resolution images of each page of the Constitution.
http://www.nara.gov/exhall/charters/constitution/conmain.html

A Revolutionary People, 1775–1828

Susan Butler, who teaches American and women's history at Cerritos College, has gathered together an impressive list of sites on the revolutionary period. Included are more than two dozen links to sites on Thomas Jefferson.
http://www3.cerritos.edu/sbutler/part2rev.htm

History of Compromise Legislation:
An Annotated Chronology

This page links to sources on compromise legislation in the United States, from the Northwest Ordinance in 1787 to the *Dredd Scott* decision in 1856. Much of the focus is on slavery, but it also examines the first two-party system, Indian removal policies of the 1830s, and the First and Second Banks of the United States.
http://www.wfu.edu/~zulick/340/compromise.html

PART 2

Revolution and the New Nation

The American Revolution led to independence from England and to the establishment of a new nation. As the United States matured, its people and leaders struggled to implement fully the ideals that had sparked the Revolution. What had been abstractions before the formation of the new government had to be applied and refined in day-to-day practice. The nature of post-Revolutionary America, government stability, the transition of power against the backdrop of political factionalism, and the extension of democracy had to be worked out.

■ Were the Founding Fathers Democratic Reformers?

■ Did Thomas Jefferson Abandon His Political Ideals in Purchasing the Louisiana Territory?

■ Was Andrew Jackson's Indian Removal Policy Motivated by Humanitarian Impulses?

ISSUE 6

Were the Founding Fathers Democratic Reformers?

YES: John P. Roche, from "The Founding Fathers: A Reform Caucus in Action," *American Political Science Review* (December 1961)

NO: Alfred F. Young, from "The Framers of the Constitution and the 'Genius' of the People," *Radical History Review* (vol. 42, 1988)

ISSUE SUMMARY

YES: Political scientist John P. Roche asserts that the Founding Fathers were not only revolutionaries but also superb democratic politicians who created a Constitution that supported the needs of the nation and at the same time was acceptable to the people.

NO: Historian Alfred F. Young argues that the Founding Fathers were an elite group of college-educated lawyers, merchants, slaveholding planters, and "monied men" who strengthened the power of the central government yet, at the same time, were forced to make some democratic accommodations in writing the Constitution in order to ensure its acceptance in the democratically controlled ratifying conventions.

The United States possesses the oldest written constitution of any major power. The 55 men who attended the Philadelphia Convention of 1787 could scarcely have dreamed that 200 years later the nation would venerate them as the most "enlightened statesmen" of their time. James Madison, the principal architect of the document, may have argued that the Founding Fathers had created a system that might "decide forever the fate of Republican Government which we wish to last for ages," but Madison also told Thomas Jefferson in October 1787 that he did not think the document would be adopted, and if it was, it would not work.

The enlightened statesmen view of the Founding Fathers, presented by nineteenth-century historians like John Fiske, became the accepted interpretation among the general public until the Progressive Era. In 1913 Columbia University professor Charles A. Beard's *An Economic Interpretation of the Constitution of the United States* (Free Press, 1913, 1986) caused a storm of controversy because it questioned the motivations of the Founding Fathers. The Founding Fathers supported the creation of a stronger central government, argued Beard, not for patriotic reasons but because they wanted to protect their own economic interests.

114

Beard's research method was fairly simple. Drawing upon a collection of old, previously unexamined treasury records in the National Archives, he discovered that a number of delegates to the Philadelphia Convention and, later, the state ratifying conventions, held substantial amounts of continental securities that would sharply increase in value if a strong national government were established. In addition to attributing economic motives to the Founding Fathers, Beard included a Marxist class conflict interpretation in his book. Those who supported the Constitution, he said, represented "personalty interests which had been adversely affected under the Articles of Confederation: money, public securities, manufactures, and trade and shipping." Those who opposed ratification of the Constitution were the small farmers and debtors.

Beard's socioeconomic conflict interpretation of the supporters and opponents of the Constitution raised another issue: How was the Constitution ratified if the majority of Americans opposed it? Beard's answer was that most Americans could not vote because they did not own property. Therefore, the entire process, from the calling of the Philadelphia Convention to the state ratifying conventions, was nonrepresentative and nondemocratic.

An Economic Interpretation was a product of its times. Economists, sociologists, and political scientists had been analyzing the conflicts that resulted from the Industrial Revolution, which America had been experiencing at the turn of the twentieth century. Beard joined a group of progressive historians who were interested in reforming the society in which they lived and who also shared his discontent with the old-fashioned institutional approach. The role of the new historians was to rewrite history and discover the real reason why things happened. For the progressive historians, reality consisted of uncovering the hidden social and economic conflicts within society.

In the years between the world wars, the general public held steadfastly to the enlightened statesmen view of the Founding Fathers, but Beard's thesis on the Constitution became the new orthodoxy in most college texts on American history and government. The post–World War II period witnessed the emergence of the neoconservative historians, who viewed the Beardian approach to the Constitution as overly simplistic.

In the first of the following selections, which is a good example of consensus history, John P. Roche contends that the Founding Fathers may have been revolutionaries, but they were also superb democratic politicians who framed a Constitution that supported the needs of the nation and at the same time was acceptable to the people. A good example of Beard's influence lasting into the 1990s can be found in the second selection, in which Alfred F. Young argues that although the Constitution may have strengthened the powers of the central government, the Founding Fathers were forced to make concessions to the people in the final document. Otherwise, the delegates to the state ratifying conventions would have rejected the new Constitution.

YES

John P. Roche

THE FOUNDING FATHERS:
A REFORM CAUCUS IN ACTION

The work of the Constitutional Convention and the motives of the Founding Fathers have been analyzed under a number of different ideological auspices. To one generation of historians, the hand of God was moving in the assembly; under a later dispensation, the dialectic (at various levels of philosophical sophistication) replaced the Deity: "relationships of production" moved into the niche previously reserved for Love of Country.... The Framers have undergone miraculous metamorphoses: at one time acclaimed as liberals and bold social engineers, today they appear in the guise of sound Burkean conservatives, men who in our time would subscribe to *Fortune*....

The "Fathers" have thus been admitted to our best circles; the revolutionary ferocity which confiscated all Tory property in reach ... has been converted ... into a benign dedication to "consensus" and "prescriptive rights." ... It is not my purpose here to argue that the "Fathers" were, in fact, radical revolutionaries; that proposition has been brilliantly demonstrated.... My concern is with the further position that not only were they revolutionaries, but also they were democrats. Indeed, in my view, there is one fundamental truth about the Founding Fathers ...: They were first and foremost superb democratic politicians.... As recent research into the nature of American politics in the 1780s confirms, they were committed (perhaps willy-nilly) to working within the democratic framework, within a universe of public approval.... The Philadelphia Convention was not a College of Cardinals or a council of Platonic guardians working within a manipulative, pre-democratic framework; it was a nationalist reform caucus which had to operate with great delicacy and skill in a political cosmos full of enemies to achieve the one definitive goal—popular approbation....

What they did was to hammer out a pragmatic compromise which would both bolster the "national interest" and be acceptable to the people. What inspiration they got came from their collective experience as professional politicians in a democratic society. As John Dickinson put it to his fellow delegates on August 13, "Experience must be our guide. Reason may mislead us."

From John P. Roche, "The Founding Fathers: A Reform Caucus in Action," *American Political Science Review*, vol. 55 (December 1961). Copyright © 1961 by The American Political Science Association. Reprinted by permission.

In this context, let us examine the problems they confronted and the solutions they evolved. The Convention has been described picturesquely as a counter-revolutionary junta and the Constitution as a coup d'état, but this has been accomplished by withdrawing the whole history of the movement for constitutional reform from its true context. No doubt the goals of the constitutional elite were "subversive" to the existing political order, but it is overlooked that their subversion could only have succeeded if the people of the United States endorsed it by regularized procedures. . . .

I

When the Constitutionalists went forth to subvert the Confederation, they utilized the mechanisms of political legitimacy. And the roadblocks which confronted them were formidable. At the same time, they were endowed with certain potent political assets. The history of the United States from 1786 to 1790 was largely one of a masterful employment of political expertise by the Constitutionalists as against bumbling, erratic behavior by the opponents of reform. Effectively, the Constitutionalists had to induce the states, by democratic techniques of coercion, to emasculate themselves. . . . And at the risk of becoming boring, it must be reiterated that the only weapon in the Constitutionalist arsenal was an effective mobilization of public opinion.

The group which undertook this struggle was an interesting amalgam of a few dedicated nationalists with the self-interested spokesmen of various parochial bailiwicks. The Georgians, for example, wanted a strong central authority to provide military protection for their huge, underpopulated state against the Creek Confederacy; Jerseymen and Connecticuters wanted to escape from economic bondage to New York; the Virginians hoped to establish a system which would give that great state its rightful place in the councils of the republic. The dominant figures in the politics of these states therefore cooperated in the call for the Convention. In other states, the thrust towards national reform was taken up by opposition groups who added the "national interest" to their weapons system; in Pennsylvania, for instance, the group fighting to revise the Constitution of 1776 came out four-square behind the Constitutionalists, and in New York, [Alexander] Hamilton and the Schuyler [family] ambiance took the same tack against George Clinton. There was, of course, a large element of personality in the affair: there is reason to suspect that Patrick Henry's opposition to the Convention and the Constitution was founded on his conviction that Jefferson was behind both, and a close study of local politics elsewhere would surely reveal that others supported the Constitution for the simple (and politically quite sufficient) reason that the "wrong" people were against it. . . .

What distinguished the leaders of the Constitutionalist caucus from their enemies was a "Continental" approach to political, economic and military issues. To the extent that they shared an institutional base of operations, it was the Continental Congress (thirty-nine of the delegates to the Federal Convention had served in Congress), and this was hardly a locale which inspired respect for the state governments. . . . Membership in the Congress under the Articles of Confederation worked to establish a continental frame of reference, that a Congressman from Pennsylvania and one from

North Carolina would share.... This was particularly true with respect to external affairs: the average state legislator was probably about as concerned with foreign policy than as he is today, but Congressmen were constantly forced to take the broad view of American prestige, were compelled to listen to the reports of Secretary John Jay and to the dispatches and pleas from their frustrated envoys in Britain, France and Spain. From considerations such as these, a "Continental" ideology developed which seems to have demanded a revision of our domestic institutions primarily on the ground that only by invigorating our general government could we assume our rightful place in the international arena....

Note that I am not endorsing the "Critical Period" thesis; on the contrary, Merrill Jensen seems to me quite sound in his view that for most Americans, engaged as they were in self-sustaining agriculture, the "Critical Period" was not particularly critical. In fact, the great achievement of the Constitutionalists was their ultimate success in convincing the elected representatives of a majority of the white male population that change was imperative. A small group of political leaders with a Continental vision and essentially a consciousness of the United States' international impotence, provided the matrix of the movement. To their standard other leaders rallied with their own parallel ambitions. Their great assets were (1) the presence in their caucus of the one authentic American "father figure," George Washington, whose prestige was enormous; (2) the energy and talent of their leadership (in which one must include the towering intellectuals of the time, John Adams and Thomas Jefferson, despite their absence abroad), and their communications "network," which

was far superior to anything on the opposition side; (3) the preemptive skill which made "their" issue The Issue and kept the locally oriented opposition permanently on the defensive; and (4) the subjective consideration that these men were spokesmen of a new and compelling credo: American nationalism, that ill-defined but nonetheless potent sense of collective purpose that emerged from the American Revolution....

The Constitutionalists got the jump on the "opposition" (a collective noun: oppositions would be more correct) at the outset with the demand for a Convention. Their opponents were caught in an old political trap: they were not being asked to approve any specific program of reform, but only to endorse a meeting to discuss and recommend needed reforms. If they took a hard line at the first stage, they were put in the position of glorifying the status quo and of denying the need for any changes. Moreover, the Constitutionalists could go to the people with a persuasive argument for "fair play"—"How can you condemn reform before you know precisely what is involved?" Since the state legislatures obviously would have the final say on any proposals that might emerge from the Convention, the Constitutionalists were merely reasonable men asking for a chance. Besides, since they did not make any concrete proposals at that stage, they were in a position to capitalize on every sort of generalized discontent with the Confederation.

Perhaps because of their poor intelligence system, perhaps because of overconfidence generated by the failure of all previous efforts to alter the Articles, the opposition awoke too late to the dangers that confronted them in 1787. Not only did the Constitutionalists manage to get every state but Rhode Island... to appoint delegates to Philadelphia, but when the results were in, it appeared that they dominated the delegations. Given the apathy of the opposition, this was a natural phenomenon: in an ideologically nonpolarized political atmosphere those who get appointed to a special committee are likely to be the men who supported the movement for its creation.... Much has been made of the fact that the delegates to Philadelphia were not elected by the people; some have adduced this fact as evidence of the "undemocratic" character of the gathering. But put in the context of the time, this argument is wholly specious: the central government under the Articles was considered a creature of the component states and in all the states but Rhode Island, Connecticut and New Hampshire, members of the national Congress were chosen by the state legislatures. This was not a consequence of elitism or fear of the mob; it was a logical extension of states'-rights doctrine to guarantee that the national institution did not end-run the state legislatures and make direct contact with the people.

II

With delegations safely named, the focus shifted to Philadelphia. While waiting for a quorum to assemble, James Madison got busy and drafted the so-called Randolph or Virginia Plan with the aid of the Virginia delegation. This was a political master-stroke. Its consequence was that once business got under way, the framework of discussion was established on Madison's terms. There was no interminable argument over agenda; instead the delegates took the Virginia Resolutions—"just for purposes of discussion"—as their point of departure. And

along with Madison's proposals, many of which were buried in the course of the summer, went his major premise: a new start on a Constitution rather than piecemeal amendment....

Standard treatments of the Convention divide the delegates into "nationalists" and "states'-righters" with various improvised shadings ("moderate nationalists," etc.), but these are a posteriori categories which obfuscate more than they clarify. What is striking to one who analyzes the Convention as a case-study in democratic politics is the lack of clear-cut ideological divisions in the Convention. Indeed, I submit that the evidence—Madison's Notes, the correspondence of the delegates, and debates on ratification—indicates that this was a remarkably homogeneous body on the ideological level. [Robert] Yates and [John] Lansing [of New York], who favored the New Jersey Plan]... left in disgust on July 10.... Luther Martin, Maryland's bibulous narcissist, left on September 4 in a huff when he discovered that others did not share his self-esteem; others went home for personal reasons. But the hard core of delegates accepted a grinding regimen throughout the attrition of a Philadelphia summer precisely because they shared the Constitutionalist goal.

Basic differences of opinion emerged, of course, but these were not ideological; they were structural. If the so-called "states'-rights" group had not accepted the fundamental purposes of the Convention, they could simply have pulled out and by doing so have aborted the whole enterprise. Instead of bolting, they returned day after day to argue and to compromise. An interesting symbol of this basic homogeneity was the initial agreement on secrecy: these professional politicians did not want to become prisoners of publicity; they wanted to retain that freedom of maneuver which is only possible when men are not forced to take public stands in the preliminary stages of negotiation. There was no legal means of binding the tongues of the delegates: at any stage in the game a delegate with basic principled objections to the emerging project could have taken the stump (as Luther Martin did after his exit) and denounced the convention to the skies. Yet... the delegates generally observed the injunction. Secrecy is certainly uncharacteristic of any assembly marked by strong ideological polarization....

Commentators on the Constitution who have read *The Federalist* in lieu of reading the actual debates have credited the Fathers with the invention of a sublime concept called "Federalism."... Federalism, as the theory is generally defined, was an improvisation which was later promoted into a political theory. Experts on "federalism" should take to heart the advice of David Hume, who warned... "there is no subject in which we must proceed with more caution than in [history], lest we assign causes which never existed and reduce what is merely contingent to stable and universal principles." In any event, the final balance in the Constitution between the states and the nation must have come as a great disappointment to Madison....

It is indeed astonishing how those who have glibly designated James Madison the "father" of Federalism have overlooked the solid body of fact which indicates that he shared Hamilton's quest for a unitary central government. To be specific, they have avoided examining the clear import of the Madison-Virginia Plan, and have disregarded Madison's dogged inch-by-inch retreat from the bastions of centralization. The Virginia Plan

envisioned a unitary national government effectively freed from and dominant over the states. The lower house of the national legislature was to be elected directly by the people of the states with membership proportional to population. The upper house was to be selected by the lower and the two chambers would elect the executive and choose the judges. The national legislature was to be empowered to disallow the acts of state legislatures, and the central government was vested, in addition to the powers of the nation under which the Articles of Confederation, with plenary authority wherever "... the separate States are incompetent or in which the harmony of the United States may be interrupted by the exercise of individual legislation." Finally, just to lock the door against state intrusion, the national Congress was to be given the power to use military force on recalcitrant states. This was Madison's "model" of an ideal national government, though it later received little publicity in *The Federalist*.

The interesting thing was the reaction of the Convention to this militant program for a strong autonomous central government. Some delegates were startled, some obviously leery of so comprehensive a project of reform, but nobody set off any fireworks and nobody walked out. Moreover, in the two weeks that followed, the Virginia Plan received substantial endorsement *en principe*; the initial temper of the gathering can be deduced from the approval "without debate or dissent," on May 31, of the Sixth Resolution which granted Congress the authority to disallow state legislation "... contravening in its opinion the Articles of Union." Indeed, an amendment was included to bar states from contravening national treaties.

The Virginia Plan may therefore be considered, in ideological terms, as the delegates' Utopia, but as the discussions continued and became more specific, many of those present began to have second thoughts.... They were practical politicians in a democratic society, and no matter what their private dreams might be, they had to take home an acceptable package and defend it—and their own political futures—against predictable attack. On June 14 the breaking point between dream and reality took place. Apparently realizing that under the Virginia Plan, Massachusetts, Virginia and Pennsylvania could virtually dominate the national government—and probably appreciating that to sell this program to "the folks back home" would be impossible—the delegates from the small states dug in their heels and demanded time for a consideration of alternatives....

Now the process of accommodation was put into action smoothly—and wisely, given the character and strength of the doubters. Madison had the votes, but this was one of those situations where the enforcement of mechanical majoritarianism could easily have destroyed the objectives of the majority: the Constitutionalists were in quest of a qualitative as well as a quantitative consensus; ... it was a political imperative if they were to attain ratification.

III

According to the standard script, at this point the "states'-rights" group intervened in force behind the New Jersey Plan, which has been characteristically portrayed as a revision to the status quo under the Articles of Confederation with but minor modifications. A careful examination of the evidence indicates that only

in a marginal sense is this an accurate description. It is true that the New Jersey Plan put the states back into the institutional picture, but one could argue that to do so was a recognition of political reality rather than an affirmation of states'-rights. A serious case can be made that the advocates of the New Jersey Plan, far from being ideological addicts of states'-rights, intended to substitute for the Virginia Plan a system which would both retain strong national power and have a chance of adoption in the states. The leading spokesman for the project asserted quite clearly that his views were based more on counsels of expediency than on principle.... In his preliminary speech on June 9, Paterson had stated " ... to the public mind we must accommodate ourselves," and in his notes for this and his later effort as well, the emphasis is the same. The structure of government under the Articles should be retained:

> 2. Because it accords with the Sentiments of the People
>
> > [Proof:] 1. Coms. [Commissions from state legislatures defining the jurisdiction of the delegates]
> >
> > 2. News-papers—Political Barometer. Jersey never would have sent Delegates under the first [Virginia] Plan—

Not here to sport Opinions of my own. Wt. [What] can be done. A little practicable Virtue preferrable to Theory.

This was a defense of political acumen, not of states'-rights....

In other words, the advocates of the New Jersey Plan concentrated their fire on what they held to be the political liabilities of the Virginia Plan—which were matters of institutional structure—rather than on the proposed scope of national authority. Indeed, the Supremacy Clause of the Constitution first saw the light of day in Paterson's Sixth Resolution; the New Jersey Plan contemplated the use of military force to secure compliance with national law; and finally Paterson made clear his view that under either the Virginia or the New Jersey systems, the general government would " . . . act on individuals and not on states." From the states'-rights viewpoint, this was heresy: the fundament of that doctrine was the proposition that any central government had as its constituents the states, not the people, and could only reach the people through the agency of the state government.

Paterson then reopened the agenda of the Convention, but he did so within a distinctly naturalist framework. Paterson's position was one of favoring a strong central government in principle, but opposing one which in fact put the big states in the saddle.

How attached would the Virginians have been to their reform principles if Virginia were to disappear as a component geographical unit (the largest) for representational purposes? Up to this point, the Virginians had been in the happy position of supporting high ideals with that inner confidence born of knowledge that the "public interest" they endorsed would nourish their private interest. Worse, they had shown little willingness to compromise. Now the delegates from the small states announced that they were unprepared to be offered up as sacrificial victims to a "national interest" which reflected Virginia's parochial ambition. Caustic Charles Pinckney was not far off when he remarked sardonically that " . . . the whole [conflict] comes to this: Give N. Jersey an equal vote, and she will

dismiss her scruples, and concur in the Natil. system." What he rather unfairly did not add was that the Jersey delegates were not free agents who could adhere to their private convictions; they had to take back, sponsor and risk their reputations on the reforms approved by the Convention—and in New Jersey, not in Virginia. . . .

IV

On Tuesday morning, June 19, . . . James Madison led off with a long, carefully reasoned speech analyzing the New Jersey Plan which, while intellectually vigorous in its criticisms, was quite conciliatory in mood. "The great difficulty," he observed, "lies in the affair of Representation; and if this could be adjusted, all others would be surmountable." (As events were to demonstrate, this diagnosis was correct.) When he finished, a vote was taken on whether to continue with the Virginia Plan as the nucleus for a new constitution: seven states voted "Yes"; New York, New Jersey, and Delaware voted "No"; and Maryland, whose position often depended on which delegates happened to be on the floor, divided. Paterson, it seems, lost decisively; yet in a fundamental sense he and his allies had achieved their purpose: from that day onward, it could never be forgotten that the state governments loomed ominously in the background. . . . Moreover, nobody bolted the convention: Paterson and his colleagues took their defeat in stride and set to work to modify the Virginia Plan, particularly with respect to its provisions on representation in the national legislature. Indeed, they won an immediate rhetorical bonus; when Oliver Ellsworth of Connecticut rose to move that the word "national" be expunged from the Third Virginia Resolution ("Resolved that a national Government ought to be established consisting of a supreme Legislative, Executive and Judiciary"), Randolph agreed and the motion passed unanimously. The process of compromise had begun.

For the next two weeks, the delegates circled around the problem of legislative representation. The Connecticut delegation appears to have evolved a possible compromise quite early in the debates, but the Virginians and particularly Madison (unaware that he would later be acclaimed as the prophet of "federalism") fought obdurately against providing for equal representation of states in the second chamber.... On July 2, the ice began to break when through a number of fortuitous events—and one that seems deliberate—the majority against equality of representation was converted into a dead tie. The Convention had reached the stage where it was "ripe" for a solution (presumably all the therapeutic speeches had been made), and the South Carolinians proposed a committee. Madison and James Wilson wanted none of it, but with only Pennsylvania dissenting, the body voted to establish a working party on the problem of representation.

The members of this committee, one from each state, were elected by the delegates—and a very interesting committee it was. Despite the fact that the Virginia Plan had held majority support up to that date, neither Madison nor Randolph was selected (Mason was the Virginian) and Baldwin of Georgia, whose shift in position had resulted in the tie, was chosen. From the composition, it was clear that this was not to be a "fighting" committee: the emphasis in membership was on what might be described as "second-level political entrepreneurs." On the ba-

sis of the discussions up to that time, only Luther Martin of Maryland could be described as a "bitter-ender." Admittedly, some divination enters into this sort of analysis, but one does get a sense of the mood of the delegates from these choices—including the interesting selection of Benjamin Franklin, despite his age and intellectual wobbliness, over the brilliant and incisive Wilson or the sharp, polemical Gouverneur Morris, to represent Pennsylvania. His passion for conciliation was more valuable at this juncture than Wilson's logical genius, or Morris' acerbic wit....

It would be tedious to continue a blow-by-blow analysis of the work of the delegates; the critical fight was over representation of the states and once the Connecticut Compromise was adopted on July 17, the Convention was over the hump. Madison, James Wilson, and Gouverneur Morris of New York (who was there representing Pennsylvania!) fought the compromise all the way in a last-ditch effort to get a unitary state with parliamentary supremacy. But their allies deserted them.... Moreover, once the compromise had carried (by five states to four, with one state divided), its advocates threw themselves vigorously into the job of strengthening the general government's substantive powers—as might have been predicted, indeed, from Paterson's early statements. It nourishes an increased respect for Madison's devotion to the art of politics, to realize that this dogged fighter could sit down six months later and prepare essays for *The Federalist* in contradiction to his basic convictions about the true course the Convention should have taken.

V

Two tricky issues will serve to illustrate the later process of accommodation. The first was the institutional position of the Executive. Madison argued for an executive chosen by the National Legislature and on May 29 this had been adopted with a provision that after his seven-year term was concluded, the chief magistrate should not be eligible for reelection. In late July this was reopened and for a week the matter was argued from several different points of view.... One group felt that the states should have a hand in the process; another small but influential circle urged direct election by the people. There were a number of proposals: election by the people, election by state governors, by electors chosen by state legislatures, by the National legislature, ... and there was some resemblance to three-dimensional chess in the dispute because of the presence of two other variables, length of tenure and reeligibility. Finally, after opening, reopening, and re-reopening the debate, the thorny problem was consigned to a committee for resolution.

The Brearley Committee on Postponed Matters was a superb aggregation of talent and its compromise on the Executive was a masterpiece of political improvisation. (The Electoral College, its creation, however, had little in its favor as an institution—as the delegates well appreciated.) The point of departure for all discussion about the presidency in the Convention was that in immediate terms, the problem was non-existent; in other words, everybody present knew that under any system devised, George Washington would be President. Thus they were dealing in the future tense and to a body of working politicians the merits of the Brearley proposal were obvious: everybody got a piece of cake. (Or to put it more academically, each viewpoint could leave the Convention and argue to its constituents that it had really won the day.) First, the state legislatures had the right to determine the mode of selection of the electors; second, the small states received a bonus in the Electoral College in the form of a guaranteed minimum of three votes while the big states got acceptance of the principle of proportional power; third, if the state legislatures agreed (as six did in the first presidential election), the people could be involved directly in the choice of electors; and finally, if no candidate received a majority in the College, the right of decision passed to the National Legislature with each state exercising equal strength. (In the Brearley recommendation, the election went to the Senate, but a motion from the floor substituted the House; this was accepted on the ground that the Senate already had enough authority over the executive in its treaty and appointment powers.)

This compromise was almost too good to be true, and the Framers snapped it up with little debate or controversy. No one seemed to think well of the College as an institution; indeed, what evidence there is suggests that there was an assumption that once Washington had finished his tenure as President, the electors would cease to produce majorities and the chief executive would usually be chosen in the House. George Mason observed casually that the selection would be made in the House nineteen times in twenty and no one seriously disputed this point. The vital aspect of the Electoral College was that it got the Convention over the hurdle and protected everybody's interests....

In short, the Framers did not in their wisdom endow the United States with a College of Cardinals—the Electoral College was neither an exercise in applied Platonism nor an experiment in indirect government based on elitist distrust of the masses. It was merely a jerry-rigged improvisation which has subsequently been endowed with a high theoretical content....

The second issue on which some substantial practical bargaining took place was slavery. The morality of slavery was, by design, not at issue; but in its other concrete aspects, slavery colored the arguments over taxation, commerce, and representation. The "Three-Fifths Compromise," that three-fifths of the slaves would be counted both for representation and for purposes of direct taxation (which was drawn from the past—it was a formula of Madison's utilized by Congress in 1783 to establish the basis of state contributions to the Confederation treasury) had allayed some Northern fears about Southern over-representation.... The Southerners, on the other hand, were afraid that Congressional control over commerce would lead to the exclusion of slaves or to their excessive taxation as imports. Moreover, the Southerners were disturbed over "navigation acts," i.e., tariffs or special legislation providing, for example, that exports be carried only in American ships; as a section depending upon exports, they wanted protection from the potential voracity of their commercial brethren of the Eastern states. To achieve this end, Mason and others urged that the Constitution include a proviso that navigation and commercial laws should require a two-thirds vote in Congress.

These problems came to a head in late August and, as usual were handed to a committee in the hope that, in Gouverneur Morris' words, "... these things may form a bargain among the Northern and Southern states." The Committee reported its measures of reconciliation on August 25, and on August 29 the package was wrapped up and delivered. What occurred can best be described in George Mason's dour version (he anticipated Calhoun in his conviction that permitting navigation acts to pass by majority vote would put the South in economic bondage to the North—it was mainly on this ground that he refused to sign the Constitution):

> The Constitution as agreed to till a fortnight before the Convention rose was such a one as he would have set his hand and heart to.... [Until that time] The 3 New England States were constantly with us in all questions... so that it was these three States with the 5 Southern ones against Pennsylvania, Jersey and Delaware. With respect to the importation of slaves, [decision-making] was left to Congress. This disturbed the two Southernmost States who knew that Congress would immediately suppress the importation of slaves. Those two States therefore struck up a bargain with the three New England States. If they would join to admit slaves for some years, the two Southern-most States would join in changing the clause which required the 2/3 of the Legislature in any vote [on navigation acts]. It was done.

On the floor of the Convention there was a virtual love-feast on this happy occasion. Charles Pinckney of South Carolina attempted to overturn the committee's decision, when the compromise was reported to the Convention, by insisting that the South needed protection from the imperialism of the Northern states. But his Southern colleagues were not prepared to rock the boat and General C. C.

Pinckney arose to spread oil on the suddenly ruffled waters; he admitted that:

> It was in the true interest of the S[outhern] States to have no regulation of commerce; but considering the loss brought on the commerce of the Eastern States by the Revolution, their liberal conduct towards the views of South Carolina [on the regulation of the slave trade] and the interests the weak Southn. States had in being united with the strong Eastern states, he thought it proper that no fetters should be imposed on the power of making commercial regulations; and that his constituents, though prejudiced against the Eastern States, would be reconciled to this liberality. He had himself prejudices against the Eastern States before he came here, but would acknowledge that he had found them as liberal and candid as any men whatever.

Pierce Butler took the same tack, essentially arguing that he was not too happy about the possible consequences, but that a deal was a deal....

VI

Drawing on their vast collective political experience, utilizing every weapon in the politician's arsenal, looking constantly over their shoulders at their constituents, the delegates put together a Constitution. It was a makeshift affair; some sticky issues (for example, the qualification of voters) they ducked entirely; others they mastered with that ancient instrument of political sagacity, studied ambiguity (for example, citizenship), and some they just overlooked. In this last category, I suspect, fell the matter of the power of the federal courts to determine the constitutionality of acts of Congress. When the judicial article was formulated (Article III of the Constitution), deliberations were still in the stage where the legislature was endowed with broad power under the Randolph formulation, authority which by its own terms was scarcely amenable to judicial review. In essence, courts could hardly determine when " . . . the separate States are incompetent or . . . the harmony of the United States may be interrupted"; the National Legislature, as critics pointed out, was free to define its own jurisdiction. Later the definition of legislative authority was changed into the form we know, a series of stipulated powers, but the delegates never seriously reexamined the jurisdiction of the judiciary under this new limited formulation. All arguments on the intention of the Framers in this matter are thus deductive and a posteriori, though some obviously make more sense than others.

The Framers were busy and distinguished men, anxious to get back to their families, their positions, and their constituents.... They were trying to do an important job, and do it in such a fashion that their handiwork would be acceptable to very diverse constituencies. No one was rhapsodic about the final document, but it was a beginning, a move in the right direction, and one they had reason to believe the people would endorse. In addition, since they had modified the impossible amendment provisions of the Articles ... to one demanding approval by only three-quarters of the states, they seemed confident that gaps in the fabric which experience would reveal could be rewoven without undue difficulty.

So with a neat phrase introduced by Benjamin Franklin (but devised by Gouverneur Morris) which made their decision sound unanimous, and an inspired benediction by the Old Doctor urging doubters to doubt their own infallibility, the Constitution was accepted and signed. Curiously, Edmund Randolph, who had played so vital a role throughout, refused to sign, as did his fellow Virginian George Mason and Elbridge Gerry of Massachusetts. Randolph's behavior was eccentric;... the best explanation seems to be that he was afraid that the Constitution would prove to be a liability in Virginia politics, where Patrick Henry was burning up the countryside with impassioned denunciations. Presumably, Randolph wanted to check the temper of the populace before he risked his reputation, and perhaps his job, in a fight with both Henry and Richard Henry Lee. Events lend some justification to this speculation: after much temporizing ... Randolph endorsed ratification in Virginia and ended up getting the best of both worlds....

The Constitution, then, was an apotheosis of "constitutionalism," a triumph of architectonic genius; it was a patchwork sewn together under the pressure of both time and events by a group of extremely talented democratic politicians. They refused to attempt the establishment of a strong, centralized sovereignty on the principle of legislative supremacy for the excellent reason that the people would not accept it. They risked their political fortunes by opposing the established doctrines of state sovereignty because they were convinced that the existing system was leading to national impotence and probably foreign domination. For two years, they worked to get a convention established. For over three months, in what must have seemed to the faithful participants an endless process of give-and-take, they reasoned, cajoled, threatened, and bargained amongst themselves. The result was a Constitution which the people, in fact, by democratic processes, did accept, and a new and far better national government was established....

To conclude, the Constitution was neither a victory for abstract theory nor a great practical success. Well over half a million men had to die on the battlefields of the Civil War before certain constitutional principles could be defined—a baleful consideration which is somehow overlooked in our customary tributes to the farsighted genius of the Framers and to the supposed American talent for "constitutionalism." The Constitution was, however, a vivid demonstration of effective democratic political action, and of the forging of a national elite which literally persuaded its countrymen to hoist themselves by their own boot straps.

NO

Alfred F. Young

THE FRAMERS OF THE CONSTITUTION
AND THE "GENIUS" OF THE PEOPLE

On June 18, 1787, about three weeks into the Constitutional Convention at Philadelphia, Alexander Hamilton delivered a six-hour address that was easily the longest and most conservative the Convention would hear. Gouverneur Morris, a delegate from Pennsylvania, thought it was "the most able and impressive he had ever heard."

Beginning with the premise that "all communities divide themselves into the few and the many," "the wealthy well born" and "the people," Hamilton added the corollary that the "people are turbulent and changing; they seldom judge or determine right." Moving through history, the delegate from New York developed his ideal for a national government that would protect the few from "the imprudence of democracy" and guarantee "stability and permanence": a president and senate indirectly elected for life ("to serve during good behavior") to balance a house directly elected by a popular vote every three years. This "elective monarch" would have an absolute veto over laws passed by Congress. And the national government would appoint the governors of the states, who in turn would have the power to veto any laws by the state legislatures.

If others quickly saw a resemblance in all of this to the King, House of Lords and House of Commons of Great Britain, with the states reduced to colonies ruled by royal governors, they were not mistaken. The British constitution, in Hamilton's view, remained "the best model the world has ever produced."

Three days later a delegate reported that Hamilton's proposals "had been praised by everybody," but "he has been supported by none." Acknowledging that his plan "went beyond the ideas of most members," Hamilton said he had brought it forward not "as a thing attainable by us, but as a model which we ought to approach as near as possible." When he signed the Constitution the framers finally agreed to on September 17, 1787, Hamilton could accurately say, "no plan was more remote from his own."

Why did the framers reject a plan so many admired? To ask this question is to go down a dark path into the heart of the Constitution few of its celebrants care to take. We have heard so much in our elementary and high school

From Alfred F. Young, "The Framers of the Constitution and the 'Genius' of the People," *Radical History Review*, vol. 42 (1988). Copyright © 1988 by Cambridge University Press. Reprinted by permission.

civics books about the "great compromises" within the Convention—between the large states and the small states, between the slaveholders and non-slaveholders, between North and South —that we have missed the much larger accommodation that was taking place between the delegates as a whole at the Convention and what they called "the people out of doors."

The Convention was unmistakably an elite body. [In 1987] the official exhibit for the bicentennial, "Miracle at Philadelphia," [opened] appropriately enough with a large oil portrait of Robert Morris, a delegate from Philadelphia, one of the richest merchants in America, and points out elsewhere that 11 out of 55 delegates were business associates of Morris'. The 55 were weighted with merchants, slaveholding planters and "monied men" who loaned money at interest. Among them were numerous lawyers and college graduates in a country where most men and only a few women had the rudiments of a formal education. They were far from a cross section of the four million or so Americans of that day, most of whom were farmers or artisans, fishermen or seamen, indentured servants or laborers, half of whom were women and about 600,000 of whom were African-American slaves.

THE FIRST ACCOMMODATION

Why did this elite reject Hamilton's plan that many of them praised? James Madison, the Constitution's chief architect, had the nub of the matter. The Constitution was "intended for the ages." To last it had to conform to the "genius" of the American people. "Genius" was a word eighteenth-century political thinkers used to mean spirit: we might say character or underlying values.

James Wilson, second only to Madison in his influence at Philadelphia, elaborated on the idea. "The British government cannot be our model. We have no materials for a similar one. Our manners, our law, the abolition of entail and primogeniture," which made for a more equal distribution of property among sons, "the whole genius of the people, are opposed to it."

This was long-range political philosophy. There was a short-range political problem that moved other realistic delegates in the same direction. Called together to revise the old Articles of Confederation, the delegates instead decided to scrap it and frame an entirely new constitution. It would have to be submitted to the people for ratification, most likely to conventions elected especially for the purpose. Repeatedly, conservatives recoiled from extreme proposals for which they knew they could not win popular support.

In response to a proposal to extend the federal judiciary into the states, Pierce Butler, a South Carolina planter, argued, "the people will not bear such innovations. The states will revolt at such encroachments." His assumption was "we must follow the example of Solomon, who gave the Athenians not the best government he could devise but the best they would receive."

The suffrage debate epitomized this line of thinking. Gouverneur Morris, Hamilton's admirer, proposed that the national government limit voting for the House to men who owned a freehold, i.e. a substantial farm, or its equivalent. "Give the vote to people who have no property and they will sell them to the rich who will be able to buy them," he said with some prescience. George Mason, author of Virginia's Bill of Rights, was aghast. "Eight or nine states have extended the right of suffrage beyond the freeholders. What will people there say if they should be disfranchised?"

Benjamin Franklin, the patriarch, speaking for one of the few times in the convention, paid tribute to "the lower class of freemen" who should not be disfranchised. James Wilson explained, "it would be very hard and disagreeable for the same person" who could vote for representatives for the state legislatures "to be excluded from a vote for this in the national legislature." Nathaniel Gorham, a Boston merchant, returned to the guiding principle: "the people will never allow" existing rights to suffrage to be abridged. "We must consult their rooted prejudices if we expect their concurrence in our propositions."

The result? Morris' proposal was defeated and the convention decided that whoever each state allowed to vote for its own assembly could vote for the House. It was a compromise that left the door open and in a matter of decades allowed states to introduce universal white male suffrage.

GHOSTS OF YEARS PAST

Clearly there was a process of accommodation at work here. The popular movements of the Revolutionary Era were a presence at the Philadelphia Convention even if they were not present. The delegates, one might say, were haunted by ghosts, symbols of the broadly based movements elites had confronted in the making of the Revolution from 1765 to 1775, in waging the war from 1775 to 1781 and in the years since 1781 within their own states.

The first was the ghost of Thomas Paine, the most influential radical democrat of the Revolutionary Era. In 1776 Paine's pamphlet *Common Sense* (which sold at least 150,000 copies), in arguing for independence, rejected not only King George III but the principle of monarchy and the so-called checks and balances of the unwritten English constitution. In its place he offered a vision of a democratic government in which a single legislature would be supreme, the executive minimal, and representatives would be elected from small districts by a broad electorate for short terms so they could "return and mix again with the voters." John Adams considered *Common Sense* too "democratical," without even an attempt at "mixed government" that would balance "democracy" with "aristocracy."

The second ghost was that of Abraham Yates, a member of the state senate of New York typical of the new men who had risen to power in the 1780s in the state legislatures. We have forgotten him; Hamilton, who was very conscious of him, called him "an old Booby." He had begun as a shoemaker and was a self-taught lawyer and warm foe of the landlord aristocracy of the Hudson Valley which Hamilton had married into. As James Madison identified the "vices of the political system of the United States" in a memorandum in 1787, the Abraham Yateses were the number-one problem. The state legislatures had "an itch for paper money" laws, laws that prevented foreclosure on farm mortgages, and tax laws that soaked the rich. As Madison saw it, this meant that "debtors defrauded their creditors" and "the landed interest has borne hard on the mercantile interest." This, too, is what Hamilton had in mind when he spoke of the "depredations which the democratic spirit is apt to make on property" and what others meant by the "excess of democracy" in the states.

The third ghost was a very fresh one —Daniel Shays. In 1786 Shays, a captain in the Revolution, led a rebellion of debtor farmers in western Massachusetts which the state quelled with its own somewhat unreliable militia. There were "combustibles in every state," as George Washington put it, raising the specter of "Shaysism." This Madison enumerated among the "vices" of the system as "a want of guaranty to the states against internal violence." Worse still, Shaysites in many states were turning to the political system to elect their own kind. If they succeeded they would produce legal Shaysism, a danger for which the elites had no remedy.

The fourth ghost we can name was the ghost of Thomas Peters, although he had a thousand other names. In 1775, Peters, a Virginia slave, responded to a plea by the British to fight in their army and win their freedom. He served in an "Ethiopian Regiment," some of whose members bore the emblem "Liberty to Slaves" on their uniforms. After the war the British transported Peters and several thousand escaped slaves to Nova Scotia from whence Peters eventually led a group to return to Africa and the colony of Sierra Leone, a long odyssey to freedom. Eighteenth-century slaveholders, with no illusions about happy or contented slaves, were haunted by the specter of slaves in arms.

ELITE DIVISIONS

During the Revolutionary Era elites divided in response to these varied threats from below. One group, out of fear of "the mob" and then "the rabble in arms," embraced the British and became active Loyalists. After the war most of them went into exile. Another group who became patriots never lost their obsession with coercing popular movements....

Far more important, however, were those patriot leaders who adopted a strategy of "swimming with a stream which it is impossible to stem." This was the metaphor of Robert R. Livingston, Jr., ... a gentleman with a large tenanted estate in New York. Men of his class had to learn to "yield to the torrent if they hoped to direct its course."

Livingston and his group were able to shape New York's constitution, which some called a perfect blend of "aristocracy" and "democracy." John Hancock, the richest merchant in New England, had mastered this kind of politics and emerged as the most popular politician in Massachusetts. In Maryland Charles Carroll, a wealthy planter, instructed his anxious father about the need to "submit to partial losses" because "no great revolution can happen in a state without revolutions or mutations of private property. If we can save a third of our personal estate and all of our lands and Negroes, I shall think ourselves well off."

The major leaders at the Constitutional Convention in 1787 were heirs to both traditions: coercion and accommodation —Hamilton and Gouverneur Morris to the former, James Madison and James Wilson much more to the latter.

They all agreed on coercion to slay the ghosts of Daniel Shays and Thomas Peters. The Constitution gave the national government the power to "suppress insurrections" and protect the states from "domestic violence." There would be a national army under the command of the president, and authority to nationalize the state militias and suspend the right of habeas corpus in "cases of rebellion or invasion." In 1794 Hamilton, as secretary of the treasury, would exercise such powers fully (and needlessly) to suppress the Whiskey Rebellion in western Pennsylvania.

Southern slaveholders correctly interpreted the same powers as available to shackle the ghost of Thomas Peters. As it turned out, Virginia would not need a federal army to deal with Gabriel Prosser's insurrection in 1800 or Nat Turner's rebellion in 1830, but a federal army would capture John Brown after his raid at Harpers Ferry in 1859.

But how to deal with the ghosts of Thomas Paine and Abraham Yates? Here Madison and Wilson blended coercion with accommodation. They had three solutions to the threat of democratic majorities in the states.

Their first was clearly coercive. Like Hamilton, Madison wanted some kind of national veto over the state legislatures. He got several very specific curbs on the states written into fundamental law: no state could "emit" paper money or pass "laws impairing the obligation of contracts." Wilson was so overjoyed with these two clauses that he argued that if they alone "were inserted in the Constitution I think they would be worth our adoption."

But Madison considered the overall mechanism adopted to curb the states "short of the mark." The Constitution, laws and treaties were the "supreme law of the land" and ultimately a federal court could declare state laws unconstitutional. But this, Madison lamented, would only catch "mischiefs" after the fact. Thus they had clipped the wings of Abraham Yates but he could still fly.

The second solution to the problem of the states was decidedly democratic. They wanted to do an end-run around the state legislatures. The Articles of Confederation, said Madison, rested on "the pillars" of the state legislatures who elected delegates to Congress. The "great fabric to be raised would be more stable and durable if it should rest on the solid grounds of the people themselves"; hence, there would be popular elections to the House.

Wilson altered only the metaphor. He was for "raising the federal pyramid to a considerable altitude and for that reason wanted to give it as broad a base as possible." They would slay the ghost of Abraham Yates with the ghost of Thomas Paine.

This was risky business. They would reduce the risk by keeping the House of Representatives small. Under a ratio of one representative for every 30,000 people, the first house would have only 65 members; in 1776 Thomas Paine had suggested 390. But still, the House would be elected every two years, and with each state allowed to determine its own qualifications for voting, there was no telling who might end up in Congress.

There was also a risk in Madison's third solution to the problem of protecting propertied interests from democratic majorities: "extending the sphere" of government. Prevailing wisdom held that a republic could only succeed in a small geographic area; to rule an "extensive" country, some kind of despotism was considered inevitable.

Madison turned this idea on its head in his since famous *Federalist* essay No. 10. In a small republic, he argued, it was relatively easy for a majority to gang up on a particular "interest." "Extend the sphere," he wrote, and "you take in a greater variety of parties and interests." Then it would be more difficult for a majority "to discover their own strength and to act in unison with each other."

This was a prescription for a non-colonial empire that would expand across the continent, taking in new states as it dispossessed the Indians. The risk was there was no telling how far the "democratic" or "leveling" spirit might go in such likely would-be states as frontier Vermont, Kentucky and Tennessee.

DEMOCRATIC DIVISIONS

In the spectrum of state constitutions adopted in the Revolutionary era, the federal Constitution of 1787 was, like New York's, somewhere between "aristocracy" and "democracy." It therefore should not surprise us—although it has eluded many modern critics of the Constitution—that in the contest over ratification in 1787–1788, the democratic minded were divided.

Among agrarian democrats there was a gut feeling that the Constitution was the work of an old class enemy. "These lawyers and men of learning and monied men," argued Amos Singletary, a working farmer at the Massachusetts ratifying convention, "expect to be managers of this Constitution and get all the power and all the money into their own hands and then will swallow up all of us little folks ... just as the whale swallowed up Jonah."

Democratic leaders like Melancton Smith of New York focused on the small size of the proposed House. Arguing from Paine's premise that the members of the legislature should "resemble those they represent," Smith feared that "a substantial yeoman of sense and discernment will hardly ever be chosen" and the government "will fall into the hands of the few and the great." Urban democrats, on the other hand, including a majority of the mechanics and tradesmen of the major cities who in the Revolution had been a bulwark of Paineite radicalism, were generally enthusiastic about the Constitution. They were impelled by their urgent stake in a stronger national government that would advance ocean-going commerce and protect American manufacturers from competition. But they would not have been as ardent about the new frame of government without its saving graces. It clearly preserved their rights to suffrage. And the process of ratification, like the Constitution itself, guaranteed them a voice. As early as 1776 the New York Committee of Mechanics held it as "a right which God has given them in common with all men to judge whether it be consistent with their interest to accept or reject a constitution."

Mechanics turned out en masse in the parades celebrating ratification, marching trade by trade. The slogans and symbols they carried expressed their political ideals. In New York the upholsterers had a float with an elegant "Federal Chair of State" flanked by the symbols of Liberty and Justice that they identified with the Constitution. In Philadelphia the bricklayers put on their banner "Both buildings and rulers are the work of our hands."

Democrats who were skeptical found it easier to come over because of the Constitution's redeeming features. Thomas Paine, off in Paris, considered the Constitution "a copy, though not quite as base as the original, of the form of the British government." He had always opposed a single executive and he objected to the "long duration of the Senate." But he was so convinced of "the absolute necessity" of a stronger federal government that "I would have voted for it myself had I been in America or even for a worse, rather than have none." It was crucial to Paine that there was an amending process, the means of "remedying its defects by the same appeal to the people by which it was to be established."

THE SECOND ACCOMMODATION

In drafting the Constitution in 1787 the framers, self-styled Federalists, made their first accommodation with the "genius" of the people. In campaigning for its ratification in 1788 they made their second. At the outset, the conventions in the key states—Massachusetts, New York and Virginia—either had an anti-Federalist majority or were closely divided. To swing over a small group of "antis" in each state, Federalists had to promise that they would consider amendments. This was enough to secure ratification by narrow margins in Massachusetts, 187 to 168; in New York, 30 to 27; and in Virginia, 89 to 79.

What the anti-Federalists wanted were dozens of changes in the structure of the government that would cut back national power over the states, curb the powers of the presidency as well as protect individual liberties. What they got was far less. But in the first Congress in 1789, James Madison, true to his pledge, considered all the amendments and shepherded 12 amendments through both houses. The first two of these failed in the states; one would have enlarged the House. The 10 that were ratified by December 1791 were what we have since called the Bill of Rights,

protecting freedom of expression and the rights of the accused before the law. Abraham Yates considered them "trivial and unimportant." But other democrats looked on them much more favorably. In time the limited meaning of freedom of speech in the First Amendment was broadened far beyond the framers' original intent. Later popular movements thought of the Bill of Rights as an essential part of the "constitutional" and "republican" rights that belonged to the people.

THE "LOSER'S" ROLE

There is a cautionary tale here that surely goes beyond the process of framing and adopting the Constitution and Bill of Rights from 1787 to 1791. The Constitution was as democratic as it was because of the influence of popular movements that were a presence, even if not present. The losers helped shape the results. We owe the Bill of Rights to the opponents of the Constitution, as we do many other features in the Constitution put in to anticipate opposition.

In American history popular movements often shaped elites, especially in times of crisis when elites were concerned with the "system." Elites have often divided in response to such threats and according to their perception of the "genius" of the people. Some have turned to coercion, others to accommodation. We run serious risk if we ignore this distinction. Would that we had fewer Gouverneur Morrises and Alexander Hamiltons and more James Madisons and James Wilsons to respond to the "genius" of the people.

POSTSCRIPT

Were the Founding Fathers Democratic Reformers?

Roche stresses the political reasons for writing a new Constitution. In a spirited essay that reflects great admiration for the Founding Fathers as enlightened politicians, Roche describes the Constitution as "a triumph of architectonic genius; it was a patch-work sewn together under the pressure of both time and events by a group of extremely talented democratic politicians."

Roche narrates the events of the convention of 1787 with a clarity rarely seen in the writings on this period. He makes the telling point that once the dissenters left Philadelphia, the delegates were able to hammer out a new Constitution. All the Founding Fathers agreed to create a stronger national government, but differences centered around the shape the new government would take. The delegates' major concern was to create as strong a national government as possible that would be acceptable to all states. Had the ratifying conventions rejected the new Constitution, the United States might have disintegrated into 13 separate countries.

Young asserts that the Constitution was written by an elite group of people to strengthen the powers of the national government against those of the people. He believes that four ghosts that made their presence felt at the Philadelphia Convention caused the Founding Fathers to react in a paradoxical manner. On the one hand, the shadows of the radical Democrat Thomas Paine and arch anti-Federalist Abraham Yates of the New York State senate forced the Founding Fathers to support universal white male suffrage, a House of Representatives directly elected by the people every two years, and a bill of rights to protect the individual liberties of people from a tyrannical government. On the other hand, the national government was able to quell the ghosts of Daniel Shays and ex-slave Thomas Peters with its power to "suppress insurrections" and protect the states from "domestic violence."

Historian Gordon S. Wood tries to recapture the eighteenth-century world in *The Creation of the American Republic, 1776–1787* (University of North Carolina Press, 1969), a seminal work that has replaced Beard as the starting point for scholarship on this topic. A devastating critique of the methodological fallacies of Wood and other intellectual writers on this period can be found in Ralph Lerner's "The Constitution of the Thinking Revolutionary," in Richard Beeman et al., eds., *Beyond Confederation: Origins of the Constitution and American National Identity* (University of North Carolina Press, 1987). Also see Richard B. Morris, *The Forging of the Union, 1781–1789* (Harper & Row, 1987) and Michael Kammen, *A Machine That Would Go of Itself: The Constitution in American Culture* (Alfred A. Knopf, 1986).

ISSUE 7

Did Thomas Jefferson Abandon His Political Ideals in Purchasing the Louisiana Territory?

YES: David A. Carson, from "Blank Paper of the Constitution: The Louisiana Purchase Debates," *The Historian* (Spring 1992)

NO: Barry J. Balleck, from "When the Ends Justify the Means: Thomas Jefferson and the Louisiana Purchase," *Presidential Studies Quarterly* (Fall 1992)

ISSUE SUMMARY

YES: David A. Carson, associate professor of history and social studies education, states that Thomas Jefferson initially abandoned his ideological commitment to states' rights and strict constructionism by his decision to support the acquisition of the Louisiana Territory.

NO: Barry J. Balleck, assistant professor of political science, summarizes Thomas Jefferson's political ideals and concludes that Jefferson agreed to purchase the Louisiana Territory in support of his most deeply held political principle—the protection of republican government. This was the primary goal that underlay all of his actions as president of the United States.

Between 1789 and 1796, two competing political traditions developed in the United States and were embodied in two political parties—the Federalists and the Democratic-Republicans. Most of the early debates between members of these competing factions focused on specific issues and programs, such as the creation of a central banking system, the establishment of protective tariffs, and of foreign policy matters. However, at the heart of these disagreements were differences concerning the power exercised by the newly created federal government under the Constitution of the United States.

The Federalists, who held the upper hand politically until 1800, believed that only through a strong central government could independence be guaranteed, freedom ensured, and prosperity secured. They desired an activist government that would use its powers to the highest degree possible under the Constitution. States' rights, they insisted, was an inherently divisive doctrine to be avoided at all costs.

The Democratic-Republicans, under the leadership of James Madison and Thomas Jefferson, supported the national government, but they expressed concern that an overly powerful central government could become destructive of powers residing in the states or, more seriously, carry out an assault on the individual liberties of citizens. For these leaders, the best prevention against an abusive federal government lay in a strict construction of the Constitution. Thomas Jefferson carried this political philosophy into the White House following his victory in the presidential election of 1800, but within two years he confronted an issue that seriously challenged his ability to remain consistent to his ideological views.

In 1762, France had ceded its claim to lands west of the Mississippi River to Spain. In 1801, however, Napoleon Bonaparte negotiated the transfer of Louisiana from Spain to France and announced that American shippers would no longer be allowed to deposit their goods at the port of New Orleans. Jefferson sought a peaceful negotiation with the French and sent American statesman James Monroe to Paris to attempt to purchase New Orleans. In Paris, Monroe and the American minister to France, Robert Livingston, met with the French minister of foreign affairs, Charles Maruice de Talleyrand-Périgord, who shocked the Americans with an offer to sell them all of the Louisiana Territory for $15 million. Monroe jumped at this opportunity to double the potential size of the United States, even though he lacked the authority to do so, and Jefferson supported his emissary's decision knowing full well that the Constitution did not expressly authorize the acquisition of new territory.

Jefferson's first impulse was to seek an enabling constitutional amendment, but he feared that a protracted debate over the measure might give the French too much time to reconsider their offer. Some of his supporters suggested that the power to acquire new territory could be implied from the constitutionally granted authority to make treaties, but given Jefferson's traditional opposition to such a broad interpretation, this alternative was not entirely satisfactory. Nevertheless, in light of the opportunity manifested in France's offer, Jefferson concluded that Congress should cast aside "metaphysical subtleties" and ratify the agreement.

Did Jefferson betray his most deeply held political ideals in order to acquire the Louisiana Territory from the French? David A. Carson maintains that he did. In fact, Carson argues, once having abandoned his commitment to states' rights and strict constructionism in the Louisiana Purchase, Jefferson frequently demonstrated a propensity for taking executive actions that ignored his long-time support for a limited central government.

Barry J. Balleck suggests that scholars need to pay more attention to the full range of Jefferson's ideological views. According to Balleck, foremost was the desire to protect republican government in the new United States. When other views, such as states' rights and strict constructionism, stood in the way of that ultimate goal, Jefferson was prepared to set them aside temporarily in order to achieve the greater good for the American people.

YES

David A. Carson

BLANK PAPER OF THE CONSTITUTION: THE LOUISIANA PURCHASE DEBATES

The acquisition of Louisiana was exceeded in importance during the early republic only by the signing of the Declaration of Independence and the ratification of the Constitution. The Louisiana Purchase gave the United States undisputed control of the Mississippi Valley and the heart of the North American continent, an area of centuries-old contention among France, Spain, Great Britain, and more recently the United States. The acquisition of this immense territory further opened the door to sectional rivalry, the expansion of slavery, and the eventual disruption of the Union in the Civil War. On a more fundamental level, the acquisition irrevocably altered the very nature of the Union. Thomas Jefferson himself saw that it threatened to make "blank paper" of the Constitution since it expanded the powers of the national government further than even the most die-hard Federalists could have imagined. The purchase also shifted the philosophical grounds on which the political parties in Congress had laid their foundations, and it made the author of the Kentucky Resolutions' theory of strict construction the new author of Louisiana's theory of loose construction.

This shift in political ideologies between the Republicans and Federalists stands out in the constitutional legacy of the Jefferson administration. The President had long championed the concepts of state rights, state sovereignty, and strict construction of the Constitution. With him on this philosophical ground stood James Madison (although to a lesser degree), James Monroe, and John Randolph, the Republican leader of the House. Yet these very men, so wary of the dangers of a centralized federal government, effected the greatest expansion of governmental powers yet known in the new nation.

John Randolph, because of his position in the House and his well-known life-long devotion to state rights, is a particularly interesting study. He is acknowledged by most historians to be the philosophical link between the Kentucky Resolutions of 1798 and John C. Calhoun's doctrine of nullification. Yet in this issue he has been described as a "centralizing statesman." At the time, Randolph saw no difficulty in expanding the president's powers to acquire Louisiana and, in the House, he was an obedient instrument of the

From David A. Carson, "Blank Paper of the Constitution: The Louisiana Purchase Debates," *The Historian*, vol. 54 (Spring 1992). Copyright © 1992 by David A. Carson. Reprinted by permission of the author and *The Historian*. Notes omitted.

president's will. However, Randolph soon attempted to push back time and undo the results of his own labor. In 1822, he cried out against the purchase and its effects on the Constitution, saying, "We were forewarned! I for one, although forewarned, was not forearmed. If I had been, I have no hesitation in declaring that I would have said to the imperial Dejanira of modern times, take back your fatal present!" In 1803, Randolph, like other Republican leaders and state-rights advocates, was caught up in the exhilaration of an expanding nation. On the issue of Louisiana, the resolve of the executive and the legislature, with the exception of the Northeastern Federalists, was fixed and Congress followed the president's lead.

On July 16, two days after Jefferson received the purchase treaty, he called his cabinet to help plot the course of the agreements through Congress. Since the treaty had to be ratified by both nations within six months of the signing, the cabinet agreed to convene Congress on October 17, which would leave sufficient time for both houses to act before the closing date of October 30. The delay would allow Jefferson to deal with political opposition and to resolve his own constitutional doubts. The cabinet also agreed to make public the substance of the treaty but not the treaty itself.

The question uppermost in Jefferson's mind at this time related to the constitutionality of such an immense acquisition. On July 17, the day after the cabinet meeting, Jefferson wrote that he had decided to call Congress early because "they will be obliged to ask from the People an amendment of the Constitution, authorizing their receiving the province into the Union, and providing for its government." Long before the ac-

quisition of Louisiana, the president had wrestled over the constitutional difficulties of adding to the original territory of the United States. In January 1803, he asked his cabinet to confront this problem and offer advice. With only the purchase of New Orleans and perhaps the Floridas anticipated, Attorney General Levi Lincoln responded to Jefferson's request with a proposal lacking both insight and consistency. He stated that the desired territory was so essential to the United States that any means of obtaining it was justified. He further advocated claiming that France had agreed by treaty to extend the boundaries of the Mississippi Territory and Georgia to the Gulf of Mexico. By adopting this indirect method, "would not the General Govt avoid some constitutional, and some political embarrassments, which a direct acquisition of a foreign territory by the Govt of the United States might occasion?"

Secretary of the Treasury Albert Gallatin pointed out the obvious flaws in Lincoln's logic and offered his own argument. Gallatin maintained that the United States as a nation had "an inherent right to acquire territory." Further, if the acquisition was made by treaty, "the same constituted authorities in whom the treaty-making power is vested have a constitutional right to sanction the acquisition." After the territory had been acquired, "Congress [has] the power either of admitting [it] into the Union as a new State, or of annexing [it] to a State with the consent of that State or [of] making regulations for the government of such territory."

Jefferson responded favorably to Gallatin's assertion: "You are right, in my opinion, as to Mr. L[incoln]'s proposition: there is no constitutional difficulty as to the acquisition of territory." But in the very next sentence the president again maintained, "I think it will be safer not to permit the enlargement of the Union but by amendment of the Constitution."

The juxtaposition of conflicting ideas reveals the debate forming in Jefferson's own mind. Although bound to his philosophy of strict construction, he was mindful of the need for expediency and practicality in government. He was willing to expand the powers of his office but was fearful enough of the consequences that he desired exceptional authorization for this one act. The internal conflict was typical of Jefferson, as is clear from the many debates between his head and his heart in his letters. During the early stages of the particular debate, Jefferson's heart, with its roots in minimal government and strict construction, held ascendancy. Only when Napoleon's attitude toward the purchase changed did Jefferson's head, with its need for practicality and expediency, gain ascendancy. Having relinquished old principles in this issue, he would find it easier and more expedient to do the same on future issues. Most Republican members of Congress would follow this course throughout his presidency. Others adhered to it only through the Louisiana issue, then charted a course of their own.

The question of the constitutionality of purchasing new territory lay dormant after the January exchange of letters among Jefferson, Lincoln, and Gallatin, but it reawakened in July with news of the acquisition of Louisiana. Jefferson immediately wrote two drafts of a constitutional amendment. Both authorized the purchase, defined Indian rights, and established an Indian zone north of the 31st parallel. The second draft also included provisions for the eventual acquisition of the Floridas and a summary of the rights and obligations of its citizens.

Jefferson explained his feelings on the constitutional issue in a letter to John Dickinson. He wrote:

> There is a difficulty in this acquisition which presents a handle to the malcontents among us, though they have not yet discovered it. Our confederation is certainly confined to the limits established by the revolution. The general government has no powers but such as the Constitution has given it; and it has not given it a power of holding foreign territory, [and] still less of incorporating it into the Union. An amendment of the Constitution seems necessary for this.

Three days later Jefferson expressed almost identical words to John Breckinridge, the faithful Republican senator from Kentucky, but added that the executive had already "done an act beyond the Constitution."

Shortly after Jefferson related his sentiments to Breckinridge, a new element entered the picture. While not completely altering Jefferson's constitutional misgivings, it caused him to view them in a different light. On August 17, the president received a letter from Robert Livingston, U.S. minister to France, about French opinion, noting that the United States had made too favorable a bargain. Livingston wrote that Napoleon was displeased with the settlement and would seize any reason to void it. The minister urged that the treaty be ratified as soon as possible if Louisiana were to become a U.S. territory.

This news so alarmed Jefferson that he immediately changed his tactics. The next day he wrote Breckinridge about his misgivings on the constitutionality of the purchase. Telling him of the news from Livingston, Jefferson warned that "nothing must be said on that subject which may give a pretext for retracting; but that we should do sub-silentio what shall be found necessary." Similar letters went out that day to Thomas Paine and James Madison. On August 23, Jefferson wrote Gallatin asking him to prepare a bill authorizing the transfer of stock with which Louisiana would be purchased. The president warned the secretary of treasury that, "It will be well to say as little as possible on the constitutional difficulty, and that Congress should act on it without talking." These letters reveal the influence that Jefferson believed he had to maintain over Congress to stifle opposition. His letter to Gallatin also reveals that the president still had misgivings, for after his warning against talk of constitutional difficulties, he immediately submitted a new draft of an amendment for Gallatin's consideration. Jefferson was a man trapped by his political philosophies; he could neither fully hold on to them nor fully let them go.

Jefferson's constitutional doubts put him in a small minority. Not only did his cabinet advisors disagree with him but so did the majority of Congress. Virginia Senator Wilson Cary Nicholas spoke for others when he wrote the president in early September: "Upon an examination of the constitution, I find the power as broad as it could well be made.... Nor do I see anything in the constitution that limits the treaty making power." Then he sagely warned, "I shou'd think it very probable if the treaty shou'd be by you declared to exceed the constitutional authority of the treaty making power, that it would be rejected by the Senate, and if that should not happen, that great use wou'd be made with the people of a wilful breech of the constitution."

The president's reply to Nicholas reveals his constitutional gymnastics in microcosm. Jefferson first advised Congress to act quickly, with little debate or reference to the constitutional difficulty, lest Napoleon void the treaty. Then Jefferson declared his belief that the Constitution provided only for the incorporation of new states into the Union out of the territory the United States possessed at the time of the revolution. He admitted that the Constitution could be read in another way, but "when an instrument admits two constructions, the one safe, the other dangerous, the one precise, the other indefinite, I prefer that which is safe & precise." Jefferson continued: "I had rather ask an enlargement of power from the nation, where it is found necessary, than to assume it by a constitution which would make our powers boundless." Then, to the heart of the matter: "Our peculiar security is in possession of a written Constitution. Let us not make it a blank paper by construction." So far, Jefferson stood on the same ground he had taken in 1798, but his statement shows that, as usual, his head was overcoming his heart. "If, however, our friends shall think differently, certainly I shall acquiesce with satisfaction; confiding that the good sense of our country will correct the evil construction when it shall produce ill effects."

Jefferson thus presented a strong argument for strict construction but left the door open for an exception to the rule. He was not being hypocritical or even ambivalent, for he sincerely believed that by their reason, Americans would also treat the purchase as an exception and not the precedent for a broad system of loose construction. If members of Congress had not been so overwhelmingly in favor of the purchase and convinced of its constitutionality,

Jefferson surely would have sought an amendment. But the majority in both Houses were unhindered by doubts, and this, along with Napoleon's change of heart, caused the president to readily "acquiesce with satisfaction." Once this had occurred, Jefferson was ready to present the treaty to Congress.

The Eighth Congress, which convened on October 17, 1803, was in many respects the ablest and most cooperative of the four in Jefferson's two terms. Federalist influence had declined since the Seventh Congress, and Republican factionalism did not arise in large measure until the Ninth. Virginia's W. C. Nicholas was the primary administrative spokesman through whom Jefferson communicated his will to the Senate. Senator John Taylor of North Carolina was a staunch state-rights advocate who generally followed party policy but pointed out inconsistencies when the administration wavered from cherished philosophies. When Nicholas resigned after the first session, he was replaced in the second session (November 5, 1804, to March 3, 1805) by William Branch Giles, another state-rights advocate and sometimes maverick but generally a straight party man. Kentucky's Breckinridge, usually the spokesman for the Western states, was another key senator upon whom Jefferson relied.

Very few moderate Federalists in the Senate voted their conscience and not always their party, but extreme Federalists followed the lead of Timothy Pickering of Massachusetts. This group included the Connecticut and Delaware delegates who predictably opposed any administration measure, regardless of its merit.

The lower House was dominated by Speaker Nathaniel Macon of North Carolina, Chairman of the Ways and Means Committee John Randolph of Virginia, and Joseph Nicholson of Maryland. This triumvirate was to the legislative branch what Jefferson, Madison, and Gallatin were to the executive. When in agreement with the administration, as they were through most of the Eighth Congress, their irresistible influence in the House was essential. Macon's ties with the administration were important because the speaker appointed all committee chairmen and could stack the deck either for or against the president. Randolph was important not only for his position on the powerful Ways and Means Committee but also for his skills as an orator and his ability to cajole, caress, or ridicule House members into line. Nicholson's importance lay in his ties with Republican leaders in all branches of government and in the personal respect he commanded throughout the House. Other leading Republican representatives in the Eighth Congress included Caesar Rodney of Delaware, and the president's two sons-in-law from Virginia, John Eppes and Thomas Randolph.

Federalist opposition in the House was again felt mainly through the New England delegates. South Carolina was the only Southern state with a significant degree of Federalist influence in the House, but sentiment toward the Louisiana Purchase among Federalists in that state, as in Virginia and North Carolina, was mixed.

Before Congress met, Jefferson wrote to Breckinridge and urged him to help get "every friend of the purchase" to attend on the first day of the session. The president asked him to "impress this necessity on the Senators of the western states by private letter." Breckinridge, who called the purchase an achievement "of which the annals of no country can furnish a parallel," responded by writing Senators William Cocke of Tennessee and Thomas Washington of Ohio to meet with him in Washington on October 15 for an "interchange of sentiments" on Louisiana. He hoped also to organize Western sympathizers against a Federalist attack on the purchase.

The outcome of this meeting is unknown, but only two of the Western senators were absent on October 17 when Congress convened and received Jefferson's third annual address, which dealt mainly with foreign affairs. The president formally announced the treaty of purchase and asked the Senate for immediate ratification. After it had acted, he would ask Congress for measures which would allow the occupation and governing of the territory, along with its incorporation into the Union. He also spoke of other matters but did not mention the problem of constitutionality.

Well before Jefferson gave his address, he sought the advice of his cabinet on the most desirable procedure for ratifying the treaty and passing the measures putting it into effect. The president wanted only to lay the treaty before both houses, probably because of his unresolved conflict over the convention's constitutionality. He may have felt that he would stand on firmer constitutional grounds if both bodies gave the documents a thorough hearing and agreed that they were within the scope of the Constitution. But James Madison warned Jefferson to avoid the constitutional difficulty of allowing the House to debate a treaty that depended on the Senate. Gallatin agreed that the treaty-making power lay solely with the president and the Senate. Madison and Gallatin were more concerned with the constitutional problem of

involving the House in the treaty debate. They may also have anticipated that, although the Republicans dominated both houses, the lower house would be more likely to question the constitutionality of the treaty, and thus place the entire transaction at risk. Therefore, they urged the path of least resistance.

On October 17, the Senate received the treaty and related documents. Despite efforts by Federalists William Wells and James Hillhouse to embarrass the administration by casting doubts on the legitimacy of France's title to Louisiana, the Senate approved the treaty on October 20, by a vote of 24 to 7. Six days later, the Senate voted 26 to 6 to allow the president to take possession of Louisiana and to provide for its temporary government.

The day after the Senate approved the treaty, Jefferson sent a message to both houses announcing ratification and requesting Congress to move quickly in passing measures for paying for, occupying, and governing the territory. The House received the message on October 22, with John Randolph moving to carry the treaty into effect. The resolution was referred to the Committee of the Whole. Two days later, Roger Griswold, a Connecticut Federalist, moved to request that the president give the House a copy of the Treaty of San Ildefonso (by which France had acquired Louisiana from Spain), a copy of the deed of cession from Spain to France, copies of correspondence between the governments of the United States and Spain showing the latter's sentiments about the cession, and any other documents that might shed light on the strength of the U.S. claim to Louisiana. This resolution, so similar to that of Wells and Hillhouse in the Senate, was another attempt to embarrass the administration by requesting documents and titles the president did not possess. Griswold maintained that the president's request to carry the treaty into effect could not be complied with until the United States could be assured of having clear title to Louisiana. If France had not received clear title, then that of the United States was highly questionable and the country would be spending millions for a territory it could not possess.

Randolph, the administration's treaty manager in the House, replied that the duty of the House was to act on legislation laid before it, not to interpret or debate the nation's treaties. Matthew Lyon of Kentucky said he might have agreed to Griswold's resolution if it had been brought forward in a respectful manner, but since it was meant to embarrass the president, he opposed it. Calvin Goddard of Connecticut, supporting the resolution, did not want to lose $15 million because France did not live up to its obligations in the Treaty of San Ildefonso. John Smilie, a Republican from Pennsylvania, read from the House journal debate on Jay's Treaty of 1796 to show that the House could not rule on the validity of a treaty. Other Republicans called Griswold's resolution indecent, unnecessary, and premature. Finally, the House decided to divide Griswold's resolution into two. The first would require the president to transmit a copy of the Treaty of San Ildefonso to the House. This resulted in a tie, 59 to 59. When Speaker Macon voted for it, the first resolution carried. The second required the president to give the House all documents, treaties, and correspondence, which reflected the validity of the U.S. claim to Louisiana or the attitude of Spain to the cession. This resolution failed by the narrow vote of 57 to 59.

These votes were closer than Jefferson or Republican leaders anticipated since their party held a majority of 103 to 39 in the House. The votes show that though the House might still support the purchase, it was not as willing as the Senate to ram legislation through blindly without thought or debate. House leaders knew the importance of time, but House members also recognized the importance of thorough examination of pertinent materials and discussion of tactics and consequences. Madison and Gallatin had been correct in their expectation of more complications in the House.

On October 25, the House once again began to debate measures for carrying out the treaty and conventions. Opening for the opposition, Federalist Gaylord Griswold of New York launched the broadside Jefferson dreaded. He asked where in the Constitution could be found provisions for the incorporation of territory and inhabitants into the United States. He could find no such powers within the Constitution, yet the president and the Senate had claimed it through their treaty-making power. Griswold maintained that the House should withhold all means of support when such a grab for undelegated power was being made. If any branch of government possessed such power, it should be the legislative. He further stated that the spirit of republican government was inconsistent with an expansive territory. He also opposed as unconstitutional the seventh article of the treaty, which gave France and Spain commercial privileges in New Orleans for twelve years. For these reasons, he hoped that the House would refuse to carry the treaty into effect.

Randolph rose to answer Griswold's questions on the constitutionality of the purchase. The Republican leader maintained that the boundaries of the United States were unknown at the time of the adoption of the Constitution. Therefore, it fell upon the executive to define and expand the boundaries through its treaty-making power. He reminded Griswold of the extension of U.S. territory to the 31st parallel by Pinckney's Treaty and maintained that the acquisition of Louisiana was no less constitutional.

In the debate that followed, only the Northeastern Federalists took a hard line against the treaty. They denounced Virginian dominance, questioned the ability of the president to admit people of a foreign nation into the United States, and debated where the treaty-making powers of the government lay. Republicans, maintaining a united front, were joined by several Federalists who usually opposed the administration. Maryland's Nicholson taunted the Federalists, who in the previous session had advocated war measures to seize the very territory they now refused to purchase. He also defended the right of the general government to extend the territory of the United States by purchase or treaty. Delaware's Rodney then put forth a line of reasoning to support the purchase's constitutionality that must have shocked even his fellow Republicans. Rodney asserted that unless the Constitution forbade the acquisition of territory there was no reason why the purchase would not fall under provision for the general welfare and common defense. He compared it with the right of the government to purchase land for the creation of forts, magazines, arsenals, dockyards, and other public buildings. If the government could purchase land from the states or from individuals, why could it not also purchase land from a foreign nation? Such an argument must have secretly delighted old Federalists who would have feared to make such a plea for a broad interpretation of the Constitution. It must also have struck a nerve among the state-rights Republicans who favored the purchase but deplored a permanent, broad extension of the powers of the national government.

Debate continued from October 25 to October 28, as Republicans persistently pressed arguments more suited to the Federalist ideology, and Northeastern Federalists cried out against the unconstitutional extension of executive powers. Nevertheless, when a vote was taken, the bill for paying for, occupying, and governing the territory was passed by a large majority. Among those in opposition were Federalists from Vermont, New York, New Hampshire, Connecticut, Massachusetts, Maryland, and Virginia. Republicans were convinced of the benefits of the purchase to their nation, their party, and their individual sections. For the moment they, like the president, put constitutional questions on the shelf and clutched at the unexpected acquisition with both hands. The fears of wide expansion of executive power were revealed only in an amendment that the House added to the Senate bill, which said the absolute power of the president to govern Louisiana would cease at the end of the session of Congress if no other government had been erected—the only attempt to limit the broad powers that the Republican Congress had granted to its ex-champion of strict construction.

On November 2, the Senate took up the second reading of "An act authorizing the creation of a stock to the amount of eleven millions two hundred and fifty thousand dollars, for the purpose of carrying into effect the convention of the 30th of April, 1803, between the United States of America and the French Republic, and making provision for the same." When the question "Shall the bill pass?" was asked, a new round of debate was touched off in which the Senate repeated the arguments heard in the House. Samuel White, a Delaware Federalist, began the debate by pointing out that Spain was hostile to the sale and might block the United States from taking possession of the territory. He then questioned Napoleon's intention of allowing the actual transfer of Louisiana to the United States. Finally, he alluded to the constitutionality of the acquisition: "But as to Louisiana, this new, immense, unbounded world, if it should ever be incorporated into this Union, which I have no idea can be done but by altering the Constitution, I believe it will be the greatest curse that could at present befall us."

Debate on the bill resumed in the Senate the next day with Pickering, a Massachusetts Federalist, heading the opposition and Breckinridge leading the administration's forces. The argument occurred over the constitutionality of the purchase itself—an issue supposedly disposed of when the Senate approved the treaty. Pickering gave the Federalist position, in this case an extreme state-rights position. He professed a belief that neither the president nor Congress had the authority to admit territory and its inhabitants into the Union. He also believed this could not be accomplished even with the amendment to the Constitution that Jefferson proposed. Rather, the assent of each individual state was needed for the admission of a foreign country into the United States. Pickering also pointed out that France had never fulfilled its obligations to Spain in the Treaty of San Ilde-

fonso (Napoleon had promised to secure a kingdom in Italy for the duke of Parma), and since France had never possessed clear title to Louisiana, the United States would never have clear title.

Pickering was answered by John Taylor, a state-rights Republican from Virginia, who upheld the constitutionality of the sale by saying that the right to acquire territory—a right possessed by all thirteen states during the Confederation —had been surrendered to the general government under the Constitution. Taylor's line of reasoning must have tasted bitter to him at a later date since he would return to champion the principles of strict construction. Connecticut's Uriah Tracy answered Taylor, expressing doubts about the constitutionality of the purchase but admitted that the question had become moot when the Senate approved the treaty. Tracy's main objection to the treaty, like that of so many Northeastern Federalists, was that it gave the Southern and Western interests a strength that was "contradictory to the principles of our original Union."

Federalist jealousy of the South and West was a common theme throughout the debate. New Hampshire Senator William Plumer had warned that the incorporation of Louisiana into the Union would divide and sever the United States. He felt the men of the Northeast possessed "the high rank that they are entitled to hold in the Union—and they have too much pride tamely to shrink into a state of insignificance." Manasseh Cutler, Federalist representative from Massachusetts, echoed Plumer, saying that the admission of Louisiana would upset the balance of the states and would "lay the foundation for the separation of the states." Josiah Quincy, another Federalist from Massachusetts, said that the extent of the nation was already a national misfortune. It was bad enough to have Kentuckians in the legislature, but if the new treaty went into effect, Congress would be crowded with "buffaloes from the head of the Missouri and alligators from the Red River."

Republicans could do little to refute such arguments. The purchase did broaden the influence of the South and West at the expense of the Northeast and laid the foundation for the spread of slavery and the eventual—albeit temporary—dissolution of the Union. Breckinridge told the Senate that the theory of a republic could work more effectively in a large area and that Louisiana would thus benefit the nation. Virginia's Nicholas expressed amazement that some senators were going to such lengths to prove unconstitutional a measure which they had already passed. Tennessee's Cocke pointed out the inconsistency of the New England Federalists. In the previous Congress, they had clamored for war and the military seizure of New Orleans and the Floridas but condemned as unconstitutional the purchase of the very lands they had wanted to seize. The question on the passage of the bill, when put to the Senate, carried 26 to 5. Only Connecticut's Hillhouse and Tracy, Delaware's Wells and White, and Pickering of Massachusetts opposed it.

Jefferson was understandably delighted with the votes in the House and Senate, but he was not surprised. The president was so certain the purchase was beneficial to the nation that his faith in the good sense of its representatives did not admit any doubt as to the outcome of the congressional vote, despite his own misgivings. After ratification of the treaty, Jefferson wrote exultingly to New York treaty proponent Robert Livingston, "Your treaty has obtained nearly a general approbation. The federalists spoke and voted against it, but they are now so reduced in their numbers as to be nothing." A few days later he noted, "The votes of both Houses on ratifying and carrying the treaties into execution have been precisely party votes."

Federalist John Quincy Adams, who, in this instance, was blinded neither by party nor president, was not yet willing to pass on the constitutionality question. Shortly after the treaty had been laid before the Senate, Adams announced to Madison that he approved the purchase but felt it his duty to introduce a constitutional amendment to carry through the Louisiana treaty. Madison coyly replied that "he did not know that it was universally agreed that it required an amendment of the Constitution." In the Senate debate over the bill to allow the president to take possession of Louisiana, Adams offered an amendment that would have inserted the words "consistently with the Constitution of the United States" into the purchase bill. This was struck down as out of order. However, even after the treaty was ratified and accompanying measures were passed, Adams persisted in pushing for an amendment. These efforts, so similar to those of the president in July, were for naught. Adams again raised the question of an amendment before the Senate on November 25, but his resolutions were voted down by a large majority. Adams' third attempt failed in December.

There is no question that Adams' fears of the effect of the purchase on the Constitution were sincere. Throughout the debate he stood practically alone as the defender of strict constitutional construction. Years later he denounced Jefferson for being elected under the banner of state-rights and for attacking the implied powers of the national government, "when the first thing he did was to purchase Louisiana—an assumption of implied powers greater in itself and more comprehensive in its consequences than all the assumptions of implied powers in the twelve years of the Washington and Adams administrations put together." Adams was especially significant in the Louisiana debate because he occupied the same constitutional position that Jefferson had abandoned in July (the same ground that would soon be reclaimed by John Randolph and the Quids, or Old Republicans). If the need for haste in approving the treaty had not been so great, Jefferson and Adams might have combined their efforts to secure a suitable constitutional amendment. Adams' objections died on the altar of expediency and public opinion.

Adams' shot was the last volley fired in the debate on the constitutionality of the Louisiana Purchase. Jefferson serenely rested on his belief that any damage done to the Constitution would be remedied by the reasonableness of the American people, and Jefferson's party seemed unperturbed by the relative ease with which party principles of strict construction had been compromised. Immediate reflection offered only images of territorial expansion and westward migration, party solidarity, and securing Jefferson another place in history.

But for Jefferson and his party, the purchase represented a potentially ominous turning point. Having championed the concepts of state-rights, state sovereignty, and strict construction of the Constitution for so long, Jefferson, in one bold stroke, threatened to reduce that Constitution to "blank paper." Abandoning his conservative philosophy in a successful and popular matter such as the acquisition of Louisiana would make it easier for Jefferson to do the same on such future issues as his pursuit of the Floridas, prosecution of an undeclared war against Tripoli, and arbitrary enforcement of the embargo. Only upon deeper reflection did some of those very Republicans who had pushed for the treaty later realize that their abandonment of party principles in 1803 had established a precedent they would later regret. Louisiana, that "fatal present" Randolph spoke of in 1822, would serve as a reminder that philosophical principles can be easy sacrifices to the god of political pragmatism.

NO

Barry J. Balleck

WHEN THE ENDS JUSTIFY THE MEANS

The Louisiana Purchase was a watershed event in the history of the United States. By this one act the size of the nation was more than doubled and a formidable potential enemy—France—was removed from among the major actors in North America. More than simply a coup for the United States, however, the Louisiana Purchase was the greatest achievement of Thomas Jefferson's presidency. With the addition of this virgin territory to the patrimony of the United States, Jefferson secured for the nation "for generations, if not centuries to come," a necessary guarantor of Republicanism—landed and commercial expansion. Moreover, Jefferson felt that the purchase of Louisiana would ensure the pastoral nature of the United States and forestall the degeneration which had befallen classical Republican governments. Jefferson was confident that the Louisiana territory would promote the development of a virtuous Republican citizenry.

In purchasing the Louisiana territory, however, Thomas Jefferson called into question his most cherished political convictions. He was a strict constitutional constructionist and a strong supporter of states' rights. The former position, as understood by Jefferson, meant that " . . . the general government has no powers but such as the constitution has given it. . . ." The latter position, as Jefferson's biographer Dumas Malone points out, was deeply inbred in Jefferson. He was "a Virginian before he became anything else, and he never ceased to be one." Yet by purchasing Louisiana, Jefferson's adherence to both strict constructionism and to states' rights were called into question. As John Quincy Adams wrote, the purchase of Louisiana entailed "an assumption of implied power greater in itself and more comprehensive in its consequence, than all the assumptions of implied power in the twelve years of the Washington and Adams Administrations put together." Echoing this criticism, Henry Adams added, "The principle of strict constructionism was the breath of his [Jefferson's] political life. The Pope could as easily trifle with the doctrine of apostolic succession as Jefferson with the limits of Executive power." Why, then, did Jefferson undertake to purchase Louisiana, an act that he understood to be contrary to the principles of strict constructionism and states' rights?

In answering this question, it is important to recognize the underlying conviction that directed all of Jefferson's actions—i.e., Republicanism. For Jefferson and many of his contemporaries, Republicanism was the only form of government suitable to the United States. However, as historical republics had demonstrated, the passage of time was a republic's worst enemy as growth and urbanization eventually led to centralized governmental power and societal decay. Republican government could thus only survive in an atmosphere of limited government and in a society of virtuous and moral citizens. As such, Republicanism relied on the aid of selected defenses aimed at forestalling decay. In general, Jefferson believed that states' rights and strict constructionism provided such defenses, though he understood that time would inevitably wear them away.

Understood in this light, the Louisiana Purchase was a case of the ends justifying the means; that is, in order to secure the desired end of Republicanism, Jefferson temporarily set aside its most dependable guarantors—states' rights and strict constructionism—by stepping for a time outside the bounds of the Constitution. This abandonment of the standard defenses of Republicanism was necessary in order to grasp an opportunity that provided for the long-term security of Republicanism—in this case the new frontiers provided by the Louisiana territory. Once secured, Jefferson returned to the normal protection of Republicanism provided by state's rights and strict constructionism. As Henry Adams noted in this regard, Jefferson believed that "in the hands of true Republicans the constitution, even though violated, was on the whole safe; the precedent, though alarming was exceptional."

Other writers have recognized Jefferson's dilemma in the case of the Louisiana Purchase. Drew McCoy (1980), for example, provided an excellent discussion of Jefferson's Republican ideals and suggests that they directly influenced his decision to purchase the Louisiana territory. Robert Tucker and David Hendrickson (1990) also suggest that in the case of Louisiana, Jefferson sacrificed his constitutional scruples in order to achieve his end of an "Empire of Liberty." Neither of these works, however, adequately relate Jefferson's abandonment of his traditional means—states' rights and strict constructionism—to his end—Republicanism.

This [selection] will demonstrate that Jefferson was consistent in his purchase of the Louisiana territory—that there was no "sell out" of his political ideals. . . .

REPUBLICANISM AS A JEFFERSONIAN IDEAL

To Jefferson, the security of Republican government seemed to depend upon states' rights and strict constructionism. After all, to secure the benefits of Republicanism to the new nation was the ultimate end of government, and both states' rights and strict constructionism would secure Republicanism by restraining the power of the national government. However, as Jefferson recognized, the general protection provided by states' rights and strict constructionism could not be expected to hold forever. The frontier would eventually fill up, cities would grow, and general societal decay would ensue. Therefore, if at a certain time an unprecedented opportunity to extend the period of Republican stability presented itself—and could only be grasped by moving temporarily away from the generally appropriate means for protecting Republicanism—one would necessarily have to seize the opportunity.

This, then, was Jefferson's rationale. After all, in the Jeffersonian sense Republicanism was much more than simply a form of government. Indeed, it was a way of life that was intensely concerned with the broader social and moral condition of the country. Thus, its vitality was paramount in advancing a virtuous citizenry, which ensured the continued existence of the United States. At the core of Republicanism stood two fundamental pillars: individualism and an agrarian way of life.

INDIVIDUALISM

In drawing a distinction between Republicans and Federalists, Jefferson noted that Republicans consisted of (1) the entire body of landholders throughout the United States, and (2) the body of laborers, not being landholders, whether in husbanding or the arts. Of particular concern for Republicans, then, was the independence accorded the individual which came through either landholding or honest labor. As Drew McCoy points out, "the abject dependence of the landless or laboring poor rendered them vulnerable to bribery, corruption, and factious dissension, a society with large numbers of these dependents was hardly suited to the Republican form."

Land thus provided the landholder with a great measure of personal independence. The landholder need not rely on other men, or any man, for his basic existence. Such independence, Republicans believed, "permitted a citizen to participate responsibly in the political process, for it allowed him to pursue spontaneously the common or public good, rather than the narrow interest of the men—or the government—on whom he depended for his support." Jefferson firmly believed in this principle. In his *Notes on the State of Virginia*, he said:

> Those who labour in the earth are the chosen people of God, if ever he had a chosen people, whose breasts he has made his peculiar deposit for substantial and genuine virtue.... While we have land to labour then, let us never wish to see our citizens occupied at a workbench, or twirling a distaff.

Farming was thus both a noble and a virtuous endeavor to Jefferson. "An industrious farmer," he said,

> occupies a more dignified place in the scale of beings, whether moral or political, than a lazy lounger, valuing himself on his family too proud to work, and drawing out a miserable existence by eating on that surplus of other men's labor, which is the sacred fund of the helpless poor. A pitiful annuity will only prevent them from exerting that industry and those talents which would soon lead them to a better fortune.

Property and its wise use was necessary, therefore, to the development of a committed and responsible Republican citizenry. Moreover, this citizenry, through its productivity, would "promote industry, population and frugality, and even morality." In short, in landowners Republicans saw "the most valuable citizens [for] they are the most vigorous, the most independant [sic], the most virtuous and they are tied to their country and wedded to its liberty and interest by the most lasting bands."

In like manner those without landed property, who nonetheless engaged in productive labor, were also believed to exhibit individualism and the virtues of Republican society. Jefferson commented that

> ... carpenters, masons, [and] smiths, are wanting in husbandry: but, for the general operation of manufacture, let our workshops remain in Europe. . . . The loss by the transportation of commodities across the Atlantic will be made up in happiness and permanence of government. The mobs of great cities add just so much to the support of pure government, as sores do to the strength of the human body.

Jefferson extolled not only farmers, then, but also artisans who labored in support of farmers. Such a reciprocal economy, Jefferson believed, "was especially conducive to Republican virtue and the diffusion of power among the people." That is, Jefferson never lost his faith in the people or in their propensity to do good. He believed, however, that when congregated into large cities, the people became susceptible to manipulation by those of the higher classes. In fact, Jefferson often wrote of the superiority of rural life over urban life. Writing to a pregnant Maria Cosway in Europe in 1790, Jefferson said, "You may make children there, but this is the country to transplant them to. . . . There is no comparison between the sum of happiness enjoyed here and

there. All the distractions of your great Cities are but feathers in the scale against the domestic enjoiments [sic] and rural occupations, and neighborly societies we live amidst here." Jefferson always urged that the people remain rural in character as it was in this state that "the manners and spirit of a people... preserve a republic in vigor. A degeneracy in these is a canker which soon eats to the heart of its laws and constitutions."

AGRARIANISM AND POLITICAL ECONOMY

Accepting that individualism was at the heart of Republicanism, why was agrarianism also emphasized by the Republicans? A partial explanation is suggested immediately above. However, to fully understand Jefferson's and the Republicans' emphasis on agrarianism, it is important to understand their political economy.

With the economic and social dislocations of the 1780s, it appeared to Jefferson and others that "old age" was advancing on the United States far more rapidly than they had ever imagined. The increasing desire on the part of many Americans for "finer" manufactures and the need to employ the increasing labor surplus weighed heavily on Republican minds as more and more the United States began to exhibit the degenerative decay of England. Some Americans came to suspect "that the Revolutionary vision of a Republican society in which there would be no 'labouring poor'—where everyone would be independent and economically secure—was a chimera." One writer even suggested that it was the "inevitable lot" of some in society to be poor and "experience a certain degree of dependence and servility."

This view, of course, did great violence to the Republican vision of industrious citizens. Moreover the suggestion that large-scale manufactures might alleviate unemployment and excess poverty was equally antithetical. Indeed, true Republicans, like Jefferson, had long held that household manufactures—those items produced by artisans and craftsmen in their homes or small shops—were sufficient for the country. Writing late in his life, Jefferson said:

Every family in the country is a manufactory within itself, and is very generally able to make within itself all the stouter and middling stuffs for its own clothing and household use. . . . The economy and thriftiness resulting from our household manufactures are such that they will never be laid aside; and nothing more salutary for us has ever happened than the British obstructions to our demands for their manufactures. Restore free intercourse when they will, their commerce with us will have totally changed its form, and their articles we shall in the future want from them will not exceed their own consumption of our produce.

Thus, Jefferson and the Republicans were confident that the United States could survive on its cottage industries and its agricultural production. The latter, of course, was particularly necessary "for a healthy society of active, enterprising, hence virtuous, Republican farmers."

To promote agrarianism, however, it was necessary to secure markets for agricultural goods. Failure to do so produced unfavorable consequences, for as the Scottish political economist Sir James Steuart warned, "agricultural surpluses that outran the capacity of available markets to absorb them created a dangerous situation; 'for if the whole be not consumed, the regorging plenty will discourage the industry of the farmer.'"

Jefferson became keenly aware, then, that to secure his vision of virtuous citizens in an agrarian nation it was necessary to not only have an adequate supply of land but adequate markets as well. As Drew McCoy points out in this regard:

If agrarian republicans were viable only so long as there was adequate markets to absorb the fruits of their republican industry, it appeared that the rest of the world had to cooperate in creating the conditions that might permit America to remain a simple republic of virtuous farmers. The full employment and moral integrity of the mass of Americans thus depended on what was happening abroad. No foreign markets, no industrious republicans; it was that simple.

Despite what might be its shortcomings, Jefferson's belief in agrarianism was strengthened, curiously enough, by the writings of Thomas Malthus. Malthus, who popularized the theory of population pressure on subsistence, indicated that all societies were destined to develop toward a state of overpopulation, corruption, and old age. Malthus intimated that old age might be postponed through an abundance of land available to a society, but it would not forestall the inevitable—societal decay. "Perpetual youth," Malthus concluded, was impossible for any nation, even a nation with "a vast reservoir of fertile land." For one to expect the United States to remain a land of relatively little poverty and misery, Malthus declared, was as reasonable as expecting "to prevent a wife or mistress from growing old by never exposing her to sun and air." "It is, undoubtedly, a most disheartening reflection," Malthus concluded, "that the great obstacle in the way to any extraordinary improvement in society, is of a nature that we can never hope to overcome."

Jefferson read Malthus with great interest. Though he found Malthus' theories "very interesting" and of "sound logic," Jefferson nevertheless disagreed with Malthus that population pressure would be an immediate problem in America. The possibility of emigration to virgin territory, Jefferson reasoned, was always available and would forestall Malthus' predictions for many years. The United States, Jefferson argued, was a notable exception to Malthus' theories for "here," he said,

> the immense extent of uncultivated and fertile lands enables every one, who will labor, to marry young, and to raise a family of any size. Our food, then, may increase geometrically with our laborers, and our births, however multiplied, become effective. Again, there the best distribution of labor is supposed to be that which places the manufacturing hands along side the agricultural; so that the one part shall feed both, and the other part furnish both with clothes and other comforts. Would that be best here? Egoism and first appearances say yes. Or would it be better that all our laborers should be employed in agriculture? . . . In solving this question . . . we should allow its just weight to the moral and physical preference of the agricultural, over the manufacturing man.

Once again, Jefferson saw the United States as an agricultural paradise where industrious, virtuous landowners and laborers could secure for themselves and their posterity the blessings of "life, liberty, and the pursuit of happiness." Jefferson was not averse, however, to padding the agricultural advantage he perceived in the United States. Indeed, he continued to hold that a predominantly agricultural society was the best support for Republicanism. This conviction was to have important implications during Jefferson's presidency, particularly in the case of the Louisiana Purchase which will now be considered.

THE LOUISIANA PURCHASE

. . .The task at hand is to apply [Jefferson's political] ideology to the most momentous event of Jefferson's two terms as President—his purchase of the Louisiana territory from France in 1803. In undertaking this task, we are less interested in how the Louisiana territory was secured from France than in the charges brought against Jefferson, by friends and enemies alike, that this act represented betrayal of his most visible political convictions; i.e., states' rights and strict constructionism. Interestingly enough, Jefferson had serious reservations about his authority to purchase Louisiana but became curiously silent on his action before laying the treaty before Congress. The question of greatest importance, then, is whether or not Jefferson "sold out" his political ideals. Through this examination we hope to demonstrate that he did not.

INITIAL REACTIONS
TO THE TREATY

News of the treaty to secure the Louisiana territory reached Washington on the eve of the fourth of July, 1803. Many citizens were overjoyed with the treaty, hailing it as the greatest American achievement since the Declaration of Independence. Others, most notably Federalist opponents of Jefferson, criticized the treaty as a monumental blunder. Fifteen million dollars, they bellowed, was a lot to pay for a "howling wilderness." George Cabot, in fact, saw the cession of Louisiana as chiefly advantageous to France. "It is," he said, "like selling us a ship after she is surrounded by a British fleet." Cabot's reasoning in the case of Louisiana was that France would have been unable to exploit the territory because of its proximity to American and British interests.

In an appeal to the average citizen's pocketbook, the Federalists attempted to display graphically what Louisiana meant to the population as a whole: a stack of dollar bills one upon another that would produce a pile three miles high; twenty dollars from every taxpayer in the United States; benefits only to southern planters and western frontiersmen. All of these arguments, and others, were offered by the Federalists in opposition to the treaty.

Yet the Federalists also saw political opportunity in Jefferson's actions. His treaty with France, they reasoned, was the first step in the dismemberment of the Union; for the purchase of Louisiana irrevocably altered the relationship between the national government and the states. Moreover, it went against Jefferson's own well-stated positions of states' rights and strict constitutional construction. Thus, in Louisiana the Federalists saw an opportunity to discredit Jefferson and recapture power from the Republicans. Indeed, Louisiana was just the fodder the Federalists needed to show Americans once and for all the rashness and pomposity of Thomas Jefferson. Interestingly enough, Jefferson recognized in the Louisiana Purchase the possibility of losing power to the Federalists, yet he proceeded with the treaty. Obviously, political tenure was not his only motivation in this case. . . .

IMPLICATIONS OF THE LOUISIANA PURCHASE

The Louisiana Purchase . . . could be considered as both the zenith and the nadir of Jefferson's presidency; for on the one hand it doubled the size of the United States and ensured that the country would have ample land for expansion for many years to come. But on the other hand, the Purchase brought into question fundamental Jeffersonian doctrines and exposed Jefferson to criticism that has lasted to this day. Indeed, Merrill Peterson sees the Louisiana Purchase as "a revolution in the American Union [which] became, a revolution in the Constitution. A momentous act of Jeffersonian statesmanship unhinged the Jeffersonian dogmas and opened, so far as precedent might control, the boundless field of power so much feared. Critics then and since found the President inconsistent."

What did the Louisiana Purchase do to the doctrines of states' rights and strict constructionism? Many, of course, claim that it enlarged the powers of the national government vis-à-vis the states and made, as Jefferson feared, a "blank paper of the Constitution." The former assertion is almost certainly true; the latter an exaggeration. It is interesting to note, however, that among the supporters of the Louisiana Purchase were some of the most avid proponents of states' rights and strict constructionism, aside from Jefferson:

> In the Senate sat John Breckinridge of Kentucky, supposed to be the author of the Kentucky Resolutions, and known as their champion in the Kentucky legislature. From Virginia came John Taylor of Caroline, the reputed father of the Virginia Resolutions, and the soundest of strict constructionists. Twenty years

later, his "Construction Construed" and "New Views on the Constitution" became the text books of the States-rights school. His colleague was Wilson Cary Nicholas, who had also taken a prominent part in supporting the Virginia Resolutions, and whose devotion to the principles of strict construction was beyond doubt. One of the South Carolina senators was Pierce Butler; one of those from North Carolina was David Stone; Georgia was represented by Abraham Baldwin and James Jackson,—staunch States-rights Republicans all.

Thus, those who had been long-time supporters of states' rights and strict constructionism sided with Jefferson on the Louisiana Purchase. The question to be asked, however, is what impact these defections had on these doctrines. States' rights, of course, would be an important issue for another sixty years, settled only by the death of 600,000 Americans during the Civil War. Strict constructionism, on the other hand, did suffer a blow with Jefferson's actions. Who is to say, however, that Jefferson did more than accelerate the inevitable growth of national government and the presidency given the inevitable growth of the country? That is, as the country became larger and more diverse, there was an almost instinctive need for stronger central control which Jefferson, through his actions, ensured, knowingly or not.

One could argue, then, that in the case of Louisiana Jefferson brought to the fore those issues that would eventually have to be reckoned with in the country's future—i.e., state vs. national power and strict vs. loose construction of the Constitution. Though the issue of state power in the U.S. federal system has been largely settled, constitutional interpretation remains an issue with no apparent resolution. Such is the inevitable consequence of being so far removed from the intent of the framers. Thus, we can only hope today that those who interpret the Constitution will do so in the same spirit as Thomas Jefferson, having always, as their ultimate end, the best interests of the United States.

CONCLUSION

Thomas Jefferson is often hailed as one of the greatest presidents of the United States. This judgment stems from many factors, not the least of which was Jefferson's commitment to his political ideals. The question posed at the outset of this [selection], however, was whether or not Jefferson "sold out" his political ideals—i.e., republicanism, states' rights and strict constructionism—in the case of the Louisiana Purchase. The majority of conventional commentary seems to think so. Indeed, there has been great criticism heaped on Jefferson for his supposed betrayal of doctrines that defined his political life. But Jefferson was a complex man. How can we know what Jefferson's real intentions were, then? Dumas Malone at least gives us a hint when he intimates that Jefferson believed the Louisiana territory to be "essential to national security." In effect, in making the choice he did, Jefferson "relented on the 'means' he would rather have employed because his political allies insisted that his preferred means might jeopardize the end sought and thereby give an advantage to his political enemies."

And what was the end which Jefferson sought? Undoubtedly, it was securing the "national security" in the broad sense of promoting an "Empire of Liberty" wherein would reside virtuous agrarian citizens who would secure for themselves and their posterity Jefferson's ideals of "life, liberty, and the pursuit of happiness" into the distant future. "The nation's best interests," Jefferson held, "demanded the extension of the empire for liberty. The world will here see such an extent of country under a free and moderate government as it has never yet seen."

For Jefferson, the Louisiana Purchase secured the virtues of Republicanism in an "Empire of Liberty." As pointed out in a popular pamphlet which celebrated it:

> The Purchase enhanced American security and lessened the danger of a corrupting war; it bolstered the influence of the agricultural class, always the best repository of republican virtue; and it laid the basis for a flourishing commerce in the West that would cultivate an active, industrious, and republican people.

The Louisiana Purchase also addressed other fundamental threats that deeply concerned the Republicans—societal decay and the problems associated with agricultural surpluses. "We see in Louisiana," a prominent Republican said, "an assurance of long life to our cause. The Atlantic States, as they advance to that condition of society, where wealth and luxury tend to vice and aristocracies, will yield to that country accessions of enterprizing [sic] men. The spirit of faction, which tends to concentrate, will be destroyed by this diffusion." Jefferson echoed this optimism: "by enlarging the empire of liberty, we multiply its auxiliaries, and provide new sources of renovation, should its principles, at any time, degenerate, in those

portions of our country which gave them birth."

Louisiana filled Jefferson's political economy bill as well. By securing for industrious farmers vast amounts of land and the transportation network offered by control of the Mississippi and Missouri Rivers, the Louisiana territory assured a market for the surplus produce of American farmers. Had this market not been available, the *Kentucky Gazette* intoned, American farmers would have "degenerated into savages, because they had no incentive to industry." Thus, "by providing the incentive to industry that shaped a republican people, it [the Louisiana Purchase] laid the necessary basis for the westward expansion of republican civilization itself."

Did Jefferson "sell out" in the case of Louisiana? Perhaps by the letter of states' rights and strict constructionism he did, but certainly not if one considers the spirit of those doctrines. After all, what was the ultimate end of government? For Jefferson it was securing the Republican ideal. All other doctrines were simply auxiliaries. While states' rights and strict constructionism were, in and of themselves, important, they were ancillary to the greater good of Republicanism. When it became necessary to secure the greater good, states' rights and strict constructionism were sacrificed, not because they were not important—they, too, promoted Republicanism—but because they were a means to an end, that end being Jefferson's "Empire of Liberty."

Jefferson is thus justly criticized by the apparent abandonment of his states' rights and strict constructionist views in the case of the Louisiana Purchase. However, this criticism has been extreme to the point of suggesting that Jefferson sold out his ideals. To the contrary, we assert that Jefferson was entirely consistent given his grand design for the American Republic. His was a vision of a land of liberty which was far beyond his time, one may even say utopian. Yet few in Jefferson's time, and even fewer today, understood the ramifications of Jefferson's actions. All that is seen are the seeming inconsistencies, which in any politician are rarely tolerated. Thus, Jefferson was left to say sadly, "Every day proves to me more and more, that this American world was not made for me."

POSTSCRIPT

Did Thomas Jefferson Abandon His Political Ideals in Purchasing the Louisiana Territory?

The peaceful inauguration of Thomas Jefferson on March 4, 1801 marked the first time under the new Constitution that executive power had been transferred from one party to another. In light of the hostility that had been articulated in the presidential campaign by Federalists and Democratic-Republicans alike, many people viewed this as nothing short of miraculous. But here was "Mad Tom" Jefferson, the "Jacobin" and "atheist," declaring in his inaugural address, "We are all Republicans, we are all Federalists." What had happened to the much-anticipated "Revolution of 1800" once Jefferson entered the White House?

The purchase of the Louisiana Territory was not the only evidence that Jefferson believed his inaugural rhetoric and was determined to "outfederal-ize" the Federalists. For example, although he criticized the elitist tendencies of the Federalists, Jefferson filled key posts in his administration with the "rich, well-born, and able" from the Democratic-Republican ranks. Also, Jefferson did not tamper with the economic policies put in place by his political nemesis, Alexander Hamilton.

However, Jefferson lost no time as president in expunging some of the Federalist party's pet measures from previous administrations, including the Alien and Sedition Acts and the Judiciary Act of 1801. He supported the impeachment of Supreme Court Associate Justice Samuel Chase, who had used the bench as a political stump. In addition, the Jeffersonian "revolution" witnessed significant changes in the government's fiscal policies as Jefferson sought a balanced federal budget by cutting costs in the executive branch, especially with regard to military expenditures.

Two older works are good starting points for a study of Jefferson: Henry Adams's classic *History of the United States During the Administrations of Thomas Jefferson and James Madison* (nine volumes, 1889–1891) and Richard Hofstadter's cogent essay, "Thomas Jefferson: The Aristocrat as Democrat," from his *The American Political Tradition and the Men Who Made It* (1948; reprint, Alfred A. Knopf, 1973). The definitive biographical study is Dumas Malone's sympathetic though magisterial *Jefferson and His Time*, 6 vols. (Little, Brown & Company, 1948–1981). Malone discusses Jefferson's handling of the Louisiana Territory in *Volume 4: Jefferson the President: First Term, 1801–1805* (Little, Brown & Company, 1970).

ISSUE 8

Was Andrew Jackson's Indian Removal Policy Motivated by Humanitarian Impulses?

YES: Robert V. Remini, from *Andrew Jackson and the Course of American Freedom, 1822–1832, vol. 2* (Harper & Row, 1981)

NO: Anthony F. C. Wallace, from *The Long, Bitter Trail: Andrew Jackson and the Indians* (Hill and Wang, 1993)

ISSUE SUMMARY

YES: Professor Robert V. Remini argues that Andrew Jackson did not seek to destroy Native American life and culture. He portrays Jackson as a national leader who sincerely believed that the Indian Removal Act of 1830 was the only way to protect Native Americans from annihilation at the hands of white settlers.

NO: Historian and anthropologist Anthony F. C. Wallace counters that Andrew Jackson oversaw a harsh policy with regard to Native Americans. This policy resulted in the usurpation of land, attempts to destroy tribal culture, and the forcible removal of Native Americans from the southeastern United States to a designated territory west of the Mississippi River.

Andrew Jackson's election to the presidency in 1828 ushered in an era marked by a growing demand for political and economic opportunities for the "common man." As the "people's president," Jackson embodied the democratic ideal in the United States. In his role as chief executive, Jackson symbolized a strong philosophical attachment to the elimination of impediments to voting (at least for adult white males), the creation of opportunities for the common man to participate directly in government through officeholding, and the destruction of vestiges of economic elitism that served only the rich, well-born, and able. In addition, Jackson was a nationalist who defended states' rights as long as those rights did not threaten the sanctity of the Union.

The rise of Jacksonian democracy occurred during a dramatic territorial growth increase in the years immediately following the War of 1812. A new state joined the Union each year between 1816 and 1821. As the populations of these states increased, white citizens demanded that their governments, at both the state and national levels, do something about the Native American tribes in their midst who held claims to land in these regions by virtue of previous treaties. (Andrew Jackson had negotiated several of these treaties. Some included provisions for the members of the southern tribes to remain on their lands in preparation for obtaining citizenship.) Most white settlers preferred the removal of Native Americans to western territories where, presumably, they could live unencumbered forever. The result was the "Trail of Tears," the brutal forced migration of Native Americans in the 1830s that resulted in the loss of thousands of lives.

According to historian Wilcomb Washburn, "No individual is more closely identified with . . . the policy of removal of the Indians east of the Mississippi to lands west of the river—than President Andrew Jackson." While most historians are in agreement with the details of Jackson's Indian removal policy, there is significant debate with respect to his motivation. Did Jackson's racist antipathy to the Indians pave the way for the "Trail of Tears"? Or did he support this policy out of a humanitarian desire to protect Native Americans from the impending wrath of white settlers and their state governments who refused to negotiate with the southern tribes as sovereign nations?

Robert Remini, Jackson's foremost biographer, states that the criticism of Jackson's Indian Removal Act is unfair. Jackson firmly believed that removal was the only policy that would prevent the decimation of Native Americans. Remini concludes that Jackson attempted to deal as fairly as possible with the representatives of the Choctaws, Cherokees, Chickasaws, Creeks, and Seminoles, known then as the "Five Civilized Tribes."

Anthony F. C. Wallace maintains that Jackson viewed Native Americans as savages and, while not proposing their extermination, he supported a policy of coercion to force their removal from the southeastern states. This approach, according to Wallace, was consistent with several powerful forces in Democratic politics, including the exaltation of the common white man, expansionism, and open acceptance of racism.

YES
Robert V. Remini

"BROTHERS, LISTEN ...
YOU MUST SUBMIT"

It is an awesome contradiction that at the moment the United States was entering a new age of economic and social betterment for its citizens—the industrial revolution underway, democracy expanding, social and political reforms in progress—the Indians were driven from their homes and forced to seek refuge in remote areas west of the Mississippi River. [Andrew] Jackson, the supreme exponent of liberty in terms of preventing government intervention and intrusion, took it upon himself to expel the Indians from their ancient haunts and decree that they must reside outside the company of civilized white men. It was a depressing and terrible commentary on American life and institutions in the 1830s.

The policy of white Americans toward Indians was a shambles, right from the beginning. Sometimes the policy was benign—such as sharing educational advantages—but more often than not it was malevolent. Colonists drove the Indians from their midst, stole their lands and, when necessary, murdered them. To the colonists, Indians were inferior and their culture a throwback to a darker age.

When independence was declared and a new government established committed to liberty and justice for all, the situation of the Indians within the continental limits of the United States contradicted the ennobling ideas of both the Declaration and the Constitution. Nevertheless, the Founding Fathers convinced themselves that men of reason, intelligence and good will could resolve the Indian problem. In their view the Indians were "noble savages," arrested in cultural development, but they would one day take their rightful place beside white society. Once they were "civilized" they would be absorbed.

President George Washington formulated a policy to encourage the "civilizing" process, and Jefferson continued it. They presumed that once the Indians adopted the practice of private property, built homes, farmed, educated their children, and embraced Christianity these Native Americans would win acceptance from white Americans. Both Presidents wished the

Indians to become cultural white men. If they did not, said Jefferson, then they must be driven to the Rocky Mountains.

The policy of removal was first suggested by Jefferson as the alternative to the "civilizing" process, and as far as many Americans were concerned removal made more sense than any other proposal. Henry Clay, for example, insisted that it was impossible to civilize these "savages." They were, he argued, inferior to white men and "their disappearance from the human family would be no great loss to the world."

Despite Clay's racist notions—shared by many Americans—the government's efforts to convert the Indians into cultural white men made considerable progress in the 1820s. The Cherokees, in particular, showed notable technological and material advances as a result of increased contact with traders, government agents, and missionaries, along with the growth of a considerable population of mixed-bloods.

As the Indians continued to resist the efforts to get rid of them—the thought of abandoning the land on which their ancestors lived and died was especially painful for them—the states insisted on exercising jurisdiction over Indian lands within their boundaries. It soon became apparent that unless the federal government instituted a policy of removal it would have to do something about protecting the Indians against the incursions of the states. But the federal government was feckless. It did neither. Men like President John Quincy Adams felt that removal was probably the only policy to follow but he could not bring himself to implement it. Nor could he face down a state like Georgia. So he did nothing. Many men of good will simply turned their faces away. They, too, did nothing.

Not Jackson. He had no hesitation about taking action. And he believed that removal was indeed the only policy available if the Indians were to be protected from certain annihilation. His ideas about the Indians developed from his life on the frontier, his expansionist dreams, his commitment to states' rights, and his intense nationalism. He saw the nation as an indivisible unit whose strength and future were dependent on its ability to repel outside foes. He wanted all Americans from every state and territory to participate in his dream of empire, but they must acknowledge allegiance to a permanent and indissoluble bond under a federal system. Although devoted to states' rights and limited government in Washington, Jackson rejected any notion that jeopardized the safety of the United States. That included nullification and secession. That also included the Indians. . . .

The Indian Removal Act of 1830 authorized Jackson to carry out the policy outlined in his first message to Congress. He could exchange unorganized public land in the trans-Mississippi west for Indian land in the east. Those Indians who moved would be given perpetual title to their new land as well as compensation for improvements on their old. The cost of their removal would be absorbed by the federal government. They would also be given assistance for their "support and subsistence" for the first year after removal. An appropriation of $500,000 was authorized to carry out these provisions.

This monumental piece of legislation spelled the doom of the American Indian. It was harsh, arrogant, racist —and inevitable. It was too late to acknowledge any rights for the Indians. As [Senator Theodore] Frelinghuysen [of New Jersey] remarked, all the white man had ever said to the Indian from the moment they first came into contact was "give!" Once stripped of his possessions the Indian was virtually abandoned.

Of the many significant predictions and warnings voiced during the debates in Congress that eventually came true, two deserve particular attention. One of them made a mockery of Jackson's concern for freedom. The President insisted that the Indians would not be forced to remove. If they wished to reside within the state they might do so but only on condition that they understood they would be subject to state law. He would never force them to remove, never compel them to surrender their lands. That high and noble sentiment as interpreted by land-greedy state officials meant absolutely nothing. Fraud and deception also accompanied the exchange of land. Jackson himself tried desperately to discourage corruption among the government agents chosen to arrange the removal, but the events as they actually transpired ran totally opposite to what he expected and promised.

The other prediction that mocked Jackson's commitment to economy was the cost of the operation. In the completed legislation the Congress had appropriated $500,000 but the actual cost of removal is incalculable. For one thing the process extended over many years and involved many tribes. Naturally some Indians resisted Jackson's will and the government was required to apply force. The resulting bloodshed and killing and the cost of these Indian wars cannot be quantified. For a political party that prized economy above almost everything else the policy of Indian removal was a ra-

dial departure from principle. Still many Democrats argued that the actual cost was a small price to pay for the enormous expanse of land that was added to the American empire. In Jackson's eight years in office seventy-odd treaties were signed and ratified, which added 100 million acres of Indian land to the public domain at a cost of roughly $68 million and 32 million acres of land west of the Mississippi River. The expense was enormous, but so was the land-grab.

Andrew Jackson has been saddled with a considerable portion of the blame for this monstrous deed. He makes an easy mark. But the criticism is unfair if it distorts the role he actually played. His objective was not the destruction of Indian life and culture. Quite the contrary. He believed that removal was the Indian's only salvation against certain extinction. Nor did he despoil Indians. He struggled to prevent fraud and corruption, and he promised there would be no coercion in winning Indian approval of his plan for removal. Yet he himself practiced a subtle kind of coercion. He told the tribes he would abandon them to the mercy of the states if they did not agree to migrate west.

The Indian problem posed a terrible dilemma and Jackson had little to gain by attempting to resolve it. He could have imitated his predecessors and done nothing. But that was not Andrew Jackson. He felt he had a duty. And when removal was accomplished he felt he had done the American people a great service. He felt he had followed the "dictates of humanity" and saved the Indians from certain death.

Not that the President was motivated by concern for the Indians—their language or customs, their culture, or anything else. Andrew Jackson was motivated principally by two considerations: first, his concern for the military safety of the United States, which dictated that Indians must not occupy areas that might jeopardize the defense of this nation; and second, his commitment to the principle that all persons residing within states are subject to the jurisdiction and laws of those states. Under no circumstances did Indian tribes constitute sovereign entities when they occupied territory within existing state boundaries. The quickest way to undermine the security of the Union, he argued, was to jeopardize the sovereignty of the states by recognizing Indian tribes as a third sovereignty.

But there was a clear inconsistency—if not a contradiction—in this argument. If the tribes were not sovereign why bother to sign treaties (requiring Senate approval) for their land? Actually Jackson appreciated the inconsistency, and it bothered him. He never really approved of bargaining or negotiating with tribes. He felt that Congress should simply determine what needed to be done and then instruct the Indians to conform to it. Congress can "occupy and possess" any part of Indian territory, he once said, "whenever the safety, interest or defence of the country" dictated. But as President, Jackson could not simply set aside the practice and tradition of generations because of a presumed contradiction. So he negotiated and signed treaties with dozens of tribes, at the same time denying that they enjoyed sovereign rights.

The reaction of the American people to Jackson's removal policy was predictable. Some were outraged, particularly the Quakers and other religious groups. Many seemed uncomfortable about it but agreed that it had to be done. Probably a larger number of Americans favored removal and applauded the President's action in settling the Indian problem once and for all. In short, there was no public outcry against it. In fact it was hardly noticed. The horror of removal with its "Trail of Tears" came much later and after Jackson had left office.

Apart from everything else, the Indian Removal Act served an important political purpose. For one thing it forced Jackson to exercise leadership as the head of the Democratic party within Congress. It prepared him for even bigger battles later on. For another it gave "greater ideological and structural coherence" to the party. It separated loyal and obedient friends of the administration from all others. It became a "distinguishing feature" of Jacksonian Democrats....

According to the Treaty of Dancing Rabbit Creek, the Choctaws agreed to evacuate all their land in Mississippi and emigrate to an area west of the Arkansas Territory to what is now Oklahoma. In addition the Indians would receive money, household and farm equipment, subsistence for one year, and reimbursement for improvements on their vacated property. In effect the Choctaws ceded to the United States 10.5 million acres of land east of the Mississippi River. They promised to emigrate in stages: the first group in the fall of 1831, the second in 1832, and the last in 1833.

Jackson immediately submitted the treaty to Congress when it reconvened in December, 1830, and [Secretary of War John] Eaton, in his annual report, assured the members that agreement was reached through persuasion only. No secret agreements, no bribes, no promises. Everything had been open and aboveboard! The Senate swallowed the lie whole and ratified the treaty on February 25, 1831, by a vote of 35 to 12.

Said one Choctaw chief: "Our doom is sealed."

Since the Treaty of Dancing Rabbit Creek was the first to win Senate approval the President was very anxious to make it a model of removal. He wanted everything to go smoothly so that the American people would understand that removal was humane and beneficial to both the Indians and the American nation at large. Furthermore, he hoped its success would encourage other tribes to capitulate to his policy and thereby send a veritable human tide streaming across the Mississippi into the plains beyond.

The actual removal of the Choctaw Nation violated every principle for which Jackson stood. From start to finish the operation was a fraud. Corruption, theft, mismanagement, inefficiency—all contributed to the destruction of a once-great people. The Choctaws asked to be guided to their new country by General George Gibson, a man they trusted and with whom they had scouted their new home. Even this was denied them. The bureaucracy dictated another choice. So they left the "land of their fathers" filled with fear and anxiety. To make matters worse the winter of 1831–1832 was "living hell." The elements conspired to add to their misery. The suffering was stupefying. Those who watched the horror never forgot it. Many wept. The Indians themselves showed not a single sign of their agony.

Jackson tried to prevent this calamity but he was too far away to exercise any real control, and the temptations and opportunities for graft and corruption were too great for some agents to resist. When he learned of the Choctaw experience and the suffering involved, Jackson was deeply offended. He did what he could to prevent its recurrence.

He proposed a new set of guidelines for future removals. He hoped they would reform the system and erase mismanagement and the opportunity for theft.

To begin with, the entire operation of Indian removal was transferred from civilian hands to the military. Then the office of commissioner of Indian affairs was established under the war department to coordinate and direct all matters pertaining to the Indians. In large part these changes reflected Jackson's anguish over what had happened to the Choctaws, but they also resulted from his concern over public opinion. Popular outrage could kill the whole program of removal....

The experience of removal is one of the horror stories of the modern era. Beginning with the Choctaws it decimated whole tribes. An entire race of people suffered. What it did to their lives, their culture, their language, their customs is a tragedy of truly staggering proportions. The irony is that removal was intended to prevent this calamity.

Would it have been worse had the Indians remained in the East? Jackson thought so. He said they would "disappear and be forgotten." One thing does seem certain: the Indians would have been forced to yield to state laws and white society. Indian Nations *per se* would have been obliterated and possibly Indian civilization with them.

In October, 1832, a year and a half after the Choctaw treaty was ratified, General [John] Coffee signed a treaty with the Chickasaws that met Jackson's complete approval. "Surely the religious enthusiasts," wrote the President in conveying his delight to Coffee, "or those who have been weeping over the oppression of the Indians will not find fault with it for want of liberality or justice to the Indians." By this time Jackson had grown callous. His promise to economize got the better of him. "The stipulation that they remove at their own expence and on their own means, is an excellent feature in it. The whole treaty is just. We want them in a state of safety removed from the states and free from colision with the whites; and if the land does this it is well disposed of and freed from being a corrupting source to our Legislature."

Coffee's success with the Chickasaws followed those with the Creeks and Seminoles. On March 24, 1832, the destruction of the Creek Nation begun with the Treaty of Fort Jackson in 1814 was completed when the chiefs signed an agreement to remove rather than fight it out in the courts. The Seminoles accepted a provisional treaty on May 9, 1832, pending approval of the site for relocation. Thus, by the close of Jackson's first administration the Choctaws, Creeks, Chickasaws, and Seminoles had capitulated. Of the so-called Five Civilized Tribes only the Cherokees held out.

Not for long. They found small consolation from the courts. The Cherokees' lawyer, William Wirt, sued in the Supreme Court for an injunction that would permit the Indians to remain in Georgia unmolested by state law. He argued that the Cherokees had a right to self-government as a foreign nation and that this right had long been recognized by the United States in its treaties with the Indians. He hoped to make it appear that Jackson himself was the nullifier of federal law. In effect he challenged the entire removal policy by asking for a restraining order against Georgia.

Chief Justice John Marshall in the case *Cherokee Nation* v. *Georgia* handed down his opinion on March 18, 1831. He rejected Wirt's contention that the Cherokees were a sovereign nation. He also rejected Jackson's insistence that they were subject to state law. The Indians, he said, were "domestic dependent nations," subject to the United States as a ward to a guardian. They were not subject to individual states, he declared. Indian territory was in fact part of the United States.

The Indians chose to regard the opinion as essentially favorable in that it commanded the United States to protect their rights and property. So they refused to submit—either to Georgia or to Jackson. Meanwhile, Georgia passed legislation in late December, 1830, prohibiting white men from entering Indian country after March 1, 1831, without a license from the state. This was clearly aimed at troublesome missionaries who encouraged Indians in their "disobedience." Samuel A. Worcester and Dr. Elizur Butler, two missionaries, defied the law; they were arrested and sentenced to four years imprisonment in a state penitentiary. They sued, and in the case *Worcester* v. *Georgia* the Supreme Court decided on March 3, 1832, that the Georgia law was unconstitutional. Speaking for the majority in a feeble voice, John Marshall croaked out the court's decision. All the laws of Georgia dealing with the Cherokees were unconstitutional, he declared. He issued a formal mandate two days later ordering the Georgia Superior Court to reverse its decision.

Georgia, of course, had refused to acknowledge the court's right to direct its actions and had boycotted the judicial proceedings. The state had no intention of obeying the court's order. Since the court adjourned almost immediately after rendering its decision nothing further could be done. According to the Judiciary Act of 1789 the Supreme Court could issue its order of compliance only when a case had already been remanded without response. Since the court would not reconvene until January, 1833, no further action by the government could take place. Thus, until the court either summoned state officials before it for contempt or issued a writ of habeas corpus for the release of the two missionaries there was nothing further to be done. The President was under no obligation to act. In fact there is some question as to whether the court itself could act since the existing habeas corpus law did not apply in this case because the missionaries were not being detained by federal authorities. And since the Superior Court of Georgia did not acknowledge in writing its refusal to obey, Marshall's decision could not be enforced. Jackson understood this. He knew there was nothing for him to do. "The decision of the supreme court has fell still born," he wrote John Coffee, "and they find that it cannot coerce Georgia to yield to its mandate."

It was later reported by Horace Greeley that Jackson's response to the Marshall decision was total defiance. "Well: John Marshall has made his decision: *now let him enforce it!*" Greeley cited George N. Briggs, a Representative from Massachusetts, as his source for the statement. The quotation certainly sounds like Jackson and many historians have chosen to believe that he said it. The fact is that Jackson did not say it because there was no reason to do so. There was nothing for him to enforce. Why, then, would he refuse an action that no one asked him to take? As he said, the decision was stillborn. The court rendered an opinion which abandoned the Indians to their inevitable fate. "It cannot coerce Georgia to yield to its mandate," said Jackson, "and I believe [Major John] Ridge has expressed despair, and that it is better for them [the Cherokees] to treat and move."

Even if Jackson did not use the exact words Greeley put into his mouth, even if no direct action was required at the moment, some historians have argued that the quotation represents in fact Jackson's true attitude. There is evidence that Jackson "sportively said in private conversation" that if summoned "to support the decree of the Court he will call on those who have brought about the decision to enforce it." Actually nobody expected Jackson to enforce the decision, including the two missionaries, and therefore a lot of people simply assumed that the President would defy the court if pressured. In the rush to show Jackson as bombastic and blustery, however, an important point is missed. What should be remembered is that Jackson reacted with extreme caution to this crisis because a precipitous act could have triggered a confrontation with Georgia. Prudence, not defiance, characterized his reaction to both the challenge of Georgia and later the threat of nullification by South Carolina. As one historian has said, Jackson deserves praise for his caution in dealing with potentially explosive issues and should not be condemned for his so-called inaction.

Still the President had encouraged Georgia in its intransigence. He shares responsibility in producing this near-confrontation. He was so desperate to achieve Indian removal that he almost produced a crisis between federal and state authorities. Nor can it be denied, as one North Carolina Congressman observed, that "Gen Jackson could by a nod of the head or a crook of the finger induce Georgia to submit to the law. It is by the promise or belief of his countenance and support that Georgia is stimulated to her disorderly and rebellious conduct."

Jackson chose not to nod his head or crook his finger for several reasons, the most important of which was his determination to remove the Cherokees. But he had other concerns. As the time neared for the Supreme Court to reconvene and deliberate on Georgia's defiance, a controversy with South Carolina over nullification developed. Jackson had to be extremely careful that no action of his induced Georgia to join South Carolina in the dispute. Nullification might lead to secession and civil war. He therefore maneuvered to isolate South Carolina and force Georgia to back away from its position of confrontation. He needed to nudge Georgia into obeying the court order and free the two missionaries. Consequently he moved swiftly to win removal of the Indians. His secretary of war worked quietly to convince the legal counsel for the missionaries and the friends of the Cherokees in Congress, such as Theodore Frelinghuysen, that the President would not budge from his position nor interfere in the operation of Georgia laws and that the best solution for everyone was for the Indians to remove. Meanwhile the Creeks capitulated, and a treaty of removal was ratified by the Senate in April, 1832.

Although Senator Frelinghuysen "prayed to God" that Georgia would peacefully acquiesce in the decision of the Supreme Court he soon concluded that the Cherokees must yield. Even Justice John McLean, who wrote a concurring opinion in the *Worcester* case, counseled the Cherokee delegation in Washington to sign a removal treaty. Van Buren's Albany Regency actively intervened because of their concern over a possible southern backlash against their leader. Van Buren himself encouraged his friend Senator John Forsyth to intercede with the newly elected governor of Georgia, Wilson Lumpkin, keeping Jackson carefully informed of his actions. More significant, however, were the letters written by the secretary of war to Lumpkin. These letters pleaded for a pardon for the two missionaries and stated that the President himself gave his unconditional endorsement of the request. Finally Forsyth conferred with William Wirt who in turn conferred with a representative of the two missionaries, and they all agreed to make no further motion before the Supreme Court. That done, Governor Lumpkin ordered the "keeper" of the penitentiary on January 14, 1833 to release Worcester and Butler under an arrangement devised by Forsyth. Thus, while the President held steady to his course and directed the activities of the men in contact with Lumpkin, both the problem of Georgia's defiance and the fate of the two missionaries were quietly resolved without injurious consequences to the rest of the nation. It was one of Jackson's finest actions as a statesman.

Ultimately, the Cherokees also yielded to the President. On December 29, 1835, at New Echota a treaty was signed arranging an exchange of land. A protracted legal argument had gained the Indians a little time but nothing else. Removal now applied to all eastern Indians, not simply the southern tribes. After the Black Hawk War of 1832 Jackson responded to the demands of Americans in the northwest to send all Indians beyond the Mississippi. A hungry band of

Sac and Fox Indians under the leadership of Black Hawk had recrossed the Mississippi in the spring of 1832 to find food. People on the frontier panicked and Governor John Reynolds of Illinois called out the militia and appealed to Jackson for assistance. Federal troops were immediately dispatched under Generals Winfield Scott and Henry Atkinson. A short and bloody war resulted, largely instigated by drunken militia troops, and when it ended the northwestern tribes were so demoralized that they offered little resistance to Jackson's steady pressure for their removal west of the Mississippi. The result of the Black Hawk War, said the President in his fourth message to Congress, had been very "creditable to the troops" engaged in the action. "Severe as is the lesson to the Indians," he lectured, "it was rendered necessary by their unprovoked aggressions, and it is to be hoped that its impression will be permanent and salutary."

It was useless for the Indians to resist Jackson's demands. Nearly 46,000 of them went west. Thousands died in transit. Even those under no treaty obligation to emigrate were eventually forced to remove. And the removal experiences were all pretty much like that of the Choctaws—all horrible, all rife with corruption and fraud, all disgraceful to the American nation.

The policy of removal formed an important part of Jackson's overall program of limiting federal authority and supporting states' rights. Despite the accusation of increased executive authority, Jackson successfully buttressed state sovereignty and jurisdiction over all inhabitants within state boundaries. This is a government of the people, Jackson argued, and the President is the agent of the people. The President and the Congress exercise their jurisdiction over "the people of the union. [W]ho are the people of the union?" he asked. Then, answering his own question, he said: "all those subject to the jurisdiction of the sovereign states, none else." Indians are also subject to the states, he went on. They are subject "to the sovereign power of the state within whose sovereign limits they reside." An "absolute independence of the Indian tribes from state authority can never bear an intelligent investigation, and a quasi independence of state authority when located within its Territorial limits is *absurd.*"

In addition to establishing the removal policy Jackson also restructured the bureaucracy handling Indian problems. Since 1824 a Bureau of Indian Affairs headed by Thomas L. McKenney had supervised the government's relations with the Indians. By the time Jackson assumed the presidency the Bureau had become an "enormous quagmire" from an administrative point of view. McKenney was retained in office to take advantage of his reputation to win passage of the Removal bill. Once Removal passed, McKenney was dismissed. (For one thing he had supported Adams in 1828). Then the Bureau was reorganized. On June 30, 1834, Congress passed the necessary legislation establishing the Office of Indian Affairs under an Indian commissioner, and this administrative machinery remained in place well into the twentieth century. The Indian service was restructured into a more cohesive operation than had previously been the case. It regularized procedures that had been practiced as a matter of custom rather than law.

Ultimately Jackson's policy of removal and reorganization of the Indian service won acceptance by most Americans. The

President was seen as a forceful executive who addressed one of the nation's most bedeviling problems and solved it. Even Americans who fretted over the fate of the Indians eventually went along with removal. The policy seemed enlightened and humane. It seemed rational and logical. It constituted, Americans thought, the only possible solution to the Indian problem.

NO

Anthony F. C. Wallace

THE LONG, BITTER TRAIL: ANDREW JACKSON AND THE INDIANS

Georgia in the late 1820s was a prosperous and rapidly developing common-wealth. The state government encouraged the growth of an extensive system of private banks that lent money to aspiring farmers and entrepreneurs. Family farms were the norm; there were few cotton plantations larger than 500 acres. Railroads and shallow-draft steamboats were opening up the agricultural interior and connecting the cotton country with seaports at Savannah and Brunswick, through which passed the trade not only with Great Britain but also with the industrial Northern states. Georgia was less inclined than her neighbor South Carolina to espouse the doctrine of nullification, so hateful to President Jackson, propounded by that state's legislature and advocated by her native son Vice President John C. Calhoun. Increasingly, too, the Georgia electorate was turning away from the faction headed by Jackson's old political rival, William H. Crawford, and was favoring the party more friendly to the President. Jackson had motives for rewarding Georgia that went beyond his commitment to Indian removal.

Thus Georgians felt that they had the right to claim the President's sympathetic attention in time of need. And now was that time. The Cherokee constitution in effect nullified Georgia law and made the Indian nation a "state within a state." Left to themselves, the Cherokees would become a prosperous, independent commonwealth, and they would never sell their land (indeed, by Cherokee law, the further sale of land to the United States was a crime). On December 20, 1828, immediately after the election of Andrew Jackson as President of the United States, the Georgia legislature passed a law extending the state's jurisdiction—i.e., its laws, its police powers, and its courts—over the Cherokees living within the state. Enforcement was to be deferred until June 1, 1830, to give the President and Congress time to act in support of Georgia.

* * *

Georgia's action forced the President's hand. He must see to it that a removal policy long covertly pursued by the White House would now be enacted into law by the Congress. The new President quickly took steps to implement a removal program that would, among other things, resolve the Georgia crisis. As his Secretary of War he appointed his old friend and political supporter from Tennessee, Senator John Eaton. No doubt with the advice of Superintendent McKenney, who had convinced himself of the need for removal, Eaton included in his first (1829) Report to the President a recommendation for wholesale removal of the Eastern Indians to a self-governing "Indian territory" in the West, where the U.S. Army would protect them from intruding whites and keep the peace among the tribes.

The Twenty-first Congress convened for its first session in December 1829, and as was (and still is) the custom, the President delivered to it a message reporting on the State of the Union and making recommendations for new legislation. Not unexpectedly, he paid considerable attention to the Indian question.... About half the discussion of Indian affairs was devoted to the constitutional issue raised by the Cherokee claim to independence and political sovereignty within the state of Georgia. Jackson stated that in his view the Native Americans residing within the boundaries of old or new states were subject to the laws of those states. He recognized the efforts of some tribes to become "civilized" but saw the only hope for their survival to be removal to a Western territory. The rhetoric was candid but compassionate in tone, no doubt intended to disarm criticism, suggesting that removal was not merely legally justified but morally necessary, and that he was responding not to the greed of land speculators and would-be settlers but to a moral imperative to save the Indians from extinction. Emigration, of course, should be strictly voluntary with individuals. Those who chose to leave would be provided with an "ample district West of the Mississippi," to be guaranteed to them as long as they occupied it. Each tribe would have its own territory and its own government and would be free to receive "benevolent" instructors in the "arts of civilization." In the future, there might arise "an interesting commonwealth, destined to perpetuate the race, and to attest the humanity and justice of this Government." For those who chose to remain, he gave assurance that they would "without doubt" be allowed to keep possession of their houses and gardens. But he warned them that they must obey the laws of the states in which they lived, and must be prepared to give up all claims to "tracts of country on which they have neither dwelt nor made improvements, merely because they have seen them from the mountain, or passed them in the chace." Eventually, those who stayed behind could expect to "become merged in the mass of our population."

On February 24, 1830, a removal bill was reported out from the House Committee on Indian Affairs (John Bell of Tennessee, chairman). The same bill was also introduced into the Senate by its Indian Committee (also chaired by a Jackson man from Tennessee). The text of the bill... was briefer than the President's message recommending it. In eight sections, it authorized the President to set aside an Indian territory on public lands west of the Mississippi; to exchange districts there for land now occupied by Indians in the East; to grant the tribes absolute ownership of their new homes "forever"; to treat with tribes for the rearrangement of boundaries in order to effect the removal; to ensure that property left behind by emigrating

Indians be properly appraised and fair compensation be paid; to give the emigrants "aid and assistance" on their journey and for the first year after their arrival in their new country; to protect the emigrants from hostile Indians in the West and from any other intruders; to continue the "superintendence" now exercised over the Indians by the Trade and Intercourse Laws. And to carry out these responsibilities, the Congress appropriated the sum (soon to prove woefully inadequate) of $500,000.

The debate on the bill was long and bitter, for the subject of Indian removal touched upon a number of very emotional issues: the constitutional question of states' rights versus federal prerogatives, Christian charity, national honor, racial and cultural prejudices, manifest destiny, and of course just plain greed. The opening salvo was the Report of the Indian Committee of the House. The report defended the constitutional right of the states to exercise sovereignty over residents, including Indians, within their borders. It discussed the nature of Indian title, naïvely asserting that in pre-Columbian times "the whole country was a common hunting ground"; they claimed as private or tribal property only their "moveable wigwams" and in some parts of the continent "their small corn patches." The committee declared that the Indians were incapable of "civilization," despite their recent "extravagant pretensions," so loudly touted by misguided zealots opposed to emigration. Among the Cherokees, the report asserted, only a small oligarchy of twenty-five or thirty families controlled the government and only these, and about two hundred mixed-blood families who made up what the report referred to as a "middle class,"

could claim to have made any progress toward what the committee regarded as "civilization." These favored few opposed emigration. But the remainder, allegedly living in indolence, poverty, and vice, were generally in favor of removal as the only way to escape destitution and eventual annihilation. Obviously, in the committee's view, it was not merely justifiable but morally imperative to save the Southern tribes from extinction by helping them to emigrate to the West.

Both Houses of Congress were deluged by hundreds of petitions and memorials, solicited by religious groups and benevolent societies opposed to Indian removal. Town meetings were held, particularly in the Northern states, demanding justice for the Native Americans. Joseph Hemphill, congressman from Pennsylvania, published a review of Cass's article "Indian Reform," excoriating him for recommending an oppressive policy toward the Indians; and he included in his condemnation the Reverend Isaac McCoy, who had written a book, *The Practicability of Indian Reform*, urging removal as the only means of civilizing the natives. The American Board of Commissioners exerted wide influence on Protestant denominations in the cause of Indian rights. Not to be outdone, friends of Jackson organized their own pro-removal missionary society, its masthead adorned with the names of prominent officials and clergymen who favored the bill. Its efforts were eclipsed by the older American Board, however, whose leader, Jeremiah Evarts, under the *nom de plume* William Penn, had already published his *Essays on the Present Crisis in the Condition of the American Indians*.

In the spring of 1830, active debate began in the chambers of Congress. The attack on the bill was launched in the Senate by Theodore Frelinghuysen of New Jersey, a distinguished lawyer whose deep religious convictions had already earned him the respect of colleagues in both parties. Frelinghuysen, a Whig, was an example of the "Christian party in politics," for at one time or another he was president of the American Board of Commissioners for Foreign Missions (sixteen years), president of the American Bible Society (sixteen years), president of the American Tract Society (six years), vice president of the American Sunday School Union (fifty years), and for many years an officer of the American Temperance Union and the American Colonization Society. His stand on the Indian question was to earn him a national reputation as "the Christian statesman" and in 1844 a place on the Whig ticket as (unsuccessful) candidate for Vice President of the United States, along with Henry Clay for President. Senator Frelinghuysen's speech, which took three days to deliver, pointed out that the Indian policy of the United States, from the time of Washington on, had been based on the principle that the United States was obligated to protect peaceful natives living in unceded territory from intrusion by whites under any pretext, by force if necessary. Treaties with the Native Americans, according to the Constitution, were, like other treaties, the law of the land. The Jackson Administration, by refusing to enforce existing treaties, was violating the Constitution.

Why was more Indian land needed now, when annual sales of public lands amounted to no more than 1 million acres? The Indian occupants of the continent had already peacefully sold more than 214 million acres, and much of that remained vacant. To be sure, hunters would eventually sell to agriculturists, but willingly and in response to reasonable argument, not by coercion, as this bill, in the hands of this administration, promised. Furthermore, many of the Native Americans, in response to the official reform policy of the United States government, were adopting white customs and could be expected to amalgamate with the whites, if left alone where they were. Frelinghuysen concluded with an essentially moral appeal:

> Sir, if we abandon these aboriginal proprietors of our soil, these early allies and adopted children of our forefathers, how shall we justify it to our country? . . . How shall we justify this trespass to ourselves? . . . Let us beware how, by oppressive encroachments upon the sacred privileges of our Indian neighbors, we minister to the agonies of future remorse.

The pro-removal reply to Frelinghuysen was delivered by Senator John Forsyth of Georgia. Like his opponent, Forsyth was a lawyer and a former attorney general of his state. He had served as a representative in Congress, as minister to Spain (he secured the King's ratification of the 1819 treaty ceding Florida to the United States), and, most recently, he had served as governor of Georgia (1827–29). He was a loyal Jackson follower, would later support Jackson and oppose Calhoun over nullification, and in 1834 he was rewarded by appointment as Secretary of State. He was a skilled orator and had the reputation of being the best debater of his time.

Forsyth dismissed Frelinghuysen's words as a mere self-interested plea by the "Christian party in politics" to create unwarranted sympathy for the Indians, among whom their missionaries lived so prosperously. He pointed to the deplorable conditions under which the Native Americans now lived and to the long history of the removal policy. Forsyth, as a true friend of the Indians, had long had doubts that removal would promote their civilization, but he would vote for this bill because it would relieve the states "from a population useless and bothersome" and would place these wild hunters in a country better supplied with game. But most of Forsyth's time was spent on legal arguments about states' rights (particularly Georgia's) to exercise sovereignty over Indians, about old treaties and proclamations, and about natural law. He concluded that Georgia had a right to expect the United States to remove the Indians (without coercion, of course) to a happier hunting ground west of the Mississippi.

The debate raged for weeks in both the Senate and the House. Amendments were proposed in the Senate that would have weakened the bill by protecting the Indians' interests; three times these amendments were defeated by a single vote. In general, delegates from the Northern and Eastern states, many of them National Republicans, anti-Masons, and moral reformers, stood against the bill, and Southern and Western delegates —many, like Jackson, with little interest in evangelical Christianity—favored it. Eventually, on April 23, 1830, the Senate voted 28 to 19 to pass the measure. On May 24, the House passed the bill by a narrower margin, 102 to 97.

President Jackson signed the Removal Act on the same day. It was, some maintained, the "leading measure" of his administration; indeed, "the greatest question that ever came before Congress, short of the question of peace and war." Jackson himself said that Indian removal was the "most arduous part of my duty" as President.

*   *   *

A fairly clear federal policy with regard to the transfer to white owners of title to newly purchased Indian lands, based on a generation of experience, was already in place when the Removal Act was passed and signed. In some cessions, individual Indians were allowed to retain small tracts, called "allotments" (in distinction to tribally owned "reservations"), generally small parcels of land around their residences. These allotments could be sold by their Indian owners to settlers or land companies by government-approved contract. The remainder of the ceded territory became part of the public lands of the United States (except for Georgia, where, by special agreement, lands purchased by the United States were turned over to the state). The usual practice of the federal government was to dispose of the public lands as quickly as possible. The lands were first surveyed and then sold, a large proportion initially at public auction at a minimum price of $1.25 an acre, and the remainder at subsequent privately arranged sales.

Meanwhile, "actual settlers" would be entering these public lands, staking out claims, building cabins, making improvements. Along with the squatters, "land lookers" sent by land companies were prowling about, identifying the best locations for speculative investment. The government did not try to stop the squatters, who often were tacitly accorded a "preemption right" to 80 or 160 acres around their improvements at the minimum price of $1.25 an acre. "Speculator" land companies, while they were condemned in political rhetoric as unfair monopolistic competitors of the "actual settler," at least sometimes supported the settlers' interests. Government did not really want to discourage the speculators any more than the settlers. After all, many politicians and officials (as we have seen, including Jackson and his friends) were speculators in Indian lands themselves, and anyway, there were rarely enough settlers on hand to buy up all the land offered for sale. Besides, some tracts like town sites required expensive development before resale to "actual settlers."

The government did not expect to realize much if any profit from the sale of the public lands. Some of the less desirable tracts, slow to move, eventually went for as little as $12\,^1/_2$ cents an acre after languishing for up to five years. Some of the more attractive sites, on the other hand, might bring prices at auction well above the $1.25-an-acre minimum. But even though the Indians would be given only a few cents an acre for their land, the government was likely to agree to pay for the expense of their relocation out of the proceeds from the sale of their former domain. And there were costs associated with preparing the public lands for sale: surveys, the opening of roads, and the operations of the Land Office itself, both in Washington and in the field. Public policy was to get the public lands into private hands, for economic development, as quickly as possible.

Thus the Jackson administration was ready to do its "land-office business" as soon as the Indians could be persuaded to sell and agree to remove. In fact, efforts to that end were already under way.

THE TRAIL OF TEARS

Responsibility for arranging the actual removal of the Indians was now in the hands of the administration. Jackson had in place a removal team: his protégé John Eaton, the Secretary of War; Thomas McKenney, Superintendent of the Indian Office, a declared supporter of removal; General Coffee, his old comrade-in-arms, always ready to serve as the situation demanded—as Indian fighter, treaty negotiator, or surveyor of purchased lands. He also had available the staff of Indian agents who served under McKenney. But McKenney, despite his support for the principle of voluntary removal, soon balked at the harassment tactics of the administration. He was removed from office in August 1830. In 1831, after another official had served for a year, the position was filled by a loyal Jacksonite, Elbert Herring, who supported the removal policy until he left in 1836. Along with McKenney, about half the experienced Indian agents in the field were replaced by Jackson men. They could be counted on to execute administration policy more readily than those whose long acquaintance with Native Americans had made them too sympathetic. In 1831, Eaton, mired in an embarrassing domestic scandal, was replaced as Secretary of War by Lewis Cass, who... was not only a loyal Democrat but also a leading advocate of removal. Not incidentally, his political leadership in the Michigan Territory, which was about to become a state, would come in handy at election time in 1832.

It was the team of Jackson, Cass, and Herring that supervised the removal of most of the Southern Indians from 1830 through 1836. By the end of 1836, the Choctaws and Creeks had emigrated, and by the close of 1837 the Chickasaws had followed. Cherokee resistance was not broken, however, until 1839, and the

Seminoles were not removed until 1842, after a long and bloody war.

* * *

In principle, emigration was to be voluntary; the Removal Act did not require Native Americans to emigrate, and those who wished to remain could do so. But the actual policy of the administration was to encourage removal by all possible means, fair or foul.

Jackson as usual spoke publicly in a tone of friendship and concern for Indian welfare. In a letter of instruction to an agent who was to visit the Choctaws in October 1829 (even before the Removal Act was passed) he outlined the message from "their father," the President, urging them to emigrate. The threats were veiled. "They and my white children are too near each other to live in harmony and peace." The state of Mississippi had the right to extend a burdensome jurisdiction over them, and "the general government will be obliged to sustain the States in the exercise of their right." He, as President, could be their friend only if they removed beyond the Mississippi, where they should have a "land of their own, which they shall possess as long as Grass grows or water runs . . . and I never speak with forked tongue."

A harsh policy was nevertheless quickly put in place. To weaken the power of the chiefs, many of whom opposed removal, the traditional practice of paying annuities in a lump sum, to be used by the chiefs on behalf of the tribe for capital improvements and education, was terminated and annuities were doled out piecemeal to individual Indians. The amounts were pitifully small—each Cherokee was to receive forty-four cents per year, for example, and even that

was to be withheld until he reached the West. Some annuities were not paid at all, being diverted by local agents to pay spurious damage claims allowed by state courts against Indians.

The principal acts of harassment, however, were carried out by the governments and citizens of the Southern states. The extension of state sovereignty over the tribes within their borders led quickly to the passage of destructive legislation. The tribal governments, so carefully organized in imitation of white institutions, were simply abolished; it became illegal for tribes to establish their own laws and to convict and punish lawbreakers. The chiefs were to have no power. Tribal assemblies were banned. Indians were subject to state taxes, militia duty, and suits for debt. Indians were denied the right to vote, to bring suit, even to testify in court (as heathens all—despite the evidence of conversion for many—they could not swear a Christian oath). Intruders were encouraged to settle on Indian territory; lands were sold even before they had been ceded. In Georgia, after gold was discovered on Cherokee property, the Indians were prohibited from digging or mining gold on their own land, while hundreds of white prospectors were allowed to trespass and steal the gold with impunity.

And all the while, the federal government stood idly by, refusing to intervene in the application of state laws. The result was chaos. Thousands of intruders swarmed over the Indian country in a frenzied quest for land and gold, destroying Indian farms and crops. The missionaries tried to persuade their Indian friends to stand firm against removal. But Georgia passed a law requiring missionaries to take an oath of loyalty to the state or leave the Indian country, and when a number refused, they were seized, imprisoned, tried, convicted, and sentenced to long prison terms. All but two were pardoned after they signed a pledge to obey the laws of Georgia. The recalcitrant ones, the famous Samuel Worcester, former head of the American Board's school at Brainerd, publisher of *The Cherokee Phoenix*, and an ardent anti-removal advocate, and an assistant missionary, Elizur Butler, chose to appeal their convictions. While they languished in prison, the case wound its way up to the Supreme Court, where the issue was interpreted in the context of Georgia's claim of state sovereignty. The Supreme Court found against Georgia's right to supersede federal authority over Indian tribes and thus set aside Georgia's assertion of state sovereignty over the Cherokees and their missionaries. Jackson was not impressed, however, and is reputed to have said, "Justice Marshall has made his decision, now let him enforce it." Whether he actually used these words has been questioned; but they represent his sentiments, for the administration did nothing to aid the missionaries or effectively to deter intruders. Worcester was not released from prison until the following year (1833).

The other major legal challenge to the state's sovereignty was an earlier suit pressed by the Cherokee nation that directly challenged the constitutionality of Georgia's attempt to execute state law within the Indian country. Former Attorney General William Wirt (who also represented Samuel Worcester) applied to the Supreme Court for an injunction. But this case was dismissed on the technical ground that an Indian nation was not a foreign state but a "domestic dependent nation," a "ward" of its "guardian," the United States, and therefore could not bring suit before the Supreme Court.

It is abundantly clear that Jackson and his administration were determined to permit the extension of state sovereignty because it would result in the harassment of Indians, powerless to resist, by speculators and intruders hungry for Indian land. Jackson, of course, was not always so indulgent of states' rights, as is shown by his famous threat later on to use military force against South Carolina if that state acted on John Calhoun's doctrine of nullification.

POSTSCRIPT

Was Andrew Jackson's Indian Removal Policy Motivated by Humanitarian Impulses?

One of the interesting sidelights of the federal government's efforts to develop a policy with regard to Native American tribes residing in individual states revolved around the questions of tribal sovereignty versus states' rights. The Cherokee, in particular, proved troublesome in this regard. Since 1791 the United States had recognized the Cherokee as a nation in a number of treaties, and in 1827 delegates of this tribe initiated action to draft a constitution that would more formally recognize this status. In doing so, Native Americans confronted a barrier in the United States Constitution that prohibited the establishment of a new state in a preexisting state without the latter's approval. In response, Georgia, where most of the Cherokee lived, opposed the plan and called for the removal of all Native Americans. At this juncture, Cherokee leaders sought an injunction to prevent the state of Georgia from enforcing its laws within Native American territory. The case reached the United States Supreme Court which, in *Cherokee Nation v. Georgia* (1831), expressed sympathy for the Native Americans' position but denied that the Cherokee held the status of a foreign nation. The following year, in the midst of efforts to remove all Native Americans from the southeastern United States, Chief Justice John Marshall, in *Worcester v. Georgia* (1832), ruled that the state had no right to extend sovereignty over the Cherokees within its borders.

Major studies of the Indian removal policy in Jacksonian America include Angie Debo's classic, *And Still the Waters Run: The Betrayal of the Five Civilized Tribes* (University of Oklahoma Press, 1940); Allen Guttman, *States Rights and Indian Removal: The Cherokee Nation vs. the State of Georgia* (D. C. Heath, 1965); John Ehle, *Trail of Tears: The Rise and Fall of the Cherokee Nation* (Doubleday, 1988); Mary E. Young, *Redskins, Ruffleshirts, and Rednecks: Indian Allotments in Alabama and Mississippi, 1830-1860* (University of Oklahoma Press, 1961); and Arthur H. DeRosier, Jr., *The Removal of the Choctaw Indians* (University of Tennessee Press, 1970). Perhaps the best analysis of Jackson's sometimes ambiguous attitude toward Native Americans is Michael Paul Rogin, *Fathers and Children: Andrew Jackson and the Subjugation of the American Indian* (Alfred A. Knopf, 1975).

For general studies of Native American history that include discussions of Jackson's attitudes and policies with regard to Native Americans, see Wilcomb E. Washburn, *The Indian in America* (Harper & Row, 1975); Robert

F. Berkhofer, Jr., *The White Man's Indian: Images of the American Indian from Columbus to the Present* (Alfred A. Knopf, 1978); and Francis Paul Prucha's edited collection of readings, *The Indian in American History* (Holt, Rinehart and Winston, 1971).

The historical literature on Jacksonian philosophy and policies is extensive. Robert Remini is Jackson's definitive, generally sympathetic biographer. His three-volume study, *Andrew Jackson and the Course of American Empire, 1767–1821* (Harper & Row, 1977), *Andrew Jackson and the Course of American Freedom, 1822–1832* (Harper & Row, 1981), and *Andrew Jackson and the Course of American Democracy, 1833–1845* (Harper & Row, 1984) is the culmination of a long career of study and writing. Older though equally excellent studies include, Arthur Schlesinger, Jr., *The Age of Jackson* (Little, Brown & Company, 1946); John William Ward, *Andrew Jackson: Symbol for an Age* (Oxford University Press, 1955); and Marvin Meyers, *The Jacksonian Persuasion: Politics and Belief* (Stanford University Press, 1957). Useful primary sources on the "age of Jackson" are collected in Edward Pessen, ed., *Jacksonian Panorama* (Bobbs-Merrill, 1976). The period is also explored in Glyndon G. Van Deusen, *The Jacksonian Era, 1828–1848* (Harper & Row, 1959); Edward Pessen, *Jacksonian America: Society, Personality, and Politics* (Dorsey Press, 1969); and Henry L. Watson, *Liberty and Power: The Politics of Jacksonian America* (Hill and Wang, 1990). Finally, Alexis de Tocqueville's classic *Democracy in America* (HarperCollins, 1988) sheds a great deal of light on the still-young nation of Jackson's time from the perspective of a foreign observer.

On the Internet . . .

http://www.dushkin.com

Black Resistance: Slavery in the United States
This slavery exhibit is part of Afro-America's Black History Museum. Compiled by Carolyn L. Bennett and designed by Matt Evans, it offers a chronology of events, a brief introduction to the transport of Africans to America, and some commentary on the attitudes of slaves.
http://www.afroam.org/history/slavery/main.html

ReenactorsWorldPlus.com
ReenactorsWorldPlus.com is dedicated to the tens of thousands of men, women, and children around the world who bring our historical heritage alive through education in our schools, living history events, and other public areas. This page is dedicated to the Mexican-American War.
http://reenactorsworldplus.com/mexican.htm

Historical Text Archive: Women's History
This archive contains an impressive collection of links related to women and their roles in history. Topics include women on the frontier in the 1800s, women and social movements in the United States, and women during the Civil War.
http://www.msstate.edu/Archives/History/women.html

PART 3

Antebellum America

Pressures and trends that began building in the early years of the American nation continued to gather momentum until conflict was almost inevitable. Population growth and territorial expansion brought the country into conflict with other nations. The United States had to respond to challenges from Americans who felt alienated from or forgotten by the new nation because the ideals of human rights and democratic participation that guided the founding of the nation had been applied only to selected segments of the population.

■ Were the Abolitionists "Unrestrained Fanatics"?

■ Did Slaves Exercise Religious Autonomy?

■ Was the Mexican War an Exercise in American Imperialism?

■ Did the Westward Movement Transform the Traditional Roles of Women in the Mid-Nineteenth Century?

ISSUE 9

Were the Abolitionists "Unrestrained Fanatics"?

YES: Avery Craven, from *The Coming of the Civil War,* 2d ed. (University of Chicago Press, 1957)

NO: Irving H. Bartlett, from "The Persistence of Wendell Phillips," in Martin Duberman, ed., *The Antislavery Vanguard: New Essays on the Abolitionists* (Princeton University Press, 1965)

ISSUE SUMMARY

YES: Historian Avery Craven asserts that the fanaticism of the abolitionist crusade created an atmosphere of crisis that resulted in the outbreak of the Civil War.

NO: Irving Bartlett, retired professor of American civilization, differentiates between agitation and fanaticism and states that abolitionists like Wendell Phillips were deeply committed to improving the quality of life for all Americans, including African Americans held as slaves.

Opposition to slavery in the area that became the United States dates back to the seventeenth and eighteenth centuries when Puritan leaders, such as Samuel Sewall, and Quakers, such as John Woolman and Anthony Benezet, published a number of pamphlets condemning the existence of the slave system. This religious link to antislavery sentiment is also evident in the writings of John Wesley as well as in the decision of the Society of Friends in 1688 to prohibit their members from owning bondservants. Slavery was said to be contrary to Christian principles. These attacks, however, did little to diminish the institution. In fact, efforts to force emancipation gained little headway in the colonies until the outbreak of the American Revolution. Complaints that the English government had instituted a series of measures that "enslaved" the colonies in British North America raised thorny questions about the presence of real slavery in those colonies. How could Americans demand their freedom from King George III, who was cast in the role of oppressive master, while denying freedom and liberty to African American bondsmen? Such a contradiction inspired a gradual emancipation movement in the North, which was often accompanied by compensation for the former slave owners.

In addition, antislavery societies sprang up throughout the nation to continue the crusade against bondage. Interestingly, the majority of these organizations were located in the South. Prior to the 1830s the most prominent antislavery organization was the American Colonization Society, which offered a two-fold program: (1) gradual, compensated emancipation of slaves, and (2) exportation of the new freedmen to colonies outside the boundaries of the United States, mostly to Africa.

In the 1830s antislavery activity underwent an important transformation. A new strain of antislavery sentiment expressed itself in the abolitionist movement. Drawing momentum from both the revivalism of the Second Great Awakening and the example set by England (which prohibited slavery in its imperial holdings in 1833), abolitionists called for the immediate end to slavery without compensation to masters for the loss of their property. Abolitionists viewed slavery not so much as a practical problem to be resolved, but rather as a moral offense incapable of resolution through traditional channels of political compromise. In January 1831 William Lloyd Garrison, who for many came to symbolize the abolitionist crusade, published the first issue of *The Liberator,* a newspaper dedicated to the immediate end of slavery. In his first editorial, Garrison expressed the indignation of many in the abolitionist movement when he warned slaveholders and their supporters to "urge me not to use moderation in a cause like the present. I am in earnest—I will not equivocate—I will not excuse—I will not retreat a single inch—AND I WILL BE HEARD...."

Unfortunately for Garrison, relatively few Americans were inclined to respond positively to his call. His newspaper generated little interest outside Boston, New York, Philadelphia, and other major urban centers of the North. This situation, however, changed within a matter of months. In August 1831 a slave preacher named Nat Turner led a rebellion of slaves in Southampton County, Virginia, that resulted in the death of fifty-eight whites. Although the revolt was quickly suppressed and Turner and his supporters (along with many slaves not involved in the uprising) were executed, the incident spread fear throughout the South. Governor John B. Floyd of Virginia turned an accusatory finger toward the abolitionists when he concluded that the Turner uprising was "undoubtedly designed and matured by unrestrained fanatics in some of the neighboring states." Moreover, it would be charged, these abolitionists contributed to a crisis environment that degenerated over the next generation and ultimately produced civil war.

Some historians have accepted the view that abolitionist fanaticism, expressed through attacks on Southern slavery, led to political deterioration in the United States which culminated in secession and war. Avery Craven, for example, blames abolitionists for inciting volatile emotions by characterizing slaveholders as sinful aristocrats willing to distort the American dream of freedom to preserve their peculiar institution.

Irving Bartlett, in contrast, surveys the abolitionist career of Wendell Phillips and concludes that he was not a fanatic but rather a practical agitator, an intellectual, and a committed philosopher of reform who clearly understood the difference between agitation and demagoguery.

YES

Avery Craven

THE NORTHERN ATTACK ON SLAVERY

The abolition movement... was closely related in origins, leadership, and expression to the peace movement, the temperance crusade, the struggles for women's rights, prison and Sabbath reform, and the improvement of education. It was not unrelated to the efforts to establish communities where social-economic justice and high thinking might prevail. It was part of the drive to unseat aristocrats and re-establish American democracy according to the Declaration of Independence. It was a clear-cut effort to apply Christianity to the American social order.

The anti-slavery effort was at first merely one among many. It rose to dominance only gradually. Fortunate from the beginning in leadership, it was always more fortunate in appeal. Human slavery more obviously violated democratic institutions than any other evil of the day; it was close enough to irritate and to inflame sensitive minds, yet far enough removed that reformers need have few personal relations with those whose interests were affected. It rasped most severely upon the moral senses of a people whose ideas of sin were comprehended largely in terms of self-indulgence and whose religious doctrines laid emphasis on social usefulness as the proper manifestation of salvation. And, what was more important, slavery was now confined to a section whose economic interests, and hence political attitudes, conflicted sharply with those of the Northeast and upper Northwest.

Almost from the beginning of the new anti-slavery movement, two distinct centers of action appeared, each with its distinct and individual approach to the problem. One developed in the industrial areas of New England. Its most important spokesman was William Lloyd Garrison, founder and editor of a Boston abolition paper called the *Liberator*. Garrison at first accepted the old idea that slavery was an *evil* to be pointed out and gradually eradicated by those among whom it existed, but he shifted his position in the early 1830's and denounced slavery as a damning crime to be unremittingly assailed and immediately destroyed. The first issue of his paper announced a program from which he never deviated: " ... *I do not wish to think or speak or write with moderation. I will not retreat a single inch, and I will be heard.*" The problem, as Garrison saw it, was one of abstract right and wrong. The Scriptures and the

Declaration of Independence had already settled the issue. Slavery could have no legal status in a Christian democracy. If the Constitution recognized it, then the Constitution should be destroyed. Slaveholders were both sinners and criminals. They could lay no claim to immunity from any mode of attack. . . .

The extreme and impractical nature of the Garrison anti-slavery drive served to attract attention and arouse antagonism rather than to solve the problem. It did, however, show how profoundly the conditions of the time had stirred the reform spirit and how wide the door had been opened to the professional reformers—men to whom the question was not so much "how shall we abolish slavery, as how shall we best discharge our duty . . . to ourselves." Garrison may be taken as typical of the group. His temperament and experiences had combined to set him in most relationships against the accepted order of things. His life would probably have been spent in protesting even if slavery had never existed. From childhood he had waged a bitter fight *against* obstacles and *for* a due recognition of his abilities. A drunken father had abandoned the family to extreme poverty before William was three years old, and the boy, denied all but the rudiments of an education, had first been placed under the care of Deacon Bartlett, and then apprenticed for seven years to one Ephraim Allen to learn the printing trade. His first venture after his apprenticeship was over failed. His second gave him the opportunity to strike back at an unfair world. He became an editor of the *National Philanthropist,* a paper devoted to the suppression of "intemperance and its Kindred vices." This publication served also as a medium through which to attack lotteries, Sabbath-breaking, and war. A new Garrison began to emerge. His personality, given opportunity for expression, asserted itself. Attending a nominating caucus in Boston, he made bold to speak, and, being resented as an upstart, he replied to his critic in a letter to the Boston *Courier:*

> It is true my acquaintance in this city is limited. . . . Let me assure him, however, that if my life be spared, my name shall one day be known to the world—at least to such an extent that common inquiry shall be unnecessary.

To another critic he reiterated this statement, adding these significant words: "I speak in the spirit of prophecy, not of vainglory—with a strong pulse, a flashing eye, and a glow of the heart. The task may be yours to write my biography."

Anti-slavery efforts entered the Garrison program when Benjamin Lundy, the pioneer abolitionist, invited him to help edit the *Genius of Universal Emancipation* in Baltimore. Hostile treatment there, climaxed by imprisonment for libel, together with the influence of extreme British opinion, changed a moderate attitude which admitted "that immediate and complete emancipation is not desirable . . . no rational man cherishes so wild a vision," into the extreme and uncompromising fanaticism expressed only two years later in the *Liberator.* From that time on Garrison was bothered only by the fact that the English language was inadequate for the expression of his violent opinions. Southerners in Congress were desperados.

> We would sooner trust the honor of the country . . . in the hands of the inmates of our penitentiaries and prisons than in their hands . . . they are the meanest of thieves and the worst of

robbers. . . . We do not acknowledge them to be within the pale of Christianity, or republicanism, or humanity!

Hatred of the South had supplanted love for the Negro!

In such an approach as this, there could be no delay, no moderation. Right was right, and wrong was wrong. The Slaveholder could not be spared or given time to learn the evil of his ways. Action immediate and untempered was demanded. Yet this was the same William Lloyd Garrison who, in 1877, replied to Susan B. Anthony's request for aid to Women's Suffrage:

> You desire me to send you a letter, to be read at the Washington Convention of the National Woman Suffrage Association, in favor of a petition to Congress, asking that body to submit to the several States a 16th Amendment for the Constitution of the United States, securing suffrage for all, irrespective of sex. On fully considering the subject, I must decline doing so, because such a petition I deem to be quite premature. If its request were complied with by the present Congress —a supposition simply preposterous— the proposed Amendment would be rejected by every State in the Union, and in nearly every instance by such an overwhelming majority as to bring the movement into needless contempt. Even as a matter of "agitation," I do not think it would pay. Look over the whole country, and see in the present state of public sentiment on the question of woman suffrage what a mighty primary work remains to be done in enlightening the masses, who know nothing and care nothing about it, and consequently are not at all prepared to cast their votes for any such thing. . . .

Evidently circumstances alter cases in reform as drastically as in other lines of human endeavor!

The second center of anti-slavery effort was in upper New York and the farther Northwest. Influences from this center included in their sweep, however, much of rural New England and the Middle States and the movement found liberal financial help in New York City. Benjamin Lundy and other Quaker leaders started the crusade, but it did not come to full and wide expression until Theodore Weld, already the ablest temperance orator in the Northwest, set about cultivating the great field prepared for social reform by the Finney revivals.

Weld was, like Garrison, unusual both in abilities and in personal characteristics. He was much given to "anti-meat, -butter, -tea, and -coffee, etc. -ism[s]." He indulged in excessive self-effacement and in extravagant confessions of selfishness, pride, impatience of contradiction, personal recklessness, and "a bad, unlovely temper." Of his pride, "the great besetment of my soul," he wrote:

> I am too proud to be ambitious, too proud to seek applause, too proud to tolerate it when lavished upon me, proud as Lucifer that I can and do scorn applause and spurn flattery, and indignantly dash down and shiver to atoms the censer in which others would burn incense to me; too proud to betray emotions, too proud ever for an instant to lose my self possession whatever the peril, too proud to ever move a hair for personal interest, too proud ever to defend my character when assailed or my motives when impeached, too proud ever to wince when the hot iron enters my soul and passes thro it.

He wrote also of his contempt of opponents—"one of the *trade* winds of my nature [which] very often . . . *blows a hurricane*," and he listed by name those "who strangely and stupidly idolize me . . . and yield themselves to my sway in all confidence and love." He boasted of his daring and told of how as a child a tremendous thunderstorm would send him whooping and hallooing through the fields like a wild Indian. He had the Puritan's love of enduring; the saint's "right" to intolerance. He was, in fact, always a revivalist—a man with a mission to perform in the great West—"the battlefield of the World."

The campaign which he launched was but an expansion of the benevolence crusade already a part of the Western revival effort. As W. C. Preston said: "Weld's agents made the anti-slavery cause 'identical with religion,' and urged men, by all they esteem[ed] holy, by all the high and exciting obligations of duty to man and God . . . to join the pious work of purging the sin of slavery from the land." The movement, as it developed, was generally temperate in tone, and tended to function through the existing agencies of religion and politics. Lane Theological Seminary, founded in Cincinnati to train leaders in the Finney tradition, became the center from which Weld worked. Here, in a series of debates, he shaped the doctrine of gradual immediatism which by insisting that *gradual emancipation* begin *at once*, saved the movement from Garrison's extremes; from here he went out to win a group of converts which included James G. Birney, Joshua Giddings, Edwin M. Stanton, Elizur Wright, and Beriah Green; and here he adapted the revival technique to the abolition crusade and prepared the way for his loyal band of Seventy to carry that crusade throughout the whole Northwest.

There was, however, another aspect to the movement in this region—a very hard-headed practical aspect. Its leaders believed in action as well as agitation. And action here meant political action.

Western men had a way of viewing evil as something there ought to be a law against. They thought it was the business of government to secure morality as well as prosperity. They were even inclined to regard the absence of prosperity as the result of the existence of evil. Naturally, therefore, in spite of the revival-meeting procedure used to spread the gospel of abolition, action against slavery followed political precedent. This action began with petitions to Congress for such a practical end as the abolition of slavery in the District of Columbia. When Southern resentment of such a measure brought the adoption of gag rule methods, the contest was broadened into a fight on the floors of Congress for the constitutional rights of petition and free speech. This proved to be an excellent way to keep the slavery question before the public and to force slaveholders to reveal their undemocratic attitudes. Petitions arrived in such quantities as to clog the work of Congress. A Washington organization for agitation and lobbying became necessary. Weld himself went to Washington to advise with John Quincy Adams and his fellow workers. Slavery thus again entered national politics, this time by way of the Northwest. Anti-slavery politicians, such as Joshua Giddings and Salmon P. Chase of Ohio, quickly proved the value of the cause as a stepping-stone to public office. . . .

With the new growth and new importance of the movement, the technique of its propaganda also reached new efficiency. Never before or since has a cause been urged upon the American people with such consummate skill and such lasting effects. Every agency possible in that day was brought into use; even now the predominating opinions of most of the American people regarding the antebellum South and its ways are the product of that campaign of education.

Indoctrination began with the child's A B C's which were learned from booklets containing verses like the following:

A is an Abolitionist
A man who wants to free
The wretched slave, and give to all
An equal liberty.

B is a Brother with a skin
Of somewhat darker hue,
But in our Heavenly Father's sight,
He is as dear as you.

C is the Cotton field, to which
This injured brother's driven,
When, as the white man's *slave*, he
    toils
From early morn till even.

D is the Driver, cold and stern,
Who follows, whip in hand,
To punish those who dare to rest,
Or disobey command.

. . . .

I is the Infant, from the arms
Of its fond mother torn,
And at a public auction sold
With horses, cows, and corn.

. . . .

Q is the Quarter, where the slave
On coarsest food is fed
And where, with toil and sorrow worn
He seeks his wretched bed.

. . . .

W is the Whipping post,
To which the slave is bound,
While on his naked back, the lash
Makes many a bleeding wound.

. . . .

Z is a Zealous man, sincere,
Faithful, and just, and true;

An earnest pleader for the slave—
Will you not be so too?

For children able to read, a wider variety of literature was written. One volume in verse urged "little children" to "plead with men, that they buy not slaves again" and called attention to the fact that

They may harken what *you* say,
Though from *us* they turn away.

Another verse suggested that:

Sometimes when from school you
    walk,
You can with your playmates talk,
Tell them of the slave child's fate,
Motherless and desolate.
And you can refuse to take
Candy, sweetmeat, pie or cake,
Saying "No"—unless 'tis free—
"The slave shall not work for me."

Juvenile story books, with some parts written in verse and printed in large and bold type and the rest written in prose and set in smaller type, were issued with the explanation that the verses were adapted to the capacity of the youngest reader, while the prose was well suited for being read aloud in the family circle. "It is presumed," said the preface, "that [with the prose] our younger friends will claim the assistance of their older brothers and sisters, or appeal to the ready aid of their mamma." Such volumes might contain pictures and stories from *Uncle Tom's Cabin* or they might consist of equally appealing tales of slave children cruelly torn from their parents or tortured by ingenious methods.

For adults the appeal was widened. No approach was neglected. Hymn books offered abolition songs set to familiar tunes. To the strains of "Old Hundred" eager voices invited "ye Yeomen brave" to rescue "the bleeding slave," or, to the "Missionary Hymn," asked them to consider

The frantic mother
Lamenting for her child,
Till falling lashes smother
Her cries of anguish wild!

Almanacs, carrying the usual information about weather and crops, filled their other pages with abolition propaganda. In one of these, readers found the story of Liburn Lewis, who, for a trifling offense, bound his slave, George, to a meat block and then, while all the other slaves looked on, proceeded slowly to chop him to pieces with a broad ax, and to cast the parts into a fire. Local, state, and national societies were organized for more efficient action in petitioning, presenting public speakers, distributing tracts, and publishing anti-slavery periodicals. The American Anti-Slavery Society "in the year 1837–38, published 7,877 bound volumes, 47,256 tracts and pamphlets, 4,100 circulars, and 10,490 prints. Its quarterly *Anti-Slavery Magazine* had an annual circulation of 9,000; the *Slave Friend*, for children, had 131,050; the monthly *Human Rights*, 189,400, and the weekly *Emancipator*, 217,000." From 1854 to 1858 it spent $3281 on a series of tracts discussing every phase of slavery, under such suggestive titles as "Disunion, our Wisdom and our Duty," "Relations of Anti-Slavery to Religion," and "To Mothers in the Free States." Its "several corps of lecturers of the highest ability and worth... occupied the field" every year in different states. Its Annual Reports, with their stories of atrocities and their biased discussion of issues, constituted a veritable arsenal from which weapons of attack could be drawn. Like other anti-slavery soci-

eties, it maintained an official organ, issued weekly, and held its regular conventions for the generation of greater force.

Where argument and appeal to reason failed, the abolitionists tried entertainment and appeal to emotion. *Uncle Tom's Cabin* was written because its author, "as a woman, as a mother," was "oppressed and broken hearted, with the sorrows & injustice" seen, and "because as a Christian" she "felt the dishonor to Christianity—because as a lover of [her] country, [she] trembled at the coming day of wrath." It became a best seller in the most complete sense. Only the Bible exceeded it in numbers sold and in the thoroughness with which it was read in England and America. Editions were adapted to every pocketbook, and translations carried it throughout the world. Dramatized and put on the stage, it did more to make the theatre respectable in rural America than any other single influence. The fictitious Uncle Tom became the stereotype of all American Negro slaves; Simon Legree became the typical slaveholder. A generation and more formed its ideas of Southern life and labor from the pages of this novel. A romantic South, of planter-gentlemen and poor whites, of chivalry and dissipation, of "sweet but worthless" women, was given an imaginative reality so wide and so gripping that no amount of patient research and sane history writing could alter it. Other novels, such as *Our World: or the Slaveholder's Daughter*, built their plots about the love affairs of Southern planters with their Negro slaves. Jealousies between wives and mistresses, struggles between brothers for the possession of some particularly desirable wench, or the inner conflict of a master over his obligation to his mulatto bastards, constituted the main appeal in such works. The object was always the same: to reveal the licentious character of Southern men, the unhappy status of Southern homes, and the horrible violation of Negro chastity everywhere existing under slavery.

Reformed slaveholders and escaped slaves were especially valuable in the crusade. Under the warming influence of sympathetic audiences their stories of cruelty and depravity grew apace. Persecution and contempt from old friends increased their zeal. Birney, the Grimké sisters, Frederick Douglass, and many others influenced the movement and were influenced by it in a way comparable only to the relation of reformed drunkards to the temperance cause.

By means of such agencies and methods a well-defined picture of the South and slavery became slowly fixed in Northern minds. The Southern people were divided into two distinct classes—slaveholders and poor whites. The former constituted an aristocracy, living in great white-pillared houses on extended plantations. The latter, ignorant and impotent, made up a rural slum which clung hopelessly to the pine barrens or the worn-out acres on the fringes of the plantations. Planters, who lived by the theft of Negro labor, completely dominated the section. They alone were educated; they alone held office. Non-slaveholders were too poor to "buy an education for themselves and their children," and the planters, not wishing to "endanger their supremacy," refused to establish public schools. Few poor whites could either read or write. They gained their opinions and their principles from "stump speeches and tavern conversations." They were "absolutely in the slaveholder's power." He sent "them to the polls to vote him into office and in so doing to vote down their own rights and

interests...." They knew "no more what they [were] about, than so many children or so many Russian serfs...."

Social-economic conditions in the South were described as tumble-down and backward. The slave, lacking the incentive of personal gain, was inefficient. The master, ruined by power, self-indulgence, and laziness, was incapable of sound management. James Birney described the section as one

> whose Agriculture is desolation—whose Commerce is mainly confined to a crazy wagon and half fed team of oxen or mules as a means of carrying it on —whose manufacturing "Machinery" is limited to the bones and sinews of reluctant slaves—whose currency is individual notes always to *be* paid (it may be at some broken bank) and mortgages on men and women and children who may run away or die, and on land, which without them is of little value....

Others went so far as to charge the panic of 1837 to Southern profligacy. "The existence of Slavery," resolved the American Anti-Slavery Society in 1840, "is the grand cause of the pecuniary embarrassments of the country; and... no real or permanent relief is to be expected... until the total abolition of that execrable system." Joshua Leavitt called the slave system "a bottomless gulf of extravagance and thriftlessness." Another explained its "withering and impoverishing effect["] by the fact that it was the "rule of violence and arbitrary will.... It would be quite in character with its theory and practice," he said, "if slave-drivers should refuse to pay their debts and meet the sheriff with dirk and pistol." Leavitt estimated that the South had "taken from the North, within five years, more than $100,000,000, by notes which will never be paid," and quoted an

English writer to the effect that "planters are always in debt. The system of society in a slaveholding community is such as to lead to the contraction of debt, which the system itself does not furnish the means of paying. . . ."

Nor did the Southern shortcomings, according to the anti-slavery view, end with things material. Moral weaknesses were even more offensive. Sexual virtue was scarcely known. "The Slave States," wrote an abolitionist, "are Sodoms, and almost every village family is a brothel." Another writer declared that "in the slaveholding settlements of Middle and Southern Mississippi . . . there [was] not a virtuous young man of twenty years of age." "To send a lad to a male academy in Mississippi," he said, "is moral murder." An anti-slavery pamphlet told of "a million and a half of slave women, some of them without even the tinge of African blood . . . given up a lawful prey to the unbridled lusts of their masters." Another widely circulated tract described a slave market in which one dealer "devoted himself exclusively to the sale of young mulatto women." The author pictured the sale of "the most beautiful woman I ever saw," without "*a single trace of the African about her features*" and with "a pair of eyes that pierced one through and through" to "one of the most lecherous-looking old brutes" that he had ever seen. The narrative closed with the shrieking appeal: "God shield the helpless victim of that bad man's power —it may be, ere now, that bad man's lust!" The conclusion was inescapable. Slavery and unrestrained sexual indulgence at Negro expense were inseparable.

In such a section and in the hands of such men, abolitionists assumed that slavery realized its most vicious possibilities. Anti-slavery men early set themselves to the task of collecting stories of cruelty. These were passed about from one to another, often gaining in ferocity as they travelled. Weld gathered them together in a volume entitled *American Slavery As It Is* and scattered them broadcast over the North. The annual reports of the anti-slavery societies, their tracts and periodicals, also revelled in atrocities, asking no more proof of their absolute truth than the word of a fellow fanatic.

The attempt to picture slavery "as it was," therefore, came to consist almost entirely of a recital of brutalities. Now and then a kind master and seemingly contented slaves were introduced for the purpose of contrast—as a device to deepen shadows. But, as a rule, Southerners, according to these tracts, spent their time in idleness broken only by brutal cock-fights, gander pullings, and horse races so barbarous that "the blood of the tortured animal drips from the lash and flies at every leap from the stroke of the rowel." Slavery was one continual round of abuse. The killing of a slave was a matter of no consequence. Even respectable ladies might cause "several to be *whipped to death*." Brandings, ear cropping, and body-maiming were the rule. David L. Child honestly declared: "From all that I have read and heard upon the subject of whipping done by masters and overseers to slaves . . . I have come to the conclusion that some hundreds of *cart whips* and cowskin instruments, which I am told make the skin fly like feathers, and cut frequently to the bone, are in *perpetual daily motion* in the slave states." John Rankin told of Negroes stripped, hung up and stretched and then "whipped until their bodies [were] covered with blood and mangled flesh," some dying "under the lash, others linger[ing] about for a time, and at length die[ing] of their *wounds...."* The recital was indeed one of *"groans, tears, and blood."*

To abuse was added other great wrongs. Everywhere slaves were overworked, underfed, and insufficiently clothed and sheltered. Family ties were cut without the slightest regard for Negro feelings—infants were torn from the mother's breast, husbands separated from their wives and families. Marriage was unknown among slaves, and the right to worship God generally denied. Strangely enough, little was said of slave-breeding for market. That charge was largely left to the politicians of the next decades and to the historians of a later day.

Two principal assumptions stood out in this anti-slavery indictment of the slaveholder. He was, in the first place, the arch-aristocrat. He was the great enemy of democracy. He was un-American, the oppressor of his fellow men, the exploiter of a weaker brother. Against him could be directed all the complaints and fears engendered by industrial captains and land speculators. He, more than any other aristocrat, threatened to destroy the American democratic dream.

In the second place, he was a flagrant sinner. His self-indulgence was unmatched. His licentious conduct with Negro women, his temperance in the use of intoxicating liquors, his mad dueling, and his passion for war against the weak were enough to mark him as the nation's moral enemy number one! The time for dealing moderately had passed. Immediate reform was imperative.

Thus it was that the slaveholder began to do scapegoat service for all aristocrats and all sinners. To him were transferred resentments and fears born out of local conditions. Because it combined in itself both the moral and the democratic appeal, and because it coincided with sectional rivalry, the abolition movement gradually swallowed up all other reforms. The South became the great object of all efforts to remake American society. Against early indifference and later persecution, a handful of deadly-in-earnest men and women slowly built into a section's consciousness the belief in a Slave Power. To the normal strength of sectional ignorance and distrust they added all the force of Calvinistic morality and American democracy and thereby surrounded every Northern interest and contention with holy sanction and reduced all opposition to abject depravity. When the politician, playing his risky game, linked expansion and slavery, Christian common folk by the thousands, with no great personal urge for reforming, accepted the Abolition attitudes toward both the South and slavery. Civil war was then in the making.

NO

Irving H. Bartlett

THE PERSISTENCE OF
WENDELL PHILLIPS

"The antislavery agitation is an important, nay, an essential part of the machinery of the state. It is not a disease nor a medicine. No; it is the normal state,— The normal state of the nation."

— Lecture on Public Opinion

Wherever Wendell Phillips walked on the Harvard campus he carried the aura of Beacon Hill with him. He was as well born as any Winthrop or Saltonstall and had been brought up in an imposing brick mansion on Beacon Hill only a few steps from the State House. The son of Boston's first mayor, a man universally respected for sound conservative principles, young Phillips seemed intent on following in his father's footsteps. He gained a reputation as being "the pet of the aristocracy," and in orations at the college exhibitions went out of his way to attack reformers and defend the standing order. One of his friends later recalled that Phillips would probably have been chosen by his classmates as the man *"least likely* to give the enthusiasm and labor of [his life] to the defense of popular rights."

Fifteen years after he left Harvard Phillips was asked by the secretary of the class of 1831 to fill out a questionnaire. He noted that he was in good health but growing bald. Under occupation he said he had prepared for the law "but grew honest and quitted what required an oath to the Constitution of the United States." Asked to note any other remarks that might be interesting to his classmates, he wrote: "My main business is to forward the abolition of slavery. I hold that the world is wrong side up and maintain the propriety of turning it upside down. I go for Disunion and have long since abjured that contemptible mockery, the Constitution of the United States."

To understand Phillips' career as an abolitionist and free-lance radical it is first necessary to account for his transformation from gentility to "fanaticism." Certainly it was not a natural development. After graduating from Harvard College Phillips entered the Harvard Law School. His career there and later as a practicing attorney was uneventful. Like most of the other sons of the old Federalists, he was happy to follow Daniel Webster into the Whig party which continued to serve the bulwarked conservatism of Massachusetts. He shared an office at this time with a man who later led a mob against abolitionists, and most of his social contacts were with the old aristocratic families who, if they knew anything about William Lloyd Garrison, naturally "supposed him to be a man who ought to be hung," and were unanimously determined to outlaw anyone, even the saintly William Ellery Channing, for expressing the slightest sympathy with his principles.

Phillips' first personal encounter with the antislavery movement came in October 1835, when he stood on a Boston street corner and watched a jeering mob drag Garrison through the street at the end of a rope. A few weeks later he met Ann Terry Greene, one of Garrison's disciples, and in less than a year, to the consternation of his mother and most of Boston society, married her. A few months later he made his first antislavery speech.

As with most of the early abolitionists, religion played a dominant role in making Phillips an abolitionist. We will never know how successful he might have been in law or politics, but his advantages in family background and education, his intelligence, and his remarkable oratorical talent suggest that the achievements of a Webster, Choate, or Sumner were not beyond his reach. The fact is, however, that between the time he graduated from college and met his wife, Phillips appears to have been in a melancholy state of mind largely because he lacked a sense of vocation. He had been brought up as a devout Calvinist, and it was a fundamental article in his belief that a man must make his life count for something. Like all new lawyers he found it slow going to get a practice started, but even more important he found no great satisfaction in

the profession. He needed to find a calling. As it turned out he fell in love and found his calling at the same time. His bride introduced him to William Lloyd Garrison and other Boston abolitionists, and in the early days of their marriage, when her health permitted, accompanied him to antislavery meetings. Phillips had undergone religious conversion years before under the powerful preaching of Lyman Beecher. As he joined hands with the abolitionists he felt he was being born a third time. "None know what it is to live," he wrote in 1841, "till they redeem life from its seeming monotony by laying it a sacrifice on the altar of some great cause."

Phillips never forgot the importance of religion to the antislavery movement. "Our enterprise is eminently a religious one," he said, "dependent for success entirely on the religious sentiment of the people." When Phillips refused to take an oath to support the "proslavery constitution" of the United States, he thought of himself as following in the tradition of his forbear, the Reverend George Phillips, who had come to America in 1630 to put the Atlantic Ocean "between himself and a corrupt church." He did not think of himself as an ordinary lecturer or orator, but as a kind of minister to the public, preaching the gospel of reform. When he was called to fill Theodore Parker's pulpit in the Boston Music Hall in 1860, it was natural for him to begin a sermon by announcing that "Christ preached on the last political and social item of the hour; and no man follows in his footsteps who does not do exactly the same thing." Phillips' sermons before Parker's congregation were the same sermons that he preached in Faneuil Hall before antislavery meetings, and he was convinced that he did his duty to

NO Irving H. Bartlett / 197

God in both places by flaying the public sinners of the day whether their names were Webster, Everett, Jefferson Davis, or Abraham Lincoln.

The idealism of the American revolutionary tradition also played a decisive role in shaping Phillips' career. When he was a boy, he remembered later, the Boston air still "trembled and burned with Otis and Sam Adams." He had been born practically next door to John Hancock's mansion, within [sight] of Bunker Hill and only a few steps from the site of the Boston massacre. When he was thirteen years old and a student at the Boston Latin School he stood for hours in a crowd on the Common to catch a glimpse of Lafayette upon his visit to the city. Two years later, while poring over his lessons at the school, the sound of tolling bells came through the open windows announcing the deaths of Thomas Jefferson and John Adams.

Phillips never doubted that the revolutionary fathers were on his side. His first antislavery speech was given to support John Quincy Adams in his fight to get the Congress to hear petitions attacking slavery. Phillips argued that the right of petition was a traditional right for free men and that in attacking it the South threatened the freedom of all men. "This is the reason we render to those who ask us why we are contending against southern slavery," he said, "*that it may not result in northern slavery . . . it is our own rights which are at issue.*"

The speech which made Phillips famous in Boston was given at a Faneuil Hall meeting to honor the memory of Elijah Lovejoy who had been killed by a mob in Alton, Illinois. The meeting was called to pay tribute to Lovejoy, but the abolitionists almost lost control of it when James Austin, the Attorney General

for Massachusetts, stood up and made a violent speech attacking Lovejoy for having published an incendiary antislavery newspaper. Austin likened the mob which destroyed Lovejoy and his press to the patriots responsible for the Boston Tea Party. Phillips was able to get the floor after Austin, and overcome the hooting and jeering of the proslavery faction in the audience with an eloquent defense of Lovejoy. Again Phillips was defending a traditional American right, freedom of the press, and he insisted that the spirit of the American revolution supported him.

> Sir, when I heard the gentleman lay down principles which place the murderers of Alton side by side with Otis and Hancock, with Quincy Adams, I thought those pictured lips would have broken into voice to rebuke the recreant American,—The slanderer of the dead. . . . In the sentiments he has uttered, on soil consecrated by the prayers of Puritans and the blood of patriots, the earth should have yawned and swallowed him up.

In his reliance on religion and the spirit of the Declaration of Independence, Phillips was like most other abolitionists. As an orator, however, despite the fact that he was part of a movement full of celebrated speakers, his uniqueness is unchallenged.

For at least a quarter of a century, from 1850 to 1875, Wendell Phillips was the commanding figure on the American lecture platform. Not only was he a spectacular success on the Lyceum circuit, but during the critical years surrounding the Civil War, his reputation as a critic of public policy was so great that each of his major addresses became a national event widely reported by the Boston and New York press and copied in papers throughout the northern and western states. Chauncey Depew, who lived to be ninety and claimed to have heard all the great speakers including Webster and Clay, declared that Phillips was "the greatest of all American orators." Thomas Wentworth Higginson placed Phillips and Webster together as the two most powerful orators in the post-revolutionary period, while Bronson Alcott said that Phillips' speeches "in range of thought, cleverness of statement, keen satire, brilliant wit, personal anecdote, wholesome moral sentiments, patriotism and Puritan spirit" were "unmatched by any of the great orators of the day." A critical piece in the *New Englander* in 1850 may be considered typical of the way in which a performance by Phillips was reviewed. Taking pains to disassociate himself from the speaker's radical doctrines, the writer went on to say that he was a "more instructive and more interesting speaker" than Clay, Webster, Choate, Adams, or Benton. Nor was Phillips' power entirely lost on the generation which grew up after his death in 1884, for as late as 1927 Senator William E. Borah, one of the few great American orators of this century, confessed to the habit of reading one of Phillips' speeches every three weeks or so to keep the famous radical's "style" fresh in his mind.

What sets Phillips off from the other lecturers within the Garrisonian camp, such colorful individuals as Parker Pillsbury and Stephen and Abby Kelly Foster, is that Phillips alone was consistently recognized as great even by those who detested his ideas. After hearing him declare in what was perhaps an unconscious parody of Webster's famous words, that he hoped to witness before he died "the convulsion of a sundering Union and a dissolving church," a New York reporter remarked that Phillips' sentiments "however repugnant to general opinion were expressed with a clear and lofty eloquence and extraordinary felicity and beauty of illustration." In Boston, where Phillips was loved and hated the most, a writer for the *Courier* made the same point in plain language. "It is a dish of tripe and onions served on silver," he wrote, "or black-strap presented in a goblet of Bohemian glass... Mr. Phillips thinks like a Billingsgate fishwoman, or a low pothouse bully, but he speaks like Cicero."

The sources of Phillips' power on the platform were deceptive. Those seeing him for the first time were invariably surprised to discover that he was not an orator in the grand manner. Shortly before the Civil War an Andover student, hearing that Phillips was to lecture in Boston, made a twenty-two-mile pilgrimage on foot to hear him. At first the trip seemed hardly worthwhile, for Phillips stood on the platform, one hand lightly resting on a table, talked for what seemed about twenty minutes and suddenly sat down. When the astonished young man consulted his watch he found that he had been listening for an hour and a half.

There was, as the Andover student discovered, nothing ponderous about Phillips as a speaker, no bombast, no flights of empty rhetoric. He spoke almost conversationally; his appearance was invariably one of calm poise, and he relied little on the kind of theatrics that led Henry Ward Beecher to auction off a slave girl from the pulpit. "The most prolonged applause could not disturb a muscle in his countenance," one listener remembered, "and a storm of hisses seemed to have as little effect on him." His customary serenity enhanced the effect of those few occasions when

Phillips did make some spectacular gesture, as for example, when after mentioning the name of the fugitive slave commissioner George Ticknor Curtis, he would rinse his mouth out with water and spit it on the floor.

Webster with his bull-like body and cavernous, smoldering eyes could overpower an audience with sheer physical magnetism. Phillips did not have this power. He was a man of average height, rather slightly built, with finely drawn features which most easily lent themselves to expressions of scorn and resolution. What everyone did notice about him was his aristocratic bearing. An Englishman visiting Boston saw Phillips and Edmund Quincy walking together down Park Street and remarked that they were the only men he had seen in this country "who looked like Gentlemen." As a matter of fact, Phillips came as close to being a native-born aristocrat as any American could. And his assurance on the platform was undoubtedly related to the fact that he did not have to make a name for himself. He had a way of treating his opponents as if they were socially beneath him as well as morally loathsome. Because of this he was nearly immune to criticism, and absolutely invulnerable to a heckling audience. He would never lose his temper, but would reply to his critics in a tone so witheringly contemptuous that it was like a blast of air from an iceberg. Neither rotten eggs nor brickbats could startle him, and hissing so consistently aroused him to his best effort that his admirers sometimes sat in a back row and hissed merely to make him warm to the subject.

By far the most sensational characteristic of Phillips as a speaker was the contrast between his perfectly controlled, poised, almost dispassionate manner, and the inflammatory language he employed. It was the apparent effortlessness of his delivery that impressed many listeners most. "Staples said the other day that he heard Phillips speak at the State House," wrote Thoreau in his *Journal*. "By thunder! he never heard a man that could speak like him. His words come so easy. It was just like picking up chips." In an effort to explain how the speaker remained somehow detached from his own eloquence, another observer compared him to "a cold but mysteriously animated statue of marble." Time and time again when Phillips was on tour, talking before new audiences, the reporter would register the audience's surprise. "They had conceived him to be a ferocious ranter and blustering man of words. They found him to be a quiet, dignified and polished gentleman and scholar, calm and logical in his argument."

One of the reasons why abolitionist meetings in the middle and later 1850's began to draw impressively large crowds, as the critics of the abolitionists pointed out, was that for many people an antislavery meeting had all the elements of a theatrical performance. The star performer was usually Wendell Phillips, and his stock in trade, according to the unconverted, was "personal abuse." To the abolitionists themselves he was, as his publisher remarked, the greatest "master of invective" in the nineteenth century. With sublime confidence, almost as if he were reading from a sheaf of statistics or reciting a series of scientific facts, Phillips would take the platform to announce that Daniel Webster was "a great mass of dough," Edward Everett "a whining spaniel," Massachusetts Senator Robert C. Winthrop "a bastard who had stolen the name of Winthrop," and the New England churches an ecclesiastical machine to manufacture hypocrisy "just as really as Lowell manufactures cotton." It was the way Phillips uttered his epithets that fascinated most critics. The shrewd Scottish traveler David Macrae who had been led "from the ferocity of his onslaughts on public men and public measures... to form a false conception of his delivery" noted with surprise that vehemence and declamation were replaced by sarcasm, "cold, keen, withering." Macrae was impressed by the relentless manner in which Phillips pursued his opponents. "He follows an enemy like an Indian upon the trail.... When he comes to strike, his strokes are like galvanic shocks; there is neither noise nor flash but their force is terrible."

A writer for an English paper who was contrasting Phillips' speeches with "the rounded periods of Mr. Seward" and "the finished artistic rhetoric of the patriotic Mr. Everett" noted one quality which grated on European ears, and that was "the concentrated bitterness, the intense spirit of hatred with which they are frequently suffused." Because Phillips did not like to talk in general terms about issues, because he always took dead aim on personalities and heaped "the concentrated bitterness" of his rhetoric upon the heads of men prominent in public life, and because the people turned out in droves to hear him, Robert C. Winthrop believed that Phillips had "gradually educated our people to relish nothing but the 'eloquence of abuse.'"

A good many later critics have been much harsher than Winthrop in criticizing Phillips. Theodore Roosevelt called him a wild-eyed fanatic and Professor [James G.] Randall has dismissed his speeches as "a kind of grandiloquent, self-righteous raving." A careful reading of his career shows these estimates to be incorrect. What distinguishes Phillips from the other abolitionists more significantly than anything else is that he was an intellectual, a philosopher of reform as well as a practical agitator. It is impossible to understand him, therefore, without knowing more about his political ideas and his conception of the role of the reformer in America.

Like other abolitionists Phillips believed in the Higher Law and judged every public question from an absolute moral standard. He believed that a man's first duty was to God, and that men should do their duty at whatever cost. He was convinced that anything right in principle had to be right in practice. He accepted Garrison's demand for immediate emancipation without question. Phillips' Calvinism, his belief in Divine Providence, made it possible for him to dismiss whatever doubts he might have had about the practicality of this radical solution. "No matter if the charter of emancipation was written in blood," he said in one of his early speeches, "and anarchy stalk abroad with giant strides—if God commanded, it was right." Phillips' Calvinism reinforced his radicalism. He did not have to worry about the consequences of his agitation. A man could only do his duty and let God do the rest.

As the most eloquent and intellectual of all the radicals, Phillips was called upon to defend the position that abolitionists should not support a constitution or government which supported slavery. Although the refusal of the radical abolitionists to vote or hold office, and their continued agitation to get the North to secede from the union seemed incomprehensible to most people, the position was perfectly consistent with

Phillips' principles. Slavery was evil and this evil was supported by a Federal government which protected slave states from insurrection, undertook to return their fugitives and gave them special representation in Congress. Therefore anything voluntarily done in support of this government (i.e. taking an oath to support the Constitution or voting for a candidate who would be required to take such an oath), supported slavery also and was evil.

Despite the fact that his position was condemned in the public mind from the beginning, Phillips, through pamphlets and lectures, did as much as anyone could do to persuade people of its worth. He never once doubted its soundness. When friends like Charles Sumner argued that the course he advocated would impede the struggle for emancipation, he replied that "honesty and truth are more important than even freeing slaves." When Sumner asked how he could consistently pay taxes or even remain in the country, he reminded him that a man's choices were always limited by the social and historical situation in which God placed him. A man had to live in the world, but he did not have to collaborate with the devil, which is what Sumner and all other "loyal citizens" were doing. "To live where God sent you and protest against your neighbor—this is certainly different from *joining him* in sinning, which the office holder of this country does."

Phillips' moralism supplied the ballast for his career. His solutions to difficult problems were both "right" and simple. When he continued to badger the government long after Garrison and other abolitionists had retired from the field after the war, it was because he sought *"justice —absolute, immediate, unmixed justice* to the negro." He did not, however, live by shibboleths alone, and his tactics as a reformer were based on a surprisingly sophisticated conception of American politics and society.

Phillips recognized that slavery was a threat to the freedom of all Americans. This conviction developed gradually out of his early experiences. He had the grisly reminiscences of the Grimké sisters to remind him of the evils of slavery in the south—the whippings and mutilations, the ruthless separation of husband and wife, of parent and child. Closer to his personal experience was what slavery had done to supposedly free American citizens. It had jailed Prudence Crandall for opening a school for Negro girls. It had publicly whipped Amos Dresser for daring to distribute antislavery literature. It had tried to gag John Quincy Adams in Congress, had mobbed Garrison within the shadow of Faneuil Hall, and had finally killed Lovejoy. The pattern seemed always to be the same; principle was overcome by power. For the first time Phillips sensed the demonic possibilities of a slave power supported by public opinion in America.

A lawyer, bred in all the technical reliance on the safeguards of Saxon liberty, I was puzzled, rather than astounded, by the fact that, outside of the law and wholly unrecognized in the theory of our institutions, was a mob power—an abnormal element which nobody had counted in, in the analysis of the system, and for whose irregular actions no check, no balance, had been provided. The gun which was aimed at the breast of Lovejoy on the banks of the Mississippi brought me to my feet conscious that I stood in the presence of a power whose motto was victory or death.

Having recognized the importance of public opinion in America Phillips began to examine American institutions more closely. He distinguished a fundamental tension between the American ideal, a society based on the rights of man, and an American political system based on numbers. "The majority rules, and law rests on numbers, not on intellect or virtue," thus "while theoretically holding that no vote of the majority can authorize injustice, we practically consider public opinion the real test of what is true and what is false; and hence, as a result, the fact which Tocqueville has noticed, that practically our institutions protect, not the interest of the whole community but the interests of the majority."

Phillips was acute enough to see that while the tyranny of the majority might occasionally express itself violently, as in the lynching of Lovejoy, a more common and insidious threat to liberty came through the intimidation of citizens holding unpopular ideas. "Entire equality and freedom in political forms" naturally tended to "make the individual subside into the mass, and lose his identity in the general whole." In an aristocratic society like England a man could afford to "despise the judgment" of most people so long as he kept the good opinion of those in his own class. In America there was no refuge. Every citizen "in his ambition, his social life, or his business" depended on the approbation and the votes of those around him. Consequently, Phillips said, "instead of being a mass of individuals, each one fearlessly blurting out his own convictions,—as a nation, compared with other nations, we are a mass of cowards. More than any other people, we are afraid of each other."

Although Phillips knew that in some nations public opinion was shaped by political leaders, he could find nothing to show that this was true in the American experience. Theoretically every American male citizen was supposed to be eligible for office, but in practice, "with a race like ours, fired with the love of material wealth," the best brains were drawn into commerce. As a result politics took up with small men, "men without grasp enough for large business ... men popular because they have no positive opinions." Even if an occasional man of the first rank (a Charles Sumner for example), did emerge in politics, he would be lost to the reformer because the whole art of politics in America was based on the ability to compromise. "The politician must conceal half his principles to carry forward the other half," Phillips said, "must regard, not rigid principle and strict right, but only such a degree of right as will allow him at the same time to secure *numbers.*"

These considerations led Phillips to conclude that the reformer in America had to confront the people directly. "Our aim," he said in his lecture *The Philosophy of Abolitionism*, "is to alter public opinion." Slavery endured and abolitionists were mobbed because a majority of Americans refused to face the moral issues involved. Phillips was too much of a realist to believe that he could suddenly convert the nation, but he did feel that he could force the issue and change the public attitude toward slavery.

Phillips knew that most people in the North disliked slavery, but he also knew that it was to their self-interest to leave it alone. To stir up controversy was dangerous: no one wanted to be known as a troublemaker; mill owners were concerned for their capital; mill hands were concerned for their jobs; the respectable middle class was concerned for its reputation. The easy thing for everyone was to turn away from the problem. The abolitionist's job was to scatter thorns on the easy road by dramatizing the moral issue and insisting that every man who did not throw his whole influence into the scales against slavery was as guilty as the slaveholder. "We will gibbet the name of every apostate so black and high," Phillips warned, "that his children's children shall blush to hear it. Yet we bear no malice—cherish no resentment. We thank God that the love of fame is shared by the ignoble."

What this could mean in practice is perhaps best seen in Phillips' criticism of Henry Gardner, a Boston politician who was the leader of Know-Nothingism in Massachusetts and Governor of the Commonwealth from 1855 to 1858. Gardner usually made a few antislavery sounds during election campaigns, but his great appeal was to nativism, and it was he who had blocked Phillips' attempt to get Judge Edward Loring recalled after the rendition of Anthony Burns. Phillips believed that Gardner dabbled in antislavery politics for personal gain and frustrated the abolitionists' effort to educate the public. He called the Governor "a consummate hypocrite, a man who if he did not have some dozen and distinct reasons for telling the truth would naturally tell a lie." On another occasion he said, "Our course is a perfect copy of Sisyphus. We always toil up, up, up the hill until we touch the soiled sandals of some Governor Gardner, and then the rock rolls down again. Always some miserable reptile that has struggled into power in the corruption of parties—reptiles who creep where *man* disdains to climb; some slight thing of no consequence till its foul mess

blocks our path; and dashes our hopes at the last minute."

The denunciation could hardly have been more savage. Phillips insisted, however, that there was nothing personal in it.

Do not say I am personal in speaking thus of Governor Gardner.... Do not blame me when I speak thus of Henry J. Gardner. What is the duty of the minority... what is the duty of a minority in this country? A minority has no right to rebel... the majority have said the thing shall be so. It is not to resist, it is to convert. And how shall we convert? If the community is in love with some monster, we must paint him truly. The duty of a minority being to convert, every tool which the human mind knows, it is their right and duty to use; a searching criticism, pitiless sarcasm, bitter invective, rigid analysis of motives, constant recurrence to the admitted facts of a man's career,—these are our rights, if our function is to save the people from delusion.

Phillips was not a fanatic. He used the most violent language dispassionately as a surgeon uses the sharpest steel. He could not actually cut away the diseased tissue with his rhetoric, but he could expose it. Thus when he called Lincoln a "slave hound" he was reminding his listeners and readers that as a Congressman Lincoln had supported a bill which would have enforced the return of fugitive slaves escaping into the District of Columbia. This was the man who expected to get the antislavery vote. Phillips' intention in attacking Lincoln so savagely was simply to dramatize the rottenness of the American conscience by showing that only a "slave hound" could be elected President. His reply to those who accused him of extravagance and distortion was that "there are far more dead hearts to be quickened, than confused intellects to be cleared up—more dumb dogs to be made to speak than doubting consciences to be enlightened. We have use, then, for something beside argument."

The easiest way to treat nettlesome reformers like the abolitionists is to dismiss them as cranks. Nothing irritated Phillips more than the attempts of his opponents to thrust him outside the mainstream of American life. The antislavery agitation, he insisted, was "an essential part of the machinery of the state... not a disease nor a medicine... the normal state of the nation."

The preceding statement takes us to the heart of Phillips' philosophy of reform. He recognized that American ideals could ultimately be translated into practice only through politics. At the same time he knew that the American politician's ability to gain and hold power was largely determined by his ability to effect compromises that appealed to numbers rather than to principle. He added to these corruptive tendencies the fact that people in a democracy always tend to have as high an opinion of themselves as possible—always tremble on the edge of national idolatry. The result, Phillips argued, was that "every government is always growing corrupt. Every Secretary of State is by the very necessity of his position an apostate." A democratic society that trusted to constitutions and political machinery to secure its liberties never would have any. "The people must be waked to a new effort," he said, "just as the church has to be regenerated in each age." In the middle of the nineteenth century the abolitionist was the agency of national regeneration, but even after he had vanished his function in the American system would still remain.

> Eternal vigilance is the price of liberty: power is ever stealing from the many to the few. The manna of popular liberty must be gathered each day, or it is rotten.... The hand entrusted with power becomes, either from human depravity or *esprit de corps*, the necessary enemy of the people. Only by continual oversight can the democrat in office be prevented from hardening into a despot: only by unintermitted agitation can a people be kept sufficiently awake to principle not to let liberty be smothered in material prosperity. All clouds, it is said, have sunshine behind them, and all evils have some good result; so slavery, by the necessity of its abolition, has saved the freedom of the white race from being melted in luxury or buried beneath the gold of its own success. Never look, therefore, for an age when the people can be quiet and safe. At such times despotism, like a shrouding mist, steals over the mirror of Freedom.

It should be clear now that Phillips believed the radical abolitionist to be justified as much by his radicalism as by his abolitionism. Phillips preferred the word agitator to radical, and since he himself was frequently accused of demagoguery, he took pains to point out the difference between the demagogue and agitator. A demagogue (he used Robespierre as an example), "rides the storm; he has never really the ability to create one. He uses it narrowly, ignorantly, and for selfish ends. If not crushed by the force which, without his will, has flung him into power, he leads it with ridiculous miscalculation against some insurmountable obstacle that scatters it forever. Dying, he leaves no mark on the elements with which he has been mixed." Quoting Sir Robert

Peel, Phillips defined agitation as "the marshalling of the conscience of a nation to mould its laws." Daniel O'Connell who, after thirty years of "patient and sagacious labor," succeeded in creating a public opinion and unity of purpose to free Ireland from British tyranny was one of Phillips' models as a successful agitator.

It was because Phillips thought of himself primarily as an agitator and Garrison thought of himself primarily as an abolitionist that the two came to a parting of the ways in 1865. With the war over and slavery prohibited by the passage of the thirteenth amendment, Garrison felt that the "covenant with death" had been annulled. The American nation had become "successor to the abolitionists," and the American Anti-Slavery Society had lost its excuse for being. Phillips did not agree. He argued that the nation needed "the constant, incessant discriminating criticism of the abolitionists as much as ever." The debate grew rancorous and resulted in Garrison's quitting the Society. Phillips was elected President in his place, and for the next five years continued to agitate as fiercely for Negro suffrage as he had for emancipation. Only after the fifteenth amendment was passed did he allow the organization to be dissolved.

Even then Phillips did not relax his efforts. He denounced the decision to remove Federal troops from the South as vehemently as he had the Fugitive Slave Law, and predicted that a " 'solid south'—the slave power under a new name" would soon control national politics. Most of the other surviving abolitionists had long since gone over to the Republican party lock, stock, and barrel, but Phillips saw through the moral pretensions of the Republicans as clearly as anyone in the country. They had waved the bloody flag with regularity, but had been unwilling to make the sacrifices and the long-term commitments in reconstruction that were necessary if the moral legacy of the war was not to be squandered away. Accusing the Republicans of "a heartless and merciless calculation" to exploit war memories and Ku Klux Klan atrocities for party purposes, Phillips claimed that no party in history had ever "fallen from such a height to such a depth of disgrace."

The rhetoric was the same but the response was not. The people had grown tired of the war, and newspapers that would have praised him in the sixties now wrote about "Mr. Phillips' Last Frenzy" and called him "the apostle of unforgiving and relentless hate."

Meanwhile, even as he decried the growing popularity of the illusion that the Negro might be safe in the hands of his old master, Phillips turned his attention to the struggle of free labor in the North. "While this delusion of peace without purity persists," he was saying in 1878, "labor claims every ear and every hand." And so, in the declining years of his life, Wendell Phillips, true to his belief that agitation was "an essential part of the machinery of the state," poured his whole influence into the struggle for social justice in an industrial society. His solutions were still simple—passage of an eight-hour law—the unlimited issuance of Greenbacks. His tactics were the same. "The only way to accomplish our object," he said, "is to shame greedy men into humanity. Poison their wealth with the tears and curses of widows and orphans. In speaking of them call things by their right names. Let men shrink from them as from slave dealers and pirates." And the response was the same he had received during the hard, bitter years before the war. If anything Phillips was even more of an outsider now than he had been then. His support of unions, the right to strike, shorter hours of work, a graduated income tax, and his derision of laissez-faire ("the bubble and chaff of 'supply and demand'") offended even the old abolitionists. If Phillips had acted "with ordinary common sense and good temper when slavery was abolished and had gone into politics," Edmund Quincy thought, "he might have been the next Senator ... but he is 'played out' as we say, and will be merely a popular lecturer and a small demagogue for the rest of his life."

Quincy was a retired reformer. Like most of his contemporaries and most of the American historians who have followed, he could not appreciate Wendell Phillips, a gentleman who understood the difference between agitation and demagoguery, and knew that the radical in America could never retire.

POSTSCRIPT

Were the Abolitionists "Unrestrained Fanatics"?

One of the weaknesses of most studies of abolitionism, which is reflected in both of the preceding essays, is that they are generally written from a monochromatic perspective. In other words, historians typically discuss whites within the abolitionist crusade and give little, if any, attention to the roles blacks played in the movement. Whites are portrayed as the active agents of reform while blacks are the passive recipients of humanitarian efforts to eliminate the scourge of slavery. Students should be aware that African Americans, slave and free, also rebelled against the institution of slavery both directly and indirectly.

Benjamin Quarles, in *Black Abolitionists* (Oxford University Press, 1969) describes a wide range of roles played by African Americans in the abolitionist movement. For example, as Garrison's *Liberator* struggled to survive in the early months of 1831, African American subscribers in the North kept the paper afloat. In addition, African Americans organized themselves into local antislavery societies, became members of national abolitionist organizations (particularly the American Anti-Slavery Society and the American and Foreign Anti-Slavery Society), contributed funds to the operations of these societies, made black churches available for abolitionist meetings, and promoted abolitionism through pamphlet-writing and speaking engagements. Between 1830 and 1835 the Negro Convention Movement sponsored annual meetings of African Americans in which protests against slavery were a central feature.

Studies that discuss the role of black abolitionists in the antislavery movement include Ronald K. Burke, *Samuel Ringgold Ward: Christian Abolitionist* (Garland, 1995); and Nell Irvin Painter, *Sojourner Truth: A Life, A Symbol* (W. W. Norton, 1997).

For general discussions of the abolitionist movement, see Gerald Sorin, *Abolitionism: A New Perspective* (Praeger, 1972); Lewis Perry, *Radical Abolitionism: Anarchy and the Government of God in Antislavery Thought* (Cornell University Press, 1973); Merton L. Dillon, *The Abolitionists: The Growth of a Dissenting Minority* (Northern Illinois Press, 1974); James Brewer Stewart, *Holy Warriors: The Abolitionists and American Slavery* (Hill and Wang, 1976); Ronald G. Walters, *The Antislavery Appeal: American Abolitionism After 1830* (Johns Hopkins University Press, 1978); Lawrence J. Friedman, *Gregarious Saints: Self and Community in American Abolitionism, 1830–1870* (Cambridge University Press, 1982); and Stanley Harrold, *The Abolitionists in the South, 1831–1861* (University Press of Kentucky, 1995).

ISSUE 10

Did Slaves Exercise Religious Autonomy?

YES: Albert J. Raboteau, from "Slave Autonomy and Religion," *Journal of Religious Thought* (Fall 1981/Winter 1982)

NO: John B. Boles, from "Introduction," in John B. Boles, ed., *Masters and Slaves in the House of the Lord: Race and Religion in the American South, 1740–1870* (University Press of Kentucky, 1988)

ISSUE SUMMARY

YES: Professor of history Albert J. Raboteau argues that the religious activities of American slaves were characterized by institutional and personal independence, which undermined the ability of the masters to exercise effective control over their chattel property.

NO: Professor of history John B. Boles recognizes that slaves often worshiped apart from their masters, but he asserts that the primary religious experience of Southern slaves occurred within a biracial setting in churches dominated by whites.

Since the mid-1950s, few issues in American history have generated more interest among scholars than the institution of slavery. Books and articles analyzing the treatment of slaves, comparative slave systems, the profitability of slavery, slave rebelliousness (or lack thereof), urban slavery, the slave family, and slave religion abound. This proliferation of scholarship, stimulated in part by the civil rights movement, contrasts sharply with the amount of historical literature written on slavery between the two world wars, a time that was monopolized by a single book—Ulrich B. Phillips's apologetic and blatantly racist *American Negro Slavery* (1918).

Phillips, a native Georgian who taught for most of his career at Yale University, based his sweeping view of the southern slave system upon plantation records left by some of the wealthiest slave owners. He concluded that American slavery was a benign institution controlled by paternalistic masters. These owners, Phillips insisted, rarely treated their bond servants cruelly but, instead, provided their childlike, acquiescent human property with food, clothing, housing, and other necessities of life.

Although black historians such as George Washington Williams, W. E. B. Du Bois, Carter G. Woodson, and John Hope Franklin produced scholarly works that emphasized the brutal impact of slavery, their views received almost no consideration from the wider academic community. Consequently, recognition of a "revisionist" interpretation of slavery was delayed until the post–World War II era when, in the wake of the *Brown* desegregation case, Kenneth Stampp, a white northern historian, published *The Peculiar Institution* (1956). Stampp also focused primarily upon antebellum plantation records, but his conclusions were literally a point-by-point rebuttal of the Phillips thesis. The institution of slavery, he said, was a harsh, oppressive system in which slave owners controlled their servants through fear of the lash. Further, in contrast to the image of the passive, happy-go-lucky "Sambo" described by Phillips, Stampp argued that slaves were "a troublesome property" who resisted their enslavement in subtle as well as overt ways.

In 1959 Stanley Elkins synthesized these seemingly contradictory interpretations in his controversial study *Slavery: A Problem in American Institutional and Intellectual Life.* Elkins clearly accepted Stampp's emphasis on the harshness of the slave system by hypothesizing that slavery was a "closed" system in which masters dominated their slaves in the same way that Nazi concentration camp guards in World War II had controlled the lives of their prisoners. Such an environment, he insisted, generated severe psychological dysfunctions that produced the personality traits of Phillips's "Sambo" character type.

As the debate over the nature of slavery moved into the 1960s and 1970s, several scholars, seeking to provide a history of the institution "from the bottom up," began to focus upon the slaves themselves. Interviews with former slaves had been conducted in the 1920s and 1930s under the auspices of Southern University in Louisiana, Fisk University in Tennessee, and the Federal Writers Project of the Works Progress Administration. Drawing upon these interviews and previously ignored slave autobiographies, sociologist George Rawick and historians John Blassingame and Eugene D. Genovese, among others, portrayed a multifaceted community life over which slaves held a significant degree of influence. This community, which operated beyond the view of the "Big House," was, according to Genovese, "the world the slaves made."

These contrasting interpretive currents are reflected in the following essays on the nature of slave religion. In the first selection, Albert J. Raboteau describes the ways in which the acceptance of Christianity produced numerous opportunities for slaves to assume control over their own religious activities, which led to an autonomy that permitted slaves to resist some of the dehumanizing elements of the slave system. John B. Boles admits that slaves in the antebellum South worshiped in a variety of ways (in independent black churches, plantation chapels, or informal, secret gatherings), but he concludes that the typical site for slave religious activities was the church of their masters.

YES

Albert J. Raboteau

SLAVE AUTONOMY AND RELIGION

One of the perennial questions in the historical study of American slavery is the question of the relationship between Christianity and the response of slaves to enslavement. Did the Christian religion serve as a tool in the hands of slaveholders to make slaves docile or did it serve in the hands of slaves as a weapon of resistance and even outright rebellion against the system of slavery? Let us acknowledge from the outset that the role of religion in human motivation and action is very complex; let us recognize also that Christianity played an ambiguous role in the stances which slaves took toward slavery, sometimes supporting resistance, sometimes accommodation. That much admitted, much more remains to be said. Specifically, we need to trace the convoluted ways in which the egalitarian impulse within Christianity overflowed the boundaries of the master-slave hierarchy, creating unexpected channels of slave autonomy on institutional as well as personal levels. To briefly sketch out some of the directions which religious autonomy took among slaves in the antebellum South is the purpose of this essay.

INSTITUTIONAL AUTONOMY

From the beginning of the Atlantic slave trade in the fifteenth century, European Christians claimed that the conversion of slaves to Christianity justified the enslavement of Africans. For more than four centuries Christian apologists for slavery would repeat this religious rationalization for one of history's greatest atrocities. Despite the justification of slavery as a method of spreading the gospel, the conversion of slaves was not a top priority for colonial planters. One of the principal reasons for the refusal of British colonists to allow their slaves religious instruction was the fear that baptism would require the manumission of their slaves, since it was illegal to hold a fellow Christian in bondage. This dilemma was solved quickly by colonial legislation stating that baptism did not alter slave status. However, the most serious obstacle to religious instruction of the slaves could not be legislated away. It was the slaveholder's deep-seated uneasiness at the prospect of a slave laying claim to Christian fellowship with his master. The concept of equality, though only

Excerpted from Albert J. Raboteau, "Slave Autonomy and Religion," *Journal of Religious Thought*, vol. 38 (Fall 1981/Winter 1982), pp. 51–64. Copyright © 1981 by *Journal of Religious Thought*. Reprinted by permission. Notes omitted.

spiritual, between master and slave threatened the stability of the system of slave control. Christianity, complained the masters, would ruin slaves by allowing them to think themselves equal to white Christians. Far worse was the fear, supported by the behavior of some Christian slaves, that religion would make them rebellious. In order to allay this fear, would-be missionaries to the slaves had to prove that Christianity would make better slaves. By arguing that Christian slaves would become obedient to their masters out of duty to God and by stressing the distinction between spiritual equality and worldly equality, the proponents of slave conversion in effect built a religious foundation to support slavery. Wary slaveholders were assured by missionaries that "Scripture, far from making an Alteration in Civil Rights, expressly directs, *that every Man abide in the Condition wherein he is called, with great Indifference of Mind* concerning outward circumstances."

In spite of missionary efforts to convince them that Christianity was no threat to the slave system, slaveowners from the colonial period on down to the Civil War remained suspicious of slave religion as a two-edged sword. Clerical assurances aside, the masters' concern was valid. Religious instruction for slaves had more than spiritual implications. No event would reveal these implications as clearly as the series of religious revivals called the Great Awakenings which preceded and followed the Revolution. The impact of revival fervor would demonstrate how difficult it was to control the egalitarian impulse of Christianity within safe channels.

The first Great Awakening of the 1740s swept the colonies with the tumultuous preaching and emotional conversions of revivalistic, evangelical Protestantism. Accounts by Whitefield, Tennent, Edwards, and other revivalists made special mention of the fact that blacks were flocking to hear the message of salvation in hitherto unseen numbers. Not only were free blacks and slaves attending revivals in significant numbers, they were taking active part in the services as exhorters and preachers. The same pattern of black activism was repeated in the rural camp meetings of the Great Awakening of the early nineteenth century.

The increase in slave conversions which accompanied the awakenings was due to several factors. The evangelical religion spread by the revivalists initiated a religious renaissance in the South where the majority of slaves lived. The revival became a means of church extension, especially for Methodists and Baptists. The mobility of the Methodist circuit rider and the local independence of the Baptist preacher were suited to the needs of the rural South. Among the Southerners swelling the ranks of these denominations, were black as well as white converts.

Moreover, the ethos of the revival meeting, with its strong emphasis upon emotional preaching and congregational response, not only permitted ecstatic religious behavior but encouraged it. Religious exercises, as they were termed, including fainting, jerking, barking, and laughing a "holy laugh," were a common, if spectacular, feature of revivals. In this heated atmosphere slaves found sanction for an outward expression of religious emotion consonant with their tradition of danced religion from Africa. While converting to belief in a "new" God, slaves were able to worship in ways hauntingly similar to those of old.

Extremely important for the development of black participation in revival religion was the intense concentration upon individual inward conversion which fostered an inclusiveness that could become egalitarianism. Evangelicals did not hesitate to preach to racially mixed congregations and had no doubt about the capacity of slaves to share the experience of conversion to Christ. Stressing plain doctrine and emotional preaching, emphasizing the conversion experience instead of religious instruction, made Christianity accessible to illiterate slave and slaveholder alike. The criterion for preachers was not seminary training but evidence of a converted heart and gifted tongue. Therefore, when an awakened slave showed talent for preaching, he preached, and not only to black congregations. The tendency of evangelical Protestantism to level the souls of all men before God reached its logical conclusion when blacks preached to and converted whites.

By the last quarter of the eighteenth century a cadre of black preachers had begun to emerge. Some of these pioneer black ministers were licensed, some not; some were slaves, others free. During the 1780s a black man named Lewis preached to crowds as large as four hundred in Westmoreland County, Virginia. Harry Hosier traveled with Methodist leaders, Asbury, Coke, Garretson, and Whatcoat and was reportedly such an eloquent preacher that he served as a "drawing card" to attract larger crowds of potential converts, white and black. In 1792 the mixed congregation of the Portsmouth, Virginia Baptist Church selected a slave, Josiah Bishop, as pastor, after purchasing his freedom and also his family's. Another black preacher, William Lemon, pastored a white Baptist church in Gloucester County, Virginia, for a time at the turn of the century.

In 1798, Joseph Willis, a freeman, duly licensed as a Baptist preacher, began his ministry in southwest Mississippi and Louisiana. He formed Louisiana's first Baptist church at Bayou Chicot in 1812 and served as its pastor. After developing several other churches in the area, he became the first moderator of the Louisiana Baptist Association in 1818. Uncle Jack, an African-born slave, joined the Baptist church and in 1792 began to preach in Nottoway County, Virginia. White church members purchased his freedom and he continued to preach for over forty years. Henry Evans, a free black licensed as a local preacher by the Methodists, was the first to bring Methodist preaching to Fayetteville, North Carolina. Initially preaching to black people only, he attracted the attention of several prominent whites and eventually the white membership of his congregation increased until the blacks were crowded out of their seats. Evans was eventually replaced by a white minister, but continued to serve as an assistant in the church he had founded until his death.

That black preachers should exhort, convert, and even pastor white Christians in the slave South was certainly antithetical to the premise of slave control. Though such occasions were rare, they were the ineluctable result of the impulse unleashed by revivalistic religion. Of greater importance for the development of autonomy in the religious life of slaves was the fact that black preachers, despite threats of punishment, continued to preach to slaves and in some few cases even founded churches.

An early historian of the Baptists applauded the anonymous but effective ministry of these black preachers:

> Among the African Baptists in the Southern states there are a multitude of preachers and exhorters whose names do not appear on the minutes of the associations. They preach principally on the plantations to those of their own color, and their preaching though broken and illiterate, is in many cases highly useful.

Several "African" Baptist churches sprang up before 1800. Some of these black congregations were independent to the extent that they called their own pastors and officers, joined local associations with white Baptist churches, and sent their own delegates to associational meetings. Though the separate black church was primarily an urban phenomenon, it drew upon surrounding rural areas for its membership, which consisted of both free blacks and slaves. Sometimes these black churches were founded amidst persecution. Such was the case with the African Baptist Church of Williamsburg, Virginia, whose history was chronicled in 1810:

> This church is composed almost, if not altogether of people of colour. Moses, a black man, first preached among them, and was often taken up and whipped, for holding meetings. Afterwards Gowan Pamphlet... became popular among the blacks, and began to baptize, as well as to preach. It seems, the association had advised that no person of colour should be allowed to preach, on the pain of excommunication; against this regulation, many of the blacks were rebellious, and continued still to hold meetings. Some were excluded, and among this number was Gowan.... Continuing still to preach and many professing faith under his ministry, not being in connexion with any church himself, he formed a kind of church out of some who had been baptized, who, sitting with him, received such as offered themselves; Gowan baptized them, and was moreover appointed their pastor; some of them knowing how to write, a churchbook was kept; they increased to a large number; so that in the year 1791, the Dover association, stat[ed] their number to be about five hundred. The association received them, so far, as to appoint persons to visit them and set things in order. These making a favourable report, they were received, and have associated ever since.

Several features of this narrative deserve emphasis as significant examples of black religious autonomy. Ignoring the threat of excommunication, not to mention physical punishment, blacks rebelled against white religious control and insisted on holding their own meetings, led by their own ministers. They gathered their own church, apparently according to the norms of Baptist polity, accepted their own members, kept their own minutes, and finally succeeded in joining the local association, all the while growing to a membership of five hundred by 1791!

In Savannah, Georgia, a slave named Andrew Bryan established an African Baptist Church, against white objection and persecution. In 1790, Bryan's church included two hundred and twenty-five full communicants and approximately three hundred and fifty converts, many of whom did not have their masters' permission to be baptized. In 1803, a Second African Church of Savannah was organized from the first, and a few years later a third came into being. Both of the new churches were led by black pastors. After Bryan's death, his nephew, Andrew Marshall, became pastor of the

First African Church and by 1830 his congregation had increased in size to two thousand, four hundred and seventeen members.

The labors of these early black preachers and their successors were crucial in the formation of slave religion. In order to adequately understand the development of Christianity among the slaves, we must realize that slaves learned Christianity not only from whites but from other slaves as well. Slave preachers, exhorters, and church-appointed watchmen instructed their fellow slaves, nurtured their religious development, and brought them to conversion in some cases without the active involvement of white missionaries or masters at all. The early independence of black preachers and churches was curtailed as the antebellum period wore on, particularly in periods of reaction to slave conspiracies, when all gatherings of blacks for whatever purpose were viewed with alarm. For slaves to participate in the organization, leadership, and governance of church structures was perceived as dangerous. Surely it was inconsistent, argued the guardians of the system, to allow blacks such authority. As the prominent South Carolinian planter, Charles Cotesworth Pinkney, declared before the Charleston Agricultural Society in 1829, the exercise of religious prerogatives left slaves too free from white control. "We look upon the habit of Negro preaching as a widespreading evil; not because a black man cannot be a good one, but . . . because they acquire an influence independent of the owner, and not subject to his control. . . . When they have possessed this power, they have been known to make an improper use of it." No doubt, Pinkney and his audience had in mind the African Methodist Church of Charleston which had served as a seedbed of rebellion for the Denmark Vesey conspiracy of 1822. (Following discovery of the plot, whites razed the church to the ground.)

Regardless of periodic harassment by civil and ecclesiastical authorities, black preachers continued to preach and separate black churches continued to be organized. Just as Pinkney and others warned, in preaching and in church life some blacks found channels for self-expression and self-governance. To be sure, the exercise of such autonomy was frequently modified by white supervision, but it was nonetheless real. In various sections of the antebellum South, black churches kept gathering members, over the years swelling in size to hundreds and in a few instances thousands of members. Certainly, the vast majority of slaves attended churches under white control. However, even in racially mixed churches some black Christians found opportunities to exercise their spiritual gifts and a measure of control over their religious life. This was so especially in Baptist churches because Baptist polity required that each congregation govern itself. In some churches committees of black members were constituted to oversee their own conduct. These committees listened to black applicants relate their religious experience and heard the replies of members charged with moral laxity. Meeting once a month, committees of "brethren in black" conducted business, reported their recommendations to the general meeting and gave to black church members experience in church governance. This experience laid a foundation upon which freedmen would rapidly build their own independent churches after emancipation.

Hampered though it was, the exercise of religious autonomy among slaves was a fact of antebellum life. It was due to the nature of the revival fervor of the Great Awakenings of the eighteenth and early nineteenth centuries which first brought the slaves to conversion in large numbers and also created a situation in which it became possible for black freemen and slaves to preach and even pastor. (By way of contrast, these avenues to spiritual authority would not open for blacks in either the Church of England or the Roman Catholic Church for a long time to come.) To the extent possible, then, black Christians proved not at all reluctant about deciding their own religious affairs and managing their own religious institutions. For the vast majority of slaves, however, institutional religious autonomy was not possible. This did not stop them from seeking religious independence from whites in more secretive ways.

PERSONAL AUTONOMY

Like their colonial predecessors, antebellum missionaries to the slaves had to face objections from whites that religion for slaves was dangerous. Beginning in the 1820s, a movement led by prominent clerics and laymen attempted to mold southern opinion in support of missions to the slaves. Plantation missionaries created an ideal image of the Christian plantation, built upon the mutual observance of duties by masters and by slaves. One leader of the plantation mission stated the movement's basic premise when he predicted that "religious instruction of the Negroes will *promote our own morality and religion.*" For, when "one class rises, so will the other; the two are so associated they are apt to rise or fall together. Therefore, servants do well by your masters and masters do well by your servants."

In this premise lay a serious fallacy; for while the interests of master and slave occasionally coincided, they could never cohere. No matter how devoted master was to the ideal of a Christian plantation, no matter how pious he might be, the slave knew that the master's religion did not countenance the slaves' freedom in this world.

Precisely because the interests of master and slave extended only so far and no further, there was a dimension of the slaves' religious life that was secret. The disparity between the master's ideal of religion on the plantation and that of the slaves led the slaves to gather secretly in the quarters or in brush arbors (aptly named hush harbors) where they could pray, preach, and sing, free from white control. Risking severe punishment, slaves disobeyed their masters and stole off under cover of secrecy to worship as they saw fit. Here it was that Christianity was fitted to their own peculiar experience.

It was the slaveholding gospel preached to them by master's preacher which drove many slaves to seek true Christian preaching at their own meetings. "Church was what they called it," recalled former slave Charlie Van Dyke, "but all that preacher talked about was for us slaves to obey our masters and not to lie and steal." To attend secret meetings was in itself an act of resistance against the will of the master and was punished as such. In the face of the absolute authority of the Divine Master, the authority of the human master shrank. Slaves persisted in their hush harbor meetings because there they found consolation and communal support, tangible relief from the exhaustion and brutality of work stretching from "day clean" to after dark, day in and day out. "Us niggers," remarked Richard Carruthers, describing a scene still vivid in his memory many years later, "used to have a prayin' ground down in the hollow and sometimes we come out of the field... scorchin' and burnin' up with nothin' to eat, and we wants to ask the good Lawd to have mercy.... We takes a pine torch... and goes down in the hollow to pray. Some gits so joyous they starts to holler loud and we has to stop up they mouth. I see niggers git so full of the Lawd and so happy they draps unconscious."

In the hush harbor slaves sought not only substantive preaching and spiritual consolation they also talked about and prayed for an end to their physical bondage. "I've heard them pray for freedom," declared one former slave. "I thought it was foolishness then, but the old time folks always felt they was to be free. It must have been something 'vealed unto 'em. Though some might be skeptical, those slaves who were confident that freedom would come, since God had revealed it, were able to cast their lives in a different light. Hope for a brighter future irradiated the darkness of the present. Their desire for freedom in this world was reaffirmed in the songs, prayers, and sermons of the hush harbor. This was just what the master—those who didn't believe in prayer, as well as those who did —tried to prevent. The external hush harbor symbolized an internal resistance, a private place at the core of the slaves' religious life which they claimed as their own and which, in the midst of bondage, could not be controlled.

For evangelical Christians, black or white, full admission into membership in the church required that the candidate give credible testimony about the inner workings of the Spirit upon his or her heart. The conversion experience, as described by ex-slaves, was typically a visionary one, inaugurated by feelings of sadness and inner turmoil. Frequently the individual "convicted of sin" envisioned Hell and realized that he was destined for damnation. Suddenly, the sinner was rescued from this danger and led to a vision of Heaven by an emissary from God. Ushered into God's presence, the person learned that he was not damned but saved. Awakening, the convert realized that he was now one of the elect and overwhelmed with the joyful feeling of being "made new" shouted out his happiness. For years afterwards, this "peak" experience remained a fixed point of identity and value in the convert's life. He knew that he was saved, and he knew it not just theoretically but experientially. Confident of their election and their value in the eyes of God, slaves who underwent conversion, gained in this radical experience a deeply rooted identity which formed the basis for a sense of purpose and an affirmation of self-worth— valuable psychic barriers to the demeaning and dehumanizing attacks of slavery.

Conversion, as an experience common to white and black Christians, occasionally led to moments of genuine emotional contact, in which the etiquette of racial relationships was forgotten. A dramatic instance of one such occasion was recounted by a former slave named Morte:

One day while in the field plowing I heard a voice... I looked but saw no one... Everything got dark, and I was unable to stand any longer... With this I began to cry, Mercy! Mercy! Mercy! As I prayed an angel came and touched me, and I looked new... and there came a soft voice saying, "My little one, I have loved you with an everlasting love. You are this day made alive and freed from hell. You are a chosen vessel unto the Lord." ... I must have been in this trance more than an hour. I went on to the barn and found my master waiting for me. ... I began to tell him of my experiences ... My master sat watching and listening to me, and then he began to cry. He turned from me and said in a broken voice, "Morte I believe you are a preacher. From now on you can preach to the people here on my place ... But tomorrow morning, Sunday, I want to preach to my family and my neighbors." ... The next morning at the time appointed I stood up on two planks in front of the porch of the big house and, without a Bible or anything, I began to preach to my master and the people. My thoughts came so fast that I could hardly speak fast enough. My soul caught on fire, and soon I had them all in tears ... I told them that they must be born again and that their souls must be freed from the shackles of hell.

The spectacle of a slave reducing his master to tears by preaching to him of his enslavement to sin certainly suggests that religion could bend human relationships into interesting shapes despite the iron rule of slavery. Morte's power over his master was spiritual and (as far as we know) it was temporary. It was also effective.

While commonality of religious belief might lead to moments of religious reciprocity between blacks and whites, by far the more common relationship, from the slaves' side, was one of alienation from the hypocrisy of slaveholding Christians. As Frederick Douglass put it, "Slaves knew enough of the orthodox theology of the time to consign all bad slaveholders to hell." On the same point, Charles Ball commented that in his experience slaves thought that heaven would not be heaven unless slaves could be avenged on their enemies. "A fortunate and kind master or mistress, may now and then be admitted into heaven, but this rather as a matter of favour, to the intercession of some slave, than as a matter of strict justice to the whites, who will, by no means, be of an equal rank with those who shall be raised from the depths of misery in this world." Ball concluded that "The idea of a revolution in the conditions of the whites and blacks, is the cornerstone of the religion of the latter. ..."

Slaves had no difficulty distinguishing the gospel of Christianity from the religion of their masters. Ex-slave Douglas Dorsey reported that after the minister on his plantation admonished the slaves to honor their masters whom they could see as they would God whom they could not see, the driver's wife who could read and write a little would say that the minister's sermon "was all lies." Charles Colcock Jones, plantation missionary, found that his slave congregation did not hesitate to reject the doctrine preached in a sermon he gave in 1833:

I was preaching to a large congregation on the *Epistle of Philemon*: and when I insisted upon fidelity and obedience as Christian virtues in servants and upon the authority of Paul, condemned the practice of *running away*, one half of my audience deliberately rose up and walked off with themselves, and those that remained looked any thing but satisfied, either with the preacher or his doctrine. After dismission, there was no small stir among them: some solemnly declared "that there was no such Epistle in the Bible;" others, "that I preached to please the masters;" others, "that it was not the Gospel;" others, "that they did not care if they ever heard me preach again!" ... There were some too, who had strong objections against me as a Preacher, because I was a *master*, and said, "his people have to work as well as we."

The slaves' rejection of white man's religion was clearly revealed in their attitudes toward morality. While white preachers repeated the command, "Do not steal," slaves simply denied that this precept allied to them since they themselves were stolen property. Josephine Howard put the argument this way: "Dey allus done tell us it am wrong to lie and steal, but why did de white folks steal my mammy and her mammy... Dat de sinfulles' stealin' dey is." Rachel Fairley demanded, "How could they help but steal when they didn't have nothin'? You didn't eat if you didn't steal." Henry Bibb declared that under slavery "I had a just right to what I took, because it was the labor of my hands." Other slaves concluded that it was not morally possible for one piece of property to steal another since both belonged to the same owner: it was merely a case of taking something out of one tub and putting it in another. This view of stealing referred only to master's goods, however, for a slave to steal from another slave was seriously wrong. As the saying went, "a slave that will steal from a slave is called *mean as master*." Or as one ex-slave remarked, "This is the lowest comparison slaves know how to use: 'just as mean as white folks.'"

Not all slaves, however, were able to distinguish master's religion from authentic Christianity, and were led to reject this religion totally. In 1839, Daniel Alexander Payne explained how this could happen:

The slaves are sensible of the oppression exercised by their masters; and they see these masters on the Lord's day worshipping in his holy Sanctuary. They hear their masters professing Christianity; they see their masters preaching the gospel; they hear these masters praying in their families, and they know that oppression and slavery are inconsistent with the Christian religion; therefore they scoff at religion itself—mock their masters, and distrust both the goodness and justice of God.

Frederick Douglass too remembered being shaken by "doubts arising... from the sham religion which everywhere prevailed" under slavery, doubts which "awakened in my mind a distrust of all religion and the conviction that prayers were unavailing and delusive." Unable to account for the evil of slavery in a world ruled by a just God, some slaves abandoned belief. "I pretended to profess religion one time," recalled one former slave, "I don't hardly know what to think about religion. They say God killed the just and unjust; I don't understand that part of it. It looks hard to think that if you ain't done nothing in the world you be punished just like the wicked. Plenty folks went crazy trying to get that straightened out." There is no way of estimating how many slaves felt these doubts, but they indicate how keenly aware slaves were of the disparity between the gospel of Christ and what they termed "white man's religion."

At the opposite extreme from the agnostic slave was the slave who developed a life of exemplary Christian virtue which placed him in a position of moral superiority over his master. William Grimes, for example, was possessed of a sense of righteousness which led him to take a surprising attitude toward his master when punished for something he had not done:

It grieved me very much to be blamed when I was innocent. I knew I had been faithful to him, perfectly so. At this time I was quite serious, and used constantly to pray to my God. I would not lie nor steal.... When I considered him accusing me of stealing, when I was so innocent, and had endeavored to make him satisfied by every means in my power, that I was so, but he still persisted in disbelieving me, I then said to myself, if this thing is done in a green tree what must be done in a dry? I forgave my master in my own heart for all this, and prayed to God to forgive him and turn his heart.

Grimes is of course alluding to the sacrifice of Christ and identifying himself with the innocent suffering servant who spoke the words concerning green and dry wood on his way to death on Calvary. From this vantage point Grimes is able to forgive his master. Note however the element of threat implied in the question, "if this thing is done in a green tree (to the innocent) what must be done in a dry (to the guilty)?" Those who are guilty of persecuting the innocent, like Grimes's master, will be judged and punished. (The full context of the biblical allusion includes a terrifying prediction of the destruction of Jerusalem.) What did it mean to Grimes's self-image to be able to have moral leverage by which he might elevate his own dignity. A similar impulse lay behind the comment of Mary Younger, a fugitive slave in Canada, "if those slaveholders were to come here, I would treat them well, just to shame them by showing that I had humanity." To assert one's humanity in the face of slavery's power to dehumanize, perhaps explained Grimes's careful adherence to righteousness, a righteousness which might at first glance seem merely servile.

CONCLUSION

In the slave society of the antebellum South, as in most societies, the Christian religion both supported and undermined the status quo. On the one hand, Nat Turner claimed that God's will moved him to slaughter whites, on the other, "good" slaves protected their masters out of a sense of duty. Slave religion, however was more complex than these alternatives suggest. Institutionally, the egalitarian impulse of evangelical Protestantism, leveling all men before God and lifting some up to declare his word with power and authority, gave slaves and free blacks the opportunity to exercise leadership. Usually this leadership was not revolutionary and from the perspective of political strategy it was overwhelmingly conservative. Yet political action is not the only measure of resistance to oppression. Despite political impotence, the black preacher was still a figure of power as an unmistakable symbol of the talent and ability of black men, a fact which contradicted the doctrine of inherent black inferiority. As white slaveholders occasionally recognized, black preachers were anomalous, if not dangerous, persons under the system of slave control precisely because their authority could not be effectively limited by whites.

Nor were slaveowners able to control the spirit of religious independence once it had been imbibed by their slaves. Continually this spirit sought to break out of the strictures confining slave life. When possible, it sought expression in separate institutions controlled by blacks. When that proved impossible, it found expression in secret religious gatherings "out from under the eye of the master." In both cases, the internal autonomy of the slave's own moral will prove[d] impossible to destroy. Throughout the history of Christianity, earthly rulers (civil and religious) have been troubled by the claim that individuals owed obedience to a higher authority than their own. Antebellum slaveholders and missionaries faced the same problem. When slaves disobeyed their masters in order to obey God, a long tradition of Christian heroism validated their assertion of human freedom.

The emotional ecstasy of slave religion has been criticized as compensatory and otherworldly, a distraction from the evils of this world. And so it was. But it was much more. Individually, slaves found not only solace in their religion but, particularly in the conversion experience, a source of personal identity and value. Collectively, slaves found in the archetypical symbol of biblical Israel their identity as a community, a new chosen people bound for Divine deliverance from bondage. From this communal identity mutual support, meaning, and hope derived. In the ecstasy of religious performance individual and communal identity and values were dramatically reaffirmed time and time again. In the hand-clapping, footstomping, headshaking fervor of the plantation praisehouse, the slaves, in prayer, sermon, and song, fit Christianity to their own peculiar experience and in the process resisted, even transcended the dehumanizing bonds of slavery.

NO

John B. Boles

MASTERS AND SLAVES IN THE HOUSE OF THE LORD

Race and religion have probably always been controversial topics in the South, as elsewhere, particularly when their intersection has called into question widely accepted folkways about the place of blacks in southern society. Different interpreters have suggested that the South has been haunted by God and preoccupied with race, so perhaps we should not expect a scholarly consensus on how the two intertwined in the decades from the Great Awakening to Reconstruction. The last generation of our own times has witnessed a remarkable burst of scholarship on blacks and race relations in the region and a similar if not quite as prolific discovery of southern religious history. . . .

Most laypersons today seem completely unaware that a century and a half ago many churches in the Old South had significant numbers of black members: black and white co-worshipers heard the same sermons, were baptized and took communion together, and upon death were buried in the same cemeteries. Such practices seem inconceivable today, when the old cliché that Sunday morning at 11:00 A.M. is the most segregated hour in America still rings true. When I was a boy in the rural South thirty years ago, we all supported the Lottie Moon Christmas offering to send missionaries to convert the "heathen" in Africa and elsewhere, but the church deacons and the congregation would have been scandalized had one of the black converts traveled from Africa expecting to worship with us. Yet a century earlier biracial attendance at Baptist churches like ours was the norm in the rural South.

Blacks worshiped in a variety of ways, and some did not participate in any Christian worship, for, especially in the colonial period, a smattering of blacks practiced Islam and others clung tenaciously to traditional African religions. All non-Christian religious activity was discouraged by most slaveowners, who were as ethnocentric as they were concerned about the potential for unrest and rebellion they sensed in their slaves' participation in what to whites were strange and exotic rites. In addition, many slaveowners in the seventeenth and eighteenth centuries were hesitant to attempt to convert their bondspeople to Christianity—if they themselves were Christians—out of fear that conversion might loosen the ties of their bondage. The English knew of slavery long before they had any New World settlements and had considered it a backward institution that might be promoted by Catholic Spain but not by the England of Elizabeth. Even so, the English believed that certain persons might be held in bondage—convicted felons, war prisoners, in some cases heathens, that is, nonbelievers in Christianity. It took several generations before Englishmen in the North American mainland colonies came to accept the practicality of African slavery, then argue the necessity of it, and finally surpass their Spanish rivals in its applications. To the extent that they needed any noneconomic justification, they assumed that the Africans not being Christians made it morally acceptable to enslave them. But if Africans' "heathenism" justified making them slaves, would not their conversion at the very least call into question the rightness of keeping them in bondage? On at least several occasions in the seventeenth century blacks had won their freedom in court by proving they had been baptized. Hence any moral uneasiness that might have existed among less-than-devout slaveowners for not sharing the gospel with their slaves was entirely overcome by their uneasiness about the stability of their work force should they do so. To clarify this ambiguity obliging laws were passed in the late seventeenth century specifying that a person's "civil state" would not be affected by his conversion to Christianity. . . .

Yet despite the difficulties inherent in converting the slaves—the whites' hesitancy to have their slaves hear Christian doctrines and no doubt a hesitancy on the part of some slaves to give up traditional beliefs, even if those beliefs had

been attenuated by a long presence in the New World—in the middle decades of the eighteenth century increasing numbers of bondspeople became members of Christian churches. A dramatic shift was occurring in the history of black Americans, most of whom before 1750 had been outside the Christian church, for within a century the majority of slaves were worshiping in one fashion or another as Christians. After emancipation, freedpersons continued to find in their churches solace from the cares of the world and joy and a purpose for living in a society that continued to oppress black people. Everyone acknowledges the significance of the church in the black community after freedom; less understood is black worship during the antebellum era and earlier. Yet the half-century following 1740 was the critical period during which some whites broke down their fears and inhibitions about sharing their religion with the slaves in their midst, and some blacks—only a few at first—came to find in Christianity a system of ideas and symbols that was genuinely attractive. . . .

Several aspects of African traditional religion bore close enough parallels to Christianity that bondspeople who were initially disinterested in the white man's religion could—once they glimpsed another side to it—see sufficient common ground between the whites' Christianity and their own folk religions to merit closer examination. That willingness, that openness, on the part of blacks to the claims of Christianity was all the entrée white Christian evangelicals needed. Most West African religions assumed a tripartite hierarchy of deities —nature gods, ancestral gods, and an omnipotent creator god who was more remote though more powerful than the others. This conception was roughly transferable to the Christian idea of the trinity. West Africans understood that spirit possession was a sure sign of contact with the divine, an experience not totally dissimilar from the emotional fervor of evangelistic services. Before the mid-eighteenth century slaves had not come into contact with white evangelicals, who were also largely of the lower social order, who worshiped with emotional abandon, and who spoke movingly of being possessed by the Holy Spirit and knowing Jesus as their personal savior. But such evangelical Christians came increasingly to minister to slaves, and they would bridge the chasm between the races and introduce large and growing numbers of slaves to evangelical Christianity.

During the second quarter of the eighteenth century, Evangelicalism and Pietism swept across England and Europe, and the quickening of heartfelt religion soon leapfrogged to the New World in the person of George Whitefield. The resulting Great Awakening occurred primarily north of Maryland, but Whitefield's preaching and the example of his life gained disciples in South Carolina and Georgia. None of Whitefield's followers were more devout than members of the prominent Bryan family in Georgia, and ... the two Bryan brothers sincerely believed Jesus' call for repentance was addressed to all persons, black and white, bond and free. Consequently, they undertook to promote Christianity among their own and neighboring slaves, but they did so in such a way as to support the institution of slavery. From today's perspective, their paternalistic efforts toward the blacks under their control seem a truncated version of Christianity, but they did present the faith to the slaves in a way that was acceptable to the larger society.

A subtle shift in rationales had occurred that would have a far-reaching influence on whites and blacks. At first it had been deemed appropriate to enslave Africans because they were considered heathens; by the mid-eighteenth century some Anglican clergy had begun to argue that it was appropriate to enslave Africans because they might thereby be converted to Christianity. In that sense this development foreshadowed an important tradition of elite white evangelism to blacks, and through such efforts then and in the future thousands of slaves came to know Christianity and, in various ways, to appropriate its message for their own ends.

Another development of the mid-eighteenth century was to be even more important for the growth of Christianity among the slaves than the limited Anglican awakening in the aftermath of Whitefield. In the quarter of a century following 1745 three evangelical Protestant groups planted their seeds in the colonial South—first the Presbyterians, then the Separate Baptists (later the term Separate was dropped as this species came almost completely to swallow all competing versions of believers in adult baptism), and finally the Methodists (first only a subset of the Church of England but after 1784 an independent denomination). These three churches grew at different rates and had different constituencies. The Presbyterians never experienced the extensive growth among rural southerners that the other two did but found increasing support from among those on the upper rungs of society, supplanting the erstwhile Anglican (the postrevolutionary Episcopal) church in influence among the elite. Presbyterian church members, disproportionately wealthy, of course owned disproportionate numbers of slaves, and continuing the elite paternalism pioneered by the Anglican Bryans in colonial Georgia, they tended to minister to blacks by providing them special ministers and separate accommodations. A form of religious noblesse oblige motivated some of them to devise ways to bring the gospel message to their blacks, especially after abolitionists charged that southern whites neglected the spiritual well-being of their slaves. Moreover, the developing argument that slavery was a progressive institution designed by God to effect the Christianization of Africans gave slaveholders a moral obligation to consider the religious needs of their bondspeople. This sentiment, especially strong among Presbyterians and Episcopalians, produced the significant "mission to the slaves" movement of the late antebellum period....

Although the Presbyterian church was to remain relatively small but influential beyond its numbers, the Baptists and Methodists experienced remarkable growth, especially after the Great Revival at the beginning of the nineteenth century. It would be inappropriate in this brief overview to rehearse the reasons for the success these two evangelical denominations had in the rural South; to an extraordinary degree they became the folk churches of the region. Certainly in their youthful decades, the 1750s through 1790s, when their appeal was even more emphatically to those whites who lived at the margins of society—poor, isolated, largely nonslaveholding—the Baptists and Methodists maintained a fairly consistent antislavery stance. Especially south of Maryland, both denominations recognized the political explosiveness of such beliefs if preached incautiously. They tended to criticize slavery in the abstract, delineate its evils both to the slaves and even more to the whites, emphasize that slaves were persons with souls precious in the sight of God, and suggest that slavery be ended "insofar as practicable" —or words to that effect. This is not to argue that they were insincere or hypocritical. Rather, they understood the realities of the economic and social-control imperatives of the institution and occasionally stated explicitly that if they boldly attacked slavery, they would not be allowed to preach to the blacks, thereby —by their lights—causing the unfortunate bondspeople not to hear the gospel. It is easy from today's perspective, and probably incorrect, to see as self-serving such remarks as Methodist Francis Asbury's summation of his position in 1809: "Would not an *amelioration* in the condition and treatment of slaves have produced more practical good to the poor Africans, than any attempt at their *emancipation*? The state of society, unhappily, does not admit of this: besides, the blacks are deprived of the means of instruction; who will take the pains to lead them into the way of salvation, and watch over them that they may not stray, but the Methodists? ... What is the personal liberty of the African which he may abuse, to the salvation of his soul; how may it be compared?"

The point is not the limited emancipationist impulse in the evangelical denominations and how it was thwarted over time by political and racial pressures. More appropriate here is the way the lower-class structure of the early Baptist and Methodist churches, most of whose members did not own slaves and felt estranged from the wealthier whites who did, enabled them to see blacks as potential fellow believers in a way that white worshipers in more elite churches seldom could. From the moment of their organization, typical Baptist or Methodist churches included black members, who often signed (or put their "X") on the founding documents of incorporation. Black membership in these two popular denominations was substantial from the last quarter of the eighteenth century through the Civil War. Without claiming too much or failing to recognize the multitude of ways slaves were not accorded genuine equality in these biracial churches, it is still fair to say that nowhere else in southern society were they treated so nearly as equals.

Because church membership statistics for the antebellum period are incomplete, and because churches varied in their definitions of membership, a quantitatively precise portrait of the extent to which blacks and white worshiped together is impossible to obtain. Historian John Blassingame has written that "an overwhelming majority of the slaves throughout the antebellum period attended church with their masters. Then, after the regular services ended, the ministers held special services for the slaves." Such special services were more typical of Episcopal and Presbyterian churches; Methodist and Baptist preachers would usually, sometimes toward the end of the service, call for something like "a special word for our black brothers and sisters" and then turn to them in the back pews or in the balcony and address them with a didactic sermon that often stressed obedience to their earthly masters. Sarah Fitzpatrick, a ninety-year-old former slave interviewed in 1938, recalled that "us 'Niggers' had our meetin' in de white fo'ks Baptist Church in de town o' Tuskegee. Dere's a place up in de loft dere now dat dey built fer de 'Nigger' slaves to 'tend church wid de white fo'ks. White preacher he preach to de white fo'ks an' when he git thu' wid dem he preach some to de 'Niggers.' Tell'em to mind dere Marster an' b'have deyself an' dey'll go to Hebben when dey die."

Slaves saw through these words and felt contempt for the self-serving attention they received. More important to them was the remainder of the service that they heard and participated in with the rest of the congregation. Here the slaves heard a more complete version of the gospel, and despite whatever social-control uses some ministers tried to put religion to in a portion of the Sunday service, most slaves found grounds for hope and a degree of spiritual liberation through their participation in these biracial churches. As Blassingame concluded, "Generally the ministers tried to expose the slaves to the major tenets of Christianity.... [And] only 15 percent of the Georgia slaves who had heard antebellum whites preach recalled admonitions to obedience."

Slaves worshiped apart from whites on some occasions, often with the knowledge of their owners and often without the white supervision the law called for. Some black churches were adjuncts to white churches, and completely independent and autonomous black churches existed in southern cities. Blacks worshiped privately and often secretly in their cabins and in the fields. Sometimes, and especially when their owner was irreligious, slaves had to slip away to hidden "brush arbors" deep in the woods to preach, shout, sing, and worship. But such practices should not lead us to forget that the normative worship experience of blacks in the antebellum South was in a biracial church. "Including black Sunday School scholars and catechumens," Blassingame writes, "there were probably 1,000,000 slaves under the regular tutelage of Southern churches in 1860."

When David T. Bailey examined some 40 autobiographies of blacks and 637 interviews of slaves on the subject of religion, he discovered that 32 percent of the autobiographers who mentioned religion reported that they had gone to white churches, 14 percent said their master led the services for them, and another 14 percent attended worship services at special plantation chapels, whereas 36 percent mentioned that they had attended black prayer meetings. Of the former slaves interviewed, 43.5 percent mentioned attending white churches, 6.5 percent reported master-led services, 6.5 percent described plantation chapels, and only 24 percent discussed attendance at black prayer meetings.

Such substantial black participation in churches normally considered white indicates that white evangelicals, even in the late antebellum period, when they had moved up the social scale, joined the establishment, and come to support the institution of slavery, still felt a Christian responsibility to include slaves in the outreach of the church. Their idea of mission assumed that slaves were persons with souls precious in God's sight. In fact, many white evangelicals came to believe that part of their responsibility to God involved Christianizing the slave work force. It was to that end, they reasoned, that God had sanctioned slavery.... [A]bolitionist charges that the southern church ignored the slaves infuriated southern clergymen and caused them to redouble their efforts to bring slaves into the church. During the Civil War clergy feared that God was chastising the region for not sufficiently supporting the mission effort to the blacks, and religiously inspired attempts to amend slavery by correcting the worst abuses, teaching bondspeople to read

(so the Scriptures would be accessible to them), and providing missionaries for them... almost reformed slavery out of existence in Confederate Georgia.

Devout white clergy often took seriously their responsibilities toward the blacks in their midst, and their paternalistic and racist assumptions should not blind us to their convictions that slaves too were God's children and that white slaveowners stood under God's judgment for the way they treated their bondspeople. It is difficult to understand today how devout whites could define blacks legally as chattel and yet show real concern for the state of their souls. Could genuine Christians so compartmentalize their charity? Apparently so, given their assumptions that blacks were a race of permanent children. A misguided sense of Christian responsibility led well-meaning, decent whites to justify slavery as the white man's duty to Africans, for it was, they argued, through the order and discipline bondage provided that slaves learned—sampled?—Christianity and Western civilization. Almost like whistling in the dark to drive away one's fears, white churchmen sometimes were particularly anxious to Christianize their slaves as though only thus could the institution be justified and their guilt be lessened.

Blacks too must have derived a substantial reward from their participation in the institutional churches or they would not have been involved with them to such an extent for so long. The manuscript records of hundreds of local Baptist churches across the South allow us to see a seldom-studied aspect of white-black interaction that helps explain the attraction biracial churches held for slaves. First,... blacks were accorded a semblance of equality when they joined antebellum Baptist churches. White members often addressed them as brother or sister, just as they did fellow white members. This equality in the terms of address may seem insignificant today, but in an age when only whites were accorded the titles of Mr. and Mrs., and it was taboo for a white to so address a black, any form of address that smacked of equality was notable. Behind it lay the familial idea, accepted by whites in principle if not always in practice, that in the sight of God all were equal and were members of His spiritual family. Incoming or outgoing members of Baptist churches were accepted or dismissed with "letters" attesting to their good standing, and slaves asking to join Baptist churches were expected to "bring their letter" just as prospective white members were. Churches seem to have routinely supplied such letters to their members of both races who moved to other locations. New members, black and white, were usually given the "right hand of fellowship" after their letters were accepted or after they came to the altar following the minister's sermon-ending call for conversion to "confess their sins and accept Christ's mercy." Individual churches often varied in this practice, as in much else in the South, where strict uniformity in anything was the exception.

Blacks usually sat in a separate section of the church, perhaps a balcony or a lean-to. There is evidence, however, that slaves sat scattered throughout Anglican churches in colonial Virginia and that sometimes they sat with or next to the pew of their master. Today, such segregated seating would seem to contradict the idea of spiritual equality, but the contradiction probably did not seem so stark to slaves, who were excluded from most other white-dominated functions.

The white women often sat apart from the white men, too; in that age segregation by gender was almost as common as that by race, and the familiarity of such separation might well have lessened the negative connotation although it accentuated each subgroup's sense of separate identity. That is, the sense of both a separate women's culture and a separate black culture might have been inadvertently strengthened by the prevalent mode of segregated seating under a common roof. In fact, for some blacks who were isolated on farms and small plantations with no or only a few fellow slaves, the gathering together on Sunday at the church house with slaves from other farms may have been the primary occasion for experiencing a sense of black community. For such slaves the forced segregation in seating may have seemed both natural and desirable because they hungered for close interaction with persons of their own kind. The interaction may have been a stronger attraction than the worship itself. No doubt many bondspeople found their marriage partners through such social involvement at church—certainly much white courtship began there. Perhaps, then, for slaves dispersed on farms outside the plantation district, the slave community was largely created and vitalized in the one arena in which slaves belonging to different owners could freely mingle—the biracial church service.

As with church membership practices, there was an important but limited degree of equality in slaves' participation in antebellum church discipline.... [C]ertainly no one would want to argue that whites completely forgot or transcended the racial mores of a slave society in the confines of the church building, but it is significant that slaves were allowed to give testimony—sometimes even conflicting with white testimony—and that on occasion their witness overruled the charges of whites. This occurred in a society that did not allow blacks to testify against whites in civil courts. Moreover, blacks were not disciplined out of proportion to their numbers; on the whole, they were charged with infractions similar to those of whites; and they were held to the same moral expectations as whites with regard to profanity, drunkenness, lying, adultery, failure to attend church, and fighting. There surely were charges against blacks that had no parallel for whites—for example, blacks alone were charged with running away. But nowhere else in southern society were slaves and whites brought together in an arena where both were held responsible to a code of behavior sanctioned by a source outside the society—the Bible. The Scriptures were interpreted in culturally sanctioned ways, but whites as well as blacks were occasionally found wanting.

Blacks discovered in the church and in church discipline a unique sphere wherein to nurture (and be recognized by whites to have) moral responsibility and what Timothy L. Smith has called "moral earnestness." Through the church slaves found a meaning for their lives that could give a touch of moral grandeur to the tragic dimension of their bondage. Images of the children of Israel and the suffering servant provided ways to accept their life predicament without feelings of self-worthlessness. The church offered a spark of joy in the midst of pain, a promise of life-affirming forgiveness to soften the hopelessness of unremitting bondage, an ultimate reward in heaven for unrewarded service in this world. Participation in the biracial churches was one of the ways slaves found the moral

and psychological strength to survive their bondage.

It is important to remember that social interaction does not necessarily imply social equality; in a variety of contexts outside the churches slaves and masters mingled closely without narrowing the gap between freedom and bondage. In many ways such interaction could even magnify the sense of enslavement. Yet it would be a mistake so to emphasize the belittling possibilities of white-black interaction that we fail to see the alternative possibilities inherent in the biracial churches. Slaves apparently had their image of being creatures of God strengthened by the sermons they heard —even when that was not the intention of the ministers—and the discipline they accepted. Their evident pleasure in occasionally hearing black preachers speak to biracial congregations no doubt augmented their sense of racial pride. Taking communion together with whites, serving as deacons or Sunday school teachers, being baptized or confirmed in the same ceremonies, even contributing their mite to the temporal upkeep of the church, could surely have been seen as symbolic ways of emphasizing their self-respect and equality before God. Slaves certainly were not dependent on white-controlled institutions to nurture their sense of self-worth, but neither were they adverse to seizing opportunities wherever they found them and using them for that purpose. In a society that offered few opportunities for blacks to practice organizational and leadership skills or hear themselves addressed and see themselves evaluated morally on an equal basis with whites, small matters could have large meanings. Blacks did not discover in the biracial churches an equality of treatment that spiritually transported them out of bondage, but they found in them a theology of hope and a recognition of self-worth that fared them well in their struggle to endure slavery.

As Robert L. Hall documents in his analysis of religion in antebellum Florida, blacks worshiped in a variety of ways in the antebellum South besides in biracial Protestant churches. In most southern cities and large towns there were completely independent black churches, with black ministers, black deacons or elders, and a panoply of self-help associations connected to and supported by the church. Usually such churches, like the St. James African Episcopal Church in Baltimore, were under the control of free blacks, although many if not most of the members were slaves. Although the surrounding white-dominated churches tended to ignore societal ills, emphasize conversion, and minister primarily to individuals, the black churches tended to minister to all the social and religious needs of their parishioners. There was a communal and social thrust in the independent black churches that was notably absent from the mainstream white churches of the South. (That difference even today sets many black churches apart from white.) Often the black churches had very large memberships, and sometimes their meeting places had the largest seating capacity in the city.

Blacks also worshiped in black churches that were adjunct to white churches. Such situations typically arose after the biracial church built a new sanctuary and, with the black members perhaps outnumbering the white, the blacks were allowed ("allowed" seems more accurate than "forced") to conduct separate services in the old structure. The motivation of the whites here is not clear; they often indicated that the blacks preferred their own services, but to what extent whites desired segregated white churches for essentially racist reasons is impossible to determine. In most cases when blacks were split off into separate "African" churches, as they were known, a committee of whites was assigned to oversee their services. The supervision seems to have been honored more in the breach, however. In a variety of other ways black church members were often given some autonomy in regulating portions of their worship life, again apparently more because the blacks desired such separation than because whites required it. These small islands of black autonomy within the biracial church were perhaps the beginning of the complete racial separation that would come after the Civil War.

Not all the organized churches in the South were Protestant, although Protestantism was far more dominant in the South than elsewhere in the nation. There were pockets of Catholic strength in Maryland, Kentucky, and Missouri, and in south Louisiana Catholicism was preponderant. Most southern cities had at least one Catholic church, usually attended primarily by immigrant workers. Louisiana and Maryland had rural Catholic churches as well, with numbers of black Catholic parishioners. Catholic masters sometimes required that their slaves worship as Catholics, though their bondspeople may have preferred the neighboring Baptist or Methodist churches either as a subtle form of rebellion against their masters or because of the appeal of the demonstrative emotionalism of the evangelical churches. In various ways the Catholic church ministered to bondspeople; separate black orders and sisterhoods were established and the sacraments extended. Because it was a minority church in a rabidly Protestant region and was concerned not to attract notoriety, the Catholic church never questioned the morality of slavery. An occasional Catholic institution or order might own slaves, as did the Jesuits in Maryland, though this property in humans was divested for reasons of ethics and economics. . . .

In addition to the various kinds of formal churches—biracial, adjunct, and independent black churches and plantation chapels—to which slaves had access, black worshipers also gathered in more informal, often secret settings. The evidence for this is to be found in black memoirs and slave narratives, although even these sources suggest that most blacks worshiped in one or another of the formal churches. There are many reasons why slaves would choose to worship in a manner less subject to white supervision or control. Some masters sought to prevent slaves from worshiping at all, which forced slaves to develop an underground religion and to meet secretly either in their cabins at night or in the brush arbors. Slaves who were allowed (or required) to attend a biracial church (or any formal service carefully monitored by whites) in which the minister placed too much emphasis on the "slaves-obey-your-master" homily and thereby neglected to preach the gospel in its fullness often sought an alternative worship experience. There must have been other times when slaves felt inhibited in the presence of whites and simply desired a time and a place to preach, sing, and shout without having to suffer the condescending glances of less emotionally involved white churchgoers. Although slaves worshiping apart and secretively may have developed a distinctly black

Christianity significantly different from that which they heard in the more formal institutions, there is no unambiguous evidence that they did so. More probably the services in the brush arbors were simply a longer, more emotionally demonstrative version of those in the biracial churches, with more congregational participation. No precise record exists of the theology implicit in such brush arbor meetings or of special emphases that might have developed, but the similarity in worship practice and ecclesiology of the autonomous black churches that emerged after the Civil War to the earlier biracial churches argues against the evolution of any fundamentally different system in the brush arbors.

A momentous change in the nature of church practice in the South took place at the beginning of Reconstruction. Blacks in significant numbers—eventually all of them—began to move out of the biracial churches and join a variety of independent black denominations. As Katharine Dvorak notes in her insightful essay, the blacks left on their own volition; they were not forced out. At first many white churchmen tried to persuade them to stay, but within several decades the degenerating racial climate of the region led these same churchmen on occasion to applaud the new segregated patterns of worship, so different from the common practice before the Civil War.

Of course, that freedpersons wanted to leave the biracial churches is a commentary on the less-than-complete equality they had enjoyed in them. Blacks had a strong sense of racial identity, reinforced by their having been slaves and, within the confines of the churches, by their segregated seating. The complete sermons they had heard for years, not just the self-serving words the white ministers directed specifically at them, had engendered in blacks a sense of their moral worth and equality in the sight of God. The biracial churches simultaneously nurtured this sense of moral equality and thwarted it by their conformity to the demands of the slave society. Black participation in the biracial churches—as preachers, deacons, stewards, and Sunday school teachers—had given them practical leadership and administrative experience, as had their islands of autonomy within the demographically biracial churches. Theologically and experientially blacks were ready to seize the moment offered by emancipation to withdraw from their old allegiances and create autonomous denominations. No better evidence of the freedom slaves had not enjoyed in the biracial churches exists than the rapidity with which blacks sought to establish separate denominations after the Civil War. And no better evidence exists of the extent to which slaves in the biracial churches accepted evangelical Christianity as their preferred expression of religious faith and molded their lives to its demands than the denominations they created after emancipation.

The worship services and institutional arrangements in the new black churches bore a very close resemblance to the biracial churches from which the blacks withdrew. In fact, black Baptist and Methodist services were closer to the early nineteenth-century post–Great Revival services of the evangelical churches than those of the postbellum all-white churches. Blacks had assimilated the theology and order of service in the biracial churches. Rejecting the modernizing tendencies of the white churches toward less emotion, shorter sermons, an emphasis on choir singing rather than congregational singing, and seminary-trained ministers, they more truly carried on the pioneer evangelical traditions. It should not have been surprising to anyone that when born-again Baptist presidential candidate Jimmy Carter wanted to appeal to blacks in 1976, he spoke to them in their churches. Despite the differences—black services are longer, the music is more expressive, emotions are more freely expressed, there is greater congregational participation—the kinship between the white and black Baptist churches of today is readily apparent, and it points back to a time more than a century ago when the religious culture of the South was fundamentally biracial.

POSTSCRIPT

Did Slaves Exercise Religious Autonomy?

One of the most intriguing issues for students of American slavery is the relationship between religion and resistance. Specifically, did slaves find in Christianity moderation that conditioned them to seek salvation only in God's heavenly kingdom, or did it steel their resolve to seek deliverance from their bondage in the earthly realm? To what extent is Karl Marx's dictum that religion is an "opiate of the masses" applicable to the slave experience?

Actually, there was a certain dualism evident in the slaves' religious life. Some obviously were pacified by a fatalistic attitude that slavery was their permanent status, yet hopeful that salvation would be achieved in the heavenly afterlife. Slave owners, of course, attempted to ensure their bond servants' loyalty and passivity by reminding them of Paul's injunction to Onesimus, the runaway servant, to return to his master. For their own part, slaves much preferred to hear Bible readings related to Moses' deliverance of the Israelites from Egypt. It should be remembered that Gabriel Prosser, Denmark Vesey, and Nat Turner all employed religious symbolism to foster their revolutionary conspiracies.

The nature of slave religion is an important topic in virtually every scholarly treatment of the institution of slavery. Raboteau's conclusions are presented more fully in *Slave Religion: The "Invisible Institution" in the Antebellum South* (Oxford University Press, 1978). Boles's description of the "biracial church" was inspired in part by Kenneth Bailey's seminal article "Protestantism and Afro-Americans in the Old South: Another Look," *Journal of Southern History* (November 1975). Eugene D. Genovese, in *Roll, Jordan, Roll: The World the Slaves Made* (Pantheon Books, 1974), argues that the religion developed in the slave quarters represented a synthesis of African traditions and Protestant Christianity, which fused Moses' promise of deliverance in this world with Jesus' promise of personal redemption. For the "dualism" of slave religion discussed above, see Vincent Harding, "Religion and Resistance Among Antebellum Negroes, 1800–1860," in August Meier and Elliott Rudwick, eds., *The Making of Black America: Volume I* (Atheneum, 1969). Lawrence Levine, in *Black Culture and Black Consciousness* (Oxford University Press, 1977), explores the latent and symbolic elements of protest contained in slave songs.

ISSUE 11

Was the Mexican War an Exercise in American Imperialism?

YES: Rodolfo Acuña, from *Occupied America: A History of Chicanos,* 3rd ed. (Harper & Row, 1988)

NO: Norman A. Graebner, from "The Mexican War: A Study in Causation," *Pacific Historical Review* (August 1980)

ISSUE SUMMARY

YES: Professor of history Rodolfo Acuña argues that Euroamericans took advantage of the young, independent, and unstable government of Mexico and waged unjust and aggressive wars against the Mexican government in the 1830s and 1840s in order to take away half of Mexico's original soil.

NO: Professor of diplomatic history Norman A. Graebner argues that President James Polk pursued an aggressive policy that he believed would force Mexico to sell New Mexico and California to the United States and to recognize the annexation of Texas without starting a war.

The American government in the early 1800s greatly benefited from the fact that European nations generally considered what was going on in North America of secondary importance to what was happening in their own countries. In 1801 President Thomas Jefferson became alarmed when he learned that France had acquired the Louisiana territory from Spain. He realized that western states might revolt if the government did not control the city of New Orleans as a seaport for shipping their goods. Jefferson dispatched negotiators to buy the port. He pulled off the real estate coup of the nineteenth century when his diplomats caught Napoleon in a moment of despair. With a stroke of the pen and $15 million, the Louisiana Purchase of 1803 nearly doubled the size of the country. The exact northern, western, and southeastern boundaries were not clearly defined. "But," as diplomatic historian Thomas Bailey has pointed out, "the American negotiators knew that they had bought the western half of perhaps the most valuable river valley on the face of the globe, stretching between the Rockies and the Mississippi, and bounded somewhere on the north by British North America."

After England fought an indecisive war with the United States from 1812 to 1815, she realized that it was to her advantage to maintain peaceful relations with her former colony. In 1817 the Great Lakes, which border on the United States and Canada, were mutually disarmed. Over the next half-century, the principle of demilitarization was extended to the land, resulting in an undefended frontier line that stretched for more that 3,000 miles. The Convention of 1818 clarified the northern boundary of the Louisiana Purchase and ran a line along the 49th parallel from Lake of the Woods in Minnesota to the Rocky Mountains. Beyond that point there was to be a 10-year joint occupancy in the Oregon Territory. In 1819 Spain sold Florida to the United States after Secretary of State John Quincy Adams sent a note telling the Spanish government to keep the Indians on their side of the border or else to get out of Florida. A few years later, the Spanish Empire crumbled in the New World and a series of Latin American republics emerged.

Afraid that the European powers might attack the newly independent Latin American republics and that Russia might expand south into the Oregon Territory, Adams convinced President James Monroe to reject a British suggestion for a joint declaration and to issue instead a unilateral policy statement. The Monroe Doctrine, as it was called by a later generation, had three parts. First, it closed the western hemisphere to any future colonization. Second, it forbade "any interposition" by the European monarchs that would "extend their system to any portion of this hemisphere as dangerous to our peace and safety." And third, the United States pledged to abstain from any involvement in the political affairs of Europe. Viewed in the context of 1823, it is clear that Monroe was merely restating the principles of unilateralism and nonintervention. Both of these were at the heart of American isolationism.

While Monroe renounced the possibility of American intervention in European affairs, he made no such disclaimer toward Latin America, as was originally suggested by Great Britain. It would be difficult to colonize in South America, but the transportation revolution, the hunger for land (which created political turmoil in Texas), and the need for ports on the Pacific to increase American trade in Asia encouraged the acquisition of new lands contiguous to the southwestern boundaries. In the 1840s journalists and politicians furnished an ideological rationale for this expansion and said it was to the Manifest Destiny of Americans to spread democracy, freedom, and white American settlers across the entire North American continent, excluding Canada because it was a possession of Great Britain. Blacks and Indians were not a part of this expansion.

In the first of the following selections, Rodolfo Acuña argues that Euroamericans took advantage of the young, independent, and unstable government of Mexico by waging an unjust and aggressive war against Mexico in the 1830s and 1840s for the purpose of taking away more than half of its original lands. In the second selection, Norman A. Graebner takes a different approach. Arguing from a "realistic" perspective, Graebner contends that President Polk pursued the aggressive policy of a stronger nation in order to force Mexico to sell New Mexico and California to the United States and to recognize America's annexation of Texas without causing a war.

YES

Rodolfo Acuña

LEGACY OF HATE: THE CONQUEST OF MEXICO'S NORTHWEST

AN OVERVIEW

The United States invaded Mexico in the mid-nineteenth century during a period of dramatic change. Rapid technological breakthroughs transformed the North American nation, from a farm society into an industrial competitor. The process converted North America into a principal in the world marketplace. The wars with Mexico, symptoms of this transformation, stemmed from the need to accumulate more land, to celebrate heroes, and to prove the nation's power by military superiority.

This [selection] examines the link between the Texas (1836) and the Mexican (1845–1848) Wars. It analyzes North American aggression, showing how European peoples known as "Americans" acquired what is today the Southwest. The words "expansion" and "invasion" are used interchangeably. The North American invasions of Mexico are equated with the forging of European empires in Asia, Africa, and Latin America. The urge to expand, in the case of the United States, was not based on the need for land—the Louisiana Purchase, central Illinois, southern Georgia, and West Virginia lay vacant. Rather, the motive was profit—and the wars proved profitable, with the Euroamerican nation seizing over half of Mexico.

North Americans fought the Texas War—that is, U.S. dollars financed it, U.S. arms were used on Mexican soil, and Euroamericans almost exclusively profited from it. President Andrew Jackson approved of the war and ignored North American neutrality laws. The so-called Republic held Texas in trusteeship until 1844, when the United States annexed it. This act amounted to a declaration of war on Mexico. When Mexico responded by breaking diplomatic relations, the North Americans used this excuse to manufacture the war. Many North Americans questioned the morality of the war but supported their government because it was their country, right or wrong.

This [selection] does not focus on the wars' battles or heroes, but on how North Americans rationalized these invasions and have developed historical amnesia about its causes and results. War is neither romantic nor just, and the United States did not act benevolently toward Mexico. North Americans committed atrocities, and, when they could, Mexicans responded. Eventually, the Treaty of Guadalupe Hidalgo ended the Mexican-American War, and northern Mexico became part of the North American empire. The treaty, however, did not stop the bitterness or the violence between the two peoples. In fact, it gave birth to a legacy of hate.

BACKGROUND TO THE INVASION OF TEXAS

Anglo justifications for the conquest have ignored or distorted events that led up to the initial clash in 1836. To Anglo-Americans, the Texas War was caused by a tyrannical or, at best, an incompetent Mexican government that was antithetical to the ideals of democracy and justice. The roots of the conflict actually extended back to as early as 1767, when Benjamin Franklin marked Mexico and Cuba for future expansion. Anglo-American filibusters* planned expeditions into Texas in the 1790s. The Louisiana Purchase, in 1803, stimulated U.S. ambitions in the Southwest, and six years later Thomas Jefferson predicted that the Spanish borderlands "are ours the first moment war is forced upon us." The war with Great Britain in 1812 intensified Anglo-American designs on the Spanish territory.

Florida set the pattern for expansionist activities in Texas. In 1818 several posts in east Florida were seized in unauthorized, but never officially condemned, U.S. military expeditions. Negotiations then

*[A *filibuster* is an adventurer who engages in insurrectionist or revolutionary activity in a foreign country.]

in progress with Spain finally terminated in the Adams-Onis, or Transcontinental, Treaty (1819), in which Spain ceded Florida to the United States and the United States, in turn, renounced its claim to Texas. Texas itself was part of Coahuila. Many North Americans still claimed that Texas belonged to the United States, repeating Jefferson's claim that Texas's boundary extended to the Río Grande and that it was part of the Louisiana Purchase. They condemned the Adams-Onis Treaty.

Anglo-Americans continued pretensions to Texas and made forays into Texas similar to those they had made into Florida. In 1819 James Long led an abortive invasion to establish the "Republic of Texas." Long, like many Anglos, believed that Texas belonged to the United States and that "Congress had no right or power to sell, exchange, or relinquish an 'American possession.'"

In spite of the hostility, the Mexican government opened Texas, provided that settlers agreed to certain conditions. Moses Austin was given permission to settle in Texas, but he died shortly afterwards, and his son continued his venture. In December 1821 Stephen Austin founded the settlement of San Félipe de Austin. Large numbers of Anglo-Americans entered Texas in the 1820s as refugees from the depression of 1819. In the 1830s entrepreneurs sought to profit from the availability of cheap land. By 1830 there were about 20,000 settlers, along with some 2,000 slaves.

Settlers agreed to obey the conditions set by the Mexican government—that all immigrants be Catholics and that they take an oath of allegiance to Mexico. However, Anglo-Americans became resentful when Mexico tried to enforce the agreements. Mexico, in turn, became increasingly alarmed at the flood of immigrants from the U.S.

Many settlers considered the native Mexicans to be the intruders. In a dispute with Mexicans and Indians, as well as with Anglo-American settlers, Hayden Edwards arbitrarily attempted to evict settlers from the land before the conflicting claims could be sorted out by the Mexican authorities. As a result Mexican authorities nullified his settlement contract and ordered him to leave the territory. Edwards and his followers seized the town of Nacogdoches and on December 21, 1826, proclaimed the Republic of Fredonia. Mexican officials, supported by some Anglo-Americans (such as Stephen Austin), suffocated the Edwards revolt. However, many U.S. newspapers played up the rebellion as "200 Men Against a Nation!" and described Edwards and his followers as "apostles of democracy crushed by an alien civilization."

In 1824 President John Quincy Adams "began putting pressure on Mexico in the hope of persuading her to rectify the frontier. Any of the Texan rivers west of the Sabine—the Brazos, the Colorado, the Nueces—was preferable to the Sabine, though the Río Grande was the one desired." In 1826 Adams offered to buy Texas for the sum of $1 million. When Mexican authorities refused the offer, the United States launched an aggressive foreign policy, attempting to coerce Mexico into selling Texas.

Mexico could not consolidate its control over Texas: the number of Anglo-American settlers and the vastness of the territory made it an almost impossible task. Anglo-Americans had already created a privileged caste, which depended in great part on the economic advantage given to them by their slaves. When Mexico abolished slavery, on September 15, 1829, Euroamericans circumvented the law by "freeing" their slaves and then signing them to lifelong contracts as indentured servants. Anglos resented the Mexican order and considered it an infringement on their personal liberties. In 1830 Mexico prohibited further Anglo-American immigration. Meanwhile, Andrew Jackson increased tensions by attempting to purchase Texas for as much as $5 million.

Mexican authorities resented the Anglo-Americans' refusal to submit to Mexican laws. Mexico moved reinforcements into Coahuila, and readied them in case of trouble. Anglos viewed this move as an act of hostility.

Anglo colonists refused to pay customs and actively supported smuggling activities. When the "war party" rioted at Anahuac in December 1831, it had the popular support of Anglos. One of its leaders was Sam Houston, who "was a known protégé of Andrew Jackson, now president of the United States.... Houston's motivation was to bring Texas into the United States." ...

THE INVASION OF TEXAS

Not all the Anglo-Americans favored the conflict. Austin, at first, belonged to the peace party. Ultimately, this faction joined the "hawks." Eugene C. Barker states that the immediate cause of the war was "the overthrow of the nominal republic [by Santa Anna] and the substitution of centralized oligarchy," which allegedly would have centralized Mexican control. Barker admits that "earnest patriots like Benjamin Lundy, William Ellery Channing, and John Quincy Adams saw in the Texas revolution a disgraceful affair promoted by the sordid slaveholders and land speculators."

Barker parallels the Texas filibuster and the American Revolution, stating: "In each, the general cause of revolt was the same—a sudden effort to extend imperial authority at the expense of local privilege." According to Barker, in both instances the central governments attempted to enforce existing laws that conflicted with the illegal activities of some very articulate people. Barker further justified the Anglo-Americans' actions by observing: "At the close of summer in 1835 the Texans saw themselves in danger of becoming the alien subjects of a people to whom they deliberately believed themselves morally, intellectually, and politically superior. The racial feeling, indeed, underlay and colored Texan-Mexican relations from the establishment of the first Anglo-American colony in 1821." The conflict, according to Barker, was inevitable and, consequently, justified.

Texas history is a mixture of selected fact and generalized myth. Many historians admit that smugglers were upset with Mexico's enforcement of her import laws, that Euroamericans were angry about emancipation laws, and that an increasing number of the new arrivals from the United States actively agitated for independence. But despite these admissions, many historians like Barker refuse to blame the United States.

Austin gave the call to arms on September 19, 1835, stating, "War is our only recourse. There is no other remedy." Anglo-Americans enjoyed very real advantages in 1835. They were "defending" terrain with which they were familiar. The 5,000 Mexicans living in the territory did not join them, but the Anglo population had swelled to almost 30,000. The Mexican nation was divided, and the centers of power were thousands of miles from Texas. From the interior of Mexico, Santa Anna led an army of about 6,000 conscripts, many of whom had been forced into the army and then marched hundreds of miles over hot, arid desert land. Many were Mayan and did not speak Spanish. In February 1836 the majority arrived in Texas, sick and ill-prepared to fight.

In San Antonio the dissidents took refuge in a former mission, the Alamo. The siege began in the first week of March. In the days that followed, the defenders inflicted heavy casualties on the Mexican forces, but eventually the Mexicans won out. A score of popular books have been written about Mexican cruelty in relation to the Alamo and about the heroics of the doomed men. The result was the creation of the Alamo myth. Within the broad framework of what actually happened—187 filibusters barricading themselves in the Alamo in defiance of Santa Anna's force, which, according to Mexican sources, numbered 1,400, and the eventual triumph of the Mexicans—there has been major distortion.

Walter Lord, in an article entitled "Myths and Realities of the Alamo," sets the record straight. Texas mythology portrays the Alamo heroes as freedom-loving defenders of their homes; supposedly they were all good Texans. Actually, two-thirds of the defenders had recently arrived from the United States, and only a half dozen had been in Texas for more than six years. The men in the Alamo were adventurers. William Barret Travis had fled to Texas after killing a man, abandoning his wife and two children. James Bowie, an infamous brawler, made a fortune running slaves and had wandered into Texas searching for lost mines and more money. The fading Davey Crockett, a legend in his own time, fought for the sake of fighting. Many in the Alamo had come to Texas for riches and glory. These defenders were hardly the sort of men who could be classified as peaceful settlers fighting for their homes.

The folklore of the Alamo goes beyond the legendary names of the defenders. According to Lord, it is riddled with dramatic half-truths that have been accepted as history. Defenders are portrayed as selfless heroes who sacrificed their lives to buy more time for their comrades-in-arms. As the story goes, William Barret Travis told his men that they were doomed; he drew a line in the sand with his sword, saying that all who crossed it would elect to remain and fight to the last. Supposedly all the men there valiantly stepped across the line, with a man in a cot begging to be carried across it. Countless Hollywood movies have dramatized the bravery of the defenders.

In reality the Alamo had little strategic value, it was the best protected fort west of the Mississippi, and the men fully expected help. The defenders had 21 cannons to the Mexicans' 8 or 10. They were expert shooters equipped with rifles with a range of 200 yards, while the Mexicans were inadequately trained and armed with smooth-bore muskets with a range of only 70 yards. The Anglos were protected by the walls and had clear shots, while the Mexicans advanced in the open and fired at concealed targets. In short, ill-prepared, ill-equipped, and ill-fed Mexicans attacked well-armed and professional soldiers. In addition, from all reliable sources, it is doubtful whether Travis ever drew a line in the sand. San Antonio survivors, females and noncombatants, did not tell the story until many years later, when the tale had gained currency and the myth

was legend. Probably the most widely circulated story was that of the last stand of the aging Davey Crockett, who fell "fighting like a tiger," killing Mexicans with his bare hands. This is a myth; seven of the defenders surrendered, and Crockett was among them. They were executed. And, finally, one man, Louis Rose, did escape.

Travis's stand delayed Santa Anna's timetable by only four days, as the Mexicans took San Antonio on March 6, 1836. At first, the stand at the Alamo did not even have propaganda value. Afterwards, Houston's army dwindled, with many volunteers rushing home to help their families flee from the advancing Mexican army. Most Anglo-Americans realized that they had been badly beaten. It did, nevertheless, result in massive aid from the United States in the form of volunteers, weapons and money. The cry of "Remember the Alamo" became a call to arms for Anglo-Americans in both Texas and the United States.

After the Alamo and the defeat of another garrison at Goliad, southeast of San Antonio, Santa Anna was in full control. He ran Sam Houston out of the territory northwest of the San Jacinto River and then camped an army of about 1,100 men near San Jacinto. There, he skirmished with Houston on April 20, 1836, but did not follow up his advantage. Predicting that Houston would attack on April 22, Santa Anna and his troops settled down and rested for the anticipated battle. The filibusters, however, attacked during the *siesta* hour on April 21. Santa Anna knew that Houston had an army of 1,000, yet he was lax in his precautionary defenses. The surprise attack caught him totally off guard. Shouts of "Remember the

Alamo! Remember Goliad!" filled the air. Houston's successful surprise attack ended the war. He captured Santa Anna, who signed the territory away. Although the Mexican Congress repudiated the treaty, Houston was elected president of the Republic of Texas.

Few Mexican prisoners were taken at the battle of San Jacinto. Those who surrendered "were clubbed and stabbed, some on their knees. The slaughter... became methodical: the Texan riflemen knelt and poured a steady fire into the packed, jostling ranks." They shot the "Meskins" down as they fled. The final count showed 630 Mexicans dead versus 2 Texans.

Even Santa Anna was not let off lightly; according to Dr. Castañeda, Santa Anna "was mercilessly dragged from the ship he had boarded, subjected to more than six months' mental torture and indignities in Texas prison camps."

The Euroamerican victory paved the way for the Mexican-American War. Officially the United States had not taken sides, but men, money, and supplies poured in to aid fellow Anglo-Americans. U.S. citizens participated in the invasion of Texas with the open support of their government. Mexico's minister to the United States, Manuel Eduardo Gorostiza, protested the "arming and shipment of troops and supplies to territory which was part of Mexico, and the dispatch of United States troops into territory clearly defined by treaty as Mexican territory." General Edmund P. Gaines, Southwest commander, was sent into western Louisiana on January 23, 1836; shortly thereafter, he crossed into Texas in an action that was interpreted to be in support of the Anglo-American filibusters in Texas: "The Jackson Administration made it plain to the Mexican minister

that it mattered little whether Mexico approved, that the important thing was to protect the border against Indians and Mexicans." U.S. citizens in and out of Texas loudly applauded Jackson's actions. The Mexican minister resigned his post in protest. "The success of the Texas Revolution thrust the Anglo-American frontier up against the Far Southwest, and the region came at once into the scope of Anglo ambition."

THE INVASION OF MEXICO

In the mid-1840s, Mexico was again the target. Expansion and capitalist development moved together. The two Mexican wars gave U.S. commerce, industry, mining, agriculture, and stock-raising a tremendous stimulus. "The truth is that [by the 1840s] the Pacific Coast belonged to the commercial empire that the United States was already building in that ocean."

The U.S. population of 17 million people of European extraction and 3 million slaves was considerably larger than Mexico's 7 million, of which 4 million were Indian and 3 million *mestizo* and European. The United States acted arrogantly in foreign affairs, partly because its citizens believed in their own cultural and racial superiority. Mexico was plagued with financial problems, internal ethnic conflicts, and poor leadership. General anarchy within the nation conspired against its cohesive development.

By 1844 war with Mexico over Texas and the Southwest was only a matter of time. James K. Polk, who strongly advocated the annexation of Texas and expansionism in general, won the presidency by only a small margin, but his election was interpreted as a mandate for national expansion. Outgoing President

Tyler acted by calling upon Congress to annex Texas by joint resolution; the measure was passed a few days before the inauguration of Polk, who accepted the arrangement. In December 1845, Texas became a state.

Mexico promptly broke off diplomatic relations with the United States, and Polk ordered General Zachary Taylor into Texas to "protect" the border. The location of the border was in doubt. The North Americans claimed it was at the Río Grande, but based on historical precedent, Mexico insisted it was 150 miles farther north, at the Nueces River. Taylor marched his forces across the Nueces into the disputed territory, wanting to provoke an attack.

In November 1845, Polk sent John Slidell on a secret mission to Mexico to negotiate for the disputed area. The presence of Anglo-American troops between the Nueces and the Río Grande and the annexation of Texas made negotiations an absurdity. They refused to accept Polk's minister's credentials, although they did offer to give him an ad hoc status. Slidell declined anything less than full recognition and returned to Washington in March 1846, convinced that Mexico would have to be "chastised" before it would negotiate. By March 28, Taylor had advanced to the Río Grande with an army of 4,000.

Polk, incensed at Mexico's refusal to meet with Slidell on his terms and at General Mairano Paredes's reaffirmation of his country's claims to all of Texas, began to draft his declaration of war when he learned of the Mexican attack on U.S. troops in the disputed territory. Polk immediately declared that the United States had been provoked into war, that Mexico had "shed American blood upon the American soil." On May 13, 1846, Congress declared war and authorized the recruitment and supplying of 50,000 troops.

Years later, Ulysses S. Grant wrote that he believed that Polk provoked the war and that the annexation of Texas was, in fact, an act of aggression. He added: "I had a horror of the Mexican War... only I had not moral courage enough to resign.... I considered my supreme duty was to my flag."

The poorly equipped and poorly led Mexican army stood little chance against the expansion-minded Anglos. Even before the war Polk planned the campaign in stages: (1) Mexicans would be cleared out of Texas; (2) Anglos would occupy California and New Mexico; and (3) U.S. forces would march to Mexico City to force the beaten government to make peace on Polk's terms. And that was the way the campaign basically went. In the end, at a relatively small cost in men and money, the war netted the United States huge territorial gains. In all, the United States took over 1 million square miles from Mexico.

THE RATIONALE FOR CONQUEST

In his *Origins of the War with Mexico: The Polk-Stockton Intrigue*, Glenn W. Price states: "Americans have found it rather more difficult than other peoples to deal rationally with their wars. We have thought of ourselves as unique, and of this society as specially planned and created to avoid the errors of all other nations." Many Anglo-American historians have attempted to dismiss it simply as a "bad war," which took place during the era of Manifest Destiny.

Manifest Destiny had its roots in Puritan ideas, which continue to influence Anglo-American thought to this day. According to the Puritan ethic, salvation is determined by God. The establishment of the City of God on earth is not only the duty of those chosen people predestined for salvation but is also the proof of their state of grace. Anglo-Americans believed that God had made them custodians of democracy and that they had a mission —that is, that they were predestined to spread its principles. As the young nation survived its infancy, established its power in the defeat of the British in the War of 1812, expanded westward, and enjoyed both commercial and industrial success, its sense of mission heightened. Many citizens believed that God had destined them to own and occupy all of the land from ocean to ocean and pole to pole. Their mission, their destiny made manifest, was to spread the principles of democracy and Christianity to the unfortunates of the hemisphere. By dismissing the war simply as part of the era of Manifest Destiny the apologists for the war ignore the consequences of the doctrine.

The Monroe Doctrine of the 1820s told the world that the Americas were no longer open for colonization or conquest; however, it did not say anything about that limitation applying to the United States. Uppermost in the minds of the U.S. government, the military, and much of the public was the acquisition of territory. No one ever intended to leave Mexico without extracting territory. Land was the main motive for the war.

This aggression was justified by a rhetoric of peace. Consider, for example, Polk's war message of May 11, 1846, in which he gave his reasons for going to war:

The strong desire to establish peace with Mexico on liberal and honorable terms, and the readiness of this Govern-

ment to regulate and adjust our boundary and other causes of difference with that power on such fair and equitable principles as would lead to permanent relations of the most friendly nature, induced me in September last to seek reopening of diplomatic relations between the two countries.

The United States, he continued, had made every effort not to provoke Mexico, but the Mexican government had refused to receive an Anglo-American minister. Polk reviewed the events leading to the war and concluded:

As war exists, and notwithstanding all our efforts to avoid it, exists by the act of Mexico herself, we are called upon by every consideration of duty and patriotism to vindicate with decision the honor, the rights, and the interests of our country.

Historical distance from the war has not lessened the need to justify U.S. aggression. In 1920 Justin H. Smith received a Pulitzer prize in history for a work that blamed the war on Mexico. What is amazing is that Smith allegedly examined over 100,000 manuscripts, 120,000 books and pamphlets, and 200 or more periodicals to come to this conclusion. He was rewarded for relieving the Anglo-American conscience. His two-volume "study," entitled *The War with Mexico*, used analyses such as the following to support its thesis that the Mexicans were at fault for the war:

At the beginning of her independent existence, our people felt earnestly and enthusiastically anxious to maintain cordial relations with our sister republic, and many crossed the line of absurd sentimentality in the cause. Friction was inevitable, however. The Americans were direct, positive, brusque, angular and pushing; and they would not understand their neighbors in the south. The Mexicans were equally unable to fathom our goodwill, sincerity, patriotism, resoluteness and courage; and certain features of their character and national condition made it far from easy to get on with them.

This attitude of self-righteousness on the part of government officials and historians toward U.S. aggressions spills over to the relationships between the majority society and minority groups. Anglo-Americans believe that the war was advantageous to the Southwest and to the Mexicans who remained or later migrated there. They now had the benefits of democracy and were liberated from their tyrannical past. In other words, Mexicans should be grateful to the Anglo-Americans. If Mexicans and the Anglo-Americans clash, the rationale runs, naturally it is because Mexicans cannot understand or appreciate the merits of a free society, which must be defended against ingrates. Therefore, domestic war, or repression, is justified by the same kind of rhetoric that justifies international aggression.

Professor Gene M. Brack questions historians who base their research on Justin Smith's outdated work: "American historians have consistently praised Justin Smith's influential and outrageously ethnocentric account."

THE MYTH OF A NONVIOLENT NATION

Most studies on the Mexican-American War dwell on the causes and results of the war, sometimes dealing with war strategy. One must go beyond this point, since the war left bitterness, and since Anglo-American actions in Mexico are vividly remembered. Mexicans' attitude toward Anglo-Americans has been influenced by the war just as the easy victory of the United States conditioned Anglo-American behavior toward Mexicans. Fortunately, some Anglo-Americans condemned this aggression and flatly accused their leaders of being insolent and land-hungry, and of having manufactured the war. Abiel Abbott Livermore in *The War with Mexico Reviewed*, accused his country, writing:

> Again, the pride of race has swollen to still greater insolence the pride of country, always quite active enough for the due observance of the claims of universal brotherhood. The Anglo-Saxons have been apparently persuaded to think themselves the chosen people, annointed race of the Lord, commissioned to drive out the heathen, and plant their religion and institutions in every Canaan they could subjugate.... Our treatment both of the red man and the black man has habituated us to feel our power and forget right.... The passion for land, also, is a leading characteristic of the American people.... The god Terminus is an unknown deity in America. Like the hunger of the pauper boy of fiction, the cry had been, 'more, more, give us more.'

Livermore's work, published in 1850, was awarded the American Peace Society prize for "the best review of the Mexican War and the principles of Christianity, and an enlightened statesmanship."

In truth, the United States conducted a violent and brutal war. Zachary Taylor's artillery leveled the Mexican city of Matamoros, killing hundreds of innocent civilians with *la bomba* (the bomb). Many Mexicans jumped into the Río Grande, relieved of their pain by a watery grave. The occupation that followed was even more terrorizing. Taylor was unable to control his volunteers:

> The regulars regarded the volunteers, of whom about two thousand had reached Matamoros by the end of May, with impatience and contempt.... They robbed Mexicans of their cattle and corn, stole their fences for firewood, got drunk, and killed several inoffensive inhabitants of the town in the streets....

THE TREATY OF GUADALUPE HIDALGO

By late August 1847 the war was almost at an end. Scott's defeat of Santa Anna in a hard-fought battle at Churubusco put Anglo-Americans at the gates of Mexico City. Santa Anna made overtures for an armistice that broke down after two weeks, and the war resumed. On September 13, 1847, Scott drove into the city. Although Mexicans fought valiantly, the battle left 4,000 dead, with another 3,000 prisoners. On September 13, before the occupation of Mexico City began, *Los Niños Héroes* (The Boy Heroes) leapt to their deaths rather than surrender. These teenage cadets were Francisco Márquez, Agustín Melgar, Juan Escutia, Fernando Montes de Oca, Vicente Suárez, and Juan de la Barrera. They became "a symbol and image of this unrighteous war."

The Mexicans continued fighting. The presiding justice of the Supreme Court, Manuel de la Peña, assumed the presidency. He knew that Mexico had lost and that he had to salvage as much as possible. Pressure increased, with U.S. troops in control of much of Mexico.

Nicholas Trist, sent to Mexico to act as peace commissioner, had arrived in Vera Cruz on May 6, 1847, but controversy with Scott over Trist's authority and illness delayed an armistice, and hostilities continued. After the fall of Mexico City, Secretary of State James Buchanan wanted to revise Trist's instructions. He ordered Trist to break off negotiations and return home. Polk wanted more land from Mexico. Trist, however, with the support of Winfield Scott, decided to ignore Polk's order, and began negotiations on January 2, 1848, on the original terms. Mexico, badly beaten, her government in a state of turmoil, had no choice but to agree to the Anglo-Americans' proposals.

On February 2, 1848, the Mexicans ratified the Treaty of Guadalupe Hidalgo, with Mexico accepting the Río Grande as the Texas border and ceding the Southwest (which incorporated the present-day states of California, New Mexico, Nevada, and parts of Colorado, Arizona, and Utah) to the United States in return for $15 million.

Polk, furious about the treaty, considered Trist "contemptibly base" for having ignored his orders. Yet he had no choice but to submit the treaty to the Senate. With the exception of Article X, which concerned the rights of Mexicans in the ceded territory, the Senate ratified the treaty on March 10, 1848, by a vote of 28 to 14. To insist on more territory would have meant more fighting, and both Polk and the Senate realized that the war was already unpopular in many circles. The treaty was sent to the Mexican Congress for ratification; although the Congress had difficulty forming a quorum, the treaty was ratified on May 19 by a 52 to 35 vote. Hostilities between the two nations officially ended. Trist, however, was branded as a "scoundrel," because Polk was disappointed in the settlement. There was considerable support in the United States for acquisition of all Mexico.

During the treaty talks Mexican negotiators, concerned about Mexicans left behind, expressed great reservations about these people being forced to "merge or blend" into Anglo-American culture. They protested the exclusion of provisions that protected Mexican citizens' rights, land titles, and religion. They wanted to protect their rights by treaty.

Articles VIII, IX, and X specifically referred to the rights of Mexicans. Under the treaty, Mexicans left behind had one year to choose whether to return to Mexico or remain in "occupied Mexico." About 2,000 elected to leave; most remained in what they considered *their* land.

Article IX of the treaty guaranteed Mexicans "the enjoyment of all the rights of citizens of the United States according to the principles of the Constitution; and in the meantime shall be maintained and protected in the free enjoyment of their liberty and property, and secured in the free exercise of their religion without restriction." Lynn I. Perrigo, in *The American Southwest*, summarizes the guarantees of Articles VIII and IX: "In other words, besides the rights and duties of American citizenship, they [the Mexicans] would have some special privileges derived from their previous customs in language, law, and religion."

The omitted Article X had comprehensive guarantees protecting "all prior and pending titles to property of every description." When Article X was deleted by the U.S. Senate, Mexican officials protested. Anglo-American emissaries reassured them by drafting a Statement of Protocol on May 26, 1848:

> The American government by suppressing the Xth article of the Treaty of Guadalupe Hidalgo did not in any way intend to annul the grants of lands made by Mexico in the ceded territories. These grants ... preserve the legal value which they may possess, and the grantees may cause their legitimate (titles) to be acknowledged before the American tribunals.
>
> Conformable to the law of the United States, legitimate titles to every description of property, personal and real, existing in the ceded territories, are those which were legitimate titles under the Mexican law of California and New Mexico up to the 13th of May, 1846, and in Texas up to the 2nd of March, 1836.

Considering the Mexican opposition to the treaty, it is doubtful whether the Mexican Congress would have ratified the treaty without this clarification. The vote was close.

The Statement of Protocol was strengthened by Articles VIII and IX, which guaranteed Mexicans rights of property and protection under the law. In addition, court decisions have generally interpreted the treaty as protecting land titles and water rights. In practice, however, the treaty was ignored and during the nineteenth century most Mexicans in the United States were considered as a class apart from the dominant race. Nearly every one of the obligations discussed above was violated, confirming the prophecy of Mexican diplomat Manuel Crescion Rejón, who, at the time the treaty was signed, commented:

> Our race, our unfortunate people will have to wander in search of hospitality in a strange land, only to be ejected later. Descendants of the Indians that we are, the North Americans hate us, their spokesmen depreciate us, even if they recognize the justice of our cause, and they consider us unworthy to form with them one nation and one society, they clearly manifest that their future

expansion begins with the territory that they take from us and pushing [sic] aside our citizens who inhabit the land.

As a result of the Texas War and the Anglo-American aggressions of 1845–1848, the occupation of conquered territory began. In material terms, in exchange for 12,000 lives and more than $100 million, the United States acquired a colony two and a half times as large as France, containing rich farmlands and natural resources such as gold, silver, zinc, copper, oil, and uranium, which would make possible its unprecedented industrial boom. It acquired ports on the Pacific that generated further economic expansion across that ocean. Mexico was left with its shrunken resources to face the continued advances of the United States.

SUMMARY

The colonial experience of the United States differs from that of Third World nations. Its history resembles that of Australia and/or South Africa, where colonizers relegated indigenous populations to fourth-class citizenship or noncitizenship. North American independence came at the right time, slightly predating the industrialization of nineteenth-century Europe. Its merchants took over a lucrative trade network from the British; the new Republic established a government that supported trade, industry, and commercial agriculture. A North American ideology which presumed that Latin Americans had stolen the name "America" and that God, the realtor, had given them the land, encouraged colonial expansion.

Mexico, like most Third World nations after independence, needed a pe-

riod of stability. North American penetration into Texas in the 1820s and 1830s threatened Mexico. The U.S. economic system encouraged expansion, and many of the first wave of migrants to Texas had lost their farms due to the depression of 1819. Land in Texas, generously cheap, provided room for the spread of slavery. Although many North Americans in all probability intended to obey Mexican laws and meet conditions for obtaining land grants, North American ethnocentricism and self-interest soon eroded those intentions. Clearly land values would zoom if Texas were part of the United States.

North American historians have frequently portrayed the Texas invasion as a second encounter in the "American War of Independence." Myths such as that of a tyrannical Mexican government have justified the war. In truth, the cause of the war was profit. Mexico did not invade Texas; it belonged to Mexico. Few if any of the North Americans in Texas had been born there or had lived in Texas for more than five years. Most had just recently arrived. Some rich Mexicans supported the North Americans for obvious reasons— it was in their economic self-interest. A stalemate resulted, with Euroamericans establishing the Texas Republic. In 1844, the United States broke the standoff and annexed Texas.

President James K. Polk manufactured the war with Mexico. Some North Americans opposed the war—not on grounds that it violated Mexico's territorial integrity, but because of the probability of the extension of slavery. Many North American military leaders admitted that the war was unjust, and that the United States had committed an act of aggression. However, patriotism and support for the war overwhelmed reason in the march "To the Halls of the Montezumas [sic]." North Americans, buoyant in their prosperity, wanted to prove that the United States was a world-class power.

The war became a Protestant Crusade. Texans made emotional pleas to avenge the Alamo. Both appeals were instrumental in arousing North Americans to the call to arms, to prove their valor and power of the young "American" democracy. North American soldiers committed atrocities against Mexican civilians; few were punished.

The Treaty of Guadalupe Hidalgo ended the war, and the United States grabbed over half of Mexico's soil. The war proved costly to Mexico and to Mexicans left behind. According to the treaty, Mexicans who elected to stay in the conquered territory would become U.S. citizens with all the rights of citizenship. However, the Treaty of Guadalupe Hidalgo, like those signed with the indigenous people of North American, depended on the good faith of the United States and its ability to keep its word.

NO

Norman A. Graebner

THE MEXICAN WAR:
A STUDY IN CAUSATION

On May 11, 1846, President James K. Polk presented his war message to Congress. After reviewing the skirmish between General Zachary Taylor's dragoons and a body of Mexican soldiers along the Rio Grande, the president asserted that Mexico "has passed the boundary of the United States, has invaded our territory and shed American blood upon the American soil.... War exists, and, notwithstanding all our efforts to avoid it, exists by act of Mexico." No country could have had a superior case for war. Democrats in large numbers (for it was largely a partisan matter) responded with the patriotic fervor which Polk expected of them. "Our government has permitted itself to be insulted long enough," wrote one Georgian. "The blood of her citizens has been spilt on her own soil. It appeals to us for vengeance." Still, some members of Congress, recalling more accurately than the president the circumstances of the conflict, soon rendered the Mexican War the most reviled in American history—at least until the Vietnam War of the 1960s. One outraged Whig termed the war "illegal, unrighteous, and damnable," and Whigs questioned both Polk's honesty and his sense of geography. Congressman Joshua R. Giddings of Ohio accused the president of "planting the standard of the United States on foreign soil, and using the military forces of the United States to violate every principle of international law and moral justice." To vote for the war, admitted Senator John C. Calhoun, was "to plunge a dagger into his own heart, and more so." Indeed, some critics in Congress openly wished the Mexicans well.

For over a century such profound differences in perception have pervaded American writings on the Mexican War. Even in the past decade, historians have reached conclusions on the question of war guilt as disparate as those which separated Polk from his wartime conservative and abolitionist critics....

In some measure the diversity of judgment on the Mexican War, as on other wars, is understandable. By basing their analyses on official rationalizations, historians often ignore the more universal causes of war which transcend individual conflicts and which can establish the bases for greater consensus.

From Norman A. Graebner, "The Mexican War: A Study in Causation," *Pacific Historical Review*, vol. 49, no. 3 (August 1980), pp. 405–426. Copyright © 1980 by American Historical Association, The Pacific Coast Branch. Reprinted by permission of The University of California Press Journals. Notes omitted.

Neither the officials in Washington nor those in Mexico City ever acknowledged any alternatives to the actions which they took. But governments generally have more choices in any controversy than they are prepared to admit. Circumstances determine their extent. The more powerful a nation, the more remote its dangers, the greater its options between action and inaction. Often for the weak, unfortunately, the alternative is capitulation or war.... Polk and his advisers developed their Mexican policies on the dual assumption that Mexico was weak and that the acquisition of certain Mexican territories would satisfy admirably the long-range interests of the United States. Within that context, Polk's policies were direct, timely, and successful. But the president had choices. Mexico, whatever its internal condition, was no direct threat to the United States. Polk, had he so desired, could have avoided war; indeed, he could have ignored Mexico in 1845 with absolute impunity.

* * *

In explaining the Mexican War historians have dwelled on the causes of friction in American-Mexican relations. In part these lay in the disparate qualities of the two populations, in part in the vast discrepancies between the two countries in energy, efficiency, power, and national wealth. Through two decades of independence Mexico had experienced a continuous rise and fall of governments; by the 1840s survival had become the primary concern of every regime. Conscious of their weakness, the successive governments in Mexico City resented the superior power and effectiveness of the United States and feared American notions of destiny that anticipated the annexation of Mexico's northern provinces.

Having failed to prevent the formation of the Texas Republic, Mexico reacted to Andrew Jackson's recognition of Texan independence in March 1837 with deep indignation. Thereafter the Mexican raids into Texas, such as the one on San Antonio in 1842, aggravated the bitterness of Texans toward Mexico, for such forays had no purpose beyond terrorizing the frontier settlements.

Such mutual animosities, extensive as they were, do not account for the Mexican War. Governments as divided and chaotic as the Mexican regimes of the 1840s usually have difficulty in maintaining positive and profitable relations with their neighbors; their behavior often produces annoyance, but seldom armed conflict. Belligerence toward other countries had flowed through U.S. history like a torrent without, in itself, setting off a war. Nations do not fight over cultural differences or verbal recriminations; they fight over perceived threats to their interests created by the ambitions or demands of others.

What increased the animosity between Mexico City and Washington was a series of specific issues over which the two countries perennially quarreled—claims, boundaries, and the future of Texas. Nations have made claims a pretext for intervention, but never a pretext for war. Every nineteenth-century effort to collect debts through force assumed the absence of effective resistance, for no debt was worth the price of war. To collect its debt from Mexico in 1838, for example, France blockaded Mexico's gulf ports and bombarded Vera Cruz. The U.S. claims against Mexico created special problems which discounted their seriousness as a rationale for war. True, the Mexican government failed to protect the possessions and the safety of Americans in Mexico from robbery, theft, and other illegal actions, but U.S. citizens were under no obligation to do business in Mexico and should have understood the risk of transporting goods and money in that country. Minister Waddy Thompson wrote from Mexico City in 1842 that it would be "with somewhat of bad grace that we should war upon a country because it could not pay its debts when so many of our own states are in the same situation." Even as the United States after 1842 attempted futilely to collect the $2 million awarded its citizens by a claims commission, it was far more deeply in debt to Britain over speculative losses. Minister Wilson Shannon reported in the summer of 1844 that the claims issue defied settlement in Mexico City and recommended that Washington take the needed action to compel Mexico to pay. If Polk would take up the challenge and sacrifice American human and material resources in a war against Mexico, he would do so for reasons other than the enforcement of claims. The president knew well that Mexico could not pay, yet as late as May 9, 1846, he was ready to ask Congress for a declaration of war on the question of unpaid claims alone.

Congress's joint resolution for Texas annexation in February 1845 raised the specter of war among editors and politicians alike. As early as 1843 the Mexican government had warned the American minister in Mexico City that annexation would render war inevitable; Mexican officials in Washington repeated that warning. To Mexico, therefore, the move to annex Texas was an unbearable affront. Within one month after Polk's inauguration on March 4, General Juan Almonte, the Mexican minister in Washington, boarded a packet in New York and sailed for Vera Cruz to sever his country's diplomatic relations with the United States. Even before the Texas Convention could meet on July 4 to vote annexation, rumors of a possible Mexican invasion of Texas prompted Polk to advance Taylor's forces from Fort Jesup in Louisiana down the Texas coast. Polk instructed Taylor to extend his protection to the Rio Grande but to avoid any areas to the north of that river occupied by Mexican troops. Simultaneously the president reinforced the American squadron in the Gulf of Mexico. "The threatened invasion of Texas by a large Mexican army," Polk informed Andrew J. Donelson, the American chargé in Texas, on June 15, "is well calculated to excite great interest here and increases our solicitude concerning the final action by the Congress and the Convention of Texas." Polk assured Donelson that he intended to defend Texas to the limit of his constitutional power. Donelson resisted the pressure of those Texans who wanted Taylor to advance to the Rio Grande; instead, he placed the general at Corpus Christi on the Nueces River. Taylor agreed that the line from the mouth of the Nueces to San Antonio covered the Texas settlements and afforded a favorable base from which to defend the frontier.

Those who took the rumors of Mexican aggressiveness seriously lauded the president's action. With Texas virtually a part of the United States, argued the *Washington Union*, "We owe it to ourselves, to the proud and elevated character which America maintains among the nations of the earth, to guard our own territory from the invasion of the ruthless Mexicans." The *New York Morning News* observed that Polk's policy would, on the whole, "command a general concurrence of the public opinion of his country." Some Democratic leaders, fearful of a Mexican attack, urged the president to strengthen Taylor's forces and order them to take the offensive should Mexican soldiers cross the Rio Grande. Others believed the reports from Mexico exaggerated, for there was no apparent relationship between the country's expressions of belligerence and its capacity to act. Secretary of War William L. Marcy admitted that his information was no better than that of other commentators. "I have at no time," he wrote in July, "felt that war with Mexico was probable—and do not now believe it is, yet it is in the range of possible occurrences. I have officially acted on the hypothesis that our peace may be temporarily disturbed without however believing it will be." Still convinced that the administration had no grounds for alarm, Marcy wrote on August 12: "The presence of a considerable force in Texas will do no hurt and possibly may be of great use." In September William S. Parrott, Polk's special agent in Mexico, assured the president that there would be neither a Mexican declaration of war nor an invasion of Texas.

Polk insisted that the administration's show of force in Texas would prevent rather than provoke war. "I do not anticipate that Mexico will be mad enough to declare war," he wrote in July, but "I think she would have done so but for the appearance of a strong naval force in the Gulf and our army moving in the direction of her frontier on land." Polk restated this judgment on July 28 in a letter to General Robert Armstrong, the U.S. consul at Liverpool: "I think there need be but little apprehension of war with Mexico. If however she shall be mad enough to make war we are prepared to meet her." The president assured Senator William H. Haywood of North Carolina that the American forces in Texas would never aggress against Mexico; however, they would prevent any Mexican forces from crossing the Rio Grande. In conversation with Senator William S. Archer of Virginia on September 1, the president added confidently that "the appearance of our land and naval forces on the borders of Mexico & in the Gulf would probably deter and prevent Mexico from either declaring war or invading Texas." Polk's continuing conviction that Mexico would not attack suggests that his deployment of U.S. land and naval forces along Mexico's periphery was designed less to protect Texas than to support an aggressive diplomacy which might extract a satisfactory treaty from Mexico without war. For Anson Jones, the last president of the Texas Republic, Polk's deployments had precisely that purpose:

Texas never actually needed the protection of the United States after I came into office.... There was no necessity for it after the 'preliminary Treaty,' as we were at peace with Mexico, and knew perfectly well that that Government, though she might bluster a little, had not the slightest idea of invading Texas either by land or water; and that nothing would provoke her to (active) hostilities, but the presence of troops in the immediate neighborhood of the Rio Grande, threatening her towns and settlements on the southwest side of that river.... But Donelson appeared so intent upon 'encumbering us with help,' that finally, to get rid of his annoyance, he was told he might give us as much protection as he pleased.... The protection asked for was only *prospective* and contingent; the *protection* he had in view was *immediate* and *aggressive*.

For Polk the exertion of military and diplomatic pressure on a disorganized Mexico was not a prelude to war. Whig critics of annexation had predicted war; this alone compelled the administration to avoid a conflict over Texas. In his memoirs Jones recalled that in 1845 Commodore Robert F. Stockton, with either the approval or the connivance of Polk, attempted to convince him that he should place Texas "in an attitude of active hostility toward Mexico, so that, when Texas was finally brought into the Union, *she might bring war with her.*" If Stockton engaged in such an intrigue, he apparently did so on his own initiative, for no evidence exists to implicate the administration. Polk not only preferred to achieve his purposes by means other than war but also assumed that his military measures in Texas, limited as they were, would convince the Mexican government that it could not escape the necessity of coming to terms with the United States. Washington's policy toward Mexico during 1845 achieved the broad national purpose of Texas annexation. Beyond that it brought U.S. power to bear on Mexico in a manner calculated to further the processes of negotiation. Whether the burgeoning tension would lead to a negotiated boundary settlement or to war hinged on two factors: the nature of Polk's demands and Mexico's response to them. The president announced his objectives to Mexico's troubled officialdom through his instructions to John Slidell, his special emissary who departed for Mexico in November 1845 with the assurance that the government there was prepared to reestablish formal diplomatic relations with the United States and negotiate a territorial settlement....

* * *

Actually, Slidell's presence in Mexico inaugurated a diplomatic crisis not unlike those which precede most wars. Fundamentally the Polk administration, in dispatching Slidell, gave the Mexicans the same two choices that the dominant power in any confrontation gives to the weaker: the acceptance of a body of concrete diplomatic demands or eventual war. Slidell's instructions described U.S. territorial objectives with considerable clarity. If Mexico knew little of Polk's growing acquisitiveness toward California during the autumn of 1845, Slidell proclaimed the president's intentions with his proposals to purchase varying portions of California for as much as $25 million. Other countries such as England and Spain had consigned important areas of the New World through peaceful negotiations, but the United States, except in its Mexican relations, had never asked any country to part with a portion of its own territory. Yet Polk could not understand why Mexico should reveal any special reluctance to part with Texas, the Rio Grande, New Mexico, or California. What made the terms of Slidell's instructions appear fair to him was Mexico's military and financial helplessness. Polk's defenders noted that California was not a sine qua non of any settlement and that the president offered to settle the immediate controversy over the acquisition of the Rio Grande boundary alone in exchange for the cancellation of claims. Unfortunately, amid the passions of December 1845, such distinctions were lost. Furthermore, a settlement of the Texas boundary would not have resolved the California question at all.

Throughout the crisis months of 1845 and 1846, spokesmen of the Polk administration repeatedly warned the Mexican government that its choices were limited. In June 1845, Polk's mouthpiece, the *Washington Union*, had observed characteristically that, if Mexico resisted Washington's demands, "a corps of properly organized volunteers... would invade, overrun, and occupy Mexico. They would enable us not only to take California, but to keep it." American officials, in their contempt for Mexico, spoke privately of the need to chastize that country for its annoyances and insults. Parrott wrote to Secretary of State James Buchanan in October that he wished "to see this people well flogged by Uncle Sam's boys, ere we enter upon negotiations.... I know [the Mexicans] better, perhaps, than any other American citizen and I am fully persuaded, they can never love or respect us, as we should be loved and respected by them, until we shall have given them a positive proof of our superiority." Mexico's pretensions would continue, wrote Slidell in late December, "until the Mexican people shall be convinced by hostile demonstrations, that our differences must be settled promptly, either by negotiation or the sword." In January 1846 the *Union* publicly threatened Mexico with war if it rejected the just demands of the United States: "The result of such a course on her part may compel us to resort to more decisive measures.... to obtain the settlement of our legitimate claims." As Slidell prepared to leave Mexico in March 1846, he again reminded the administration: "Depend upon it, we can never get along well with them, until we have given them a good drubbing." In Washington on May 8, Slidell advised the president "to take the redress of the wrongs and injuries which we had so long borne from Mexico into our own hands, and to act with promptness and energy."

Mexico responded to Polk's challenge with an outward display of belligerence and an inward dread of war. Mexicans feared above all that the United States intended to overrun their country and seize much of their territory. Polk and his advisers assumed that Mexico, to avoid an American invasion, would give up its provinces peacefully. Obviously Mexico faced growing diplomatic and military pressures to negotiate away its territories; it faced no moral obligation to do so. Herrera and Paredes had the sovereign right to protect their regimes by avoiding any formal recognition of Slidell and by rejecting any of the boundary proposals embodied in his instructions, provided that in the process they did not endanger any legitimate interests of the American people. At least to some Mexicans, Slidell's terms demanded nothing less than Mexico's capitulation. By what standard was $2 million a proper payment for the Rio Grande boundary, or $25 million a fair price for California? No government would have accepted such terms. Having rejected negotiation in the face of superior force, Mexico would meet the challenge with a final gesture of defiance. In either case it was destined to lose, but historically nations have preferred to fight than to give away territory under diplomatic pressure alone. Gene M. Brack, in his long study of Mexico's deep-seated fear and resentment of the United States, explained Mexico's ultimate behavior in such terms:

President Polk knew that Mexico could offer but feeble resistance militarily, and he knew that Mexico needed money. No proper American would exchange territory and the national honor for cash, but President Polk mistakenly believed that the application of military pressure would convince Mexicans to do so. They did not respond logically, but patriotically. Left with the choice of war or territorial concessions, the former course, however dim the prospects of success, could be the only one.

* * *

Mexico, in its resistance, gave Polk the three choices which every nation gives another in an uncompromisable confrontation: to withdraw his demands and permit the issues to drift, unresolved; to reduce his goals in the interest of an immediate settlement; or to escalate the pressures in the hope of securing an eventual settlement on his own terms. Normally when the internal conditions of a country undermine its relations with others, a diplomatic corps simply removes itself from the hostile environment and awaits a better day. Mexico, despite its animosity, did not endanger the security interests of the United States; it had not invaded Texas and did not contemplate doing so. Mexico had refused to pay the claims, but those claims were not equal to the price of a one-week war. Whether Mexico negotiated a boundary for Texas in 1846 mattered little; the United States had lived with unsettled boundaries for decades without considering war. Settlers, in time, would have forced a decision, but in 1846 the region between the Nueces and the Rio Grande was a vast, generally unoccupied wilderness. Thus there was nothing, other than Polk's ambitions, to prevent the United States from withdrawing its diplomats from Mexico City and permitting its relations to drift. But Polk, whatever the language of his instructions, did not send Slidell to Mexico to normalize relations with that government. He expected Slidell to negotiate an immediate boundary settlement favorable to the United States, and nothing less.

Recognizing no need to reduce his demands on Mexico, Polk, without hesitation, took the third course which Mexico offered. Congress bound the president to the annexation of Texas; thereafter the Polk administration was free to formulate its own policies toward Mexico. With the Slidell mission Polk embarked upon a program of gradual coercion to achieve a settlement, preferably without war. That program led logically from his dispatching an army to Texas and his denunciation of Mexico in his annual message of December 1845 to his new instructions of January 1846, which ordered General Taylor to the Rio Grande. Colonel Atocha, spokesman for the deposed Mexican leader, Antonio López de Santa Anna, encouraged Polk to pursue his policy of escalation. The president recorded Atocha's advice:

> He said our army should be marched at once from Corpus Christi to the Del Norte, and a strong naval force assembled at Vera Cruz, that Mr. Slidell, the U.S. Minister, should withdraw from Jalappa, and go on board one of our ships of War at Vera Cruz, and in that position should demand the payment of [the] amount due our citizens; that it was well known the Mexican Government was unable to pay in money, and that when they saw a strong force ready to strike on their coasts and border, they would, he had no doubt, feel their danger and agree to the boundary suggested. He said that Paredes, Almonte, & Gen'l Santa Anna were all willing for such an arrangement, but that they dare not make it until it was made apparent to the Archbishop of Mexico & the people generally that it was necessary to save their country from a war with the U. States.

Thereafter Polk never questioned the efficacy of coercion. He asserted at a cabinet meeting on February 17 that "it would be necessary to take strong measures towards Mexico before our difficulties with that Government could be settled." Similarly on April 18 Polk told Calhoun that "our relations with Mexico had reached a point where we could not stand still but must treat all nations whether weak or strong alike, and that I saw no alternative but strong measures towards Mexico." A week later the president again brought the Mexican question before the cabinet. "I expressed my opinion," he noted in his diary, "that we must take redress for the injuries done us into our own hands, that we had attempted to conciliate Mexico in vain, and had forborne until forbearance was no longer either a virtue or patriotic." Convinced that Paredes needed money, Polk suggested to leading senators that Congress appropriate $1 million both to encourage Paredes to negotiate and to sustain him in power until the United States could ratify the treaty. The president failed to secure Calhoun's required support.

Polk's persistence led him and the country to war. Like all escalations in the exertion of force, his decision responded less to unwanted and unanticipated resistance than to the requirements of the clearly perceived and inflexible purposes which guided the administration. What perpetuated the president's escalation to the point of war was his determination to pursue goals to the end whose achievement lay outside the possibilities of successful negotiations. Senator Thomas Hart Benton of Missouri saw this situation when he wrote: "It is impossible to conceive of an administration less warlike, or more intriguing, than that of Mr. Polk. They were *men of peace, with objects to be accomplished by means of war*;

so that war was a necessity and an indispensability to their purpose."

Polk understood fully the state of Mexican opinion. In placing General Taylor on the Rio Grande he revealed again his contempt for Mexico. Under no national obligation to expose the country's armed forces, he would not have advanced Taylor in the face of a superior military force. Mexico had been undiplomatic; its denunciations of the United States were insulting and provocative. But if Mexico's behavior antagonized Polk, it did not antagonize the Whigs, the abolitionists, or even much of the Democratic party. Such groups did not regard Mexico as a threat; they warned the administration repeatedly that Taylor's presence on the Rio Grande would provoke war. But in the balance against peace was the pressure of American expansionism. Much of the Democratic and expansionist press, having accepted without restraint both the purposes of the Polk administration and its charges of Mexican perfidy, urged the president on to more vigorous action....

Confronted with the prospect of further decline which they could neither accept nor prevent, [the Mexicans] lashed out with the intention of protecting their self-esteem and compelling the United States, if it was determined to have the Rio Grande, New Mexico, and California, to pay for its prizes with something other than money. On April 23, Paredes issued a proclamation declaring a defensive war against the United States. Predictably, one day later the Mexicans fired on a detachment of U.S. dragoons. Taylor's report of the attack reached Polk on Saturday evening, May 9. On Sunday the president drafted his war message and delivered it to Congress on the following day. Had Polk avoided the crisis, he might have gained the time required to permit the emigrants of 1845 and 1846 to settle the California issue without war.

What clouds the issue of the Mexican War's justification was the acquisition of New Mexico and California, for contemporaries and historians could not logically condemn the war and laud the Polk administration for its territorial achievements. Perhaps it is true that time would have permitted American pioneers to transform California into another Texas. But even then California's acquisition by the United States would have emanated from the use of force, for the elimination of Mexican sovereignty, whether through revolution or war, demanded the successful use of power. If the power employed in revolution would have been less obtrusive than that exerted in war, its role would have been no less essential. There simply was no way that the United States could acquire California peacefully. If the distraught Mexico of 1845 would not sell the distant province, no regime thereafter would have done so. Without forceful destruction of Mexico's sovereign power, California would have entered the twentieth century as an increasingly important region of another country.

Thus the Mexican War poses the dilemma of all international relations. Nations whose geographic and political status fails to coincide with their ambition and power can balance the two sets of factors in only one manner: through the employment of force. They succeed or fail according to circumstances; and for the United States, the conditions for achieving its empire in the Southwest and its desired frontage on the Pacific were so ideal that later generations could refer to the process as the mere fulfillment of destiny. "The Mexican Republic," lamented a Mexican writer in 1848, " ... had among other misfortunes of less account, the great one of being in the vicinity of a strong and energetic people." What the Mexican War revealed in equal measure is the simple fact that only those countries which have achieved their destiny, whatever that may be, can afford to extol the virtues of peaceful change.

POSTSCRIPT

Was the Mexican War an Exercise in American Imperialism?

According to Graebner, President James Polk assumed that Mexico was weak and that acquiring certain Mexican territories would satisfy "the long-range interests" of the United States. But when Mexico refused Polk's attempts to purchase New Mexico and California, he was left with three options: withdraw his demands, modify and soften his proposals, or aggressively pursue his original goals. According to Graebner, the president chose the third option.

Graebner is one of the most prominent members of the "realist" school of diplomatic historians. His writings were influenced by the cold war realists, political scientists, diplomats, and journalists of the 1950s who believed that American foreign policy oscillated between heedless isolationism and crusading wars without developing coherent policies that suited the national interests of the United States.

Graebner's views on the Mexican War have not gone unchallenged. For example, both David M. Pletcher's *The Diplomacy of Annexation* (University of Missouri Press, 1973), which remains the definitive study of the Polk administration, and Charles Seller's biography *James K. Polk*, 2 vols. (Princeton University Press, 1957–1966) are critical of Polk's actions in pushing the Mexican government to assert its authority in the disputed territory.

Acuña offers a Mexican perspective on the war in the first chapter of his book *Occupied America: A History of Chicanos,* 3rd ed. (Harper & Row, 1988), from which his selection is taken. He rejects the cool, detached, realistic analysis of Graebner and argues in very passionate terms that the North Americans waged an unjust aggressive war against their weaker neighbor to the south for the purpose of profit.

Acuña disagrees with older historians like Justin Smith and Eugene Barker, who justified the war as an inevitable conflict between a unique, nonviolent, capitalist, Protestant, democratic nation whose economic, religious, and political values were superior to a backward, feudal, Catholic, and authoritarian country.

Acuña also takes issue with Graebner, who considers Manifest Destiny to be mere political rhetoric with very limited goals. In Acuña's analysis, Manifest Destiny "had its roots in Puritan ideas, which continue to influence Anglo-American thought to this day.... Many citizens believed that God had destined them to own and occupy all of the land from ocean to ocean and pole to pole. Their mission, their destiny made manifest, was to spread the principles of democracy and Christianity to the unfortunates of the hemisphere."

Acuña receives support for his views from American historians like William Appleman Williams, who influenced an entire generation of diplomatic historians with the thesis that economic expansion resulted in *The Tragedy of American Diplomacy* (Delta, 1962). Mexican historian Ramón Eduardo Ruiz, in his book *Triumphs and Tragedy: A History of the Mexican People* (W. W. Norton, 1992), is more balanced and nuanced than Acuña but is just as critical of the racist ideology behind the rhetoric of Manifest Destiny that justified taking land away from not only Mexican Americans but also the North American Indians. In his article "Manifest Destiny and the Mexican War," in Howard H. Quint et al., eds., *Main Problems in American History*, vol. 1, 5th ed. (Dorsey Press, 1988), Ruiz maintains that Mexico never recovered economically from the loss of its territories to the United States 150 years ago. In an interesting twist, Ruiz also contends that the United States did not absorb all of Mexico into the United States after the Mexican War because it did not want any further increase to its nonwhite population base.

Both Graebner and Acuña appear ethnocentric in their analysis of the origins of the war. Graebner neglects the emotionalism and instability of Mexican politics at the time, which may have precluded the rational analysis a realistic historian might have expected in the decision-making process. Acuña also oversimplifies the motives of the Euroamericans, and he appears blinded to the political divisions between slaveholders and nonslaveholders and between Whig and Democratic politicians over the wisdom of going to war with Mexico.

The best two collections of readings from the major writers on the Mexican War are old but essential: see Archie McDonald, ed., *The Mexican War: Crisis for American Democracy* (D. C. Heath, 1969) and Ramón Eduardo Ruiz, ed., *The Mexican War: Was It Manifest Destiny?* (Holt, Rinehart & Winston, 1963).

There are several nontraditional books that cover the Mexican War, including John H. Schroeder, *Mr. Polk's War: American Opposition and Dissent, 1846–1848* (Wisconsin, 1973). Robert W. Johannsen summarizes the ways in which contemporaries viewed the war in *To the Halls of the Montezumas: The Mexican War in the American Imagination* (Oxford University Press, 1985).

ISSUE 12

Did the Westward Movement Transform the Traditional Roles of Women in the Mid-Nineteenth Century?

YES: Sandra L. Myres, from *Westering Women and the Frontier Experience, 1800–1915* (University of New Mexico Press, 1982)

NO: John Mack Faragher, from *Women and Men on the Overland Trail* (Yale University Press, 1979)

ISSUE SUMMARY

YES: Professor of history Sandra L. Myres (1933–1991) argues that first- and second-generation American women often worked outside the home as teachers, missionaries, doctors, lawyers, ranchers, miners, and business people instead of simply assuming the traditional roles of wife and mother.

NO: According to professor John Mack Faragher, women were reluctant pioneers because they were unwilling to break away from their close network of female relatives and friends. However, nineteenth century marital laws gave their husbands the sole authority to make the decision to move west.

In 1893 historian Frederick Jackson Turner (1861–1932) delivered an address before the American Historical Association entitled "The Significance of the Frontier in American History." According to Turner, American civilization was unique and different from European civilization because America contained an abundance of land that was settled in four major waves of migration from 1607 through 1890. During this migration European heritage was shed, and the American characteristics of individualism, mobility, nationalism, and democracy developed.

This frontier theory of American history did not go unchallenged. Other historians stated that Turner's definition of the frontier was too vague; that he underestimated the cultural forces that came to the West from Europe and the eastern states; that he neglected the forces of urbanization and industrialization in colonizing the West; that he placed an undue emphasis on sectional developments and neglected class struggles for power; and that his provincial view of American history prolonged the isolationist views of a nation that had become involved in world affairs in the twentieth century. By the time Turner died, his thesis had been widely discredited. Historians continued to write about the West, but new fields and new theories were competing for attention.

Until recently, most historians did not consider women a part of western history. One scholar who searched 2,000 pages of Turner's work could find only one paragraph devoted to women. Men built railroads, drove cattle, led military expeditions, and governed territories. "Women," concluded one writer, "were invisible, few in number, and not important to the taming of the West."

When scholars did acknowledge the presence of women on the frontier, perceptions were usually based upon stereotypes that were created by male observers and had become prevalent in American literature. According to Sandra L. Myres, there were three main images. The first image was that of a frightened, tearful woman who lived in a hostile environment and who was overworked, overbirthed, depressed, lonely, and resigned to a hard life and an early death. The second image, in contrast, was that of a helpmate and a civilizer of the frontier who could fight Native Americans as well as take care of the cooking, the cleaning, and the rearing of children. A third image of the westering women was that of the "bad woman," who was more masculine than feminine in her behavior and who was "hefty, grotesque and mean with a pistol."

The proliferation of primary source materials found since the early 1970s —letters, diaries, and memoirs written by frontierswomen—has led to a reassessment of the role of westering women. They are no longer what Joan Hoff Wilson once referred to as the "orphans of women's history." There are disagreements in interpretation, but these disagreements are now based upon sound scholarship. One area where scholars disagree concerns the following issue: Were the traditional roles of women changed by their participation in the westward movements of the nineteenth century?

In the first selection, Sandra L. Myres applies the Turner thesis to women in a positive fashion. Myres states that first- and second-generation women often worked in various fields outside of the home. In the second selection, John Mack Faragher maintains that women were reluctant pioneers because the nineteenth century marital laws gave their husbands the sole authority to make decisions to move west, thereby forcing their wives to break away from their close network of female relatives and friends.

YES   Sandra L. Myres

WOMEN AS FRONTIER ENTREPRENEURS

The West offered challenges to women's skills and provided opportunities for them to develop and test new talents and to broaden the scope of their home and community activities. It also offered, for whatever reason, a significant degree of political participation. But did the West offer economic opportunity as well? Frederick Jackson Turner maintained that the West was a liberating influence in American life and that the frontier setting offered westering Americans, at least westering males, both economic and political opportunity. "So long as free land exists," he wrote in his famous essay on the significance of the frontier, "the opportunity for a competency exists and economic power secures political power." In recent years, a number of historians have attacked portions of Turner's frontier hypothesis and especially its relevance to westering women. Indeed, several radical feminist authors have maintained that the West exerted a regressive rather than a progressive influence on women's lives. These authors contended that women on the frontiers were forced into unfamiliar, demeaning roles, and that although women in the Western settlements continued to try to reinstate a culture of domesticity, their work as virtual hired hands prevented them either from returning to older, more familiar roles in the social structure or from creating positive new roles. Unable to "appropriate their new work to their own ends and advantage," the authors of one article concluded, frontier women "remained estranged from their function as able bodies." . . .

Writing from a somewhat different perspective, several historians questioned the application of Turner's thesis to women's frontier experiences and concluded that women did not share in the freedom and opportunities the West offered to men. The stereotype of American women as the "virtuous, religious, progenitor of democracy—the cornerstone of the family and society," one maintained, was a product of an agrarian mythology (and by implication a frontier mythology as well). He argued that it was not on the farm, or on the frontier, that women won political and legal rights, but rather in the city. "It was the city," he wrote, "which became the catalyst for all the aspirations of freedom and equality held by American women." The frontier influenced women as well as men, another historian agreed, but "If we accept Turner's

From Sandra L. Myres, *Westering Women and the Frontier Experience 1800–1915* (University of New Mexico Press, 1982). Copyright © 1982 by University of New Mexico Press. Reprinted by permission. Notes omitted.

own assumption that economic opportunity is what matters, and that the frontier was significant as the context within which economic opportunity occurred, then we must observe that for American women... opportunity began pretty much where the frontier left off." In a similar vein, another historian wrote that although there were independent Western women who may have been different from women in the urban East, industrialism and the city, not the Western farm, opened new avenues for women. The frontier, according to his interpretation, "strongly reinforced the traditional role of the sexes," and, he concluded, mill girls were likely to be "potentially far more 'revolutionary' than their rural, Western counterparts."

Yet despite arguments to the contrary, there is clear evidence that Western women did not confine themselves to purely traditional domestic and community concerns. It is true that most Western women were not revolutionary. Like Western men, they did not completely break with tradition nor, with very few exceptions, attempt radically to change women's lives and role in society. They did enlarge the scope of woman's place, however, and countered prevailing Eastern arguments about woman's sphere and the cult of true womanhood. Indeed, the ideals of true womanhood never really applied to a large number of women. As one historian has pointed out, at the very time that domesticity and true womanhood were being expounded as an American ideal, an increasing number of women were leaving their homes to become factory workers and wage earners. Factory work was obviously not available in frontier areas, but like many of their Eastern sisters, Western women were employed in a number of economic activities, and some of them engaged in new fields of endeavor outside what was considered their competency, skills, or proper sphere.

On the Western frontiers, as in other rural areas, much of women's work was tied to domestic manufacture. Historians have estimated that in the colonial period, when the United States was still predominantly rural, 60 to 75 percent of domestic manufacture, particularly in textiles, was carried out by women....

Such domestic manufacture continued on the Western frontiers for many years after it had ceased in the East. Although by the nineteenth century, factories were beginning to produce foodstuffs, clothing, and other goods previously provided by home production, frontier women continued to manufacture such items themselves because "neither the goods, nor the cash to obtain them were readily available." Long, and often primitive, transportation made factory goods scarce and therefore expensive, and few frontier families, at least during the first years of settlement, had extra money to purchase what the women could, and did, produce at home. It was the women, as one Iowa man recalled, who saw that "the garden [was] tended, the turkeys dressed, the deer flesh cured and the fat prepared for candles or culinary use, the wild fruits were garnered and preserved or dried, that the spinning and knitting was done and the clothing made." Such production was not considered gainful employment, of course, and female home manufacturers were rarely, if ever, listed by census takers as employed or working women. Yet such employment was essential to the family economy. Women, as one historian wrote, were "to their families what the factory was to an industrialized society;" they were "the key link in turning unusable raw materials into consumable finished goods."

Not only did women provide needed goods and services for their families, which otherwise would have had to be purchased, but they often exchanged the produce of such work for needed goods or for cash. Margaret Murray recalled that her mother "sold Butter Eggs & Beeswax & anything we could spare off the farm, [and] in the summer and fall we gathered Black Berries wild grapes & anything we raised on the farm that would bring money or exchange for groceries." ...

Through these contributions some women came to exert a good deal of influence on the family decision-making process. "The women were not unaware" of their contributions, one reported, and were "quite capable of scoring a point on occasion when masculine attitudes became too bumptious." Some women were openly aggressive or even contradictory in opposing male decisions, while others worked more subtly and were "careful to maintain the idea of male superiority." For example, one woman bought some milk cows and began a small dairy business while her husband was away doing carpenter work, but when he returned, he sold the cows since such work "did not appeal to him." The woman, however, without raising a fuss, simply took some inheritance money and reinvested in cows and "eventually the family acquired hogs to help consume the milk ... [and] stock raising ended as the family's main economic activity."

Often women's domestic skills became the basis for a profitable business. Cooks, seamstresses, and washerwomen were in demand, especially in the mining camps and in other areas where the population included a number of single men. Although such work was laborious, it was usually well paid, particularly during the early frontier period. "I know girls that is ritch," one woman reported, "just working out bie the month," while another wrote that wages for women's work were high, "$50 to $75 a month." ...

Most of this type of work could be done at home, and women thus provided a small income for their families while they continued to carry out their household chores and care for their children within a familiar setting. ...

In frontier areas, women also served an important function as hotel and boardinghouse keepers. Women frequently boarded hired hands or seasonal workers. One California woman wrote that during the harvesting she had ten men in the family. "Washing and cooking for this crew," she reported, "takes me all the time. ..." A Texas woman recorded that her husband owned a cotton gin for twenty-two years, and "I had my part to play in this business as we boarded the hands and I did the cooking." Other women opened their homes to boarders or operated small hotels to provide an income for themselves or their families. Shortly after her husband died, Amelia Barr wrote, "I have opened my house last week for boarders and intend to take about eight steady boarders," and a Texas woman recalled that her grandmother "kept a boarding house" to support her family when her Unionist husband left for Mexico.

Boardinghouses varied in size and type of services provided. Some boarding establishments furnished only meals while others supplied both meals and lodging. Others offered a combination of services. A Kansas woman recorded that she had two lodgers for whom she provided breakfast and supper and two others who "cook their own food and lodge in our little hut." Most boarding establishments were relatively small operations. With limited space and cooking facilities, most women could not accommodate more than eight to ten boarders at a time, but a few attempted to run fairly substantial operations....

On the frontier, women were actively sought not only as wives but as contributors to the local economy. Many community builders believed that a few good women would not only help in civilizing and taming the frontier but would add to its economic development as well. The Western agents for R. G. Dun and Company (the forerunner of Dun and Bradstreet) certainly were aware of women's potential economic contributions and recommended "equality of economic opportunity when it came to finding credit endorsements." Indeed, according to one analysis of Denver credit ratings for the period 1859 to 1877, "women without collateral could usually get recommendations for credit where men could not, even when everything was equal except their sex."

However remunerative, domestic work was often boring as well as laborious, and it kept women confined within their domestic spaces. "There is something dull in sitting here day by day, planning this garment and making that, but that seems to be my destiny just now," mourned a young Nebraska girl who made a good living as a seamstress. "There does not seem to be much that a girl can do here." Other women, equally bored by dull work, tried to find an outlet for their energies and creative urges in quiltmaking, fancy sewing, or by adding artistic touches to their home manufactures. Texas pioneer Ella Bird-Dumont longed to be a sculptress but, denied the opportunity to study in her Panhandle home,

she settled instead for creating beauty in the gloves and vests she made and sold to neighboring ranch hands and cowmen....

Some frontier women refused to subvert their artistic talents to the tasks of sewing, butter making, and other home chores. A number of women were able to combine pioneering and domestic tasks and at the same time open new avenues into the "life of the mind." By the nineteenth century, writing was considered a fairly respectable occupation for women, and a number of them combined the pen with homemaking and child care. According to a recent study, between 1784 and 1860 at least one hundred magazines, most of which were devoted to women's interests, were founded in the United States and provided a market for articles by and for women. Many of these articles were about what women knew best —homemaking and the domestic arts— but the journals also published poetry, essays, and short stories by women. Women also became increasingly active in writing books as well as articles. Of the 1150 novels by American authors published in the United States between 1830 and 1850, a large proportion (perhaps as many as one-third) were written by women. So successful were some of these works that Nathaniel Hawthorne felt compelled to complain to his publisher that "America is wholly given over to a damned mob of scribbling women...." Although many of the "damned mob" admittedly produced third and fourth-rate works, their books were nonetheless popular and brought their authoresses a good deal of attention as well as a source of income....

Aside from the arts, teaching was about the only profession open to respectable women in the nineteenth century.... [E]ducation was considered an extension of women's traditional roles as child rearers and moral and cultural guardians, and American education became increasingly feminized during the nineteenth century. As Catherine Beecher pointed out, teaching young children not only provided an essential service to the community, but it helped women prepare themselves for "the great purpose of a woman's life—the happy superintendence of a family." Beecher's advice did not go unheeded: a number of women taught school at one time or another.

Although most women teachers were single, some women continued at least part-time teaching after their marriage. Especially in Western communities where men were engaged in the "multitudes of other employments that will... lead to wealth" (as Beecher so bluntly wrote), educated women, whatever their marital status, were frequently urged to help begin schools and teach for a term or two. The scarcity of teachers and the desire of frontier dwellers to provide an education for their children led to many attempts to recruit young women from the East. "We want good female teachers, who could obtain constant employment and the best of wages," a Kansas settler wrote home to a New England newspaper; "we want them immediately, and they would do much good." Various Eastern groups attempted to respond to the demand. Catherine Beecher began a campaign to send women teachers to the West, warning that "Western children were growing up without the benefit of either a practical or a moral education." Beecher, and the Board of National Popular Education, formed in 1847, did recruit some teachers. The Board served as an agency for single teachers and provided job training as well as placement services, but the number of Eastern teachers provided by the group never approached the 90,000 young women Beecher believed were needed "if the tides of barbarism were to be pushed back." Far more helpful in recruiting teachers in the West than the actions of Eastern groups and agencies were the more practical solutions found by frontier residents who relied on the resources available and found local women with at least a modicum of education to fulfill the communities' educational needs....

Despite poor working conditions, rowdy pupils, low salaries, and increasing educational requirements, some women chose full-time, lifetime careers in teaching and were able to advance themselves professionally. Many young women took advantage of the more liberal educational opportunities available to them in Western colleges and universities to improve their academic skills and qualify them for better-paying and more professionally fulfilling jobs in the educational system. When the franchise was opened to Western women, elective school offices were opened to them as well, and in most Western states, women held posts as principals, superintendents, and served on state boards of education....

A number of women combined a desire to teach with religious zeal and entered the mission field. Indeed, for some women the principal motivation for going West was not family desires or economic betterment but an answer to a religious calling to minister to the Indians....

During the 1790s, the Second Awakening "spawned a whole family of state, regional, and national societies." Thus, by the beginning of the nineteenth century most denominations sponsored both foreign and home missions, and several interdenominational societies had been formed to carry the gospel to both the Indians and the white inhabitants of new Western settlements.

The boards which organized and controlled Western missions were made up entirely of men, and decisions about the establishment and conduct of the missions were made in the East, not in the West. Nonetheless, it was the missionaries in the field who were crucial to the success of the missionary effort, and women, living and working in the West, made important and significant contributions to mission work. At first a number of mission boards refused to allow women to enter the field, fearing the frontier and Indian villages too dangerous and unseemly a place for delicate females. Women filled with missionary ardor had to content themselves with fund-raising activities and quiet support of the mission effort. Eventually, however, mission boards actively recruited both married and single women to wash, cook, and clean at the mission stations and to assist the male missionaries in teaching in the mission schools, in evangelizing among the Indian women, and in other aspects of mission work. Between 1820 and 1850, a growing number of women joined missions in the trans-Appalachian West and in Indian Territory. As the frontier moved further West, new mission fields opened, and women became increasingly prominent in missionary work. They broadened the scope of their activities, preached as well as taught, and occasionally had full responsibility for the establishment and operation of mission schools and churches. A few were ordained to the regular ministry, in order, as one put it, "to add in some ways to her power to serve." ...

Conservative and traditional in most of their views towards social progress and the role of women, the missionaries nonetheless helped broaden women's place within Western society and in the nation as a whole. Certainly they proved the ability of women to undertake successfully this strenuous and difficult calling. A number of them became strong advocates for improved education for women so that they could more effectively serve in the mission field, and their books about their mission life, their letters to newspapers and magazines, and their public speaking tours to raise funds provided a greater visibility for women as public rather than private participants in American life.

At the opposite end of the social scale from the missionaries were the practitioners of a very different, publically visible, but traditional and exclusively female occupation, the so-called soiled doves or ladies of the night. A great deal has been written about Western prostitutes; much of it, of a popular, and often sensational, nature, concentrated on such colorful characters as Poker Alice, Tit Bit, Big Nose Kate, and Rose of the Cimarron. These women were often portrayed as nice girls gone wrong, women of some character and experience who drank, gambled, and sold their favors but who still were of a basically honest nature and had "hearts of pure gold." Or they were pictured as women of "evil name and fame," depraved, vicious, and cruel "Cyprian sisters." Several recent and more scholarly studies have suggested that some girls entered the profession in order to advance themselves economically or to escape dull and dreary lives on isolated farms and ranches. Many were attracted by the bright lights and excitement of the mining camps and cattle towns and hoped to earn a little nest egg, meet a cowboy, farmer, or rancher, and eventually settle down to a respectable life. Others hoped to become economically independent and viewed prostitution as one of the few professions where women had some chance of financial success. As one Denver woman succinctly noted, "I went into the sporting life for business reasons and no other. It was a way for a woman in those days to make money and I made it." ...

Brothel owners and operators and girls who worked in the better establishments generally scorned the dance hall and saloon girls who rented upstairs rooms over the taverns and the "crib" girls who sold their wares from small two-room establishments with a bedroom with a window on the street and a kitchen in the rear. At the bottom of the scale were the women who walked the streets and who were often ill and frequently subjected to cruel and violent treatment at the hands of both customers and law enforcement officials. But whatever their social or economic level—madame, parlor girl, saloon or crib girl, or streetwalker, their life was a hard one. Many committed suicide, died of disease and alcoholism, drifted away into other occupations or, among the more fortunate, found a husband or protector. One survey of prostitutes in the Kansas cattle towns found that the average age of these women was 23.1 years, and very few were over the age of thirty. Despite the legendary success of a few women, prostitution was neither an attractive nor a rewarding occupation.

Prostitution was a town or city occupation as were other more respectable occupations such as domestic service, hotel and boardinghouse management, and teaching. The economic opportunities for rural women, especially in frontier areas, were more limited. Yet a surprising number of farm and ranch women were able to turn their knowledge of domestic production and farm and ranch management into prosperous business enterprises. In addition to their domestic occupations such as cloth production, and chicken, egg, dairy, and butter businesses, many rural women actually ran the family farm.... [W]omen often had to take over farm management when the men were ill or incapacitated or were gone from home prospecting, fighting Indians, working in town for cash, or just wandering. This was particularly true in Mormon settlements where the men were often required to be gone for one or two years on missions for the church or were involved in other church activities. Meanwhile, the women stayed at home to "milk the cows, plant the crops, and care for the children." In many instances, women (non-Mormon as well as Mormon) provided most of the support for themselves and their families. Even when their menfolk remained at home, most rural women worked with their husbands during especially busy times of the year, and they thus came to have a good understanding of the various farm operations. Wrote one young Iowa farm girl, "I can't describe a thrashing floor so you understand but some day I can show you just how it was done...." Such experience stood women in good stead when they were widowed or left alone and had to take over. In the East, single or widowed women probably would have relied on a father, brothers, or uncles to aid them, but in the West they had fewer of these support networks to draw on, hired help was scarce and expensive, and most simply took over and continued to operate the family farm until they remarried or retired and left the property to their children....

A surprising number of Western women, both single and married, took up land in their own name. In the former Mexican states and territories, where Spanish rather than English law prevailed, married women could hold separate property in their own name, and many took advantage of the opportunity to purchase and adminster their own land. Indeed, Jane McManus Storms Cazneau applied for, and received, an empresario grant from the Mexican government. During the Texas Revolution she offered to borrow money against her landholdings. "As a female, I cannot bear arms for my adopted country," she wrote in 1835, "but if the interest I possess in her soil, will be a guarantee for any money, I will with joy contribute my mite to purchase arms for her brave defenders." In other former Mexican states other women, both of Mexican and English ancestry, owned farm and ranch property which they administered themselves.

Between 1800 and 1850, many changes occurred in the social, economic, and legal position of women, and a number of states and territories outside the former Mexican provinces passed more liberal laws governing women's property rights. As one legal historian pointed out, the number of women with a stake in society increased rapidly during this period, and the English common law, primarily geared to the needs of the landed gentry, no longer was satisfactory for American needs. In fact, he wrote, "the tangle of rules and practices was potentially an impediment to the speed and efficiency of the land market. The statutes spoke of rights of husband and wife, as if the real issue was the intimate relations between the sexes. But the real point of the statutes was to rationalize more cold-blooded matters, such as the rights of a creditor to collect debts out of land owned by husbands and wives, or both." In 1839, Mississippi made the first tentative reforms in the laws relating to married women's property, and other states and territories soon followed suit. By 1850, seventeen states, many of them in the West, had granted married women legal control over their property, while in Oregon, the Donation Land Law of 1850 allowed wives of settlers to claim a half-section (320 acres) in their own right. Most Western states' legal codes made some provision for women to purchase homestead land and own and operate businesses in their own name. Husbands sometimes took advantage of these laws to escape debts or bankruptcy by transferring property to the wife's name, but this device often backfired, for women, once in legal possession of the property, frequently refused to return it, assisted in its administration, and used their legal ownership as a weapon to force their husbands to comply with their wishes....

Whether ranchwomen confined themselves to more traditional roles or actively participated in ranch operations, they tended to become increasingly self-reliant and independent. According to Nannie Alderson, "the new country offered greater personal liberty than an old and settled one," and although she admitted that her years of ranch life never taught her any business sense, she nonetheless believed that Western ranch life instilled a good deal of self-reliance in women and children. This opinion was shared by a number of outside observers. The English visitor Anthony Trollope wrote in 1862 that ranchwomen were "sharp as nails and just as hard." They were rarely obedient to their menfolk, he reported, and "they know much more than they ought to. If Eve had been a ranchwoman, she would never have tempted Adam with an apple. She would have ordered him to make his [own] meal." This was particularly true of girls who grew up on Western farms and ranches. They were even more likely than their mothers to learn riding and roping skills, participate in ranch work, and understand business operations. According to one such young woman, "it is as beneficial for a woman as for a man to be independent," and, she continued, she knew of no reasons "why the judgement of women should not be as good as that of men if they gave the subject attention." In later life, many of these ranch girls assisted their husbands in the ranching business, operated ranches of their own, or turned their talents into careers in rodeo and wild west shows. . . .

Some women turned their farm and ranch experience to the development of large-scale commercial agricultural enterprises, and others became very successful real estate investors. As early as 1742, a young frontiers-woman, Eliza Lucas, assumed management of her father's extensive Carolina estates and developed a profitable indigo market. Mention has already been made of Margaret Brent who managed not only her own lands but was executrix for Leonard Calvert's estate as well. These women established an early pattern for other women. By the late nineteenth century, a Western traveler commented on the number of "bright-minded women from other parts of the country" who were "engaged in real estate transactions in this country. . . . [I]t is not a rare thing," she continued, "for numbers of feminine speculators to attend the auction sales of land," and she estimated that of the sixty-five women teachers in the Los Angeles schools, "almost all own some land." . . .

In addition to real estate and commercial agriculture, Western women engaged in many other business and professional enterprises. A survey of the R. G. Dun and Company reports revealed a number of women in the Western states and territories owned and operated millinery shops, dressmaking establishments, grocery and dry goods stores, hotels and restaurants, and other similar establishments. For some, these enterprises served as a basis for other businesses or professions. For example, an Oregon woman, Bethenia Owens-Adair, opened a millinery shop in order to earn money for medical school, and other women reported that the income from their shops helped to underwrite real estate and mining investments. Two enterprising westering women purchased a supply of cloth and other dry goods which they sold from the back of their spring wagon to help pay their expenses to California.

Other women engaged in less-traditional businesses including manufacturing, mining, printing, and editing. Frontier women who had learned to "make-do" and who had devised various means to overcome shortages or unavailable goods applied for patents on various inventions, many of them developed out of their frontier experience. Most of these inventions were closely related to domestic and farm work—improvements for milk coolers, separators and churns, new types of wash tubs, quilting frames, beekeeping equipment, and new strains of farm and garden plants; but others, like Harriet Strong's patent for a "method and means for impounding debris and storing water," provided the basis for other businesses. Strong used her patents and her knowledge of engineering to develop an irrigation and water company in the San Gabriel Valley and became an expert on underground water storage and flood control. . . .

Women were also employed as reporters and contributors for many Western journals and newspapers. After 1850, Ladies' Department columns began to appear in newspapers, often run by the editor's wife or one of the paper's more notable female contributors. Talented women journalists, however, also wrote regular columns or contributed articles on topics of general interest. . . .

By the end of the nineteenth century, according to a recent survey, 1,238 women were engaged in printing and publication and another 1,127 were employed as compositors, linotype operators, and typesetters in eleven far-Western states. A separate study identified twenty-five women newspaper owners and editors in Missouri in the same period.

Western women were also active in other professions including medicine and law. Although these women faced many of the same obstacles and discriminations as Eastern professional women, they had less difficulty in establishing themselves and gaining recognition of their professional status. . . . [F]rontier women often had to render medical assistance and treatment, and many were recognized as professional or near-professional practitioners of the healing arts. In Mexican-American communities and in many Indian societies, women were believed to have special gifts as healers, and *curanderas* and medicine women were valued for their skills in treating illness and reducing pain. A number of women assisted their physician-husbands and sometimes substituted for them in emergencies. Midwifery and nursing were common occupations for frontier women, although these services rarely earned them monetary remuneration, and they were not acknowledged as gainfully employed in the census or other official documents. After Elizabeth Blackwell's successful assault on male domination of medicine in 1847, an increasing number of women attended medical school and became licensed physicians. In Utah, the Mormon community actively supported women's work in all aspects of medicine and dentistry and produced one of "the most remarkable groups of women doctors in American history." In 1873 Church leader Brigham Young suggested that women's classes be formed in Salt Lake City to study physiology and obstetrics and that "the Bishops see that such women be supported." . . .

Although Utah undoubtedly had the highest percentage of women doctors, other Western states and territories also had a fairly high percentage of professional women. By 1893, a number of coeducational medical schools had been established in the West and enrolled a number of women—19 percent at the University of Michigan, 20 percent at the University of Oregon, and 31 percent at Kansas Medical School.

Women had more difficulty in obtaining legal training because of statutory prohibitions based on English common law which prohibited women from being called to the bar. Nonetheless, after 1870, a few women succeeded in winning admission to legal practice, and those who did frequently vied with each other for the honor of being named the first woman admitted to practice before their state bar or the first woman to try a case before a state supreme court. . . .

Everywhere in the West, by the end of the nineteenth century, women were entering new professions and businesses and were finding new roles outside the recognized scope of woman's place. Many of these Western female entrepreneurs first learned business skills by assisting their husbands, but others learned because of necessity and gained economic and technical expertise through hard work and often bitter experience.... Other women were forced to become independent because of the absence or death of their husbands. Certainly some were reluctant capitalists and businesswomen, but others, often to their own amazement, found that they enjoyed earning their own livelihood and controlling their own lives, and they became enthusiastic entrepreneurs. "I am a great believer in the independence of women," one wrote. "I think married women should be allowed to go on with their career if they wish...." Another, the very successful California businesswoman Harriet Strong, advocated business and economic education for all women so that they would be prepared to assume management of their property if necessary. She hoped to organize a Ladies Business League of America and establish a series of business colleges and training schools to teach women the basic principles of economics and business management. It was not easy for women to succeed in business, she cautioned. "Whatever vocation a woman would enter, she must give it the same scientific study and hard work that a man would in order to make a success." Moreover, she warned:

> A woman needs to have five times as much ability as a man in order to do the same thing. She may be permitted to conduct her own ranch and be a success in a small business enterprise —yes, but let her go into the business of incorporating a large enterprise and bonding it, as a man would ... and then see if the word does not go forth, "This woman is going too far; she must be put down."...

Whether the frontier provided a liberating experience and economic as well as social and political opportunities for women is still a question of much debate. Certainly there is some evidence that it did not. As noted at the beginning of this chapter, some historians have concluded, based on women's reminiscences, diaries, and letters, that the frontier did not offer as many opportunities for women as it did for men and that women often failed to take advantage of the frontier experience as a means of liberating themselves from constricting and sexist patterns of behavior. Yet these same reminiscences, diaries, and letters also contain evidence to support the contention that women on the frontiers modified existing norms and adopted flexible attitudes and experimental behavior patterns. For some these changes were easily made and enthusiastically accepted; for others they were reluctantly made and strongly resisted. What has perhaps confused the various interpretations of woman's place and the westering experience is that the *reality* of women's lives changed dramatically as a result of adaptation to frontier conditions while the public *image* remained relatively static. Image, myth, and stereotype were contrary to what women were actually experiencing and doing. The ideal for women in the late nineteenth century moved more and more toward a romanticized view of the wife, mother, and lady, if not of leisure, at least of withdrawn and demure refinement. If frontier necessity, practice, and even law recognized female economic and political independence, social custom and tradition ignored it. Despite a growing emphasis on women's rights, nineteenth-century writers overlooked—or at least chose not to draw attention to—Western life models on which other women might pattern their own lives. Temperance and suffrage rather than economic education and independence for women dominated the feminist literature, often to the detriment of effective women's rights. Women who did not marry or who effectively ran businesses or professional enterprises were often viewed as being not quite respectable or at least unfeminine no matter how efficiently they also ran their homes or carried on family responsibilities in addition to challenging male domination of the marketplace.

Yet women who survived the first or even the second wave of adjustment to frontier conditions and changed roles for women tended to ignore, or at least not slavishly strive toward, Eastern-dictated models of femininity or the ideal of true womanhood. These hardy and self-sufficient women stepped out of woman's place with few regrets. If they did not glory in their new freedom, they did express pride in their newfound talents and accomplishments. It was the later generations of Western women, those who no longer lived on a frontier, who began to emulate Eastern models of propriety and sought to perpetuate the myths of woman's proper sphere. Yet even these later generations betrayed their frontier heritage in their personal values and attitudes. This heritage was reflected in a survey in 1943 which showed that Western women, as compared to those in the North and the South, were far better educated, held a wider variety of jobs, and were more likely to continue working, were less prone to adhere to traditional religious and denominational beliefs, were more excited and more optimistic about their lives, were more open to change, and were more likely to approve equal standards for men and women. Thus, the westering experience continued to influence Western women's values and attitudes long after the passing of the frontier.

NO   John Mack Faragher

THE WORLD OF THE FAMILY

The law of midwestern states provided official endorsement of notions of reciprocal marriage. Congress, in the Northwest Ordinance of 1787, and in the 1816 organization of the Missouri Territory, placed the areas that later became the states of Indiana, Illinois, Iowa, and Missouri under the protection of English common law; thus, in the Midwest, as in nearly all other areas of the United States, common-law definitions of marriage prevailed until amended by state statutes after mid-century. Through the common law the conventional roles of husband and wife were legally enshrined: a husband was obligated to provide a residence and household for his family, and to supply his wife with the means of feeding and clothing herself and her children; a wife was legally obligated to be her husband's helpmeet, to perform household and domestic duties freely and willingly without compensation. Both partners to the marriage contract had the exclusive legal right to the society, companionship, and conjugal affections of their spouse; there was a mutual obligation to love, to care for, and to labor faithfully to advance the interests of one's spouse.

But marriage legally obligated more than reciprocity. Legal marriage, like the marital relation in practice, gave the husband extraordinary power over the life and affairs of his wife. The law was the cultural capstone of the system of male privilege which extended from the uneven division of domestic labor through male control of the public world. Although each couple had ultimately to work out the relations of power and authority within their own marriage, the law represented the limits of the permissible and offered a sanctioned model of female subordination. The law, written by men and enforced by men, was a principal vehicle for furthering the ideological and social dominance of the patriarchy.

All women in nineteenth-century North American society, whether married or single, were without the benefits of the most basic civil rights: women could not vote, could not serve on juries, and in most places could not hold public office, all aspects of their general exclusion from the public world. Single women did enjoy almost equal legal status with men in contractual and property rights, but once married, women lost these rights as well, and very few women, of course, remained single. Married women were no longer responsible citizens but dependents, like children and idiots, relying for protection on the legal status of their husband-guardians. More than convention was operating when women dropped their maiden names and assumed the names of their husbands, since according to common-law doctrine, a man and a woman became a single legal person upon marriage, and, as Blackstone opined for every country lawyer in those hundreds of midwestern villages, that person was the husband.

The legal oppression of married women read like a bill of attainder. Since wives had no legal identity they could make no independent legal arrangements or contracts; they could neither sue nor be sued; they could not make an independent will; any contractual obligations undertaken before their marriages became the responsibility of husbands to fulfill. Wives forfeited to their husbands control and management of any and all real property they might have held before their marriage; husbands retained the rights to that property until their deaths, and indeed, if there were living issue of the marriage, the property previously owned by wives could then even be placed in trust for the children and kept out of women's hands. Husbands gained outright ownership of all the prenuptial personal property and chattels of their wives, and to husbands fell the right to proceed with any suits initiated by their wives and receive the settlements as their own. Husbands owned their wives' labor power; any wages wives received while married were legally owed to their husbands. Finally, since husbands and wives were legally one person, men could under no circumstances be charged with stealing from their wives, which gave men the widest possible leeway in their actions.

Husbands were recognized by law as the heads of their families; to them was delegated the obligation to control and discipline their wives. Hence husbands were permitted to physically punish their spouses within "reasonable limits," which by common law meant wives could be beaten as long as the instrument was no bigger around than the man's thumb. Wives were deprived of redress in the courts for injuries received at their husbands' hands. Husbands could legally confine their wives at home, refuse them visitors, even forcibly separate them from their parents. Divorce was difficult to obtain in most midwestern states; petition had to be made for a special legislative divorce. If there was a divorce, the legal assumption was that the custody of minor children went with the head of the family—the husband. For women, therefore, divorce usually meant giving up their children.

It is little wonder that the nascent women's rights movement took reform of the marriage law as one of its first objectives. Feminists supported the Married Women's Property Acts, which proposed to amend the law to allow married women to hold their prenuptial property in their own (married) names and reform women's contractual rights. Feminists had the powerful support, in most states, of legal reformers, wealthy families who wished to protect the dower property of their daughters from unscrupulous suitors, and impoverished farmers who hoped to save some of their estate from creditors by placing it in their wives' names. In the Midwest these reforms of the common law were in step with the rest of the nation, beginning during the 1850s. But the implementation of the intent of the laws was delayed many years by the determined rear guard of the exclusively male bench and bar which demonstrated real hostility to the acts. In any event, the general rule of common law continued to apply to relations between husband and wife, despite the fact that the Married Women's Acts logically renounced the legal fiction of two in one.

The property and contractual reforms would not have had much of a bearing upon the lives of most farm women in any case. Only rarely did any of these women enter a marriage with more than a modest personal dowry. The importance of the law lay rather in the considerable official authority it lent to the exercise of husbands' power. The common law sanctioned the existing power relations between midwestern men and women; it was patriarchal law.

It is interesting to look at the decision to emigrate to Oregon or California in the light of the legal model of husbands' power. In their diaries and recollections many women discussed the way in which the decision to move was made. Not one wife initiated the idea; it was always the husband. Less than a quarter of the women writers recorded agreeing with their restless husbands; most of them accepted it as a husband-made decision to which they could only acquiesce. But nearly a third wrote of their objections and how they moved only reluctantly. When John Jones informed his wife Mary of his plans, she remembered answering impulsively, "Oh, let us not go! But," she added, "it made no difference." One woman, writing of her own reluctance to move to Oregon, was reminded of the time her father had moved their family from Sangamon County to Missouri:

> I came in one evening to see a look on dear mother's face that I had never seen before. I walked away after the usual greeting and sat silent. After a time her voice strengthened and she said, "what do you think your father has done.... He has sold the farm and as soon as school closes we are to move to Missouri." ... What a shock these words gave me.

In her later years Lucy Deady wrote that her mother had known "nothing of this move until father had decided to go."

The decision to emigrate was the kind where husbands' patriarchal power made the difference: legally, after all, husbands had the right to enforce their own independent choice of domicile for the family; it was fully within a husband's prerogative to move his family without even consulting his wife....

We have no way of knowing, of course, how many wives were successful in either getting their restless husbands to take them along or in leashing them. But whatever power wives brought to bear was clearly defensive and responsive. Men held the customary authority to make these decisions, and they did so. Perhaps only when husbands proposed leaving alone, threatening the family unity upon which their authority was based, did wives most successfully challenge their dominance in worldly affairs. It is clear, at any rate, that many emigrating women had been given little if any opportunity to participate in the decision to emigrate. Enos Ellmaker described the process by which most couples probably decided to go: "After my fine [Iowa] farm had received so much improvements yet I was not satisfied with the country; *I finally got the consent of my wife to sell and move* to the far-distant Oregon." Their passive role necessarily meant that many women were reluctant participants in the crossing. "From Mrs Morrison's own lips I learned," wrote John Minto, "that the journey for which she was bending all her energies in preparation, was not in her judgement a wise business movement; but 'Wilson wished to go,' and that settled the question with her."

Women worked valiantly to preserve their domestic environment in transit, for if women had a power it was dependent upon their ability to meet their own, their husband's, and their children's domestic needs. It was in homemaking that women acquired their status, and homemaking, consequently, took up their time on the trail. For their task women demanded more equipment than men alone thought necessary. Sarah Royce remembered that family wagons "were easily distinguished by the greater number of conveniences, and household articles they carried." Some families came outfitted out of all proportion to the load limitations. Hugh Campbell remembered that their family traveled in a spring wagon built extrawide to accommodate a built-in stove, beds, and a rocking chair for his mother. The famous family wagon of the ill-fated Reed family—the Prairie Palace Car—also boasted a stove and even had a stovepipe sprouting from the canvas cover.

Most women made do with much less and yet were able, in the early stages at least, to create an air of homeyness about their camps. Sarah Royce noted the domestic articles of women—culinary equipment, food, boxes of clothing, tubs for washing—"disposed about the outside of the wagon in a home-like way," not simply strewn here and there as in the nearby male camps. "And

where bushes, trees or logs formed partial enclosures, a kitchen or sitting room quite easily suggested itself to the feminine heart, yearning for home." Tents became living rooms where women held, as best they could, to the amenities they tried to teach at home. Ed Bryant was received by Nancy Thornton in her tent "as she would have done in her parlor at home." In these settings it was sometimes possible to pretend that home really did abide with the heart. "Mrs Fox and her daughter are with us and everything is so still and quiet we can almost imagine ourselves at home again. We took out our Daguerrotypes and tried to live over again some of the happy days of 'Auld Lang Syne.'" "In the evening the young ladies came over to our house and we had a concert with both guitars. Indeed it seemed almost like a pleasant evening at home. We could none of us realize that we were almost at the summit of the Rocky Mountains."

By this stage of the trip, ascending the foothills of the Rockies, most women had been badly frustrated in their domestic work and needed no reminding of where they were. Along the Platte, the easiest leg of the journey, the water supply was muddy and crowded with "wigglers"; "this unsanitary condition," Charles True remembered, "was difficult for mother, with her life-long habits of scrupulous cleanliness and neatness to reconcile." The animal and human excrement that littered the trail were a constant injury to women's habits. When the captain of their train selected an evening campsite filthy from earlier travelers, normally passive Lavinia Porter threatened her husband; "If you do not drive me to a cleaner place to camp and sleep tonight I will take my blankets and go alone." They moved on, and "the other women looked on my daring unsubordination with wondering eyes, and envious of my cleanly quarters, at last plucked up courage to follow my example, and with much profanity [on the part of the men] the camp was moved." But some conditions could not easily be overcome.

> Our tents stand in what we should style a barnyard at home and I am sure if I were there I should as soon think of setting a table there as in such a place. The stench is sometimes almost unendurable, it arises from a ravene that is resorted to for special purposes by all the Emigration, but such things we must put up with.

As the emigrants moved up the grade approaching the Rockies, it became obvious that the overloaded wagons had to be lightened, and gradually they discarded materials not essential for survival. Domestic goods, of course, were most easily excluded from the essential category, much to the dismay of the women. "We came across a heavy old fashioned cook stove which some emigrant had hauled all those weary miles of mountain and desert, only to discard it at last," wrote Lavinia Porter. "No doubt some poor forlorn woman was now compelled to do her cooking by the primitive camp fire, perhaps much against her will." True recalled that by the time his party reached the Great Basin all his mother's camping conveniences had been discarded, greatly adding to her labors and filling her days with anxiety. This anxiety was not only an effect of added work. Books, furniture, knickknacks, china, daguerreotypes, guitars—the very articles that most helped to establish a domestic feel about the camps were the first things to be discarded. Lightening the wagons, however necessary, was interpreted by women as a process operating against their interests. In one party a woman "exclaimed over an escritoire of rare workmanship" she had found along the trail "and pitied the poor woman who had to part with it."

The loss of a sense of home—the inability to "keep house" on the trail—was perhaps the hardest loss to bear, the thing that drove women closest to desperation. In their diary entries, women wished fervently for a return to the familiar routines of home and farm life. Those routines objectively required more than a fair share from women, but they were comforting in their conventionality and, perhaps more important, comforting in the way they reserved a unique position for women. "If I were in the states now I would be sitting in a comfortable house besides a fire; but our house now is in the open air," Esther Hanna wrote. Louisa Frizzell, a strong and determined woman, nonetheless echoed her younger and more delicate sister: "I feel tired and weary, O the luxury of a house, a house!... I would have given all my interest in California, to have been seated around my own fireside." Velina Williams added her lament: "Oh, for a little home to call my own!" The trip was so long, so extended, that women began to feel that the physical foundations of domesticity—their homes—had slipped irretrievably from them, that they were moving into a wild and savage land where, perhaps, they would discover that homes were nonexistent and women frightfully oppressed.

Women, then, clung to the things that belonged to them in the homestead marriage: clearly segregated work, a physical sphere for their activity, important work in reproducing the next generation and rearing healthy and happy young farmers and farm wives. They showed little inclination to trade these roles for the more socially active work that necessity demanded from them on the trail; rather, they attempted to preserve at least the semblance of their traditional roles. Feminine farm roles had little to do with the fetishized domesticity that was a part of the womanly cult flowering in the East, for in most ways these pioneer wives and mothers were the very antithesis of that antiseptic and anesthetized version of femininity. These were working women who accepted, with their husbands, a view of marriage that was oppressive to women in practice but promised meaningful work and the rewards of achievement at tasks distinctively feminine and separate from men. For all the tensions and inadequacies of marriage, when placed under extraordinary stress women's vision could extend only far enough to wish themselves back on their well-ordered homesteads.

* * *

Denied the chance to participate in the decision to move, essentially because of the patriarchal bias of marital decision making, failing to accept as their own husbands' reasons for undertaking the move, women went not because they wanted to but because social expectations left them no choice. Understandably then, many women secretly blamed their husbands for their hardships on the trail. Lucy Rutledge Cook recorded in her letters home that her mother-in-law had vocally but privately complained to her, "Oh, I wish we never had started.... She looks so sorrowful and dejected," Lucy worried; "I think if Pa had not passengers to take through she would urge him to return; not that he would be so inclined, for returning is hopeless."

The elder Mrs. Cook declared that "no argument used to induce her to leave there seems to have any weight now" and placed the blame for the move on those who had persuaded her against her better judgment—her husband and sons. A few days later Lucy herself was echoing her mother-in-law: "Oh, how I wish we never had started for the Golden Land," but she kept her own laments private too, secreted in her letters home.

A few nights into Indian territory the Hecox–Aram party was joined at their camp one evening by a small group of Indian men who sat up around their fire all night, drinking, dancing, and loudly boasting of war exploits. Margaret Hecox retreated with her four children to the cold, damp wagon where she spent the night "hugging my baby to my bosom, with three badly scared little girls crouched at my feet." A single question reverberated in her head: "What had possessed my husband, anyway, that he should have thought of bringing us away out through this God-forsaken country?" At about the same stage of their journey, Lucy Ide wrote in her diary, "Well, well, this is not so romantic; thoughts will stray back (in spite of all our attempts to the contrary) to the comfortable homes we left and the question arises in my mind —is this a good move—but echo answers not a word."

Women reluctantly agreed to the emigration because they were dependent upon their families for society and companionship and upon their husbands for livelihood and support. Husbands and families were crucial to women's identities; the options for women left behind were lonely ones at best and could be socially and psychologically disastrous. But women were not dragged screaming to the wagons; in this sense no one forced them to go. There were a few examples of resistance; occasional anxiety or bewilderment erupted into open revolt against going forward.

> This morning our company moved on, except one family. The woman got mad and wouldn't go or let the children go. He had the cattle hitched on for three hours and coaxed her to go, but she wouldn't stir. I told my husband the circumstances and he and Adam Polk and Mr Kimball went and each one took a young one and crammed them into the wagon, and the husband drove off and left her sitting. She got up, took the back track and traveled out of sight. Cut across, overtook her husband. Meantime he sent his boy back to camp after a horse that he had left and when she came up her husband says "Did you meet John?" "Yes," was the reply, "and I picked up a stone and knocked out his brains." Her husband went back to ascertain the truth, and when he was gone she set one of his wagons on fire, which was loaded with store goods. The cover burnt off and some valuable articles. He saw the flames and came running and put it out, and then mustered spunk enough to give her a good flogging.

Short of violent resistance, it was always possible that circumstances would force a family to reconsider and turn back. Mary Ellen Todd's family traveled in 1852, when cholera was a scourge along the trails. "There was great discouragement among the emigrants..., and everyday there were some who were going back.... Women cried, begging their menfolk to take them back. It is no wonder that stout hearts began to waver. Consequently, after many heated discussions and more tears," the reluctant men finally consented to return. Mary Ellen remembered that the men "did the hooking up of their oxen in a spiritless sort of way.

Yet some of the girls and women were laughing." It would have been no surprise if some women had complained to their husbands as well as to their diaries. The carping woman was a standard image of overland folklore.

> The ladies have the hardest that
> emigrate by land,
>
> For when they cook with buffalo
> wood they often burn a hand;
>
> And when they jaw their husbands
> 'round, get mad and spill the tea.
>
> Wish to the Lord they'd be taken
> down with a turn of the di-a-ree.

Open resistance, constant complaining: these reactions would certainly have fit the disorder of women's powerlessness. But such stereotypical behavior rarely has an active existence; few women, if any, secretly plotted to sabotage the trip, and the wag who composed that verse about feminine emigrants was probably reflecting male fears of wifely resentment more than the abundance of shrews on the trail. Life is always richer and more complex than such reductionist images suggest. Women's leaving was determined by their social dependency, to be sure, and there was ample room for women to build and feel massive resentments; but their leaving was activated by the things women believed and expected of themselves. Their own social and personal values demanded that they be loving and obedient wives, faithful and ever-present mothers. They struggled with their men about the foolishness of going, but only until threatened with the loss of their wifely status; then they capitulated and packed the trunks. Past this point resistance was hopeless, as Lucy Cook recognized, more important, it would be destructive.

If we are to trust and respect their revelations in their diaries and recollections, the greatest struggle of women on the trail was the struggle to endure the hardship and suffering without becoming bitter and resentful, without becoming the carping wife, without burdening their marital relationship with the bad feelings that burned inside them. If we are to judge them not by our standards but their own, we will not resurrect and applaud every little act of womanly resistance and mean feminine spirit but examine and attempt to understand the powers of endurance that permitted them to act out the role of good wife through the whole hated experience. The women's materials give us a penetrating look at the feminine psychology of social dependency.

"Some there were, no doubt, who would have turned back," Sarah Royce later wrote, in a description which applies well to women, "but they were involved either in family or business relations with others more resolute—or more rash—and, seeing the uselessness of resistance they took up their part of the daily toil, in most cases, without complaining." Indeed, as we have seen, women not only took up their part, but over the long haul they assumed more than their 50 percent, often substituting for men, driving wagons and stock in addition to doing their own wifely work. Wholehearted work may have been a way of overcoming the inward resistance many women felt to working at all for unwanted goals.

Fears and doubts too fearful to be spoken aloud to men were whispered between mothers and daughters, sisters, or traveling female acquaintances. Most women diarists used their daily entries as an opportunity to express their feelings silently. Lavinia Porter recounted in the most melancholy terms her "sad parting" from her sister on the plains of eastern Kansas but added, "Such sorrows are to be endured not described." Endurance was the dominant emotional theme of Lavinia's overland account. "As the days wore on the irksome monotony of the journey began to pall upon me, and I spent many unhappy hours which I tried to conceal within my own breast, sometimes confiding to my journal my woes and disappointments, but managed to keep up a cheerful exterior before my husband and brother." Her resolve was to be "the courageous and valiant frontierswoman," but this outward appearance took a heavy inward toll.

> I would make a brave effort to be cheerful and patient until the camp work was done. Then starting out ahead of the team and my men folks, when I thought I had gone beyond hearing distance, I would throw myself down on the unfriendly desert and give way like a child to sobs and tears, wishing myself back home with my friends and chiding myself for consenting to take this wild goose chase. . . .

Disquiet, anxiety, melancholy, and anger were repressed and hidden from husbands, brothers, and fathers, those most responsible for such feelings. I have previously drawn the inference that woman-to-woman relations encouraged articulation and expression. In their relationships with their menfolk, however, the dynamics of family psychology compelled women to adopt the contradictory emotional mode of inexpression and seeming passivity. Lavinia Porter ran ahead to hide her tears, and [others] struggled to "hold in" and "repress" their sadness, not wanting to reveal themselves to the men about them. The second day out of Council Bluffs, Catherine Haun had an attack of homesickness, but she composed herself. "Then wiping away my tears, lest they betray me to my husband, I prepared to continue my trip. I have often thought that had I confided in him he would have certainly turned back for he, as well as the other men of the party, was disheartened and was struggling not to betray it." Here she protected her husband from his own uncertainty and helped to uphold his manhood; but might she not also have been protecting herself against the later eventuality that she would be blamed as the *sole* cause of their joint failure of will?

There was, as well, a self-motivation to this enduring mode. Especially in the context of the man's world of the trail, it would have been strange had the standards of perseverance which men successfully demonstrated not been, in part, inwardly accepted by women as well. Women might well have despised their own doubts and fears and worked to overcome them, in spite of the detachment they felt from the emigration. Thus did Rebecca Ketcham characterize her anxieties as "wicked fears" and resolve to "try to be patient." Like Rebecca, . . . many women somehow felt that repression of feelings and patient endurance would reap a heavenly reward; they looked on the trail as a kind of cross for women to bear. Maria Belshaw comforted herself, "Thy will be done O God not mine, that I may receive a crown of righteousness at thy right hand." And Sarah Royce, after successfully "holding in" during the first of many late-night bouts of home-sickness, wrote later that "in the morning there was a mildly exultant feeling which comes from having kept silent through a cowardly fit, and finding the fit gone off."

For men the trip West was an active test of competition, strength, and manliness. It meant measuring themselves against the already romanticized images of their heroic pioneer fathers and grandfathers traversing the Wilderness Road and the Cumberland Gap. For women the trip West was a test of their inner strength. They did their part and more; they were comforting wives and attentive mothers, to the many single men of the trail as well as their husbands. They did all this, because of, not in spite of, their not wanting to leave home in the first place.

The psychology of social dependency, with its costs and rewards, was the result of the systematic oppression of women, of which their marital relations were the key link. Their induction onto the trail, not as full and willing participants but more as reluctant draftees, was the cause not of rebellion and resistance, although there were occasional examples of those, but of self-denial, a kind of active passivity and endurance. The trail experience was, of course, an extreme case; daily life was more amiable to women, with smaller subjugations. But considering the weight of these small evidences of powerlessness over years of marriage, the lives of women had to be largely lives of endurance. On the trail women called up resources of courage and will which were stockpiled for just such emergencies.

POSTSCRIPT

Did the Westward Movement Transform the Traditional Roles of Women in the Mid-Nineteenth Century?

Faragher argues that frontier women were pioneers only because they were subordinate to their husbands. In spite of legal changes in the marriage laws made by many states in the mid-nineteenth century, husbands were still the controlling authority in the family. Most men made the decision to migrate west without consulting their wives.

Myres, on the other hand, gives a much more upbeat portrayal of westering women. Myres uses many diaries and letters of middle-class white women as sources, but she also includes materials on African American, Hispanic, and Native American women (but not immigrant women), and covers a broad time period. Myres sees frontier women as extremely active in business, manufacturing, agriculture, and the traditional teaching and nursing professions. Many of these jobs were located outside of the home.

A third study, Julie Roy Jeffrey's *Frontier Women: The Trans-Mississippi West 1840–1880* (Hill & Wang, 1979), emphasizes the conservative behavior of western women. Jeffrey states in her introduction, "I hoped to find that pioneer women used the frontier as a means of liberating themselves from stereotypes and behaviors which I found constricting and sexist. I discovered they did not. More important, I discovered why they did not."

The current scholarship on women has moved beyond literate white women who settled in the West and focuses upon minority women. Papers from the conferences held by the Coalition for Western Women's History and the Southwest Institute for Research on Women are published in Susan Armitage et al., eds., *The Women's West* (University of Oklahoma Press, 1987); Lillian Schlissel et al., eds., *Western Women: Their Land, Their Lives* (University of New Mexico Press, 1988); Elizabeth Jameson and Susan Armitage, eds., *Writing the Range: Race, Class, and Culture in the Women's West* (University of Oklahoma Press, 1997).

The two best overviews of the new western history are Patricia Nelson Limerick, *The Legacy of Conquest: The Unbroken Part of the American West* (W.W. Norton, 1987) and Richard White, *It's Your Misfortune and None of My Own: A New History of the American West* (University of Oklahoma Press, 1992).

On the Internet ...

http://www.dushkin.com

American Slavery in Historical Context
The primary purpose of the American Slavery in Historical Context home page is to provide a gateway to the Internet's various resources concerned with the historical institution of American slavery. It also includes links to resources concerned with the related subjects of the American Civil War and African American history in general. *http://ils.unc.edu/ingham/index.html*

Index of Civil War Information
Available on the Internet
The United States Civil War Center boasts over 2,400 indexed Civil War–related links at this site. *http://www.cwc.lsu.edu/cwc/civlink.htm*

Abraham Lincoln Online
Dedicated to the 16th president of the United States, Abraham Lincoln Online offers educational links, Lincoln's speeches and writings, historic places, and much more. *http://www.netins.net/showcase/creative/lincoln.html*

POTUS: Presidents of the United States
This page of the Internet Public Library offers some factual information on Andrew Johnson, the 17th U.S. president, and links to biographies of Johnson, related historical documents, and other resources on the Internet. *http://www.ipl.org/ref/POTUS/ajohnson.html*

PART 4

Conflict and Resolution

The changing nature of the United States and the demands of its own principles finally erupted into violent conflict. Perhaps it was an inevitable step in the process of building a coherent nation from a number of distinct and diverse groups. The leaders, attitudes, and resources that were available to the North and the South were to determine the course of the war itself, as well as the national healing process that followed.

■ Have Historians Overemphasized the Slavery Issue as a Cause of the Civil War?

■ Was the North's Victory Over the South Inevitable?

■ Did Abraham Lincoln Free the Slaves?

■ Was It Wrong to Impeach Andrew Johnson?

ISSUE 13

Have Historians Overemphasized the Slavery Issue as a Cause of the Civil War?

YES: Joel H. Silbey, from *The Partisan Imperative: The Dynamics of American Politics Before the Civil War* (Oxford University Press, 1985)

NO: Michael F. Holt, from *The Political Crisis of the 1850s* (John Wiley & Sons, 1978)

ISSUE SUMMARY

YES: Professor of history Joel H. Silbey argues that historians have overemphasized the sectional conflict over slavery and have neglected to analyze local enthnocultural issues among the events leading to the Civil War.

NO: Professor of history Michael F. Holt maintains that both northern Republicans and southern Democrats seized the slavery issue to sharply distinguish party differences and thus reinvigorate the loyalty of party voters.

In the 85 years between the start of the American Revolution and the coming of the Civil War, Americans made the necessary political compromises on the slavery issue in order not to split the nation apart. The Northwest Ordinance of 1787 forbade slavery from spreading into those designated territories under its control, and the new Constitution written in the same year prohibited the slave trade from Africa after 1808.

There was some hope in the early nineteenth century that slavery might die from natural causes. The Revolutionary generation was well aware of the contradiction between the values of an egalitarian society and the practices of a slave-holding aristocracy. Philosophically, slavery was viewed as a necessary evil, not a positive good. Several northern states abolished slavery after 1800, and the erosion of the tobacco lands in Virginia and Maryland contributed to the lessening importance of a slave labor system.

Unfortunately, two factors—territorial expansion and the market economy—made slavery the key to the South's wealth in the 35 years before the Civil War. First, new slave states were created out of a population expanding into lands ceded to the United States as a result of the Treaty of Paris of 1783 and the Louisiana Purchase of 1803. Second, slaves were sold from the upper to the lower regions of the South because the cotton gin (invented by Eli Whitney in 1793) made it possible to harvest large quantities of cotton, ship it to the textile mills of New England and the British Isles, and turn it into cloth and finished clothing as part of the new, specialized market economy.

The slavery issue came to the forefront in 1819 when some northern congressmen proposed that slavery be banned from the states being carved out of the Louisiana Purchase. A heated debate ensued, but the Missouri Compromise of 1821 drew a line that preserved the balance between free and slave states and that (with the exception of Missouri) prohibited slavery north of the 36° 30' latitude.

The annexation of Texas in 1845 and the acquisition of New Mexico, Utah, and California three years later reopened the slavery question. The question of whether or not to annex Texas to the union, after she gained her independence from Mexico in 1836, scared politicians from all sections because they were afraid of upsetting the political balance between free and slave states. Attempts at compromises in 1850 and 1854 only accelerated the situation. In 1854 Stephen A. Douglas, a senator from Illinois, hoped to boost Chicago's burgeoning market economy by encouraging the building of a transcontinental railroad. The Kansas-Nebraska Act of 1854, which repealed the Missouri Compromise, allowed the citizens of those territories to decide whether or not they wanted slavery. Abolitionists were furious because Douglas's doctrine of "popular sovereignty" had the potential to allow slavery to spread to territories where it was previously forbidden by the Missouri Compromise. For the next three years, Kansas became a battleground between pro-slavery forces and "Free-Soilers" who voted to keep slavery out of the territory.

The Kansas-Nebraska Act had major political implications. The second party system of Whigs versus Democrats fell apart, and a new realignment took place. The Whig party disappeared. In the South the need to defend slavery caused pro-business and yeoman-farmer Whigs from the back country to join the southern Democrats in a unified alliance against the North. Major and minor parties in the North joined to form the new Republican party whose unifying principle was to confine slavery to states where it already existed but not to allow it to spread to any new territories. Quickly the Republicans mounted a successful challenge against the Democrats.

The 1860 presidential election was won by the Republican Abraham Lincoln. However, the southern states refused to accept the election of Lincoln. Seven states seceded from the Union before he was inaugurated on March 4, 1861. When Lincoln refused to abandon the federal forts off the coast of Charleston in April 1861, the governor of South Carolina fired on Fort Sumter. The Civil War had begun. Four more states then joined the Confederacy.

Have historians overemphasized the sectional conflict over the slavery question as a cause of the Civil War? In the first of the following selections, Joel H. Silbey argues that historians have overemphasized the sectional conflict over slavery and have neglected to analyze local ethnocultural issues among the events leading to the Civil War. In the second selection, Michael F. Holt counters that politicians in the 1850s used the slavery issue to sharply distinguish party differences.

YES

Joel H. Silbey

THE CIVIL WAR SYNTHESIS IN AMERICAN POLITICAL HISTORY

The Civil War has dominated our studies of the period between the Age of Jackson and 1861. Most historians of the era have devoted their principal attention to investigating and analyzing the reasons for differences between the North and South, the resulting sectional conflict, and the degeneration of this strife into a complete breakdown of our political system in war. Because of this focus, most scholars have accepted, without question, that differences between the North and the South were the major political influences at work among the American people in the years between the mid-1840s and the war. Despite occasional warnings about the dangers of overemphasizing sectional influences, the sectional interpretation holds an honored and secure place in the historiography of the antebellum years. We now possess a formidable number of works which, in one way or another, center attention on the politics of sectionalism and clearly demonstrate how much the Civil War dominates our study of American political history before 1861.

Obviously nothing is wrong in such emphasis if sectionalism was indeed the dominant political influence in the antebellum era. However, there is the danger in such emphasis of claiming too much, that in centering attention on the war and its causes we may ignore or play down other contemporary political influences and fail to weigh adequately the importance of nonsectional forces in antebellum politics. And, in fact, several recent studies of American political behavior have raised serious doubts about the importance of sectional differences as far as most Americans were concerned. These have even suggested that the sectional emphasis has created a false synthesis in our study of history which increases the importance of one factor, ignores the significance of other factors, and ultimately distorts the reality of American political life between 1844 and 1861.

* * *

Scholars long have used the presidential election of 1844 as one of their major starting points for the sectional analysis of American political history. In a general sense they have considered American expansion into Texas to be the

From Joel H. Silbey, *The Partisan Imperative: The Dynamics of American Politics Before the Civil War* (Oxford University Press, 1985). Adapted from Joel H. Silbey, "The Civil War Synthesis in American Political History," *Civil War History* (June 1964). Copyright © 1964 by Kent State University Press. Reprinted by permission. Notes omitted.

most important issue of that campaign. The issue stemmed from the fact that Texas was a slave area and many articulate Northerners attacked the movement to annex Texas as a slave plot designed to enhance Southern influence within the Union. Allegedly because of these attacks, and the Southerners' defending themselves, many people in both North and South found themselves caught up in such sectional bitterness that the United States took a major step toward civil war. Part of this bitterness can be seen, it is pointed out, in the popular vote in New York State where the Whig candidate for the presidency, Henry Clay, lost votes to the abolitionist Liberty party because he was a slaveholder. The loss of these votes cost him New York and ultimately the election. As a result of Clay's defeat, historians have concluded that as early as 1844 the problem of slavery extension was important enough to arouse people to act primarily in sectional terms and thus for this episode to be a milestone on the road to war.

Recently Professor Lee Benson published a study of New York State politics in the Jacksonian era. Although Benson mainly concerned himself with other problems, some of his findings directly challenge the conception that slavery and sectional matters were of major importance in New York in 1844. In his analysis Benson utilized a more systematic statistical compilation of data than have previous workers in the field of political history. Observing that scholars traditionally have looked at what people said they did rather than at what they actually did, Benson compiled a great number of election returns for New York State in this period. His purpose was to see who actually voted for whom and to place the election in historical perspective by pin-

pointing changes in voting over time and thus identifying the basic trends of political behavior. Through such analysis Benson arrived at a major revision of the nature of New York State voting in 1844.

Benson pointed out, first of all, that the abolitionist, anti-Texas Liberty party whose vote total should have increased if the New York population wanted to strike against a slave plot in Texas, actually lost votes over what it had received in the most immediate previous election, that of 1843. Further analysis indicated that there was no widespread reaction to the Texas issue in New York State on the part of any large group of voters, although a high degree of anti-Texas feeling indeed existed among certain limited groups in the population. Such sentiment, however, did not affect voting margins in New York State. Finally, Benson concluded that mass voting in New York in 1844 pivoted not on the sectional issue but rather on more traditional divisions between ethnic and religious groups whose voting was a reaction to matters closer to home. These proved of a more personal and psychological nature than that of Texas and its related issue of slavery extension. Sectional bitterness, contrary to previous historical conceptions, neither dominated nor seriously influenced the 1844 vote in New York. Although Benson confined his study to one state, his conclusions introduce doubts about the influence of sectionalism in other supposedly less pivotal states.

* * *

Another aspect of the sectional interpretation of American politics in the pre–Civil War era involves Congress. Political historians have considered that body to be both a forum wherein leaders personally expressed attitudes that intensified sectional bitterness, as well as an arena which reflected the general pattern of influences operative in the country at large. Therefore, writers on the period have considered the behavior of congressmen to have been more and more dominated by sectionalism, particularly after David Wilmot introduced his antislavery extension proviso into the House of Representatives in 1846. Although there may have been other issues and influences present, it is accepted that these were almost completely overborne in the late 1840s and 1850s in favor of a widespread reaction to sectional differences.

In a recently completed study, I have analyzed congressional voting in the allegedly crucial pivotal decade 1841–52, the period which historians identify as embodying the transition from nationalism to sectionalism in congressional behavior. This examination indicates that a picture of the decade as one in which sectional influences steadily grew stronger, overwhelmed all other bases of divisions, and became a permanent feature of the voting behavior of a majority of congressmen, is grossly oversimplified and a distortion of reality. In brief, although sectional influences, issues, and voting did exist, particularly between 1846 and 1850, sectional matters were not the only problems confronting congressmen. In the period before the introduction of the Wilmot Proviso in 1846, national issues such as the tariff, financial policy, foreign affairs, and land policy divided congressmen along political, not sectional, lines. Furthermore, in this earlier period issues which many believed to have shown a high degree of sectional content, such as admittance of Texas and Oregon, reveal highly partisan national divisions and little sectional voting.

Even after the rise of the slavery-extension issue, other questions of a national character remained important. Slavery was but one of several issues before Congress and it was quite possible for congressmen to vote against one another as Northern and Southern sectionalists on an issue and then to join together, regardless of section, against other Northerners and Southerners on another matter. Certainly some men from both geographic areas were primarily influenced by sectional considerations at all times on all issues, but they were a minority of all congressmen in the period. The majority of congressmen were not so overwhelmingly influenced by their being Northerners or Southerners, but continued to think and act in national terms, and even resisted attempts by several sectionally minded congressmen to forge coalitions, regardless of party, against the other section.

A careful study of congressional voting in these years also demonstrates that another assumption of historians about the nature of politics is oversimplified: the period around 1846 did *not* begin the steady forward movement of congressional politics toward sectionalism and war. Rather, it was quite possible in the period between 1846 and 1852 for congressmen to assail one another bitterly in sectional terms, physically attack one another, and even threaten secession, and still for the majority of them to return in the following session to a different approach—that of nonsectional political differences with a concomitant restoration of nonsectional coalitions. For example, it was possible in 1850, after several years of sectional fighting, for a national coalition of Senators and Representatives to join together and settle in compromise terms the differences between North and

South over expansion. And they were able to do this despite the simultaneous existence of a great deal of sectional maneuvering by some congressmen in an attempt to prevent any such compromise. Furthermore, during this same session Congress also dealt with matters of railroad land grants in a way that eschewed sectional biases. Obviously the usual picture of an inexorable growth of sectional partisanship after 1846 is quite overdone. And lest these examples appeared to be isolated phenomena, preliminary research both by Gerald Wolff and by myself demonstrates that as late as 1854 there was still no complete or overwhelming sectional voting even on such an issue as the Kansas-Nebraska Act.

Such analyses of congressional behavior in an alleged transition period reinforce what Lee Benson's work on New York politics demonstrated: many varieties and many complexities existed with respect to political behavior in the antebellum period, so that even slavery failed to be a dominating influence among all people at all times—or even among most people at most times—during the 1840s and early 1850s. Again, our previous image of American politics in this period must be reconsidered in light of this fact and despite the emergence of a Civil War in 1861.

* * *

Perhaps no aspect of antebellum politics should demonstrate more fully the overpowering importance of sectional influences than the presidential election of 1860. In the preliminaries to that contest the Democratic party split on the rock of slavery, the Republican party emerged as a power in the Northern states with a good chance of winning the presidency, and loud voices in the Southern states

called for secession because of Northern attacks on their institutions. In dealing with these events, historians, as in their treatment of other aspects of antebellum politics, have devoted their primary attention to sectional bickering and maneuvering among party leaders, because they considered this activity to be the most important facet of the campaign and the key to explaining the election. Although such a focus obviously has merit if one is thinking in terms of the armed conflict which broke out only five months after the election, once again, as in the earlier cases considered here, recent research has raised pertinent questions about the political realities of the situation. We may indeed ask what were the issues of the campaign as seen by the majority of voters.

Earlier studies of the 1860 election, in concerning themselves primarily with the responses and activities of political leaders, have taken popular voting behavior for granted. This aspect has either been ignored or else characterized as reflecting the same influences and attitudes as that of the leadership. Therefore, the mass of men, it is alleged, voted in response to sectional influences in 1860. For instance, several scholars concerned with the Germans in the Middle West in this period have characterized the attitudes of that group as overwhelmingly antislavery. Thus the Republican party attracted the mass of the German vote because the liberal "Forty-Eighters" saw casting a Lincoln vote as a way to strike a blow against slavery in the United States. Going beyond this, some historians have reached similar conclusions about other Middle Western immigrant groups. As a result, according to most historians, although narrowly divided, the area went for Lincoln thanks in large part to its newest citizens, who were Northern sectionalists in their political behavior. Such conclusions obviously reinforce the apparent importance of geographic partisanship in 1860.

Testing this hypothesis, two recent scholars systematically studied and analyzed election returns in Iowa during 1860. Such examinations are important because they should reveal, if the sectional theory is correct, preoccupation among Iowa voters—especially immigrants—with the slavery question and the increasingly bitter differences between North and South. Only one of these studies, that of Professor George H. Daniels of Northwestern University, has appeared in print. But Daniels's findings shatter earlier interpretations which pinpointed sectional concerns as the central theme of the 1860 election.

Briefly stated, Daniels isolated the predominantly German townships in Iowa and, following Lee Benson's methodological lead, analyzed their vote. He found that, far from being solidly Republican voters, or moved primarily by the slavery question, the Germans of Iowa voted overwhelmingly in favor of the Democratic party. And Daniels discovered that the primary issue motivating the Germans in 1860 was an ethnic one. They were conscious of the anti-alien Know-Nothing movement which had been so strong in the United States during the 1850s and they identified the Republican party as the heir and last refuge of Know-Nothingism. If the Germans of Iowa were attracted to the Republicans by the latter's antislavery attitudes, such attraction was more than overcome by the Republicans' aura of antiforeignism. Furthermore, the Republicans were also identified in the minds of the Iowa Germans as the party of prohibitionism, a social view strongly opposed

by most Germans. Thus, as Daniels concludes, "... The rank and file Germans who did the bulk of the voting considered their own liberty to be of paramount importance. Apparently ignoring the advice of their leaders, they cast their ballots for the party which consistently promised them liberty from prohibition and native-American legislation." As a result, the Germans of Iowa voted Democratic, not Republican, in 1860.

Lest this appear to be an isolated case, the research of Robert Swierenga on Dutch voting behavior in Iowa in 1860 confirms Daniels's findings. Swierenga demonstrated that the Dutch also voted Democratic despite their vaunted antislavery attitudes; again, revulsion from certain Republican ideals overpowered any attraction toward that party on the slavery issue.

Such research into the election of 1860, as in the earlier cases of the election of 1844 and congressional voting behavior in the 1840s and early 1850s, suggests how far the sectional and slavery preconceptions of American historians have distorted reality. Many nonsectional issues were apparently more immediately important to the groups involved than any imminent concern with Northern-Southern differences. Once again, the Civil War synthesis appears to be historically inaccurate and in need of serious revision.

* * *

Several other provocative studies recently have appeared which, while dealing with nonpolitical subjects, support the conclusion that sectional problems, the slavery issue, and increasing bitterness between North and South were not always uppermost concerns to most Americans in the fifteen years before the outbreak of the war. Building upon the work of Leon Litwack, which emphasizes the general Northern antagonism toward the Negro before 1860, and that of Larry Gara demonstrating the fallacy of the idea that a well-organized and widespread underground railroad existed in the North, Professor C. Vann Woodward has cautioned students against an easy acceptance of a "North-Star" image—a picture of a universally militant Northern population determined to ease the burden of the slave in America. Rather, as Woodward points out, a great many Northerners remained indifferent to the plight of the slave and hostile to the would-be antislavery reformer in their midst.

In this same tenor, Milton Powell of Michigan State University has challenged long-held assumptions that the Northern Methodist church was a bulwark of antislavery sentiment after splitting with its Southern branch in 1844. As Powell makes clear, Northern Methodists were concerned about many other problems in which slavery played no part, as well as being beset by conditions which served to tone down any antislavery attitudes they may have held. More importantly, this led many of them to ignore slavery as an issue because of its latent tendency to divide the organization to which they belonged. Thus, even in areas outside of the political realm, the actual conditions of antebellum society challenge the validity of the sectional concept in its most general and far-reaching form.

* * *

This review of recent research indicates that much of our previous work on the prewar period should be reexamined free from the bias caused by looking first at the fact of the Civil War and then turning back to view the events of the previous decade in relation only to that fact. Although it is true that the studies discussed here are few in number and by no means include the entire realm of American politics in the antebellum era, their diversity in time and their revisionist conclusions do strongly suggest the fallacy of many previous assumptions. No longer should any historian blithely accept the traditional concept of a universal preoccupation with the sectional issue.

But a larger matter is also pointed up by this recent research and the destruction of this particular myth about political sectionalism. For a question immediately arises as to how historians generally could have accepted so readily and for so long such oversimplifications and inaccuracies. Fortunately for future research, answers to this question have been implicitly given by the scholars under review, and involve methodological problems concerning evidence and a certain naïveté about the political process.

Historians generally have utilized as evidence the writings and commentaries of contemporary observers of, and participants in, the events being examined. But, as both Benson and Daniels emphasize, this can endanger our understanding of reality. For instance, not enough attention has been paid to who actually said what, or of the motives of a given reporter or the position he was in to know and understand what was going on around him. Most particularly, scholars have not always been properly skeptical about whether the observer's comments truly reflected actuality. As Daniels pointed out in his article on German voting behavior, "contemporary opinion, including that of newspapers, is a poor guide."

If such is true, and the evidence presented by these studies indicates that it is, a question is raised as to how a historian is to discover contemporary opinion if newspapers are not always reliable as sources. The work of Benson, Daniels, and myself suggests an answer: the wider use of statistics. When we talk of public opinion (that is, how the mass of men acted or thought) we are talking in terms of aggregate numbers, of majorities. One way of determining what the public thought is by measuring majority opinion in certain circumstances—elections, for example, or the voting of congressmen—and then analyzing the content and breakdown of the figures derived. If, for example, 80 percent of the Germans in Iowa voted Democratic in 1860, this tells us more about German public opinion in 1860 than does a sprightly quote from one of the Germans in the other 20 percent who voted Republican "to uphold freedom." Historians are making much more use of statistics than formerly and are utilizing more sophisticated techniques of quantitative analysis. And such usage seems to be prelude to, judging by the works discussed here, a fuller and more accurate understanding of our past.

There are also other ways of approaching the problems posed by the 1850s. Not enough attention has been paid, it seems to me, to the fact that there are many different levels of political behavior—mass voting, legislative activity, leadership manipulation, for example—and that what is influential and important on one level of politics may not be on another. Certainly the Germans and Dutch of Iowa in 1860 were not paying much attention to the desires of their leaders. They were responding to influences deemed more important than those influences shaping the responses of their

leaders. As Swierenga pointed out in his analysis of Dutch voting:

> While Scholte [a leader of the Dutch community] fulminated against Democrats as slave mongers, as opponents of the Pacific Railroad and Homestead Bills, and as destroyers of the Constitution, the Dutch citizens blithely ignored him and the national issues he propounded and voted their personal prejudices against Republican nativists and prohibitionists.

Obviously, when historians generalize about the nature of political behavior they must also be sure which group and level of political activity they mean, and so identify it, and not confuse different levels or assume positive correlations between the actions of people on one level with those on another level. Such precision will contribute greatly to accuracy and overcome tendencies toward distortion.

Finally, based on the work under discussion here, it is clear that historians must become more aware of the complexities of human behavior. All people, even of the same stratum of society or living in the same geographic area, do not respond with the same intensity to the same social or political stimuli. Not everyone perceives his best interests in the same way, or considers the same things to be the most important problems confronting him. Depending upon time and circumstances, one man may respond primarily to economic influences; another one, at the same time and place, to religious influences; and so on. Sometimes most people in a given community will respond to the same influences equally, but we must be careful to observe *when* this is true and not generalize from it that this is *always* true. Single-factor explanations for human behavior do not seem to work, and we must remain aware of that fact.

With improved methodological tools and concepts historians may begin to engage in more systematic and complete analyses of popular voting, legislative voting, and the motivations and actions of political leaders. They will be able to weigh the relative influence of sectional problems against other items of interest and concern on all levels of political behavior. Until this is done, however, we do know on the basis of what already has been suggested that we cannot really accept glib explanations about the antebellum period. The Civil War has had a pernicious influence on the study of American political development that preceded it—pernicious because it has distorted the reality of political behavior in the era and has caused an overemphasis on sectionalism. It has led us to look not for what was occurring in American politics in those years, but rather for what was occurring in American politics that tended toward sectional breakdown and civil war—a quite different matter.

NO

Michael F. Holt

THE POLITICAL CRISIS OF THE 1850s

Historians have long looked to politics for the origins of the Civil War, and they have offered two major interpretations of political developments between 1845 and 1860. Both are primarily concerned with the breakdown of the old party system and the rise of the Republicans and not with the second aspect of the crisis—the loss of faith in politicians, the desire for reform, and their relationship to republican ideology. By spelling out my reservations about and disagreements with these interpretations, the assumptions behind and, I hope, the logic of my own approach to the political crisis of the 1850s will become clearer.

The standard interpretation maintains that intensifying sectional disagreements over slavery inevitably burst into the political arena, smashed the old national parties, and forced the formation of new, sectionally oriented ones. The Second Party System was artificial, some historians contend, since it could survive only by avoiding divisive sectional issues and by confining political debate to sectionally neutral economic questions on which the national parties had coherent stands. Once sectional pressure was reaggravated by the events of the late 1840s and early 1850s, those fragile structures shattered and were replaced. "On the level of politics," writes Eric Foner, "the coming of the Civil War is the intrusion of sectional ideology into the political system, despite the efforts of political leaders of both parties [Whigs and Democrats] to keep it out. Once this happened, political competition worked to exacerbate, rather than to solve, social and sectional conflicts."

There is much to be said for this interpretation. The Republican party did rise to dominance in the North largely because of an increase of Northern hostility toward the South, and its ascendance worsened relations between the sections. Attributing the political developments prior to its rise to the same sectional force that caused the rise has the virtue of simplicity. But that argument distorts a rapidly changing and very complex political situation between 1845 and 1860. There were three discrete, sequential political developments in those years that shaped the political crisis that led to war—the disappearance of the Whig party and with it of the old framework of two-party competition, a realignment of voters as they switched party affiliation, and a shift from a nationally balanced party system where both major parties competed on fairly even terms in all parts of the nation to a sectionally polarized one with Republicans dominant in the North and Democrats in the South. Although related, these were distinct phases, occurring with some exceptions in that order, and they were caused by different things. Although the inflammation of sectional antagonism between 1855 and 1860 helped to account for the new sectional alignment of parties, sectional conflict by itself caused neither the voter realignment of middecade nor the most crucial event of the period—the death of the Whig party, especially its death at the state level. It bears repeating that the demise of the Whig party, and with it of the traditional framework of two-party competition at the local, state, and national levels, was the most critical development in this sequence. Its disappearance helped foster popular doubts about the legitimacy of politics as usual, raised fears that powerful conspiracies were undermining republicanism, allowed the rise of the Republican party in the North, and created the situation in the lower South that produced secession there and not elsewhere.

The theory that the Second Party System was artificial and was shattered once the slavery issue arose, like the larger theory of the war's causation it reflects, founders on the problem of timing. There is considerable evidence that sectional conflict over slavery characterized the Second Party System throughout its history. Slavery was not swept under the rug; it was often the stuff of political debate. Proponents of the traditional interpretation, indeed, have often confused internal divisions within the national par-

ties with their demise. Although they point to different dates when the rupture was fatal, they have assumed that once the national parties were split into Northern and Southern wings over slavery, the parties were finished. Yet the Whig and Jacksonian parties, like almost all political organizations at any time, had frequently been divided—over slavery as well as other issues. They functioned for years in that condition. To establish the existence of sectional splits within the national parties is not to answer the vexed question of why those divisions were fatal in the 1850s and not in the 1830s and 1840s. If it was the sectional conflict that destroyed the old party system, the crucial question is why the parties were able to manage that conflict at some times and not at others. For a number of reasons, the easy reply that the volatile slavery issue simply became more explosive in the 1850s than earlier is not an adequate answer to this question.

The second major interpretation of the politics of the 1850s also has its merits and liabilities. Arguing that traditional historians have viewed events in the 1850s with the hindsight knowledge that the Civil War occurred, a new group of political historians insist that the extent to which sectionalism affected political behavior, especially popular voting behavior at the grass-roots level, has been exaggerated. Local social tensions, especially ethnic and religious tensions, motivated voters in the 1850s, they contend, not national issues like slavery, which was of so much concern to national political elites. What applies to Congress and national leaders, these new political historians say in effect, does not apply to the local level of politics. Prohibitionism, nativism, and anti-Catholicism produced the voter realignment in which the Whigs disappeared and new parties emerged in the North.

By focusing on voting behavior, this ethnocultural interpretation presents a compelling analysis of why an anti-Democratic majority was created in many parts of the North. Explaining why Northern voters realigned between 1853 and 1856, however, does not answer why the Republican party appeared or why party politics were sectionally polarized at the end of the decade. Prophets of the ethnocultural thesis, moreover, have done little to explain Southern politics, yet developments in Dixie where Catholics and immigrants were few were just as important as events in the North in leading to war. Nor do voting studies really explain the crucial first phase —the death of the Whig party. Party reorganization accompanied voter realignment in the 1850s, and ethnocultural tensions alone do not explain why new parties were necessary. Why didn't anti-Democratic voters simply become Whigs? This question has a particular urgency when one realizes that in the 1840s ethnocultural issues had also been present and that the Whigs and Democrats had aligned on opposite sides of them. The problem with stressing ethnocultural issues, as with stressing sectionalism, is why those issues could be contained within, indeed could invigorate, old party lines at one time yet could help to destroy them at another.

The fundamental weakness of previous interpretations of why the old two-party system broke down is their misunderstanding of how and why it worked. They have not adequately explored either the relationship between political parties and issues or the impact of the federal system with its divided responsibilities among local, state, and national governments on the parties and the party system. Whether historians stress sectionalism or ethnocultural issues, their central assumption seems to be that issues arising from the society at large caused political events. The Second Party System functioned because it dealt with "safe" economic questions, but once those issues were replaced or displaced by new disruptive matters the parties broke down and realignment followed. Yet what made the Second Party System work in the end was not issues *per se* or the presence of safe issues and absence of dangerous ones. In the end what made the two-party system operate was its ability to allow political competition on a broad range of issues that varied from time to time and place to place. If the genius of the American political system has been the peaceful resolution of conflict, what has supported two-party systems has been the conflict itself, not its resolution. As long as parties fought with each other over issues or took opposing stands even when they failed to promote opposing programs, as long as they defined alternative ways to secure republican ideals, voters perceived them as different and maintained their loyalty to them. Party health and popular faith in the political process depended on the perception of party difference, which in turn depended on the reality—or at least the appearance—of interparty conflict. As long as parties seemed different from each other, voters viewed them as viable vehicles through which to influence government.

Politicians had long recognized that group conflict was endemic to American society and that the vitality of individual parties depended on the intensity of their competition with opposing parties. Thomas Jefferson had perceived in

1798 that "in every free and deliberating society, there must, from the nature of man, be opposite parties, and violent dissensions and discords." "Seeing that we must have somebody to quarrel with," he wrote John Taylor, "I had rather keep our New England associates for that purpose, than to see our bickerings transferred to others." Even more explicit in their recognition of what made parties work were the founders of New York's Albany Regency in the 1820s. They deplored the lack of internal discipline and cohesion in the Jeffersonian Republican party once the Federalists disappeared, and they moved quickly to remedy it. Although any party might suffer defeats, they realized, "it is certain to acquire additional strength... by the attacks of adverse parties." A political party, indeed, was "most in jeopardy when an opposition is not sufficiently defined." During "the contest between the great rival parties [Federalists and Jeffersonians] each found in the strength of the other a powerful motive of union and vigor." Significantly, those like Daniel Webster who deplored the emergence of mass parties in the 1820s and 1830s also recognized that strife was necessary to perpetuate party organization and that the best way to break it down was to cease opposition and work for consensus. Politicians in the 1840s and 1850s continued to believe that interparty conflict was needed to unify their own party and maintain their voting support. Thus an Alabama Democrat confessed that his party pushed a certain measure at the beginning of the 1840 legislative session explicitly as "the best means for drawing the party lines as soon as possible" while by 1852, when opposition to that state's Democracy appeared to disintegrate, another warned perceptively, "I think the only danger to the Democratic party is that it will become too much an omnibus in this State. We have nothing to fear from either the Union, or Whig party or both combined. From their friendship and adherence much." Many of the important decisions in the 1840s and 1850s reflected the search by political leaders for issues that would sharply define the lines between parties and thus reinvigorate the loyalty of party voters.

If conflict sustained the old two-party system, what destroyed it was the loss of the ability to provide interparty competition on *any* important issue at *any* level of the federal system. Because the political system's vitality and legitimacy with the voters depended on the clarity of the definition of the parties as opponents, the blurring of that definition undid the system. What destroyed the Second Party System was consensus, not conflict. The growing congruence between the parties on almost all issues by the early 1850s dulled the sense of party difference and thereby eroded voters' loyalty to the old parties. Once competing groups in society decided that the party system no longer provided them viable alternatives in which they could carry on conflict with each other, they repudiated the old system by dropping out, seeking third parties that would meet their needs, or turning to nonpartisan or extrapolitical action to achieve their goals. Because the collapse of the Second Party System was such a vital link in the war's causation, therefore, one arrives at a paradox. While the Civil War is normally viewed as the one time when conflict prevailed over consensus in American politics, the prevalence of consensus over conflict in crucial parts of the political system contributed in a very real way to the outbreak of war in the first place....

The sectionalization of American politics was emphatically *not* simply a reflection or product of basic popular disagreements over black slavery. Those had long existed without such a complete polarization developing. Even though a series of events beginning with the Kansas-Nebraska Act greatly increased sectional consciousness, it is a mistake to think of sectional antagonism as a spontaneous and self-perpetuating force that imposed itself on the political arena against the will of politicians and coerced parties to conform to the lines of sectional conflict. Popular grievances, no matter how intense, do not dictate party strategies. Political leaders do. Some one has to politicize events, to define their political relevance in terms of a choice between or among parties, before popular grievances can have political impact. It was not events alone that caused Northerners and Southerners to view each other as enemies of the basic rights they both cherished. Politicians who pursued very traditional partisan strategies were largely responsible for the ultimate breakdown of the political process. Much of the story of the coming of the Civil War is the story of the successful efforts of Democratic politicians in the South and Republican politicians in the North to keep the sectional conflict at the center of political debate and to defeat political rivals who hoped to exploit other issues to achieve election.

For at least thirty years political leaders had recognized that the way to build political parties, to create voter loyalty and mobilize support, and to win elections was to find issues or positions on issues that distinguished them from their opponents and that therefore could appeal to various groups who disliked their opponents by offering them an alternative for political action—in sociological terms, to make their party a vehicle for negative reference group behavior. Because of the American ethos, the most successful tactic had been to pose as a champion of republican values and to portray the opponent as antirepublican, as unlawful, tyrannical, or aristocratic. Jackson, Van Buren, and Polk, Antimasons and Whigs, had all followed this dynamic of the political system. Stephen A. Douglas and William H. Seward had pursued the same strategy in their unsuccessful attempt to rebuild the disintegrating Second Party System with the Kansas-Nebraska Act in 1854. After faith in the old parties had collapsed irreparably, when the shape of future political alignments was uncertain, Republican politicians quite consciously seized on the slavery and sectional issue in order to build a new party. Claiming to be the exclusive Northern Party that was necessary to halt slavery extension and defeat the Slave Power conspiracy was the way they chose to distinguish themselves from Democrats, whom they denounced as pro-Southern, and from the Know Nothings, who had chosen a different organizing principle—anti-Catholicism and nativism—to construct their new party.

To say that Republican politicians agitated and exploited sectional grievances in order to build a winning party is a simple description of fact. It is not meant to imply that winning was their only objective or to be a value judgment about the sincerity or insincerity of their personal hatred of black slavery. Some undoubtedly found slavery morally intolerable and hoped to use the national government to weaken it by preventing its expansion, abolishing it in federal enclaves like the District of Columbia, and undermining it within Southern states by whatever means were constitutionally possible, such as opening the mails to abolitionist literature and prohibiting the interstate slave trade. The antislavery pedigree of Republican leaders, however, was in a sense irrelevant to the triumph of the Republican party. The leaders were divided over the policies they might pursue if they won control of the national government, and leadership views were often far in advance of those held by their electorate. Much more important was the campaign they ran to obtain power, their skill in politicizing the issues at hand in such a way as to convince Northern voters that control of the national government by an exclusive Northern party was necessary to resist Slave Power aggressions. The Republicans won more because of what they were against than because of what they were for, because of what they wanted to stop, not what they hoped to do....

The key to unraveling the paradoxes in Republican rhetoric, the juxtaposition of egalitarianism and racism, of pledges not to interfere with slavery in the South alongside calls to end slavery and join a great crusade for freedom, is to remember that the word "slavery" had long had a definite meaning aside from the institution of black slavery in the South. It was in this sense that many Republicans used the word. Slavery implied subordination to tyranny, the loss of liberty and equality, the absence of republicanism. Slavery resulted when republican government was overthrown or usurped, and that, charged Republicans, was exactly what the Slave Power was trying to do. Hence the slavery that many Republicans objected to most was not the bondage of blacks in the South but the subjugation of Northern whites to the despotism of a tiny oligarchy of slaveholders bent on destroying their rights, a minority who controlled the Democratic party and through it the machinery of the federal government. Thus one Republican complained privately in 1857, "The Slave power will not submit. The tyrants of the lash will not withhold until they have put padlocks on the lives of freemen. The Union which our fathers formed seventy years ago is not the Union today ... the sons of the Revolutionary fathers are becoming *slaves* or *masters*." Thus a Chicago Republican congressman, after reciting a litany of supposed Slave Power aggressions against the North, later recalled, "All these things followed the taking possession of the Government and lands by the slave power, until we [in the North] were the slaves of slaves, being chained to the car of this Slave Juggernaut." Thus the black abolitionist Frederick Douglass perceptively observed, "The cry of Free Men was raised, not for the extension of liberty to the black man, but for the protection of the liberty of the white."

The basic objective of Republican campaigns from 1856 to 1860, therefore, was to persuade Northerners that slaveholders meant to enslave them through their control of the national government and to enlist Northern voters behind the Republican party in a defensive phalanx to ward off *that* slavery, and not in an offensive crusade to end black slavery, by driving the Slave Power from its control of the national government. For such a tactic to succeed, the Republicans required two things. First, to make an asset and not a liability of their existence as an exclusive Northern party, they needed events to increase Northern antagonism toward the South so that men believed the South, and not foreigners and Catholics or the Republicans themselves, posed the chief threat to the republic. More important, they had successfully to identify the Democratic party as an agent or lackey of the South. Because the Republicans campaigned only in the North, because Northern voters chose among Northern candidates instead of between Northerners and Southerners, only by making Northern Democrats surrogates for the Slave Power could they make their case that Republicans alone, and not simply any Northern politicians, were needed to resist and overthrow the slavocracy. Because they dared not promise overt action against slaveholders except for stopping slavery expansion, in other words, Republicans could not exploit Northern anger, no matter how intense it was, unless they could convince Northern voters that supporting the Republicans and defeating Northern Democrats was an efficacious and constitutional way to defeat the Slave Power itself.

By the summer of 1856 it was much easier to identify the Democracy with the South than it had been earlier. For one thing, the results of the congressional elections of 1854 and 1855 had dramatically shifted the balance of sectional power within the Democratic party, a result that was plainly evident when the 34th Congress met during 1856. From 1834 to 1854 the Democratic congressional delegation had usually been reasonably balanced between North and South. In the 33rd Congress, Northern Democrats had even outnumbered Southern Democrats in the House by a margin of 91 to 67. But in 1856 there were only 25 Northerners as compared to 63 Southerners, and even though Northern Democratic representation would increase after the 1856 elections, the sectional balance would never be restored before the Civil War. The South seemed to dominate the Democracy, and that fact was especially difficult to hide during a presidential election year. Because the Democrats, unlike the Republicans, met in a common national convention with Southerners and campaigned in both sections, Democrats could not deny their Southern connection. The democratic platform endorsing the Kansas-Nebraska Act strengthened that identification, thereby flushing out regular Northern Democrats who had tried to evade the Nebraska issue in 1854 and 1855 and infuriating anti-Nebraska Democrats who had clung to the party in hopes of reversing its policy but who now bolted to the Republicans....

The Democratic party within the Deep South had, in fact, changed in significant ways. During the 1830s and 1840s, it had normally been controlled by and represented the interests of nonslaveholders from the hill country and piney woods regions. Even at that time slaveholders and their lawyer allies from the normally Whig black belt areas had contested for leadership of the Democracy. Sharing the same economic concerns as their Whig neighbors in those plantation regions, concerns that nonslaveholding Democrats generally opposed, Democrats from the black belt had bid for control of the party by trying to shift attention to national issues and asserting that the threat to Southern equality posed the greatest menace to the liberties of all Southern voters. During the 1850s, for a variety of reasons, those slaveholding elements took over the Democracy, and in state after state it became much less receptive at the state level to the wishes of the nonslaveholding majority who nonetheless remained Democrats because of traditional Jacksonian loyalties. For one thing, Franklin Pierce favored Southern Rights Democrats in the distribution of federal patronage. Second, as the Whig party dissolved, Democratic politicians from the slaveholding regions won over some of its former adherents by stressing the menace to slaveholders' interests, thereby increasing their own power within the Democratic party. Finally, during the 1850s, the cotton culture spread away from the old black belt to staunchly Democratic regions, thus enlarging the constituency that would respond to politicians riding the slavery issue.

As a result of this transformation, the economic priorities of the Democratic party changed. Democratic newspapers openly advised Democratic legislators not to offend their new Whig allies, and the new Democratic leaders wanted positive economic programs in any case. Occasionally the nonslaveholders found individual champions of the old Jacksonian orthodoxy like Governor George Winston of Alabama and Governor Joe Brown of Georgia who vetoed probusiness legislation, but Democratic legislatures invariably overrode those vetoes. To nonslaveholders, the Democratic party, as a party, and the political process as a whole no longer seemed as responsive as they once had been.

The shift of power within the dominant Democracy hastened the almost exclusive concentration of political rhetoric on the slavery and sectional issues. For one thing, slaveholders were more genuinely concerned about potential threats to black slavery than nonslaveholders. For another, the Democrats attributed their rise to dominance by 1852 to their ability to appear more pro-Southern than the Whigs, and they saw no reason to change a winning strategy. Third, the new leaders of the party continued to feel the need of holding the loyalty of the nonslaveholding backbone of the Democratic electorate. That support had always been won by identifying and crusading against antirepublican monsters. Because the new leaders did not want to attack the economic programs they were themselves promoting and because internal opposition was so weak from former Whigs who approved of those programs, they more and more portrayed the external Republican party as the chief danger to the liberty, equality, and self-esteem of all Southerners, slaveholders and nonslaveholders alike. Like the Republicans in the North, they translated the sectional conflict into the republican idiom in order to win the votes of men who were not primarily concerned with black slavery.

POSTSCRIPT

Have Historians Overemphasized the Slavery Issue as a Cause of the Civil War?

Silbey's selection represents the first sustained attack on the sectional interpretation of the events leading to the Civil War. Historians, he claims, have created a false "Civil War synthesis" that positioned slavery as the major issue that divided America, thereby distorting "the reality of American political life between 1844 and 1861."

Silbey is one of the "new political historians" who have applied the techniques of modern-day political scientists in analyzing the election returns and voting patterns of Americans' nineteenth- and early-twentieth-century predecessors. These historians use computers and regression analysis of voting patterns, they favor a quantitative analysis of past behavior, and they reject the traditional sources of quotes from partisan newspapers and major politicians because these sources provide anecdotal and often misleading portraits of our past. Silbey and other new political historians maintain that all politics are local. Therefore, the primary issues in the 1860 election for voters and their politicians were ethnic and cultural, and party loyalty was more important than sectional considerations.

Holt is also interested in analyzing the struggles for power at the state and local levels by the major political parties, but he is critical of the ethnocultural school that Silbey represents. In Holt's view, Silbey's emphasis on voter analysis explains why an anti-Democratic bloc of voters developed in the North. But it does not explain why the Whig party disappeared nor why the Republican party became the majority party in the northern and western states by 1850. More important, since Silbey and other ethnoculturalists have little to say about southern politics, reasons why secession and the subsequent Civil War took place are left unanswered.

Holt also rejects the more traditional view that the Civil War resulted from the "intensifying sectional disagreements over slavery." Instead, he promotes a more complicated picture of the events leading to the Civil War. Between 1845 and 1860, he maintains, three important things happened: the breakdown of the Whig party; the realignment of voters; and "a shift from a nationally balanced party system where both major parties competed on fairly even terms in all parts of the nation to a sectionally polarized one with Republicans dominant in the North and Democrats in the South."

Holt builds his argument on the assumption that two-party competition at the state and local levels is healthy in resolving conflicts. With the demise of the Whig party in the middle 1850s, the two-party system of competition broke down at the state and local levels. A national realignment was completed by 1860: Republicans controlled northern states while Democrats dominated the southern ones. Holt maintains that the Whig and Democratic parties had argued over the slavery issue in the 1830s and 1840s but that they did not fragment into state and local parties. He implies that if the second-party system continued through the 1850s, the slavery issue might have been resolved in a more peaceful manner.

One criticism of both Silbey and Holt is that neither author interprets the political events leading up to the Civil War within the context of the socio-economic changes taking place in the country. Both authors explain how many Americans manifested their hostility to the Irish Catholics who came here in the 1840s and 1850s by joining the Know-Nothing party, which in turn caused a realignment of the political parties. But they make no mention of the reasons why the Irish and other immigrants came here: the market revolution and the need for workers to build and staff the canals, railroads, and factories.

The list of books about the Civil War is extensive. Two good starting points are John Niven, *The Coming of the Civil War, 1837–1861* (Harlan Davidson, 1990) and Bruce Levine, *Half Slave and Half Free* (Hill & Wang, 1992). An older, extensive work with a compelling narrative and sound interpretations is David Potter, *The Impending Crisis, 1848–1861* (Harper & Row, 1976). Michael Perman has updated the well-worn problems of American civilization in *The Coming of the American Civil War*, 3rd ed. (D.C. Heath, 1993).

Both Silbey and Holt have published numerous articles in scholarly journals. Silbey, who has extensive knowledge of the nineteenth-century Democratic party, has collected his articles in *The American Political Nation 1838–1893* (Stanford University Press, 1991). A collection of Holt's articles can be found in *Political Parties and American Political Development from the Age of Jackson to the Age of Lincoln* (Louisiana State University Press, 1992).

Historians who reject the ethnocultural school, which minimizes the slavery issue as the cause of the Civil War, include Eric Foner and Kenneth M. Stampp. Foner's *Free Soil, Free Labor, Free Men* (Oxford University Press, 1970) is an excellent study of the bourgeois capitalism and conservative idealism that formed the ideological basis of the Republican party before the Civil War. In *America in 1857: A Nation on the Brink* (Oxford University Press, 1990), Stampp argues that conflict became inevitable after the election of James Buchanan to the presidency, the firestorm in Kansas, and the Supreme Court's decision in *Dred Scott v. Sandford*. A summary of the traditional view is found in Richard H. Sewell's *House Divided: Sectionalism and Civil War, 1848–1865* (Johns Hopkins University Press, 1988).

On the Internet, see http://ils.unc.edu/ingham/index.html, which is the American Slavery in Historical Context home page.

ISSUE 14

Was the North's Victory Over the South Inevitable?

YES: Richard N. Current, from "God and the Strongest Battalions," in David Donald, ed., *Why the North Won the Civil War* (Louisiana State University Press, 1960)

NO: Albert Castel, from *Winning and Losing in the Civil War: Essays and Stories* (University of South Carolina Press, 1996)

ISSUE SUMMARY

YES: Professor Richard N. Current maintains that it was the South's lack of manpower and economic resources and not the North's military superiority that doomed the Confederacy. Therefore, the North's victory over the South was inevitable.

NO: Professor Albert Castel argues that the North's victory over the South was due to luck. Also, Northern military successes in the fall of 1864 helped to reelect President Abraham Lincoln, destroying the chance for a negotiated settlement rather than a defeat for the South.

Over the past 125 years contemporaries and historians have advanced dozens of explanations for the defeat of the Confederacy in the Civil War. Most explanations can be divided into two categories: external and internal.

There are two external reasons for the Confederacy's failure, according to some historians: the Union's overwhelming resources and the uneven quality of leadership between the two sides.

In the first selection, Richard N. Current argues that the South's lack of resources in comparison with the North doomed the Confederacy. Contemporaries and historians blamed Jefferson Davis, president of the Confederacy, as well as his cabinet and military leaders for being unable to properly manage the South's economy and military campaigns. They could not overcome the weak Southern industrial infrastructure.

The second external reason for the defeat of the Confederacy is that the Union appears to have had better leadership. Lincoln is ranked by some as America's greatest president because he united his political objectives of saving the Union and freeing the slaves with a military strategy designed to defeat the Confederacy.

Internal conflicts were another problem for the Confederacy, according to some historians. In his book *State Rights in the Confederacy* (Peter Smith

Publishers, 1986), Frank Owsley maintains that governors in North Carolina and Georgia withheld men and equipment from the Confederate armies in order to build up their own state militias. The Confederate tombstone, he said, should be inscribed: "Died of State Rights."

A second version of the internal conflict argument appeared in a 1960 essay in a symposium entitled *Why the North Won the Civil War* (Touchstone Books, 1996). The editor, David Herbert Donald, argued that the resistance of Southerners to conscription, taxes, and limitations on speeches that were critical of the war effort fatally crippled the Confederacy. According to Donald, instead of state rights, the Confederate tombstone should be inscribed: "Died of Democracy."

A third variant of the internal conflict argument has recently been promoted by four Southern scholars: Richard E. Beringer, Herman Hattaway, Archer Jones, and William N. Still, Jr. Their main assertion is that the Confederacy lacked the will to win because of its inability to fashion a viable Southern nationalism, increasing religious doubts that God was on the Confederacy's side, and guilt over slavery.

In a Gettysburg symposium, edited by Gabor S. Borritt, entitled *Why the Confederacy Lost* (Oxford University Press, 1992), James M. McPherson dismisses all of the external and internal explanations for the South's defeat listed above. In his critique, McPherson applies the theory of reversibility. Briefly stated, the hindsight provided by knowing the outcome of the war allows the writer to attribute causes that explain the Northern victory.

But what if the South had won the Civil War? Could the same external explanations that are attributed to the Union victory also be used to explain a Confederate victory? Would Davis's leadership emerge as superior to Lincoln's? Would the great military leaders be Robert E. Lee, Thomas Jackson, and Braxton Bragg instead of Ulysses S. Grant, William T. Sherman, and Philip H. Sheridan? Would one Confederate soldier be considered equal to four Union soldiers? Would a triumvirate of yeoman farmers, slaveholding planters, and small industrialists have proven the superiority of agrarian values over industrial ones?

In the second selection, Albert Castel rejects the traditional internal and external explanations as well as the theory of reversibility. According to Castel, the accidental discovery of the Confederate's battleplan at Antietam, Maryland in the fall of 1862 helped the Union armies fight the Confederates to a standstill. Union victories in the West and Sherman's capture of Atlanta in the fall of 1864 were instrumental in reelecting Lincoln and spoiled the Confederacy's hopes for a negotiated settlement.

YES
Richard N. Current

GOD AND THE STRONGEST BATTALIONS

When war began in 1861, the statistics from the latest federal census decidedly favored the twenty-three states remaining in the Union as against the eleven that had withdrawn from it. In population the North had an advantage of almost five to two, and this advantage appears even greater if the slaves (more than one-third of the Southern people) are counted as somewhat less than the same number of freemen. In wealth and capacity to produce, the North held a still greater edge: in value of real and personal property, more than three to one (even with the inclusion of $2 billion for the slave property of the South); in capital of incorporated banks, more than four to one; in value of products annually manufactured, more than ten to one. The seceded states probably had a much less than proportional share of the national income. Besides, they contained only about a third of the total railroad mileage and practically none of the registered shipping. Though these comparisons are incomplete and inexact, they will serve to illustrate the point that the Union went to war with an overwhelming preponderance in most sources of economic power.

If wars are won by riches, there can be no question why the North eventually prevailed. The only question will be: How did the South manage to stave off defeat so long? Or perhaps the question ought to be: Why did the South even risk a war in which she was all but beaten before the first shot was fired?

Indeed, this last question occurred to at least a few Southerners during the secession winter. For example, the editor of the Lynchburg *Virginian* wrote: "Dependent upon Europe and the North for almost every yard of cloth, and every coat and boot and hat that we wear, for our axes, scythes, tubs and buckets, in short, for everything except our bread and meat, it must occur to the South that if our relations with the North are ever severed,—and how soon they may be none can know; may God forbid it long!—we should, in all the South, not be able to clothe ourselves; we could not fill our firesides, plough our fields, nor mow our meadows; in fact, we should be reduced to a state more abject than we are willing to look at even prospectively. And yet, all of these things staring us in the face, we shut our eyes and go in blindfold." Of course, the view of the Lynchburg *Virginian* was not the prevailing attitude

From Richard N. Current, "God and the Strongest Battalions," in David Donald, ed., *Why the North Won the Civil War* (Louisiana State University Press, 1960). Copyright © 1960 by Richard N. Current. Reprinted by permission.

of Southerners at that time. If it had been, most likely there would have been no war.

Nor was this the opinion of most leading Southerners afterwards, when the war had been lost and they were casting about for reasons why it had been. These men refused to adopt the handy and easy rationalization that the North simply had been too much and too many for the South. These men could not very well accept such an explanation, for it would have convicted them of blindness, stupidity, or even worse in going into a conflict they could not hope to win. In his memoirs General Joseph E. Johnston defended his fellow Southerners against such a possible charge. "That people," he wrote, "was not guilty of the high crime of undertaking a war without the means of waging it successfully."

As Johnston looked back, it seemed to him that the Confederacy had possessed "ample means." Other Southerners agreed with him. General P. G. T. Beauregard, for one, declared that "no people ever warred for independence with more relative advantages than the Confederacy; and if, as a military question, they must have failed, then no country must aim at freedom by means of war." The outcome was not to be explained, Beauregard insisted, by "mere material contrast" between the North and the South. So, too, the Richmond journalist and historian Edward A. Pollard maintained that "something more than numbers makes armies" and that "against the vast superiority of the North in material resources," the South had "a set-off in certain advantages."

Among these presumed advantages of the South, the first was psychological. Her people, fighting as they did for the high ideal of independence, for the protection of their very homes, were moved by a "superiour animation," a more determined spirit than the enemy could attain. The second point in the South's favor was geographic. She possessed rivers, swamps, and mountains that were "equivalent to successive lines of fortification"; she had the "immense advantage of the interior lines"; and, besides all this, she was favored with "one single advantage" which, alone, "should have been decisive of the contest." "That advantage was *space*." Even some economic aspects favored the South: At the beginning of the war it was a "remarkable fact" that "the South was richer than the North in all the *necessaries* of life," producing as she did more corn and livestock per person. The fourth and most important item might be viewed as either economic or diplomatic. This was cotton—a magic word, a magic staple, which theoretically ought to have done wonders for the Confederacy.

If statistics were on the side of the North, history seemed to be on the side of the South. In previous struggles for liberty the Dutch had beaten the Spaniards, the Russians had repelled the French, and the Americans had won out over the British against odds as bad or worse than those the Southerners faced in 1861. "In an intelligent view of the precedents of history," Pollard concluded, "it might safely [have been] predicted that the South... would be victor in the contest, however unequally matched in men and the materials of war, *unless the management of her affairs should become insane, or her people lose the virtue of endurance*." ...

In economic policy the chief errors commonly attributed to the Confederate government are these: its failure to exploit cotton promptly as a basis for foreign credit; its unwillingness to tax its people and its reliance, instead, on issues of paper money in the form of treasury notes; its impressment, or seizure at arbitrary prices, of the goods of its citizens; and its lack of thoroughness in the promotion of manufactures and in the control of transportation, especially by railroad. A brief re-examination of these matters may throw light on the question of whether the Confederacy was more handicapped by human or by material shortcomings.

In cotton, the South had a cash crop of great value, and yet, in the midst of war, Southerners reduced their planting, burned some of the bales they had on hand, and discouraged shipments abroad. "Instead of making the best use of this resource," B. J. Hendrick observes, "the [Jefferson] Davis government deliberately did all in its power to make it useless." At first glance the policy appears downright insane.

Surely there were alternatives, and in fact the Vice-President of the Confederacy, Alexander H. Stephens, proposed a different course during the war. Take two million bales from the 1860 and another two million from the 1861 crop, Stephens recommended. Pay for these with $100 million in government bonds. Buy fifty ironclad steamers to carry the cotton safely to Europe. Store it there until the price rises to fifty cents a pound, then sell it. Thus, Stephens thought, the Confederacy could net a profit of $800 million! Afterwards General Johnston was positive that this plan, if promptly put into effect, would have won the war. The cotton money, Johnston averred, would have procured arms for half a million men, who could have been ready and in the field by the time the very first battle was fought. The first battle, he implied, might well have been the last. In any event, "the Confederate treasury would have been much richer than that of the United States," and the South would have had the means of eventual success.

That the Confederacy failed to seize this splendid and obvious opportunity during the first year of the war— before the blockade had become too tight—must prove the stupidity if not the insanity of government leaders, of President Davis and his Secretary of the Treasury, Christopher G. Memminger. So it afterward seemed to historian Pollard, who berated Memminger for not having purchased cotton and sent it abroad while he had the chance....

The truth is that neither Davis nor Memminger had foisted upon the South the idea of withholding cotton. When the war began, not only these two men but practically all Southern leaders believed that cotton—or rather the lack of it— would win the war for the South. On the Southern staple Great Britain presumably depended for its prosperity, and so did France, and so too did the United States. Without cotton, Great Britain and France would face economic prostration, and to avert this they would have to come to the Confederacy's aid. Without cotton, the United States would suffer the closing of its textile mills and, more important, would have no export crop sufficient for obtaining indispensable foreign exchange. If the notions about "King Cotton" were delusions, they were not the private dreams of Memminger or Davis.

In the light of the times, these ideas were not quite so crazy as they seem in retrospect. True, the cotton shortage failed to accomplish what Southerners had expected it to do. Yet it did create a serious problem for the North, the problem of finding means of payment for necessary imports. Unfortunately for Southern hopes, the North was able to make up for her lack of cotton shipments by means of increased exports of wheat. Unfortunately, also, there were British economic interests that ran counter to the British interest in continued cotton shipments from the South, as Frank L. Owsley has demonstrated.

The Stephens-Johnston-Pollard view regarding cotton exports was at least as visionary as the King Cotton theory itself. There simply was not so much cotton available in 1861 as Stephens estimated: there were not two million bales left over from the 1860 crop, but only a few hundred thousand. Then, too, it is doubtful whether many owners of this cotton would have given it up in return for Confederate bonds. Even if enough money were obtained, the fifty ironclads probably could not have been purchased, and without them the South did not have enough shipping to send the cotton overseas. "Finally," Rembert W. Patrick concludes, "the idea ... that with four million bales in storage the price of cotton would have risen to fifty cents a pound, was fanciful."

Granting that Stephens' gigantic cotton-export scheme was not feasible in 1861, there remains the question whether *something* could not have been accomplished by a more prompt and vigorous export policy than was adopted. Whether or not Davis and Memminger should have done more than they did to base financing upon cotton, the fact is that they did more than their critics have credited them with doing. The cotton embargo, it must be remembered, was not the work of the Davis administration or of the Confederate Congress. It was the work of state and local officials and pri-

vate groups, who had the backing of an almost unanimous public opinion. It did not have the official support of Memminger and Davis, who used their influence to prevent Congress from passing an embargo act, and who encouraged shipments of cotton in so far as vessels were available. Almost from the outset, the Confederate government sought to obtain cotton by purchase or by produce loan, keeping some of it at home as a basis of credit for the purchase of foreign supplies, and sending the rest abroad. The fiasco of the Erlanger loan resulted from an attempt to use cotton for bolstering the foreign credit of the Confederacy. Not until the third year of the war, however, did the government take complete control of cotton exports and push them with determination. If this program had been undertaken earlier, probably Confederate finances could have been made much stronger than they actually became.

Certainly, Confederate financing was much less sound and less successful than Union financing. Of the Confederacy's income, to October 1864, almost 60 per cent was derived from the issue of paper money, about 30 per cent from the sale of bonds, and less than 5 per cent from taxation (the remaining 5 per cent arising from miscellaneous sources). Of the Union's income, by contrast, 13 per cent was raised by paper money, 62 per cent by bonds, and 21 per cent by taxes (and 4 per cent by other means). Thus the Confederacy relied much more upon government notes and much less upon taxation and borrowing than the Union did. Exactly how much paper money was afloat in the wartime South, nobody knows for sure. "Even if we knew the successive amounts of Confederate treasury notes in the hands of the public during the war," John C. Schwab remarks, "this would signify little, as they formed but a part of the currency; the State, municipal, bank, corporate, and individual notes formed the other, and... no inconsiderable part." The economist Eugene M. Lerner estimates that the stock of money in the South increased approximately eleven fold in the three years from January, 1861, to January, 1864. In any case, the prices of gold and other commodities were multiplied by much more than eleven. The price of gold, in Confederate dollars, rose eventually to sixty-one (in United States greenbacks it never rose even as high as three). The general price level, in Confederate dollars, soared to ninety or a hundred times its original level. The Confederacy suffered the worst inflation that Americans had known since the Revolutionary War.

In its effort to escape the evils of inflation the Confederate government but compounded them. The Funding Act of 1864, designed to force the exchange of treasury notes for bonds by threatening a partial repudiation of the notes, only speeded the loss in value of the currency. The impressment of government supplies, at less than the inflated market price, caused suppliers to withhold their goods and thus lessened the available amount. Unwittingly, the government defeated its own purposes. "The army suffered from want of food," as Schwab has observed, "though in the country at large there was no serious lack of it."

To the later critics of the Davis government it was perfectly obvious that the government should have taxed and taxed and borrowed and borrowed, rather than relying so heavily on the printing of batch after batch of treasury notes. These critics blamed Secretary Memminger, and some historians still blame him (Owsley refers to him as the "measly" Memminger). In truth, however, Memminger was just as well aware of the dangers of inflation as any of his denouncers. They were to have hindsight; he had at least a degree of foresight. But there was little he could do, especially since he lacked the force of personality to carry the Congress with him. As for taxes, he favored them, but at the start of the war he had no going machinery of tax collection to work with, and he was dealing with people who had even more than the typical American's resistance to taxation. Besides, cash was comparatively scarce in the Confederacy. The Secretary and the Congress had little choice but to resort to the 1861 requisition upon the states, which the states raised almost entirely by borrowing instead of taxing. As for issuing bonds to sop up the excess currency, Memminger favored that too, but the plain fact was that the people would not or could not buy the bonds in sufficient quantities. Hence his recommendation of the funding scheme to force the sale of bonds—a scheme that Congress carried even farther than he had intended.

There can be no doubt that the government's fiscal policies failed in their main object, namely, to transfer goods efficiently from private to public hands. There is considerable doubt, however, whether Davis or Memminger or any individual was to blame. There also is doubt whether the paper money issues, alone, accounted for the extent of inflation in the South. Actually, the price rise was uneven, and the prices that rose the most were those of goods in short supply, such as leather, wool, coffee, salt, tea, and drugs. So the actual scarcity of some items, as well as the overabundance of money, seems to have been responsible for soaring prices. Moreover, the flight from the currency, at least during the last couple of years of the war, must have been due in part to a growing popular skepticism as to the chances of the Confederacy's ever winning the war and making good on its promises to pay.

By interfering with the free market, the Davis government unintentionally discouraged production, both agricultural and industrial. At the same time the government did not interfere enough by means of positive measures to make the most of manufacturing possibilities. "The failure of the Confederacy, though predictable from the start," Ella Lonn writes, "was immediately attributable to errors of judgment in not anticipating and justly estimating its inability to supply certain indispensable necessities." This is the main conclusion of Miss Lonn in her study of *Salt as a Factor in the Confederacy,* and it is a conclusion which may be applied to other items as well as salt. In controlling manufacturers the government never aimed to do more than provide the army with essential supplies. Even the efforts in this direction were slow, halting, and indirect. The chief methods of influencing industrial production were the assignment or withholding of labor through manipulation of the draft, and the provision or denial of raw materials through control of the railroads.

Yet the government was "loath to enforce the kind of transportation policy the war effort demanded." At the start the railroad system of the South was, of course, defective. There were not enough railroad lines, and few of these were located where, strategically, they would do the most good. Besides, there were too many gaps, and there was too little rolling stock and too few mechanics and facilities for upkeep or repair. Despite these shortcomings, the railroads gave as much reality to the concept of "interior lines" as this concept ever attained. At the first battle of Bull Run the Confederates reinforced an army by railroad, in the midst of battle, for the first time in history. In moving General James Longstreet's men from Virginia to Tennessee before the battle of Chickamauga the Confederates again made history in the military use of railroads. Still, in the judgment of R. C. Black, historian of Confederate railroads, "the Confederates by no means made the best use of what they had." The government delayed too long in taking over and operating all the lines as a unified system. Confederate transportation often had to depend on wagons or carts, mule teams, and dirt roads. Instead of leaving teams and vehicles in the hands of owners, so as to let the economy go on functioning efficiently, the government too often impressed these things for strictly military uses. The resulting transportation difficulties, in the opinion of Charles W. Ramsdell, ranked next to fiscal policies in their "deleterious consequences" for the Confederacy. Without adequate transportation, the geographical advantages of the South were largely lost.

In their handling of finances, manufacturers, and transportation, the Confederate leaders made a number of errors that have become clear enough in retrospect. So the question persists: Were the South's economic disasters to be blamed upon human failings rather than material inadequacies? Was Davis inferior to Lincoln, and Memminger to Salmon P. Chase, the Union treasury head, in economic statesmanship? Were Southern civilians inferior to Northern in business ability and capacity for work? It has been said that the Confederate civil leaders in general and Memminger in particular proved themselves incompetent. And yet, if we imagine Chase in Memminger's position, it is hard to believe that he could have made a reputation as a successful financier. Memminger had to deal with problems in comparison with which those of the Union treasury were almost child's play. As for the Southern people as a whole, they unquestionably lagged behind Northerners in business experience and in education and literacy, if not also in physical health. Yet it is hard to agree with the emphasis of Pollard when he concludes: "He who seeks to solve the problem of the downfall of the Southern Confederacy must take largely into consideration the absence of any intelligent and steady system in the conduct of public affairs; the little circles that bounded the Richmond administration; the deplorable want of the commercial or business facility in the Southern mind."

It is hard to believe, and impossible to prove, that the Southerners did a worse job with economic affairs than Northerners would have done in the same circumstances. It is unimportant and unnecessary to try to prove this. The point is that the North had an economic strength several times greater to start with. In order to overcome this handicap and attain even so much as equality in economic power, the civilians of the South would have had to be *several times* as able, man for man, as those of the North. And this, obviously, is too much to have expected of any people, however willing and determined they might have been.

If the South could not meet the North on anything like an equal economic footing, she would have to compensate in some other respect. She would have to be blessed with better luck or higher

achievement in matters political, diplomatic, military, or psychological. A mere glance at these other considerations reveals at once that they cannot be appraised apart from one another, or the economic apart from any of them. These categories, after all, are purely arbitrary: we distinguish among them only for our own convenience.

In waging war, the Confederacy faced problems of politics and government that vastly complicated its problems of economic mobilization. Always the Southerners had to struggle with the incubus of John C. Calhoun, with the idea of state rights, with that fatal principle upon which their new government had been based. A Confederacy formed by particularist politicians could hardly be expected to adopt promptly those centralist policies—for marshaling resources and transportation—which victory demanded. Even apart from this ideological handicap, the Confederacy faced insuperable difficulties in attempting to set up, from scratch, a going administration in the midst of war. Professor Ramsdell has put the matter admirably: "... the southern people and their governments failed, with a few exceptions, to conserve, develop, and efficiently administer their resources; but it must be said that these were gigantic tasks, intricate, complex, and baffling. That they did not succeed better is not surprising when we remember the simplicity of southern economic and political organization before secession. There was not time, while a powerful and determined enemy was crashing at the gate, to reorganize their whole system and, without previous experience, create a complex administration, and train administrators. Problems had to be met as they arose.... All in all, it is not surprising that they could not be solved, or that, in the end, the collapse was complete."

By successful diplomacy, by winning the support of Great Britain or France, the South most likely could have canceled out all the economic advantages of the North. The Confederate financial policies, by the way, were not always easy to distinguish from the Confederate foreign policies. Thus, for example, the Erlanger loan, at least from the point of view of Judah P. Benjamin, was more a diplomatic than an economic measure, intended to elicit the support of France rather than, primarily, to raise funds. To explain why Southern hopes for foreign aid finally were dashed, it is necessary to look into a tangle of international economic relationships. It is necessary also to look into the world politics of the time, especially the divergent interests of Great Britain, France, and Russia. It is necessary even to look into the internal politics of England.

Certainly the economic history of the Confederacy cannot be told without including also the military and naval history (nor, for that matter, the military and naval without the economic). Bad as Southern transportation was at the start of the war, it soon was made worse by the advance of Union forces on land and sea. River and coastal waterways were occupied or blockaded and thus rendered useless to the Confederacy. Rail centers, like Chattanooga and Atlanta, were taken and new gaps thereby made in the already defective railroad system. The capture of New Orleans, only a year after the fighting had begun, meant the loss of the Confederacy's financial heart. As the Union armies took over more and more Southern territory, there was a continual shrinking of the area within which Confederate notes passed

as money. And as this area contracted, the quantity of paper money in it increased even more rapidly than the treasury put forth new issues, for Southerners living in the occupied territory got rid of their Confederate money by sending it to places where it still had at least a little value—to places where the Stars and Bars still waved. The more ground the Confederacy lost in battle, the worse the problem of inflation became. Meanwhile, in filling her armies, the South had to draw off from the economy a much higher proportion of her manpower than the North did of hers. The South's capacity to produce, already so small by comparison, was made even smaller by a disproportionate reduction of her labor supply. While Union military power was weakening the Southern economy, Union naval power had the same effect in perhaps even greater degree. The blockade, by bringing about serious shortages in strategic items, not only added to the inflationary trends but also frustrated efforts to maintain the transportation network and to increase industrial output. And, toward the end of the war, the Southern loss of faith in victory, as has been seen, contributed to the currency depreciation and to the economic disorganization that ensued.

Thus psychological influences, resulting from military events, fatally affected economic conditions. The reverse is equally true. Economic conditions gave rise to psychological influences that seriously affected military events.

Strategy itself at times conformed to economic facts. When the South resorted to the draft, in April, 1862, the congressional critics of Davis blamed him for having made such an extreme measure necessary. They charged that he had adopted a strategy of the "dispersed defensive" and that this, in turn, had chilled the enthusiasm of Southern men, who would have volunteered in ample numbers for an aggressive, concentrated campaign against the North. In reply to his critics Davis explained that the Confederacy lacked the means for such a campaign. "Without military stores," he said, "without the workshops to create them, without the power to import them, necessity not choice has compelled us to occupy strong positions and everywhere to confront the enemy without reserves."

Soldier morale, presumably hurt by the dispersed defensive, was further damaged by economic developments behind the lines. As General Johnston remarks, "after the Confederate currency had become almost worthless" the married soldiers from the farms "had to choose between their military service and the strongest obligations they knew —their duties to wives and children." The dilemma of these soldiers was made especially poignant by the actions of Confederate impressment officials. Those officials, as Johnston says, frequently preyed upon the most defenseless of the citizens, especially upon farm women whose husbands were away in the army. Hard beset by inflation and impressment, wives summoned their soldier-husbands home, and, faced with a torturing choice of loyalties, the soldiers often placed family above country. In other ways, too, the fiscal policies of the Confederacy no doubt impaired the morale of both soldiers and civilians. Amid the wild inflation some people grew rich overnight, at least on paper, and others lost their fortunes just as suddenly. A gambling spirit infected the land, and almost everybody became a speculator of some kind. Those gamblers who lost—and practically all of them lost in the end—naturally were prone to feelings of bitterness and envy. And they directed these feelings against one another as well as against the Yankee foe.

Since so much of the Southern despair was induced by objective conditions and events, on the battlefield and on the home front, it is difficult to accept the... thesis that the Confederacy collapsed because of a failure of the spirit. In most respects the loss of morale seems to have been a secondary rather than a primary cause of defeat.

The prime cause must have been economic. Given the vast superiority of the North in men and materials, in instruments of production, in communication facilities, in business organization and skill—and assuming for the sake of the argument no more than rough equality in statecraft and generalship—the final outcome seems all but inevitable. At least, it seems to have become inevitable once two dangers for the Union had been passed. One of these was the threat of interference from abroad. The other was the possibility of military disaster resulting from the enemy's superior skill or luck on the battlefield, from his ability to make decisive use of his power-in-being before the stronger potential of the Union could be fully developed and brought into play. Both dangers appear to have been over by midsummer, 1863, if not already by autumn, 1862. Thereafter, month by month, the resources of the North began increasingly to tell, in what became more and more a war of attrition.

True, the victory is not always to the rich. The record of mankind offers many an example of a wealthy and fat and decadent people overcome by an enemy who was poor and lean and vigorous. Indeed, these historical examples heartened those Southerners who, at the outset, assumed that all Yankees had been corrupted by commerce and industry, that the "mud-sills" of the factory and the money-grubbers of the counting-house would lack the fortitude that victory required. On the other hand, many in the North looked upon Southerners as a people debased, debauched, and incapacitated by contact with the institution of slavery. Today, at this distance in time, we can see that the two sides must have been about even in virtue and vice, devotion and disloyalty, human strength and weakness.

For the North to win, she had only to draw upon her resources as fully and as efficiently as the South drew upon hers; or, rather, the North had to make good use of only a fraction of her economic potential. Her material strength was so much greater that she could, as it were, almost lick the South with one hand tied behind her back. In fact, the North during the war years did devote a large part of her energies and resources to nonmilitary enterprise. Once the financial crisis of late 1861 was past, the Union entered upon an economic boom. She actually grew in material strength, while the South wasted away. From 1861 to 1865 nearly 5,000,000 acres of the public domain in the West were transferred to settlers and corporations. Railroad mileage lengthened from about 31,000 to more than 35,000 miles—an increase of approximately one-eighth. The value of imports for the North alone in 1864 was almost as great as it had been for the entire country, the South included, in 1860.

NO   Albert Castel

COULD THE NORTH *NOT* HAVE
WON THE CIVIL WAR?

While visiting an Ann Arbor [Michigan] bookstore in the autumn of 1992 I came across a recently published tome entitled *Guns of the South* by an author named Harry Turtledove. On the front of the dust-jacket was a picture of Robert E. Lee, attired in his Confederate general's uniform and carrying an AK-47 assault rifle. At once I assumed that this book was one of historical fiction and not historical fact. Reading it confirmed this assumption. *Guns of the South* is a novel in which the Confederates win the Civil War thanks to being supplied, via South African whites of the twenty-first century and a time machine, with large quantities of AK-47's and the requisite ammunition. Employing these rapid-firing, magazine-fed automatic rifles Lee's soldiers easily and totally defeat the much bigger Union army, equipped as it was with single-shot muzzleloaders, and thus secure Northern recognition of Confederate independence.

The implication of this story, whether author Turtledove realized it or not when he wrote it, is that without the intervention of what might be termed a technological miracle, the South could not have won the Civil War —or, to put it another way, the North could not have lost that war. What novelist Turtledove implies has been asserted quite explicitly by a goodly number of good historians. For example, Charles Beard in his *The Rise of American Civilization*—probably the most influential book about American history ever written—maintains that the triumph of the industrial North over the agricultural South in what he calls "The Second American Revolution" was inevitable:

> When the armed conflict was precipitated, the eleven states in the southern Confederacy were confronted by twenty-three states in the federal union. Nine million people, more than one-third of whom were slaves, faced twenty-two million people nearly all white. . . . Practically all of the iron, steel, textile, and munition industries of the country were in federal control. By far the major portion of the foreign commerce had long centered in the ports above the Potomac; even most of the foreign goods destined for the South had poured through the warehouses of northern cities. More than two-thirds of the banking capital of the country

From Albert Castel, *Winning and Losing in the Civil War: Essays and Stories* (University of South Carolina Press, 1996). Copyright © 1996 by University of South Carolina Press. Reprinted by permission. Notes omitted.

was in northern hands. The North also had an almost complete monopoly of the science and skilled labor required to furnish the sinews of warfare. In fact the real revolution —the silent shift of social and material power—had occurred before the southern states declared their independence and precipitated the revolution of violence. As Seward warned the planters, they would accept the inescapable either in peace or in battle.

In short, the South according to Beard was defeated even before the war started —defeated because it was "fighting the census returns." Hence Beard devotes only two paragraphs of his 1,661-page book to the battles and campaigns of the Civil War. These, he asserts, were just a "fleeting incident," and the descriptions of them are best left "to those who have chartered the science of military tactics or mastered the art of depicting tragedy and romance."

Perhaps the most masterly depiction of the tragedy and romance of the Civil War is Shelby Foote's three-volume *The Civil War, A Narrative*. Basically it is a military history of the war, one that describes its battles in great and eloquent detail. Yet Foote, like Beard, believes that the South was doomed to defeat. During one of his commentaries on Ken Burns's TV documentary, "The Civil War," Foote says that "The North fought that war with one hand behind its back." Had it needed to do so to win, "the North simply would have brought that other arm out from behind its back. I don't think the South ever had a chance to win that war."

No doubt Foote, when he said this, had in mind mainly the North's immense manpower superiority over the South. In 1860 the North had 3,500,000 men of military age (18–45), the South slightly over 1,000,000. Also, as the war went on, the North could and did draw on tens of thousands of blacks, pro-Union Southern whites, and European immigrants. Altogether at least 2,000,000 men served at one time or another in the Union armed forces, 350,000 of whom were killed in battle or by illness. On the other hand the South, although mobilizing virtually all of its available able-bodied men and even boys, could muster just 750,000 soldiers and sailors, more than one-third of whom died. Hence the North overall enjoyed close to a three-to-one advantage in numbers. Furthermore, it could have increased the ratio to four-to-one or five-to-one had it wanted to. This is why Foote contended that the North fought the war with one hand behind its back. Statistically he is correct.

Another prominent historian who argues that the North in effect was predestined to victory is William C. Davis, author and editor of numerous excellent books pertaining to the Civil War. In his biography of Confederate President Jefferson Davis, he states:

> Any final verdict on Davis as war president must be predicated on the assumption that the Confederacy could not have won the war under the conditions it faced. The material and manpower resources arrayed against it were simply too overwhelming. Barring completely unforeseeable events, only a massive intervention of European powers or the loss of will to use its own resources to full victory could have cost the Union the war.

Such, then, is the case made by those historians who believe that the North could not have lost the Civil War and accordingly that the South could not have won it. It is a powerful case, based on calculations of comparative power, and made all the more persuasive by the undeniable and indubitable fact that the North, after all, *did* win the war and the South *did* lose it.

But is it a valid case? I think not, and what follows are my reasons for so thinking. Most, if not all, of these reasons, I should point out, are as such not original with me, but have been put forth in different words by other historians, among them James M. McPherson, whose *Battle Cry of Freedom* is the best single-volume account of the Civil War era. As far as I am concerned, however, their lack of originality strengthens rather than weakens the arguments I am about to present. When it comes to a subject that has been written about so long and so much as the Civil War it is extremely difficult to be truly original and at the same time sensible.…

Broadly speaking I have two reasons for rejecting what I call the Thesis of Automatic Northern Victory. The first is philosophical. Just because something happened in a certain way in the past does not necessarily mean that it had to happen that way. Was it inevitable that the Ancient Greeks defeat the attempt of the Persians to dominate them? That Rome establish its mighty empire? That Charles Martel turn back the Saracens at Tours, thereby in Gibbon's words savings Western Europe from the "civil and religious yoke of the Koran?" That William become the Conqueror at Hastings? That the Reformation occur? That the French Revolution take the course it did? That the Americans win the Battle of Midway? Even a superficial study of these events will reveal numerous ways in which they could have had a different outcome, and in fact almost did.

To be sure, there are many occurrences in history that assuredly deserve to be termed inevitable. The military victory of the United States and its allies in the Gulf War would seem to qualify, given the one-sided ease with which it was gained. But was that war itself inevitable? Only by the narrowest of margins did Congress authorize President George Bush to employ military force against what turned out to be Saddam Hussein's badly over-rated legions. And was the decision not to exploit that victory by deposing the Iraqi tyrant also inevitable, or was it merely a mistake committed by a leader of limited foresight seeking a limited goal? Simply by asking such questions we can see the danger inherent in labeling historical events as inevitable. Maybe they were—but also maybe they were not.

My second reason for doubting that the North could not have lost the Civil War is historical. From the conquest of the Persian Empire by Alexander the Great on to the failure of the American effort to prevent the Communist conquest of South Vietnam, history is filled with wars wherein the side that was weaker in numbers, weapons, wealth, and all the other material indices of power prevailed over a stronger, oft-times far stronger, foe. Napoleon—or was it Frederick the Great?—supposedly said that God is on the side of the strongest battalions. In the sense that the side with the most men, etc., wins most of the time, that is true. But as the career of Napoleon (or Frederick the Great) amply demonstrates, it is not always true. That is because there are other factors besides the materialistic or brute force that can and do determine the outcome of wars. Chief among them are quality of leadership, combat efficiency, chance or luck, and last, but not least, the will to fight, to endure, to win. Let us now apply these factors to the waging of the Civil War. We will begin with quality of leadership.

The North's immense superiority in manpower and material would have been to little avail had the North failed to produce leadership, civilian and military, capable of making effective use of this superiority, or had the South produced leaders of such brilliance that even highly competent Northern leaders would have been no match for them. As it was, owing to the military genius of Robert E. Lee, seconded by that of Thomas J. "Stonewall" Jackson, the South came potentially close to victory in the summers of 1862 and 1863, and there are those who say it lost the war when it lost Jackson. Unfortunately for the South, however, it did not equal the North in civilian leadership (although it would have made no difference as to the ultimate outcome of the war had Lincoln been president of the Confederacy and Jefferson Davis president of the Union), and its superiority in military leadership was confined to the East. In the West the North had the better top generals —Ulysses S. Grant, George H. Thomas, William T. Sherman, and (shocking as this may seem to some) William S. Rosecrans —whereas the South failed to come up with an army commander who did not suffer from serious flaws. Consequently, while the South was able to hold, and more than hold, its own in the East, it lost the war in the West and thus as a whole. It needed two Lees. It had but one.

Another way in which the Confederacy might have negated the North's quantitative superiority was by qualitative superiority achieved through a deci-sively higher level of combat efficiency on the battlefield. Throughout history smaller armies have defeated larger ones because they were better equipped, organized, trained, and disciplined, employed a more effective tactical system, and fought with greater skill and determination. These qualities enabled first the Greeks, then the Romans, to dominate the Ancient World; at the peak of their power any reasonably competent Greek or Roman commander was virtually guaranteed of victory against his "barbarian" opponent, regardless of the numerical odds. Likewise, during the first four years of World War II the Germans, with their blitzkrieg tactics, scored awesome victories against the French and British, who matched them in soldiers and material but did not know how to use them as well, and against the Soviets, who vastly outnumbered them and even had in some categories better weapons, notably the T-34 tank. Following the collapse of the Soviet Union, when it became safe to speak the truth about "The Great Patriotic War," a Russian veteran declared: "We did not defeat the Germans, we smothered them with our bodies."

To a degree the South did achieve a superiority in combat efficiency, but like its superiority in military leadership it was confined largely to the East and to Lee's Army of Northern Virginia. In the West this did not happen. The Confederacy's Western troops were equal in courage and their endurance of hardship to those of the East but on the whole did not display an equal skill in battle. Why this was so is a complex matter that cannot be adequately explained in the space available here. Suffice, therefore, to say that such is the conclusion reached by Richard M. McMurry, an excellent historian and a Southerner, in his fine book *Two Great*

Rebel Armies, where he presents the evidence and arguments supporting this judgment. And, to repeat, the war was won by the North and lost by the South in the West.

Karl von Clausewitz, the most profound of military philosophers, states that war belongs to the province of chance. That is true, very true. Rarely in war do things go as planned, and the only thing that can be expected with absolute confidence is the unexpected. That being the case, conceivably the North could have failed to win the war had chance, in the form of good luck, consistently favored the South, or else been on its side at some crucial juncture in the conflict. Although the Confederates had some lucky breaks—as, for example, when at Chickamauga a whole division pulled out of the Union front, thereby enabling the Confederates to gain their sole major offensive victory of the entire war in the West —too often fortune favored the North, particularly on occasions when the South could least afford an adverse turn of the wheel of fortune. Thus, to cite the most famous instance of Southern bad luck, during the Antietam Campaign of September 1862 an Indiana private, while poking around in an abandoned Confederate camp, discovered an order issued by Lee that revealed he had divided his army. Supplied with this information, the Union commander, Major General George B. McClellan, who hitherto had been waiting apprehensively for Lee to move against him, advanced against Lee, causing him to fight a desperate battle wherein he barely escaped destruction and was so reduced in strength that he had no choice except to retreat from Maryland back into Virginia. Had it not been for this "lost dispatch" which a Confederate staff officer had left behind in the camp, wrapped around some cigars, there is no reason to doubt and every reason to believe that McClellan would have continued to perform like McClellan, with the result that Lee would have been able to regroup his army before McClellan took advantage of its dispersed condition, carried out as planned his invasion of Pennsylvania, continued to outmaneuver, out-march, and out-smart McClellan, and then gained a resounding success, either in the form of a battlefield victory or the occupation of some major Northern city or cities, that could have led to Southern independence, for in the late summer of 1862 the North's morale had sunk dangerously low and the British government was giving serious consideration to recognizing the Confederacy, an act that would have led to French recognition as well. British and French recognition of Southern independence, in turn, almost surely would have led to Northern defeat, for the North then would have been in a position where it either would have had to declare war on those two powers, thus bringing them into the conflict on the side of the Confederacy, or else acquiesce to their recognition by doing the same.

This is why the Battle of Antietam probably was the most decisive engagement of the Civil War from a political standpoint. By compelling Lee to abandon his first attempt to invade the North it enabled the Union to go on with the war and deprived the South of its best potential opportunity of the entire conflict to gain independence. Furthermore, Antietam provided Lincoln with the occasion for issuing the Preliminary Emancipation Proclamation, thereby transforming the war from one being waged by the North to preserve the Union into one which also was being fought to destroy slavery—

a transformation with consequences that reverberate down to the present. And all of this came about because of the carelessness of a Confederate officer who liked to smoke cigars. What was "inevitable" about that?

The final non-materialistic factor that helps determine the outcome of wars is the morale, will, and determination of the belligerents, or the lack thereof. In fact, the very object of war, as a usual thing, is to break the will of one's opponent to keep on fighting. To accomplish this, one seeks to inflict on the enemy such losses and damage that he will decide that it is useless and hopeless to continue the struggle and so call it quits. Rarely is it necessary or deemed desirable to achieve a "Carthaginian peace" in which you totally destroy or exterminate the foe.

The Civil War offers a classic case of a contest of wills, made all the more so because it is one of the few instances in all history of an armed conflict between democracies. In this war the North's basic objective, to which emancipation was secondary and supplementary, was to force the South back into the Union. To realize this goal the North had to invade the South, seize its key strategic and economic areas, defeat and demolish its armies, and cause so much suffering among the civilian population that ultimately the Southerners, or at least most of them, would realize that their cause was a lost one and so lay down their arms. (That it had to do these things, by the way, meant that the North faced a much more difficult military task than the Confederacy, one that could not be accomplished without a large superiority in numbers, one that also reduced the North's advantage in manpower, for the Union armies had to use a far greater proportion of their troops for occupation and non-combat duties, whereas the Confederates could employ a higher percentage of their soldiers where it counted most—on the firing line. As a result, during the first three years of the war the Confederates often had roughly equal or even superior strength in combat).

The South, on the other hand, could achieve its political goal—Northern acceptance of its independence—simply by frustrating the military efforts of the North to subdue it. If it was able to defend itself well enough and long enough, then sooner or later the Northern people, or enough of them, would conclude that the war could not be won, or that the cost of trying to win it was too high, and so abandon the effort to restore the Union and free the slaves. In sum, in order to win the war the North had to gain total military victory, whereas the South could win simply by not losing.

That this was so is an historical fact, not mere historical speculation. Three times during the war the South did come close to potential victory because of Northern defeatism. The first time, as already noted, was in the late summer of 1862 when Lee moved northward across the Potomac. His advance followed the repulse of a mighty Union attempt to capture Richmond and the humiliating rout of the Federal forces at the Battle of Second Bull Run, and it soon was followed by another Confederate offensive, that of Braxton Bragg's army up through Tennessee into Kentucky, an offensive that threatened to cancel out all that had been gained by the Union victories at Fort Henry, Fort Donelson, Shiloh, and Corinth. Had Lee won a major victory on Northern soil and/or seized a major Northern city or two, and had Bragg been able at least to maintain his army in

Kentucky—more than that could not be realistically expected of *him*—it is quite possible if not probable that a majority of the Northern people would have come to agree with the British leaders who were declaring that the North's effort to restore the Union by military means was an exercise in futility that should cease at once in the name of common sense and humanity. Indeed, even though Lee was compelled to withdraw to Virginia after Antietam and Bragg had to retreat into Tennessee, Northern discouragement with the war remained so strong that it, along with widespread disapproval of the Emancipation Proclamation, caused the Republicans to suffer substantial losses in the congressional and state elections in the fall of 1862. Had Lincoln been up for re-election then, probably he would have been defeated.

The second occasion when the North tottered on the brink of not winning the war was during the first six months of 1863. In the East there had been Ambrose Burnside's bloodbath at Fredericksburg and Joseph Hooker's fiasco at Chancellorsville. In the West Rosecran's army seemed stalled in Tennessee and Grant's forces bogged down—literally—among the swamps and bayous above Vicksburg, unable to reach the place, much less take it. In the North despair was on the ascendant, in the South hope. Not until July, when Lee was repulsed at Gettysburg and Grant captured Vicksburg, did the North emerge from the gloom of anticipated defeat into the glow of anticipated victory. Had Lee won at Gettysburg and Grant continued to be baffled in his attempts to seize Vicksburg, it is doubtful that the North would have retained sufficient will and determination to continue the war much longer. To my knowledge no historian worthy of the name has ever argued that the Union victories at Gettysburg and Vicksburg were "inevitable."

The third and final time the North nearly lost the will to win and with it the war was during the summer of 1864. In the spring of that year Grant had moved against Lee and Richmond, Sherman against Joseph Johnston and Atlanta. Their purpose was to crush the opposing Confederate armies and/or take those cities. Should either Grant or Sherman succeed, the Confederacy would be defeated, for Lee's and Johnston's armies, and Richmond and Atlanta, had become the symbol and the substance of the South's ability to maintain its struggle for independence. By the same token, to avoid defeat the Confederates had to hold both Grant and Sherman at bay until the North's presidential election in the fall of 1864. If they were able to do so, then there was an excellent chance that Lincoln and the Republicans would be turned out of power by the Democrats, who were declaring that the Union could not be restored by war but only by peace, a peace to be attained by negotiating an agreement with the Southern states whereby they would return to the Union in exchange for ironclad guarantees of their constitutional rights, the right of slavery among them. Although the Confederates had no intention of rejoining the Union no matter what terms were offered—they had fought too long and suffered too much to settle for anything less than full independence—they believed, with good cause, that should the Democrats take power in Washington the North would be unable to go on with the war, at least not successfully.

In Virginia Lee again did what had to be done if the South was to stave off defeat. In spite of being outnumbered more than two to one he inflicted such heavy losses on Grant's army that its offensive capability was wrecked for the remainder of 1864. In Georgia, by contrast, Johnston not only failed to halt Sherman's advance on Atlanta but he also failed to give any assurance that he would make a determined effort to that end. Hence in mid-July Jefferson Davis removed him from command and replaced him with John Bell Hood. Hood could be depended on to fight, and fight he did, attacking Sherman's army three times in less than two weeks. Each attack was beaten back with casualties that Hood could ill-afford, but he did keep Sherman out of Atlanta. By August it seemed that Sherman's campaign in Georgia, like Grant's in Virginia, had ended in stalemate. Once again Northern morale plunged.

As it plunged, the Democrats became increasingly confident that they would win the upcoming presidential election and the Republicans became increasingly convinced that they would lose it. Henry Raymond, editor of the *New York Times* and national chairman of the Republican Party, warned Lincoln that he faced defeat. Horace Greeley, editor of the *New York Tribune,* joined with other top Republican leaders in an endeavor to have Lincoln replaced with another candidate on the grounds that he could not win. And Lincoln himself despaired. On August 23, 1864, he summoned his cabinet to the White House. There he had each member sign, without reading, a memorandum that he had written. It stated:

> This morning, as for some days past, it seems exceedingly probable that this Administration will not be reelected. Then it will be my duty to so cooperate with the President-elect, as to save the Union between the election and the

> inauguration; as he will have secured his election on such grounds that he cannot possibly save it afterwards.

It is too bad that Charles Beard was not on hand to tell Lincoln that he need not worry—that the South was fighting against the census returns and thus the North could not possibly lose. As for the North bringing its other arm out from behind its back to fight, by August of 1864 Lincoln—not a bad judge of public attitudes—obviously feared that it was disposed to put the arm that already was fighting behind its back.

On August 31 the Democrats, who had postponed their national convention until the last possible moment to make sure that the military situation did not take an unexpected turn for the better, which from their standpoint would be a turn for the worse politically, nominated McClellan for president on a platform that declared the war a failure and called for "a cessation of hostilities, with a view to an ultimate convention of the States or other peaceable means, to the end that at the earliest practicable moment peace may be restored on the basis of the Federal Union of the States."

Two days later Sherman's army, having forced the Confederates to evacuate the city by cutting its sole remaining railroad supply line, occupied Atlanta: "Atlanta is ours, and fairly won," Sherman telegraphed the War Department in Washington. The fall of Atlanta wrecked the Democratic platform and ruined McClellan's candidacy. At the same time it assured Lincoln's re-election and Northern victory. The majority of Northerners now believed that the war could be won, was being won, and would be won. On the other hand the South's hope of winning by not losing, of outlasting the North in a contest of wills, was destroyed. Henceforth it no longer was a question of whether the Confederacy would be defeated but simply one of when.

So much, then, for the view that the North could not have lost the Civil War. Not only could it have lost it, it almost did. Its great superiority in manpower, manufacturing, materiel, etc. was the main ingredient of its victory. In fact, it was the essential ingredient, for without it the North would not have won. But that superiority, of and by itself, did not guarantee its victory. That required in addition able leadership, hard and skilled fighting, a certain measure of luck, and above all the will to go on with the struggle despite discouraging defeats, frustrating stalemates, and staggering casualties. Had not the North possessed and displayed these qualities to a sufficient degree, then what Lincoln had called the "house divided" would have remained divided. As it was, the house was reunited, and at the same time, again to quote Lincoln, "a new birth of freedom" occurred in the form of the abolition of slavery.

Desirable outcomes? Yes. Inevitable? No.

POSTSCRIPT

Was the North's Victory Over the South Inevitable?

Current advances a familiar argument in an unusual manner. Rather than focusing on the North's superior resources, Current discusses the inadequacies of the South's economic infrastructure. However, he argues that Southern officials, if one takes into account the ideological values of the South and its limited resources, ran the Confederacy in the best possible fashion. Ideologically, the South was committed to a confederation system similar in structure to the early government of the United States under the Articles of Confederation in the 1780s.

Castel takes issue with historians who believe that the North's superior resources guaranteed an inevitable victory in the Civil War. Castel challenges the inevitability thesis on philosophical and historical grounds. He maintains that just because an event turns out a certain way doesn't mean that there were no other alternative outcomes possible. There are historical examples from the Civil War where an unexpected and lucky event could have changed the outcome. Would the South have won the battle of Antietam if an Indiana private had not found Robert E. Lee's battle plans wrapped around a cigar in an abandoned Confederate camp?

Both essays in this issue are influenced by the times in which the authors wrote. Current is well aware of the differences between the South's failed efforts at mobilizing its resources for war in the 1860s with the changed attitude toward the use of government power and the nation's efforts in harnessing its resources in both world wars. Castel and McPherson write with full knowledge that North Vietnam defeated the United States even though they were totally inferior in the number of soliders, machines, and weapons systems.

Readers who wish to visit some of the battlefields should start with James I. Robertson Jr., *The Concise Illustrated History of the Civil War* (Stackpole Books, 1971). The best detailed reference is David J. Eicher, *Civil War Battlefields: A Touring Guide* (Taylor Publishing, 1995).

ISSUE 15

Did Abraham Lincoln Free the Slaves?

YES: James M. McPherson, from *Drawn With the Sword: Reflections on the American Civil War* (Oxford University Press, 1996)

NO: Vincent Harding, from *There Is a River: The Black Struggle for Freedom in America* (Vintage Books, 1981)

ISSUE SUMMARY

YES: Historian James M. McPherson maintains that Abraham Lincoln was the indispensable agent in emancipating the slaves through his condemnation of slavery as a moral evil, his refusal to compromise on the question of slavery's expansion, his skillful political leadership, and his implementation and direction of Union troops as an army of liberation.

NO: Professor Vincent Harding credits slaves themselves for engaging in a dramatic movement of self-liberation. Abraham Lincoln initially refused to declare the destruction of slavery as a war aim and then issued the Emancipation Proclamation, which failed to free any slaves in areas over which he had any authority.

Numerous explanations have been offered for the Civil War. Some historians see the conflict as the product of a conspiracy housed either in the North or South, depending upon one's regional perspective. For many in the Northern states, the chief culprits were the planters and their political allies who were willing to defend Southern institutions at all costs. South of the Mason-Dixon line, blame was given to the abolitionists and the free-soil architects of the Republican party. Some viewed secession and war as the consequence of a constitutional struggle between states' rights advocates and defenders of the federal government, while others focused upon the economic rivalries or the cultural differences between North and South. Embedded in each of these interpretations, however, is the powerful influence of the institution of slavery.

Abraham Lincoln fully understood the role slavery had played in the outbreak of the Civil War. In March 1865, as the war was nearing its end, he presented the following analysis: "One eighth of the whole population [in 1861] was colored slaves, not distributed generally over the Union, but localized in the Southern part of it. These slaves constituted a peculiar and powerful interest. All knew that this interest was somehow the cause of the war. To strengthen, perpetuate, and extend this interest was the object [of the South]..., while the [North]... claimed no right to do more than to restrict the territorial enlargement of it."

In light of Lincoln's recognition of the role slavery played in the clash between North and South, none should find it surprising that the Emancipation Proclamation that he issued in September 1862 established a policy to end slavery. Hence, the demise of slavery became a war aim, and Lincoln seemed to have earned his place in history as "the Great Emancipator." Upon learning of the President's announcement, the fugitive slave and abolitionist, Frederick Douglass, was ecstatic. "We shout for joy," he declared, "that we live to record this righteous decree."

But Douglass had not always been so encouraged by Lincoln's commitment to freedom. Lincoln was not an abolitionist by any stretch of the imagination, but Douglass was convinced that the Republican victory in the presidential election of 1860 had brought to the White House a leader with a deserved reputation as an antislavery man. That confidence declined, however, in the early months of Lincoln's presidency as Douglass and other abolitionists lobbied for emancipation during the secession crisis only to have their demands fall on deaf ears. Lincoln consistently avoided any public pronouncements that would suggest his desire to end slavery as a war aim. The priority was preserving the Union, and Lincoln did not view emancipation as essential to that goal.

Until Lincoln changed his course in 1862, it appeared that the slaves would have to free themselves. This is precisely what some scholars insist happened. Southern slaves, they argue, became the key agents for liberation by abandoning their masters, undermining the plantation routine, serving as spies for Union troops, and taking up arms against the Confederacy. Black Northerners pitched in as well by enlisting in the United States Army and risking their lives to defeat the Confederacy and end slavery.

The question "Who freed the slaves?" is the focus of the following essays. James McPherson reinforces the conclusion that Lincoln freed the slaves. McPherson recognizes the limited nature of the Emancipation Proclamation, but he insists that Lincoln's commitment to an antislavery philosophy, exercise of skillful political leadership, and direction of the Union armies made him perhaps the only person who could have brought an end to the institution of slavery by 1865.

For Vincent Harding, credit for the end of slavery belongs not to the alleged "Great Emancipator," who took only halting steps toward eliminating slavery, but to the masses of slaves who sought self-liberation by running away from their masters, undermining plantation operations, engaging in local insurrections, and offering their services to the Union Army and Navy.

YES

James M. McPherson

WHO FREED THE SLAVES?

If we were to go out on the streets of almost any town in America and ask the question posed by the title of this [selection], probably nine out of ten respondents would answer unhesitatingly, "Abraham Lincoln." Most of them would cite the Emancipation Proclamation as the key document. Some of the more reflective and better informed respondents would add the Thirteenth Amendment and point to Lincoln's important role in its adoption. And a few might qualify their answer by noting that without Union military victory the Emancipation Proclamation and Thirteenth Amendment would never have gone into effect, or at least would not have applied to the states where most of the slaves lived. But, of course, Lincoln was commander in chief of Union armies, so the credit for their victories would belong mainly to him. The answer would still be the same: Lincoln freed the slaves.

In recent years, though, this answer has been challenged as another example of elitist history, of focusing only on the actions of great white males and ignoring the actions of the overwhelming majority of the people, who also make history. If we were to ask our question of professional historians, the reply would be quite different. For one thing, it would not be simple or clear-cut. Many of them would answer along the lines of "On the one hand . . . but on the other. . . ." They would speak of ambivalence, ambiguity, nuances, paradox, irony. They would point to Lincoln's gradualism, his slow and apparently reluctant decision for emancipation, his revocation of emancipation orders by Generals John C. Frémont and David Hunter, his exemption of border states and parts of the Confederacy from the Emancipation Proclamation, his statements seemingly endorsing white supremacy. They would say that the whole issue is more complex than it appears—in other words many historians, as is their wont, would not give a straight answer to the question.

But of those who did, a growing number would reply, as did a historian speaking to the Civil War Institute at Gettysburg College in 1991: "THE SLAVES FREED THEMSELVES." They saw the Civil War as a potential war for abolition well before Lincoln did. By flooding into Union military camps in the South, they forced the issue of emancipation on the Lincoln administration. By creating a situation in which Northern officials would either have to return them to slavery or acknowledge their freedom, these "contrabands," as they came to be called, "acted resolutely to place their freedom—and that of their posterity—on the wartime agenda." Union officers, then Congress, and finally Lincoln decided to confiscate this human property belonging to the enemy and put it to work for the Union in the form of servants, teamsters, laborers, and eventually soldiers in Northern armies. Weighed in the scale of war, these 190,000 black soldiers and sailors (and probably a larger number of black army laborers) tipped the balance in favor of Union victory. Even deep in the Confederate interior remote from the fighting fronts, with the departure of masters and overseers to the army, "leaving women and old men in charge, the balance of power gradually shifted in favor of slaves, undermining slavery on farms and plantations far from the line of battle."

One of the leading exponents of the black self-emancipation thesis is the historian and theologian Vincent Harding, whose book *There Is a River: The Black Struggle for Freedom in America* has become almost a Bible for the argument. "While Lincoln continued to hesitate about the legal, constitutional, moral, and military aspects of the matter," Harding writes, "the relentless movement of the self-liberated fugitives into the Union lines" soon "approached and surpassed every level of force previously known.... Making themselves an unavoidable military and political issue ... this overwhelming human movement ... of self-freed men and women ... took their freedom into their own hands." The Emancipation Proclamation, when it finally and belatedly came, merely "confirmed and gave ambiguous legal stand-

ing to the freedom which black people had already claimed through their own surging, living proclamations."

During the 1980s this self-emancipation theme achieved the status of orthodoxy among social historians. The largest scholarly enterprise on the history of emancipation and the transition from a slave to a free society during the Civil War era, the Freedmen and Southern Society project at the University of Maryland, stamped its imprimatur on the interpretation. The slaves, wrote the editors of this project, were "the prime movers in securing their own liberty." The Columbia University historian Barbara J. Fields gave wide publicity to this thesis. On camera in the PBS television documentary *The Civil War* and in an essay in the lavishly illustrated volume accompanying the series, she insisted that "freedom did not come to the slaves from words on paper, either the words of Congress or those of the President," but "from the initiative of the slaves" themselves. "It was they who taught the nation that it must place the abolition of slavery at the head of its agenda.... The slaves themselves had to make their freedom real."

Two important corollaries of the self-emancipation thesis are the arguments, first, that Lincoln hindered more than he helped the cause, and second, that the image of him as the Great Emancipator is a myth created by whites to deprive blacks of credit for achieving their own freedom. This "reluctant ally of black freedom," wrote Vincent Harding, "played an actively conservative role in a situation which ... needed to be pushed toward its most profound revolutionary implications." Lincoln repeatedly "placed the preservation of the white Union above the death of black slavery"; even as late as August 1862, when he wrote his famous letter to Horace Greeley stating that "if I could save the Union without freeing *any* slave, I would do it," he was "still trapped in his own obsession with saving the white Union at all costs, even the cost of continued black slavery." By exempting one-third of the South from the Emancipation Proclamation, wrote Barbara Fields, "Lincoln was more determined to retain the goodwill of the slaveowners than to secure the liberty of the slaves." Despite Lincoln, though, "no human being alive could have held back the tide that swept toward freedom" by 1863.

Nevertheless, lamented Vincent Harding, "while the concrete historical realities of the time testified to the costly, daring, courageous activities of hundreds of thousands of black people breaking loose from slavery and setting themselves free, the myth gave the credit for this freedom to a white Republican president." University of Pennsylvania historian Robert Engs goes even farther; he thinks the "fiction" that " 'Massa Lincoln' freed the slaves" was a sort of tacit conspiracy among whites to convince blacks that "white America, personified by Abraham Lincoln, had *given* them their freedom [rather] than allow them to realize the *empowerment* that their taking of it implied. The poor, uneducated freedman fell for that masterful propaganda stroke. But so have most of the rest of us, black and white, for over a century!"

How valid are these statements? First, we must recognize the considerable degree of truth in the main thesis. By coming into Union lines, by withdrawing their labor from Confederate owners, by working for the Union army and fighting as soldiers in it, slaves did play an active part in achieving their own freedom and, for that matter, in preserving the Union. Like workers, immigrants, women, and other nonelites, slaves were neither passive victims nor pawns of powerful white males who loom so large in our traditional image of American history. They too played a part in determining their own destiny; they too made a history that historians have finally discovered. That is all to the good. But by challenging the "myth" that Lincoln freed the slaves, proponents of the self-emancipation thesis are in danger of creating another myth—that he had little to do with it. It may turn out, upon close examination, that the traditional answer to the question "Who Freed the Slaves?" is closer to being the right answer than is the new and currently more fashionable answer.

First, one must ask what was the sine qua non of emancipation in the 1860s —the essential condition, the one thing without which it would not have happened. The clear answer is the war. Without the Civil War there would have been no confiscation act, no Emancipation Proclamation, no Thirteenth Amendment (not to mention the Fourteenth and Fifteenth), certainly no self-emancipation, and almost certainly no end of slavery for several more decades at least. Slavery had existed in North America for more than two centuries before 1861, but except for a tiny fraction of slaves who fought in the Revolution, or escaped, or bought their freedom, there had been no self-emancipation during that time. Every slave insurrection or insurrection conspiracy failed in the end. On the eve of the Civil War, plantation agriculture was more profitable, slavery more entrenched, slave owners more prosperous, and the "slave power" more dominant within the South if not in the nation at large than it had ever been. Without the war, the door to freedom would have remained closed for an indeterminate length of time.

What brought the war and opened that door? The answer, of course, is complex as well as controversial. A short and simplified summary is that secession and the refusal of the United States government to recognize the legitimacy of secession brought on the war. In both of these matters Abraham Lincoln moves to center stage. Seven states seceded and formed the Confederacy because he won election to the presidency on an antislavery platform; four more seceded after shooting broke out when he refused to evacuate Fort Sumter; the shooting escalated to full-scale war because he called out the troops to suppress rebellion. The common denominator in all of the steps that opened the door to freedom was the active agency of Abraham Lincoln as antislavery political leader, president-elect, president, and commander in chief.

The statement quoted above, that Lincoln "placed the preservation of the white Union above the death of black slavery," while true in a narrow sense, is highly misleading when shorn of its context. From 1854, when he returned to politics, until nominated for president in 1860, the dominant, unifying theme of Lincoln's career was opposition to the expansion of slavery as the vital first step toward placing it in the course of ultimate extinction. A student of Lincoln's oratory has estimated that he gave 175 political speeches during those six years. The "central message" of these speeches showed Lincoln to be a "one-issue" man —the issue being slavery. Over and over again, Lincoln denounced slavery as a "monstrous injustice," "an unqualified evil to the negro, to the white man, to the soil, and to the State." He attacked his main political rival, Stephen A. Douglas,

for his "*declared* indifference" to the moral wrong of slavery. Douglas "*looks to no end of the institution of slavery*," said Lincoln.

That is the real issue. That is the issue that will continue in this country when these poor tongues of Judge Douglas and myself shall be silent. It is the eternal struggle between these two principles —right and wrong—throughout the world.... One is the common right of humanity and the other the divine right of kings.... No matter in what shape it comes, whether from the mouth of a king who seeks to bestride the people of his own nation and live by the fruit of their labor, or from one race of men as an apology for enslaving another race, it is the same tyrannical principle.

Southerners read Lincoln's speeches; they knew by heart his words about the house divided and the ultimate extinction of slavery. Lincoln's election in 1860 was a sign that they had lost control of the national government; if they remained in the Union, they feared that ultimate extinction of their way of life would be their destiny. That is why they seceded. It was not merely Lincoln's election but his election as a *principled opponent of slavery on moral grounds* that precipitated secession. Militant abolitionists critical of Lincoln for falling short of their own standard nevertheless recognized this truth. No longer would the slave power rule the nation, said Frederick Douglass. "Lincoln's election has vitiated their authority, and broken their power." Without Lincoln's election, Southern states would not have seceded in 1861, the war would not have come when and as it did, the door of emancipation would not have been opened as it was. Here was an event that qualifies as a sine qua non, and it proceeded more from the ideas and agency of Abraham Lincoln than from any other single cause.

But, we must ask, would not the election of *any* Republican in 1860 have provoked secession? Probably not, if the candidate had been Edward Bates—who might conceivably have won the election but had no chance of winning the nomination. Yes, almost certainly, if William H. Seward had been the nominee. Seward's earlier talk of a "higher law" and an "irrepressible conflict" had given him a more radical reputation than Lincoln. But Seward might not have won the election. More to the point, if he had won, seven states would undoubtedly have seceded but Seward would have favored compromises and concessions to keep others from going out and perhaps to lure those seven back in. Most important of all, he would have evacuated Fort Sumter and thereby extinguished the spark that threatened to flame into war.

As it was, Seward did his best to compel Lincoln into concessions and evacuation of the fort. But Lincoln stood firm. When Seward flirted with the notion of supporting the Crittenden Compromise, which would have repudiated the Republican platform by permitting the expansion of slavery, Lincoln stiffened the backbones of Seward and other key Republican leaders. "Entertain no proposition for a compromise in regard to the *extension* of slavery," he wrote to them. "The tug has to come, & better now, than any time hereafter." Crittenden's compromise "would lose us everything we gained by the election." It "acknowledges that slavery has equal rights with liberty, and surrenders all we have contended for.... We have just carried an election on principles fairly stated to the people. Now we are told in advance, the government shall be broken up, unless we sur-

render to those we have beaten.... If we surrender, it is the end of us. They will repeat the experiment upon us *ad libitum*. A year will not pass, till we shall have to take Cuba as a condition upon which they will stay in the Union."

It is worth emphasizing here that the common denominator in these letters from Lincoln to Republican leaders was slavery. To be sure, on the matters of slavery where it already existed and enforcement of the fugitive slave provision of the Constitution, Lincoln was willing to reassure the South. But on the crucial issue of 1860, slavery in the territories, he refused to compromise, and this refusal kept his party in line. Seward, or any other person who might conceivably have been elected president in 1860, would have pursued a different course. This sheds a different light on the assertion that Lincoln "placed the preservation of the white Union above the death of black slavery." The Crittenden Compromise did indeed place preservation of the Union above the death of slavery. So did Seward; so did most white Americans during the secession crisis. But that assertion does *not* describe Lincoln. He refused to yield the core of his antislavery position to stay the breakup of the Union. As Lincoln expressed it in a private letter to his old friend Alexander Stephens, "You think slavery is *right* and ought to be extended; while we think it is *wrong* and ought to be restricted. That I suppose is the rub."

It was indeed the rub. Even more than in his election to the presidency, Lincoln's refusal to compromise on the expansion of slavery or on Fort Sumter proved decisive. If another person had been in his place, the course of history—and of emancipation—would have been different. Here again we have without question a sine qua non.

It is quite true that once the war started, Lincoln moved more slowly and apparently more reluctantly toward making it a war for emancipation than black leaders, abolitionists, radical Republicans, and the slaves themselves wanted him to move. He did reassure Southern whites that he had no intention and no constitutional power to interfere with slavery in the states. In September 1861 and May 1862 he revoked orders by Generals Frémont and Hunter freeing the slaves of Confederates in their military districts. In December 1861 he forced Secretary of War Simon Cameron to delete from his annual report a paragraph recommending the freeing and arming of slaves. And though Lincoln signed the confiscation acts of August 1861 and July 1862 that freed some slaves owned by Confederates, this legislation did not come from his initiative. Out in the field it was the slaves who escaped to Union lines and officers like General Benjamin Butler who accepted them as "contraband of war" that took the initiative.

All of this appears to support the thesis that slaves emancipated themselves and that Lincoln's image as emancipator is a myth. But let us take a closer look. It seems clear today, as it did in 1861, that no matter how many thousands of slaves came into Union lines, the ultimate fate of the millions who did not, as well as the fate of the institution of slavery itself, depended on the outcome of the war. If the North won, slavery would be weakened if not destroyed; if the Confederacy won, slavery would survive and perhaps grow stronger from the postwar territorial expansion of an independent and confident slave power. Thus Lincoln's emphasis on the priority of Union had positive implications for emancipation, while precipitate or premature actions against slavery might jeopardize the cause of Union and therefore boomerang in favor of slavery.

Lincoln's chief concern in 1861 was to maintain a united coalition of War Democrats and border-state Unionists as well as Republicans in support of the war effort. To do this he considered it essential to define the war as being waged solely for Union, which united this coalition, and not a war against slavery, which would fragment it. When General Frémont issued his emancipation edict in Missouri on August 30, 1861, the political and military efforts to prevent Kentucky, Maryland, and Missouri from seceding and to cultivate Unionists in western Virginia and eastern Tennessee were at a crucial stage, balancing on a knife edge. To keep his fragile coalition from falling apart, therefore, Lincoln rescinded Frémont's order.

Almost certainly this was the right decision at the time. Lincoln's greatest skills as a political leader were his sensitivity to public opinion and his sense of timing. Within six months of his revocation of Frémont's order, he began moving toward a stronger antislavery position. During the spring and early summer of 1862 he alternately coaxed and prodded border-state Unionists toward recognition of the inevitable escalation of the conflict into a war against slavery and toward acceptance of his plan for compensated emancipation in their states. He warned them that the "friction and abrasion" of a war that had by this time swept every institution into its maelstrom could not leave slavery untouched. But the border states remained deaf to Lincoln's warnings and refused to consider his offer of federally compensated emancipation.

By July 1862, Lincoln turned a decisive corner toward abolition. He made up his mind to issue an emancipation proclamation. Whereas a year earlier, even three months earlier, Lincoln had believed that avoidance of such a drastic step was necessary to maintain that knife-edge balance in the Union coalition, things had now changed. The escalation of the war in scope and fury had mobilized all the resources of both sides, including the slave labor force of the Confederacy. The imminent prospect of Union victory in the spring had been shredded by Robert E. Lee's successful counteroffensives in the Seven Days. The risks of alienating the border states and Northern Democrats, Lincoln now believed, were outweighed by the opportunity to energize the Republican majority and to mobilize part of the slave population for the cause of Union—and freedom. When Lincoln told his cabinet on July 22, 1862, that he had decided to issue an emancipation proclamation, Montgomery Blair, speaking for the forces of conservatism in the North and border states, warned of the consequences among these groups if he did so. But Lincoln was done conciliating them. He had tried to make the border states see reason; now "we must make the forward movement" without them. "They [will] acquiesce, if not immediately, soon." As for the Northern Democrats, "their clubs would be used against us take what course we might."

Two years later, speaking to a visiting delegation of abolitionists, Lincoln explained why he had moved more slowly against slavery than they had urged. Having taken an oath to preserve and defend the Constitution, which protected slavery, "I did not consider that I had a *right* to touch the 'State' institution of 'Slavery' until all other measures for restoring the Union had failed.... The moment came when I felt that slavery must die that the nation might live!... Many of my strongest supporters urged *Emancipation* before I thought it indispensable, and, I may say, before I thought the country ready for it. It is my conviction that, had the proclamation been issued even six months earlier than it was, public sentiment would not have sustained it."

Lincoln actually could have made a case that the country had not been ready for the Emancipation Proclamation in September 1862, even in January 1863. Democratic gains in the Northern congressional elections of 1862 resulted in part from a voter backlash against the preliminary Emancipation Proclamation. The morale crisis in Union armies and swelling Copperhead strength during the winter of 1863 grew in part from a resentful conviction that Lincoln had unconstitutionally transformed the purpose of the war from restoring the Union to freeing the slaves. Without question, this issue bitterly divided the Northern people and threatened fatally to erode support for the war effort—the very consequence Lincoln had feared in 1861 and Montgomery Blair had warned against in 1862. Not until after the twin military victories at Gettysburg and Vicksburg did this divisiveness diminish and emancipation gain a clear mandate in the off-year elections of 1863. In his annual message of December 1863, Lincoln conceded that the Emancipation Proclamation a year earlier had been "followed by dark and doubtful days." But now, he added, "the crisis which threatened to divide the friends of the Union is past."

Even that statement turned out to be premature and overoptimistic. In the summer of 1864, Northern morale again plummeted and the emancipation issue once more threatened to undermine the war effort. By August, Grant's campaign in Virginia had bogged down in the trenches after enormous casualties. Sherman seemed similarly thwarted before Atlanta and smaller Union armies elsewhere appeared to be accomplishing nothing. War weariness and defeatism corroded the will of Northerners as they contemplated the staggering cost of this conflict in the lives of their young men. Lincoln came under enormous pressure to open peace negotiations to end the slaughter. Even though Jefferson Davis insisted that Confederate independence was his essential condition for peace, Northern Democrats managed to convince many Northern people that only Lincoln's insistence on emancipation blocked peace. A typical Democratic newspaper editorial declared that "tens of thousands of white men must yet bite the dust to allay the negro mania of the President."

Even Republicans like Horace Greeley, who had criticized Lincoln two years earlier for slowness to embrace emancipation, now criticized him for refusing to abandon it as a precondition for negotiations. The Democratic national convention adopted a platform for the 1864 presidential election calling for peace negotiations to restore the Union with slavery. Every political observer, including Lincoln himself, believed in August that the Republicans would lose the election. The *New York Times* editor and Republican national chairman Henry Raymond told Lincoln that "two special causes are assigned [for] this great reaction in public sentiment,—the want of military suc-

cess, and the impression... that we *can* have peace with Union if we would... [but that you are] fighting not for Union but for the abolition of slavery."

The pressure on Lincoln to back down on emancipation caused him to waver temporarily but not to buckle. Instead, he told weak-kneed Republicans that "no human power can subdue this rebellion without using the Emancipation lever as I have done." More than one hundred thousand black soldiers and sailors were fighting for the Union, said Lincoln. They would not do so if they thought the North intended to "betray them.... If they stake their lives for us they must be prompted by the strongest motive... There have been men who proposed to me to return to slavery the black warriors" who had fought for the Union. "I should be damned in time & in eternity for so doing. The world shall know that I will keep my faith to friends and enemies, come what will."

When Lincoln said this, he fully expected to lose the election. In effect, he was saying that he would rather be right than president. In many ways this was his finest hour. As matters turned out, of course, he was both right and president. Sherman's capture of Atlanta, Sheridan's victories in the Shenandoah Valley, and military success elsewhere transformed the Northern mood from deepest despair in August 1864 to determined confidence by November, and Lincoln was triumphantly reelected. He won without compromising one inch on the emancipation question.

It is instructive to consider two possible alternatives to this outcome. If the Democrats had won, at best the Union would have been restored without a Thirteenth Amendment; at worst the Confederacy would have achieved its independence. In either case the institution of slavery would have survived. That this did not happen was owing more to the steadfast purpose of Abraham Lincoln than to any other single factor.

The proponents of the self-emancipation thesis, however, would avow that all of this is irrelevant. If it is true, as Barbara Fields maintains, that by the time of the Emancipation Proclamation "no human being alive could have held back the tide that swept toward freedom," that tide must have been even stronger by the fall of 1864. But I disagree. The tide of freedom could have been swept back. On numerous occasions during the war, it was. When Union forces moved through or were compelled to retreat from areas of the Confederacy where their presence had attracted and liberated contrabands, the tide of slavery closed in behind them and reenslaved those who could not keep up with the advancing or retreating armies. Many of the thousands who did keep up with the Army of the Ohio when it was forced out of Alabama and Tennessee by the Confederate invasion of Kentucky in the fall of 1862 were seized and sold as slaves by Kentuckians. Lee's army captured dozens of black people in Pennsylvania in June 1863 and sent them back South into slavery. Hundreds of black Union soldiers captured by Confederate forces were reenslaved. Lincoln took note of this phenomenon when he warned that if "the pressure of the war should call off our forces from New Orleans to defend some other point, what is to prevent the masters from reducing the blacks to slavery again; for I am told that whenever the rebels take any black prisoners, free or slave, they immediately auction them off!" The editors of the Freedmen's and Southern Society project,

the most scholarly advocates of the self-emancipation thesis, acknowledge that "Southern armies could recapture black people who had already reached Union lines.... Indeed, any Union retreat could reverse the process of liberation and throw men and women who had tasted freedom back into bondage.... Their travail testified to the link between the military success of the Northern armies and the liberty of Southern slaves."

Precisely. That is the crucial point. Slaves did not emancipate themselves; they were liberated by Union armies. Freedom quite literally came from the barrel of a gun. And who was the commander in chief that called these armies into being, appointed their generals, and gave them direction and purpose? There, indubitably, is our sine qua non.

But let us grant that once the war was carried into slave territory, no matter how it came out the ensuring "friction and abrasion" would have enabled thousands of slaves to escape to freedom. In that respect, a degree of self-emancipation did occur. But even on a large scale, such emancipation was very different from *the abolition of the institution of slavery*. During the American Revolution almost as large a percentage of the slaves won freedom by coming within British lines as achieved liberation by coming within Union lines during the Civil War. Yet slavery survived the Revolution. Ending the institution of bondage required Union victory; it required Lincoln's reelection in 1864; it required the Thirteenth Amendment. Lincoln played a vital role, indeed the central role, in all of these achievements. It was also his policies and his skillful political leadership that set in motion the processes by which the reconstructed or Unionist states of Louisiana, Arkansas, Tennessee, Maryland, and Missouri abolished the institution in those states during the war itself.

Regrettably, Lincoln did not live to see the final ratification of the Thirteenth Amendment. But if he had never lived, it seems safe to say that we would not have had a Thirteenth Amendment in 1865. In that sense, the traditional answer to the question "Who Freed the Slaves?" is the right answer. Lincoln did not accomplish this in the manner sometimes symbolically portrayed, breaking the chains of helpless and passive bondsmen with the stroke of a pen by signing the Emancipation Proclamation. But by pronouncing slavery a moral evil that must come to an end and then winning the presidency in 1860, provoking the South to secede, by refusing to compromise on the issue of slavery's expansion or on Fort Sumter, by careful leadership and timing that kept a fragile Unionist coalition together in the first year of war and committed it to emancipation in the second, by refusing to compromise this policy once he had adopted it, and by prosecuting the war to unconditional victory as commander in chief of an army of liberation, Abraham Lincoln freed the slaves.

NO

Vincent Harding

THE BLOOD-RED IRONIES OF GOD

Although the destruction of the oppressors God may not effect by the oppressed,
yet the Lord our God will surely bring other destructions upon them—for not
infrequently will he cause them to rise up against one another, to be split and
divided, and to oppress each other, and sometimes to open hostilities with sword
in hand.

— David Walker, 1829

On certain stark and bloody levels, a terrible irony seemed to be at work. For
those who interpreted the events of their own times through the wisdom and
anguish of the past, the guns of Charleston certainly sounded like the signal
for the fulfillment of David Walker's radical prophecies. Here at last was the
coming of the righteous God in judgment, preparing to bring "destructions"
upon America. Here was the divine culmination of the struggle toward freedom and justice long waged by the oppressed black people. From such a
vantage point, the conflict now bursting out was the ultimate justification of
the costly freedom movement, a welcome vindication of the trust in Providence. And yet the war was not simply an ally. Like all wars, it brought with
it a train of demoralizing, destructive elements, deeply affecting even those
persons and causes which seemed to be its chief beneficiaries. In the case of
black people, the guns broke in upon their freedom struggle at many levels,
diverted and diffused certain of its significant radical elements, and became a
source of profound confusion and disarray among its most committed forces.
This was especially the case where independent radical black struggle for
justice and self-determination was concerned. . . .

When the war broke out, black men and women were convinced that it
had to destroy slavery. Especially in the North, this inner certainty flooded
their consciousness, buoyed up their hopes. Now it appeared that God was
providing a way out of the darkness of slavery and degradation, a way which
would release some of the frightening tension of the previous decade. Because
they wanted a way out so desperately, because it was hard to be driven by a
fierce urgency, fearsome to experience the personal honing in spite of one's
own softer and blunter ways, the children of Africa in America clutched

at a solution which would not cause them to be driven into the depths of radicalism. For they must have realized that the chances were good that they might not survive without being seriously, unpredictably transformed. Therefore, when the guns began, black people shunted aside the knowledge of certain fierce realities.

In that mood their men surged forward to volunteer for service in the Union cause, repressing bitter memories. In spite of their misgivings, disregarding the fact that it was not the North which had initiated this righteous war, they offered their bodies for the Northern cause, believing that it was—or would be—the cause of black freedom. If the excited, forgetful young volunteers sought justification, they could find it in the *Anglo-African*: "Talk as we may, we are concerned in this fight and our fate hangs upon its issues. The South must be subjugated, or we shall be enslaved. In aiding the Federal government in whatever way we can, we are aiding to secure our own liberty; for this war can end only in the subjugation of the North or the South." When hard pressed, the journal, like the young men it encouraged, knew very well the nature of the "liberty" they had found so far in the unsubjugated North, and the writer admitted that the North was not consciously fighting for black rights. However, the *Anglo-African* chose to see a power beyond the councils of the North: "Circumstances have been so arranged by the decrees of Providence, that in struggling for their own nationality they are forced to defend our rights." . . .

And what of the South? What of those sometimes God-obsessed black believers who had long lifted their cries for deliverance in songs and shouts, in poetry filled with rich and vibrant images? Did they sense the coming of Moses now? Was this finally the day of the delivering God, when he would set his people free? Did they hear Nat Turner's spirit speaking in the guns? Did they believe he was calling them to freedom through all the lines of skirmishers who left their blood upon the leaves? Did they have any difficulty knowing which of the white armies was Pharaoh's?

The answers were as complex as life itself. In many parts of the nation and the world there had been predictions that secession, disunion, and war would lead to a massive black insurrection which would finally vindicate Turner and Walker, and drown the South in blood. Such predictions were made without knowledge of the profound racism and fear which pervaded the white North, and certainly without awareness of the keen perceptions of black people in the South. For most of the enslaved people knew their oppressors, and certainly realized that such a black uprising would expose the presence of Pharaoh's armies everywhere. To choose that path to freedom would surely unite the white North and South more quickly than any other single development, making black men, women, and children the enemy—the isolated, unprepared enemy. For anyone who needed concrete evidence, Gen. George B. McClellan, the commander of the Union's Army of the Ohio, had supplied it in his "Proclamation to the people of Western Virginia" on May 26, 1861: "Not only will we abstain from all interferences with your slaves, but we will, with an iron hand, crush any attempt at insurrection on their part."

So, heeding their own intuitive political wisdom, the black masses confirmed in their actions certain words which had recently appeared in the *Anglo-African.* Thomas Hamilton, the editor, had heard of Lincoln's decision to countermand an emancipation order issued by one of his most fervent Republican generals, John C. Fremont, in Missouri. Hamilton predicted: "The forlorn hope of insurrection among the slaves may as well be abandoned. They are too well informed and too *wise* to court destruction at the hands of the combined Northern and Southern armies—for the man who had reduced back to slavery the slaves of rebels in Missouri would order the army of the United States to put down a slave insurrection in Virginia or Georgia." He was right, of course, and the enslaved population was also right. Therefore, instead of mass insurrection, the Civil War created the context for a vast broadening and intensifying of the self-liberating black movement which had developed prior to the war. Central to this black freedom action, as always, was the continuing series of breaks with the system of slavery, the denials of the system's power, the self-emancipation of steadily increasing thousands of fugitives. Thus, wherever possible, black people avoided the deadly prospects of massive, sustained confrontation, for their ultimate objective was freedom, not martyrdom.

As the guns resounded across the Southern lands, the movement of black folk out of slavery began to build. Quickly it approached and surpassed every level of force previously known. Eventually the flood of fugitives amazed all observers and dismayed not a few, as it sent waves of men, women, and children rushing into the camps of the Northern armies. In this overwhelming human movement, black people of the South offered their own responses to the war, to its conundrums and mysteries. Their action testified to their belief that deliverance was indeed coming through the war, but for thousands of them it was not a deliverance to be bestowed by others. Rather it was to be independently seized and transformed through all the courage, wisdom, and strength of their waiting black lives.

This rapidly increasing movement of black runaways had been noted as soon as the reality of Southern secession had been clearly established. Shortly after the guns of April began to sound in Charleston harbor, large companies of fugitives broke loose from Virginia and the Carolinas and moved toward Richmond. Again, one day in Virginia in the spring of 1861, a black fugitive appeared at the Union-held Fortress Monroe. Two days later eight more arrived, the next day more than fifty, soon hundreds. The word spread throughout the area: there was a "freedom fort," as the fugitives called it, and within a short time thousands were flooding toward it. Similarly, in Louisiana two families waded six miles across a swamp, "spending two days and nights in mud and water to their waists, their children clinging to their backs, and with nothing to eat." In Georgia, a woman with her twenty-two children and grandchildren floated down the river on "a dilapidated flatboat" until she made contact with the Union armies. In South Carolina, black folk floated to freedom on "basket boats made out of reeds," thus reviving an ancient African craft. A contemporary source said of the black surge toward freedom in those first two years of the war: "Many thousands of blacks of all ages, ragged, with no possessions, except the bundles which they carried, had assembled at Norfolk, Hampton, Alexandria and Washington. Others ... in multitudes ... flocked north from Tennessee, Kentucky, Arkansas, and Missouri."

This was black struggle in the South as the guns roared, coming out of loyal and disloyal states, creating their own liberty. This was the black movement toward a new history, a new life, a new beginning. W. E. B. Du Bois later said, "The whole move was not dramatic or hysterical, rather it was like the great unbroken swell of the ocean before it dashes on the reefs." Yet there was great drama as that flowing movement of courageous black men and women and children sensed the movement of history, heard the voice of God, created and signed their own emancipation proclamations, and seized the time. Their God was moving and they moved with him.

And wherever this moving army of self-free men and women and children went, wherever they stopped to wait and rest and eat and work, and watch the movement of the armies in the fields and forests—in all these unlikely sanctuaries, they sent up their poetry of freedom. Some of them were old songs, taking on new meaning:

Thus said the Lord, Bold Moses said
Let my people go
If not I'll smite your first-born dead
Let my people go.
No more shall they in bondage toil
Let my people go.

But now there was no need to hide behind the stories of thousands of years gone by, now it was clearly a song of black struggle, of deliverance for their own time of need. Now the singers themselves understood more fully what they meant when they sang again:

One of dese mornings, five o'clock
Dis ole world gonna reel and rock,
Pharaoh's Army got drownded
Oh, Mary, don't you weep.

They were part of the drowning river. Out there, overlooking the battlefields of the South, they were the witnesses to the terrible truth of their own sons, to the this-worldliness of their prayers and aspirations. Remembering that morning in Charleston harbor, who could say they were wrong? "Dis ole world gonna reel and rock..."

Every day they came into the Northern lines, in every condition, in every season of the year, in every state of health. Children came wandering, set in the right direction by falling, dying parents who finally knew why they had lived until then. Women came, stumbling and screaming, their wombs bursting with the promise of new and free black life. Old folks who had lost all track of their age, who knew only that they had once heard of a war against "the Redcoats," also came, some blind, some deaf, yet no less eager to taste a bit of that long-anticipated freedom of their dreams. No more auction block, no more driver's lash, many thousands gone.

This was the river of black struggle in the South, waiting for no one to declare freedom for them, hearing only the declarations of God in the sound of the guns, and moving.

By land, by river, creating their own pilgrim armies and their own modes of travel, they moved south as well as north, heading down to the captured areas of the coast of South Carolina. *Frederick Douglass's Monthly* of February 1862 quoted the report of a *New York Times* correspondent in Port Royal: "Everywhere I find the same state of things existing; everywhere the blacks hurry in droves to our lines; they crowd in small boats around our ships; they swarm upon our decks; they hurry to our officers from the cotton houses of their masters, in an hour or two after our guns are fired.... I mean each statement I make to be taken literally; it is not garnished for rhetorical effect." As usual, black people were prepared to take advantage of every disruption in the life of the oppressing white community. When they heard the guns, they were ready, grasping freedom with their own hands, walking to it, swimming to it, sailing to it—determined that it should be theirs. By all these ways, defying masters, patrols, Confederate soldiers, slowly, surely, they pressed themselves into the central reality of the war.

... By the end of the spring of 1862, tens of thousands [of self-liberated fugitives] were camped out in whatever areas the Northern armies had occupied, thereby making themselves an unavoidable military and political issue. In Washington, D.C., the commander-in-chief of the Union armies had developed no serious plans for the channeling of the black river. Consequently, in the confusion which all war engenders, his generals in the field made and carried out their own plans. They were badly strapped for manpower, and the black fugitives provided some answers to whatever prayers generals pray. The blacks could relieve white fighting men from garrison duties. They could serve as spies, scouts, and couriers in the countryside they knew so well. They could work the familiar land, growing crops for the food and profit of the Union armies. But as the war dragged on and Northern whites lost some of their early enthusiasm, many Union comman-

ders saw the black men among them primarily as potential soldiers. Many of the black men were eager to fight, but Lincoln was still not prepared to go that far.

Nevertheless, some Union commanders like Gen. David Hunter in South Carolina were again issuing their own emancipation proclamations and beginning to recruit black soldiers. In places like occupied New Orleans it was the unmanageable and threatening movement of the blacks themselves which placed additional pressures on the Union's leader. Reports were pouring into Washington which told not only of the flood of fugitives, but of black unrest everywhere. Black men were literally fighting their way past the local police forces to get themselves and their families into the Union encampments. There was word of agricultural workers killing or otherwise getting rid of their overseers, and taking over entire plantations. Commanders like Gen. Ben Butler warned that only Union bayonets prevented widespread black insurrection. (In August 1862, to preserve order and satisfy his need for manpower, Butler himself had begun to recruit black troops in New Orleans, beginning with the well-known Louisiana Native Guards.) The dark presence at the center of the national conflict could no longer be denied. Lincoln's armies were in the midst of a surging movement of black people who were in effect freeing themselves from slavery. His generals were at once desperate for the military resources represented by the so-called contrabands, and convinced that only through military discipline could this volatile, potentially revolutionary black element be contained. As a result, before 1862 was over, black troops were being enlisted to fight for their own freedom in both South Carolina and Louisiana.

In Washington, Congress was discussing its own plans for emancipation, primarily as a weapon against the South, hoping to deprive the Confederacy of a major source of human power and transfer it into Union hands. Their debates and imminent action represented another critical focus of pressure on the President. While Lincoln continued to hesitate about the legal, constitutional, moral, and military aspects of the matter, he was also being constantly attacked in the North for his conduct of the war. The whites were weary and wanted far better news from the fronts. The blacks were angry about his continued refusal to speak clearly to the issue of their people's freedom and the black right to military service. In the summer of 1862 Frederick Douglass declared in his newspaper: "Abraham Lincoln is no more fit for the place he holds than was James Buchanan.... The country is destined to become sick of both [Gen. George B.] McClellan and Lincoln, and the sooner the better. The one plays lawyer for the benefit of the rebels, and the other handles the army for the benefit of the traitors. We should not be surprised if both should be hurled from their places before this rebellion is ended.... The signs of the times indicate that the people will have to take this war into their own hands." But Frederick Douglass was not one to dwell on such revolutionary options. (Besides, had he considered what would happen to the black cause, if the white "people" really did take the war into their own hands?) Fortunately, by the time Douglass's words were published, he had seen new and far more hopeful signs of the times.

In September 1862 Abraham Lincoln, in a double-minded attempt both to bargain with and weaken the South while replying to the pressures of the North, finally made public his proposed Emancipation Proclamation. Under its ambiguous terms, the states in rebellion would be given until the close of the year to end their rebellious action. If any did so, their captive black people would not be affected; otherwise, the Emancipation Proclamation would go into effect on January 1, 1863, theoretically freeing all the enslaved population of the Confederate states and promising federal power to maintain that freedom.

What actually was involved was quite another matter. Of great import was the fact that the proclamation excluded from its provisions the "loyal" slave states of Missouri, Kentucky, Delaware, and Maryland, the anti-Confederate West Virginia Territory, and loyal areas in certain other Confederate states. Legally, then, nearly one million black people whose masters were "loyal" to the Union had no part of the emancipation offered. In effect, Lincoln was announcing freedom to the captives over whom he had least control, while allowing those in states clearly under the rule of his government to remain in slavery. However, on another more legalistic level, Lincoln was justifying his armies' use of the Confederates' black "property," and preparing the way for an even more extensive use of black power by the military forces of the Union. Here, the logic of his move was clear, providing an executive confirmation and extension of Congress's Second Confiscation Act of 1862: once the Emancipation Proclamation went into effect, the tens of thousands of black people who were creating their own freedom, and making themselves available as workers in the Union camps, could be used by the North without legal qualms. Technically, they would no longer be private property, no longer cause problems for a President concerned about property rights.

It was indeed a strange vessel that the Lord had chosen, but black folk in the South were not waiting on such legal niceties. Not long after the preliminary proclamation, an insurrectionary plot was uncovered among a group of blacks in Culpepper County, Virginia. Some were slaves and some free, and the message of their action carried a special resonance for South and North alike, and perhaps for the President himself. For a copy of Lincoln's preliminary proclamation was reportedly found among the possessions of one of the conspirators. Though at least seventeen of the group were executed, their death could not expunge the fact that they had attempted to seize the time, to wrest their emancipation out of the hands of an uncertain President. On Nat's old "gaining ground" they had perhaps heard the voice of his God and, forming their own small army, were once again searching for Jerusalem.

Such action symbolized a major difference in the movement of the Southern and Northern branches of the struggle. In the South, though most of the self-liberating black people eventually entered the camps, or came otherwise under the aegis of the Northern armies, they were undoubtedly acting on significant, independent initiatives. During the first years of the war, the mainstream of the struggle in the South continued to bear this independent, self-authenticating character, refusing to wait for an official emancipation.

In such settings black hope blossomed, fed by its own activity. Even in the ambiguous context of the contraband communities the signs were there. In 1862–63, in Corinth, Mississippi, newly free blacks in one of the best of the contraband camps organized themselves under federal oversight, and created the beginnings of an impressive, cohesive community of work, education, family life, and worship. They built their own modest homes, planted and grew their crops (creating thousands of dollars of profit for the Union), supported their own schools, and eventually developed their own military company to fight with the Union armies. It was not surprising, then, that black fugitives flocked there from as far away as Georgia. Nor was it unexpected that, in 1863, federal military plans demanded the dismantling of the model facility. Nevertheless, the self-reliant black thrust toward the future had been initiated, and Corinth was only one among many hopeful contraband communities.

Such movement, and the vision which impelled it, were integral aspects of the freedom struggle in the South. Meanwhile, to aid that struggle, by 1863 Harriet Tubman had entered the South Carolina war zone. Working on behalf of the Union forces, she organized a corps of black contrabands and traveled with them through the countryside to collect information for army raids, and to urge the still-enslaved blacks to leave their masters. Apparently the intrepid leader and her scouts were successful at both tasks, though Tubman complained that her long dresses sometimes impeded her radical activities.

In the North the situation was somewhat different. Word of Lincoln's anticipated proclamation had an electrifying effect on the black community there, but at the same time further removed the focus from the black freedom-seizing movement in the South. The promised proclamation now gave the Northerners more reason than ever to look to others for release, to invest their hope in the Union cause. Now it seemed as if they would not need to be isolated opponents of an antagonistic federal government. Again, because they wanted to believe, needed to hope, yearned to prove themselves worthy, they thought they saw ever more clearly the glory of the coming; before long, in their eyes the proclamation was clothed in what appeared to be almost angelic light. As such, it became an essentially religious rallying point for the development of a new, confusing mainstream struggle: one which, nervous and excited, approached and embraced the central government and the Republican Party as agents of deliverance. Doubts from the past were now cast aside, for their struggle was unquestionably in the hands of Providence and the Grand Army of the Republic. The voice of God was joined to that of Abraham Lincoln.

... [F]rom a certain legal point of view it could be argued that the Emancipation Proclamation set free no enslaved black people at all. Since by December 31, 1862, no Confederate state had accepted Lincoln's invitation to return to the fold with their slaves unthreatened, and since Lincoln acknowledged that he had no real way of enforcing such a proclamation within the rebellious states, the proclamation's power to set anyone free was dubious at best. (Rather, it confirmed and gave ambiguous legal standing to the freedom which black people had already claimed through their own surging, living proclamations.)

Indeed, in his annual address to Congress on December 1, 1862, Lincoln had not seemed primarily concerned with the proclamation. Instead, he had taken that crucial opportunity to propose three constitutional amendments which reaffirmed his long-standing approach to national slavery. The proposed amendments included provisions for gradual emancipation (with a deadline as late as 1900), financial compensation to the owners, and colonization for the freed people. In other words, given the opportunity to place his impending proclamation of limited, immediate emancipation into the firmer context of a constitutional amendment demanding freedom for all enslaved blacks, Lincoln chose another path, one far more in keeping with his own history.

But none of this could dampen the joy of the black North. Within that community, it was the Emancipation Proclamation of January 1, 1863, which especially symbolized all that the people so deeply longed to experience, and its formal announcement sent a storm of long-pent-up emotion surging through the churches and meeting halls. It was almost as if the Northern and Southern struggles had again been joined, this time not through wilderness flights, armed resistance, and civil disobedience, but by a nationwide, centuries-long cord of boundless ecstasy. In spite of its limitations, the proclamation was taken as the greatest sign yet provided by the hand of Providence. The river had burst its boundaries, had shattered slavery's dam. It appeared as if the theodicy of the Northern black experience was finally prevailing. For the freedom struggle, especially in the South, had begun to overwhelm the white man's war, and had forced the President and the nation officially to turn their faces toward the moving black masses. Wherever black people could assemble, by themselves or with whites, they came together to lift joyful voices of thanksgiving, to sing songs of faith, to proclaim, "Jehovah hath triumphed, his people are free." For them, a new year and a new era had been joined in one.

On the evening of December 31, 1862, Frederick Douglass was in Boston attending one of the hundreds of freedom-watch-night services being held across the North in anticipation of the proclamation. That night, a line of messengers had been set up between the telegraph office and the platform of the Tremont Temple, where the Boston meeting was being held. After waiting more than two hours in agonized hope, the crowd was finally rewarded as word of the official proclamation reached them. Douglass said: "The effect of this announcement was startling beyond description, and the scene was wild and grand. Joy and gladness exhausted all forms of expression, from shouts of praise to sobs and tears... a Negro preacher, a man of wonderful vocal power, expressed the heartfelt emotion of the hour, when he led all voice in the anthem, 'Sound the loud timbrel o'er Egypt's dark sea, Jehovah hath triumphed, his people are free.'"

Such rapture was understandable, but like all ecstatic experiences, it carried its own enigmatic penalties. Out of it was born the mythology of Abraham Lincoln as Emancipator, a myth less important in its detail than in its larger meaning and consequences for black struggle. The heart of the matter was this: while the concrete historical realities of the time testified to the costly, daring, courageous activities of hundreds of thousands of black people breaking loose from slavery and setting themselves free, the myth gave the credit for this freedom to a white Republican president. In those same times when black men and women saw visions of a new society of equals, and heard voices pressing them against the American Union of white supremacy, Abraham Lincoln was unable to see beyond the limits of his own race, class, and time, and dreamed of a Haitian island and of Central American colonies to rid the country of the constantly accusing, constantly challenging black presence. Yet in the mythology of blacks and whites alike, it was the independent, radical action of the black movement toward freedom which was diminished, and the coerced, ambiguous role of a white deliverer which gained preeminence.

POSTSCRIPT
Did Abraham Lincoln Free the Slaves?

Abraham Lincoln's reputation as "the Great Emancipator" traditionally has been based upon his decision in 1862 to issue the Emancipation Proclamation. While Harding stresses that Lincoln was forced to act by the large number of slaves who already had engaged in a process of self-liberation, he and other scholars point out the limited impact of Lincoln's emancipation policy.

Critics of Lincoln's uncertain approach to ending slavery also cite a number of other examples that draw Lincoln's commitment to freedom into question. During the presidential election campaign of 1860, candidate Lincoln had insisted that he had no desire to abolish slavery where the institution already existed. As president he stated that he would be willing to keep slavery intact if that was the best means of preserving the Union. Lincoln initially opposed arming black citizens for military service, he countermanded several of his field generals' emancipation orders, and he consistently expressed doubts that blacks and whites would be able to live in the United States as equal citizens.

In assessing Lincoln's racial attitudes and policies, care should be taken not to read this historical record solely from a late-twentieth-century perspective. Lincoln may not have been the embodiment of the unblemished racial egalitarian that some might hope for, but few whites were, including most of the abolitionists. Still, as historian Benjamin Quarles has written, Lincoln "treated Negroes as they wanted to be treated—as human beings." Unlike most white Americans of his day, Lincoln opposed slavery, developed a policy that held out hope for emancipation, and supported the Thirteenth Amendment.

Lincoln is the most written-about president. Students should consult *With Malice Toward None: The Life of Abraham Lincoln* (Harper & Row, 1977); and Philip Shaw Paludan, *The Presidency of Abraham Lincoln* (University Press of Kansas, 1994). Gabor S. Boritt, ed., *The Historian's Lincoln: Pseudohistory, Psychohistory, and History* (University of Illinois Press, 1988) is a valuable collection. John Hope Franklin's *The Emancipation Proclamation* (Harlan Davidson, 1995) is the best study of this presidential policy.

In addition to the work of Vincent Harding, the self-emancipation thesis is developed in Ira Berlin, Barbara J. Fields, Thavolia Glymph, Joseph P. Reidy, and Leslie S. Rowland, eds., *Freedom: A Documentary History of Emancipation, 1861–1867*, 3 vols. (Cambridge University Press, 1986–1991). The role of African Americans in the Civil War is the subject of James G. Hollandsworth, Jr., *The Louisiana Native Guards: The Black Military Experience During the Civil War* (Louisiana State University Press, 1995).

ISSUE 16

Was It Wrong to Impeach Andrew Johnson?

YES: Irving Brant, from *Impeachment: Trials and Errors* (Alfred A. Knopf, 1972)

NO: Harold M. Hyman, from *A More Perfect Union: The Impact of the Civil War and Reconstruction on the Constitution* (Alfred A. Knopf, 1973)

ISSUE SUMMARY

YES: Historian Irving Brant argues that President Andrew Johnson was the victim of partisan Republican politics and that the articles of impeachment passed by the House of Representatives constituted a bill of attainder in violation of the U.S. Constitution.

NO: Professor of history Harold M. Hyman contends that Congress's decision to impeach President Johnson was wholly justifiable on constitutional grounds in light of Johnson's repeated defiance of national law and his efforts to seize control of the army.

On December 19, 1998, the U.S. House of Representatives approved two articles of impeachment charging President Bill Clinton with committing "high crimes and misdemeanors" for allegedly thwarting an investigation of his personal relationship with White House intern Monica Lewinsky. As the case made its way to the Senate, media pundits and constitutional scholars across the nation provided the American people with a historical context for the first impeachment trial of an American president in 130 years. In doing so, they reminded their viewers and readers of the political drama played out in Washington, D.C., only three years after the end of the Civil War, when President Andrew Johnson escaped being removed from office by a single vote in the Senate.

Johnson, born into poverty in North Carolina in 1808, migrated to Tennessee at the age of 18 and, through a combination of ambition and hard work, made a name for himself in Democratic politics. As governor of the Volunteer State and the most prominent Southern politician to reject secession, Johnson attracted the attention of Abraham Lincoln, who offered him a spot as his vice presidential running mate on the Union party ticket in 1864. In April 1965, shortly after their electoral success, Lincoln was assassinated. As a result, Johnson became president within days of the end of the Civil War and was confronted with the enormous responsibilities associated with restoring the states of the former Confederacy to the Union.

For radical Republicans, Andrew Johnson initially seemed a preferable architect of postwar Reconstruction than the martyred Lincoln. After all, Johnson had openly expressed his desire to punish members of the planter aristocracy by prohibiting them from political participation until they had obtained a pardon from Johnson himself. In fact, Johnson envisioned a new political order in the South that would empower poor whites at the expense of the traditional political elite—the planters.

The honeymoon between congressional Republicans and the new president, however, was short-lived. Johnson adopted a Reconstruction policy that was similar to the lenient program outlined by Lincoln prior to his death, and he celebrated the rapidity with which the former Confederate states were restored to the Union. Radical Republicans were shocked when Johnson accepted the new Southern governments—many of whose elected leaders had been waging war against the United States only a few months earlier—into the national fold. They were dismayed by the president's acquiescence to the discriminatory "Black Codes" adopted by each of these states in place of the defunct slave statutes and by his refusal to seek congressional advice on the Reconstruction process. Relations further deteriorated when Johnson vetoed the Civil Rights Act of 1866 and a bill to extend the life of the Freedmen's Bureau. With the aid of moderate Republicans, the radicals succeeded in overriding these presidential vetoes, but the die had been cast. Johnson continued to resist the implementation of the Military Reconstruction Acts passed by Congress a year earlier, and he attempted to remove Secretary of War Edwin Stanton from office in apparent violation of the Tenure of Office Act. For these offenses, in 1868 the House of Representatives adopted 11 articles of impeachment against Johnson.

Were these actions justified? Had Johnson overstepped the constitutional bounds of his office? Had he threatened the sanctity of the Constitution of the United States? Was he guilty of "high crimes and misdemeanors," as charged by his congressional critics? These questions are addressed in the following selections by Irving Brant and Harold M. Hyman.

Brant agrees that Andrew Johnson did a great deal to incur the wrath of congressional Republicans. However, he argues that these actions did not warrant impeachment proceedings. In fact, Brant asserts, the Tenure of Office Act was patently unconstitutional, and the articles of impeachment adopted by the House amounted to a bill of attainder, the legality of which is rejected by the Constitution of the United States.

Hyman supports the decision to impeach Andrew Johnson. He argues that Johnson obstructed numerous congressional measures and directly violated the Tenure of Office Act. In the wake of this defiant behavior, says Hyman, the Republicans were fully within their constitutional rights to impeach the president.

YES

Irving Brant

THE JOHNSON TRIAL: ATTAINDER
BY IMPEACHMENT

The impeachment trial of President Andrew Johnson presented a strange phenomenon that has gone unnoticed in histories. Besides rebutting the specific charges against him, Johnson's counsel assailed the impeachment as a violation of the Constitution. By the nature of those charges, they contended, the proceeding violated the clause forbidding Congress to pass bills of attainder. Lawyer after lawyer hammered on that theme, but not once did a House Manager reply. The reason appears obvious: they regarded silence as a better strategy than unconvincing denials.

What is a bill of attainder? The Supreme Court defined it in the very year of the Johnson impeachment, when the Court struck down two laws passed at the close of the Civil War that required lawyers and clergymen to take loyalty oaths as a precondition to practicing their profession. Said the Court in *Cummings v. Missouri,* holding the oath for lawyers to be in violation of the Constitution:

"A bill of attainder is a legislative act which inflicts punishment without a judicial trial. If the punishment be less than death, the act is termed a bill of pains and penalties. Within the meaning of the Constitution, bills of attainder include bills of pains and penalties." ...

President Andrew Johnson did many things that invited the wrath of a Congress gripped by deep emotions after four years of civil war. Johnson, a Tennessee senator who opposed the secession of his state and adhered to the Union throughout the war, was given the vice presidential nomination in 1864 out of gratitude and party policy. The assassination of President Lincoln thrust him into the Presidency on April 15, 1865, at the moment of transition from war to peace, from preservation of the Union to the difficult and complex task of restoring national government and national unity.

The immediate question was: Should the eleven Confederate states be regarded as still legally part of the Union, and treated as if they never had left it? Or should they be regarded as conquered provinces, to be readmitted as states under such conditions as Congress should prescribe and they should agree to? President Johnson took the former view; Congress the latter. Each side invoked the name of Abraham Lincoln, but Lincoln's final policies put him much closer to the views of his successor than to those of the Radical Republican leadership in Congress.

On the crucial issue of "rebel suffrage" there were three successive postwar policies. In reorganizing Arkansas, Louisiana, Tennessee, and Virginia, Lincoln as commander in chief disfranchised only Confederate leaders. President Johnson, ruling alone in the April–December 1865 absence of Congress, extended the disfranchisement to Confederate generals and men owning property worth more than $20,000. His object was to let poor whites govern the South and to break up the big plantations. The Radical Republicans in Congress demanded full enfranchisement of the former slaves who, under the Johnson plan already in effect, were being held close to their former status.

In the Congress that convened in December 1865, Representative Thaddeus Stevens of Pennsylvania rose swiftly to leadership of the radicals by virtue of his personal drive and the intensity of his convictions. In the Senate Charles Sumner of Massachusetts, a veteran abolitionist, gained similar preeminence. In swift succession, over the President's veto, Congress passed a series of Reconstruction Acts largely designed to protect the black population. From the Radical Republicans also came the historic Thirteenth, Fourteenth, and Fifteenth Amendments, which, as far as infringement by state action is concerned, now form the bedrock of liberty and equality under the law for all American citizens and particularly safeguard Negro rights. To enforce the Reconstruction laws, the states of the late confederacy were divided into military districts ruled by Union troops.

Trouble mounted between Johnson and Congress. In the Cabinet, Secretary of War Edwin Stanton vigorously opposed the President's Reconstruction policies. Word spread that Stanton was to be asked to resign. Congress quickly passed "an Act regulating the tenure of certain offices," which became law (again over Presidential veto) on March 2, 1867. By its terms the President could not remove any head of department without the prior consent of the Senate.

This law was patently unconstitutional. The President's power to remove such officers without consent of the Senate was debated at length in 1789 and thoroughly established by a declaratory act of Congress, not conferring that authority but worded to recognize its existence as an exclusive constitutional power....

Andrew Johnson thus had constitutional warrant for disregarding the Tenure of Office Act, but nearly a year went by with Secretary Stanton still in office. On January 30, 1868, an event occurred that revealed the Stevens faction's hair-trigger attitude toward impeachment and its sweeping concept of the power to impeach. Congressman Schofield of Pennsylvania took the floor in the House and read a short editorial from the Washington *Evening Express* of the previous day. The paper asserted that at a large social gathering one of the justices of the Supreme Court "declared in the most positive terms" that all the Reconstruction acts "were unconstitutional, and that the court would be sure to pronounce them so." Warned that such remarks were indiscreet, "he at once repeated his views in a more positive manner." The Baltimore *Gazette* named the speaker: Associate Justice Stephen J. Field, whom President Lincoln had appointed to office.

Schofield moved that the Judiciary Committee make an inquiry "and report whether the facts constituted such a misdemeanor in office as to require the House to present to the Senate articles of impeachment against the said justice of the Supreme Court." The motion was instantly approved, leaving no doubt that the Radical Republican majority regarded Justice Field's remarks as impeachable. Besides being an invasion of freedom of speech, the House action clearly meant that anything its members regarded as a "misdemeanor in office" was a constitutional ground of impeachment, even though it had not the faintest taint of criminality. Field's remark was an indiscretion, but no reasonable person could call it an impeachable misdemeanor. If the Constitution means what it says, both on impeachment and on attainder, nothing could more plainly stamp such an impeachment as a bill of attainder in disguise.

In three weeks, the impeachment move against Justice Field dropped out of sight and out of mind. For on February 21 President Johnson removed Secretary Stanton from office for undercutting Presidential policies. Three days later the House of Representatives, by a majority of 126 to 47, voted articles of impeachment against the President.

Eleven articles were presented, but ten related to the Stanton episode. Primarily, the House charged as a high crime and misdemeanor that on February 21 the President did unlawfully "issue an order in writing for the removal of Edwin M. Stanton from the office of Secretary for the Department of War... which order was unlawfully issued with intent then and there to violate the act entitled 'An act regulating the tenure of certain civil offices,' passed March 2, 1867."

In the only unrelated article, the House charged that Andrew Johnson did, on August 18, 1866, "deliver with a loud voice certain intemperate, inflammatory, and scandalous harangues, and did therein utter loud threats and bitter menaces as well against Congress as the laws of the United States duly enacted thereby." These were the impeachable words of the President, cited by the House Managers:

"We have witnessed in one Department of the Government every endeavor, as it were, to prevent the restoration of peace, harmony and union... we have seen Congress pretend to be for the Union when every step they took was to perpetuate dissolution, and make disruption permanent. We have seen every step that has been taken, instead of bringing about reconciliation and harmony, has been legislation that took the character of penalties, retaliation and revenge."

The citing of such sharp but orderly political remarks as a ground of impeachment stamped the movement for what it was—a determination to oust President Johnson because of hostility to his policies, not for any impeachable misconduct.

Notable among the seven House Managers were General Benjamin F. Butler of Massachusetts, a famous orator who was embroiled in controversy throughout his life; John A. Bingham of Ohio, leading drafter and congressional expositor of the Fourteenth Amendment; George S. Boutwell of Massachusetts, later Secretary of the Treasury under President Grant; and Thaddeus Stevens. They were armed with a brief on impeachment precedents furnished by Representative William Lawrence of Ohio.

President Johnson's quintet of legal defenders included some of the outstanding lawyers of the United States. Henry Stanbury resigned as Attorney General to head the group, but illness disabled him except for the opening and closing addresses to the Senate. Benjamin R. Curtis had been appointed to the Supreme Court in 1851 at the age of forty-one, but had resigned six years later in protest against the Dred Scott decision, from which he and one other justice dissented. William M. Evarts, a recognized leader of the American bar for several decades, was also a diplomat without office: President Lincoln had sent him twice to England to dissuade the British government from aiding the Confederate navy. W. S. Groesbeck and Thomas A. R. Nelson completed the team.

The trial commenced in mid-March, three weeks after the impeachment, with General Butler opening for the Managers. He began adroitly by showing familiarity with and at the same time misrepresenting the famous trial of Warren Hastings in England:

"May it not have been that the trial then in progress [in 1787] was the determining cause why the framers of the Constitution left the description of offenses because of which the conduct of an officer might be inquired of to be defined by the laws and usages of Parliament as found in the precedents of the mother country, with which our fathers were as familiar as we are with our own?"

This question by its implications carried multiple distortions, both of the Hastings case itself and of the deductions to be drawn from it—distortions magnified by Hastings's acquittal. The seven-year Hastings trial was indeed cited by George Mason, but only as a reason for extending the grounds of impeachment beyond treason and bribery. Instead of supporting Butler's implication that the case carried impeachment beyond criminal misfeasance in office, the accusatory articles against Hastings piled crime on crime.

More subtle and even more misleading was Butler's equation of "high crimes and misdemeanors" with "the usages of Parliament as found in the precedents of the mother country." Those precedents included prosecutions forced on Parliament by omnipotent kings, prosecutions initiated by Parliaments snatching omnipotence away from the monarchs, and prosecutions that were mere outbursts of unreasoning passion. They reflected the violations more than the inclusions of the common law.

Later in the Johnson trial defense counsel Evarts exposed this perversion of history by showing that in the Hastings trial itself, British precedents on impeachment were repudiated. Lord Loughborough, said Evarts, sought "to demonstrate that the ordinary rules of proceedings in criminal cases did not apply to parliamentary impeachments, which could not be shackled by the forms observed in the Courts below" (that is, below the House of Lords). Evarts quoted the words by which Lord Thurlow overthrew this contention:

"My lords, with respect to the laws and usage of Parliament, I utterly disclaim all knowledge of such laws. It has no existence. True it is, in times of despotism and popular fury, when to impeach an individual was to crush him by the strong hand of power, of tumult, or of violence, the laws and usage of Parliament were quoted in order to justify the most iniquitous or atrocious acts. But in these days of light and constitutional government, I trust that no man will be tried except by the laws of the land, a system admirably calculated to protect innocence and to punish crime."

Thus whenever a representative or senator in Congress cites British precedent to justify going beyond the Constitution, he invokes "despotism and popular fury . . . the strong hand of power, of tumult, or of violence." Was that what the framers intended when they limited the grounds of impeachment to "high crimes and misdemeanors"?

General Butler, of course, ignored Lord Thurlow's denunciation of historic British practices that destroyed them as valid precedents. Instead, he sought to buttress his position by extended examples, contained in the brief submitted by Representative Lawrence, which he placed at this point in the record of the trial.

Lawrence cited case after case, from Hallam and other legal historians, of great lords done to death by impeachment—and then undermined his cause by placing them in Hallam's context of history, which supported Thurlow. First employed by Edward III in 1376, the impeachment process was set to one side by Tudor kings who found bills of attainder more convenient. The House of Stuart brought impeachment back. Between 1620 and 1688, it was employed forty times by Stuart kings or by a Parliament in rebellion against those kings. Attainder and impeachment as described by Hallam (as well as by historian Thomas Erskine May) were used interchangeably to destroy political offenders, and almost by the same process. Impeachment permitted a defense before the House of Lords; attainder had no standards.

It is impossible that the framers of our Constitution, knowing this history, would have prohibited bills of attainder and yet allowed the same forbidden results, actuated by the same passion, to be put into effect by a power of impeachment modeled by silent implication on British precedent. The debate in the Constitutional Convention, the wording of the impeachment clauses, the wholehearted devotion of the framers to liberty and justice, combine to forbid such a thought. In portentous contrast, the spirit of attainder ran through the trial of President Andrew Johnson. With truth, candor and impassioned rhetoric, Senator Sumner revealed the political motive for the prosecution:

"Andrew Johnson is the impersonation of the tyrannical Slave Power. In him it lives again . . . and he gathers about him . . . partisans of slavery North and South. . . . With the President at their head, they are now entrenched in the Executive Mansion. Not to dislodge them is to leave the country a prey to one of the most hateful tyrannies of history."

It was in this manner that the entire prosecution of President Johnson was conducted—in the spirit and actuality of a bill of attainder, with Johnson's counsel calling it by that name. It was brought in the form of impeachment solely because the Constitution prohibits bills of attainder. The House Managers thinly cloaked this purpose in their interpretations of the impeachment power.

General Butler put heavy reliance on Madison's remark in supporting the exclusive constitutional power of a President to remove his appointees from office, that if he made "wanton removal of meritorious officers," he would be subject to impeachment. Butler omitted the qualifying statement that the motive for such an action "must be that he may fill the place with an unworthy creature of his own." The Manager saw clear proof in this that the Senate had power to convict President Johnson for removing Secretary Stanton, regardless of the validity or invalidity of the Tenure of Office Act.

Such an argument revealed at one stroke the twin errors of Madison's statement and of the deduction Butler drew from it. In August 1867, without removing Stanton as Secretary of War, President Johnson nominated General Ulysses S. Grant to that position. The Senate, as was expected, defeated confirmation. The stage was set for Grant to seek the post by court action, thus testing the constitutionality of the Tenure of Office Act. However, the General refused to make the challenge. The Secretaryship of War was then offered to General William T. Sherman, who declined; political war was a bit too hellish. The President then removed Stanton and nominated Lieutenant General Lorenzo Thomas. None of these three men could be termed an "unworthy creature." Manager Bingham disclaimed criticism of Thomas; the crime was removal of Stanton. Thus by Madison's own terms, the President's removal of "meritorious" Secretary Stanton offered no constitutional ground of impeachment. Butler's misuse of Madison's words for such a purpose revealed the fallacy in Madison's argument, which he had thought up on the moment to score a point in polemics. General Butler summed up the Managers' position by quoting and concurring in these words of Representative Lawrence:

"We define therefore an impeachable high crime or misdemeanor to be one in its nature or consequences subversive of some fundamental or essential principle of government or highly prejudicial to the public interest, and this may consist of a violation of the Constitution, of law, of an official oath, or of duty, by an act committed or omitted, or, without violating a positive law, by the abuse of discretionary powers from improper motives, or for any improper purpose."

In other words, an impeachable misdemeanor was any action which the Senate regarded as improper, and which in its opinion proceeded from an improper motive. Butler turned to England for support:

"It is but common learning that in the English precedents the words 'high crimes and misdemeanors' are universally used; but any malversation in office highly prejudicial to the public interest, or subversive of some fundamental principle of government by which the safety of a people may be in danger, is a high crime against the nation, as the term is used in parliamentary law."

This obsolete British definition (done to death by Lord Thurlow) was the same as saying that President Johnson's 1866 speech criticizing Congress, and his transfer of the War Department from Edwin M. Stanton to Lorenzo Thomas, were impeachable either as "highly prejudicial to the nation" or as dangerous to the safety of its people. The Butler-Lawrence interpretation of "high crimes and misdemeanors" can be boiled down to the single word "maladministration," which the framers refused to put in the Constitution as a ground of impeachment. House Manager Bingham heightened this perversion of the framers' intentions by saying that in determining such grounds, the Senate was "a law unto itself"—a remark that gave the trial the precise quality of a bill of attainder.

Counsel for President Johnson referred to the 1789 debate in Congress on the President's power to remove officers, proving conclusively from Madison's speech (and acts of Congress based on it) that this power was recognized to lie in the President alone, unalterable by legislative action. General Butler conceded that if Johnson, instead of sending "his defiant message to the Senate," had said he was acting to test the constitutionality of the Tenure of Office Act, the House of Representatives might not have impeached him. So, said defense counsel Benjamin Curtis, the ground of impeachment was "not the removal of Mr. Stanton but the manner in which the President communicated the fact of that removal to the Senate after it was made."

Logically, this exchange of remarks, combined with the invalidity of the Tenure of Office Act, demolished the only charge against President Johnson that could fall within the definition of a "high misdemeanor." Curtis then proceeded to his main argument (which was a bit too broad, as it excluded all violations of state laws):

"My first position is, that when the Constitution speaks of 'treason, bribery, and other high crimes and misdemeanors,' it refers to, and includes, only high criminal offenses against the United States, made so by some law of the United States existing when the acts complained of were done, and I say that this is plainly to be inferred from each and every provision of the Constitution on the subject of impeachment."

He quoted the various clauses referring to "offenses," "conviction," "crimes," etc., in connection with impeachment, and said that the argument on this point was "vastly strengthened" by the Constitution's direct prohibition of bills of attainder and *ex post facto* laws. Curtis said:

"What is a bill of attainder? It is a case before the Parliament where the Parliament make the law for the facts they find. Each legislator (for it is in their legislative capacity they act, not in a judicial one) is, to use the phrase of the honorable Managers [Bingham], 'a law unto himself'; and according to his discretion, his views of what is politic or proper under the circumstances, he frames a law to meet the case and enacts it or votes in its enactment."

Still dwelling on Bingham's maladroit remark, Curtis went on:

"According to the doctrine now advanced bills of attainder are not prohibited by this Constitution; they are only slightly modified. It is only necessary for the House of Representatives by a majority to vote an impeachment and send up certain articles and have two thirds of this body vote in favor of conviction, and there is an attainder; and it is done by the same process and depends on identically the same principles as a bill of attainder in the English Parliament. The individual wills of the legislators, instead of the conscientious discharge of the duty of the judges, settle the result.

"I submit, then, Senators, that this view of the honorable Managers of the duties and powers of this body cannot be maintained."

In conclusion, Curtis turned to the article impeaching the President for slander of Congress in a speech. This, he said, was not only an attempt to set up an *ex post facto* law where none existed "prior to the act to punish the act"; it was a case where Congress was expressly prohibited, by the First Amendment, from making any law whatever, even to punish subsequent speech.

What was this law on freedom of speech designed to be? Was it to be, "as the honorable Managers seem to think it should be, the sense of propriety of each Senator appealed to"? That was "the same freedom of speech, Senators, in consequence of which thousands of men went to the scaffold under the Tudors and the Stuarts.... Is that the freedom of speech intended to be secured by our Constitution?"

This trial, Curtis predicted, would live in history as the most conspicuous American example either of justice or of injustice. It would (to paraphrase Edmund Burke) either exemplify that justice which is the standing policy of all civilized states, or it would produce "that injustice which is sure to be discovered, and which makes even the wise man mad, and which, in the fixed and immutable order of God's providence, is certain to return to plague its inventors."

The House Managers continued to provide defense with openings to call the impeachment a bill of attainder. Later in the trial, defense counsel Groesbeck put some of these remarks together. Without naming the Managers, he said that one of them (it was Butler) had stated that in sitting as a court of impeachment, the Senate "knew no law, either statute or common, and consulted no precedents save those of parliamentary bodies." Another (it was Bingham) had claimed that the Senate "was a law unto itself; in a word, that its jurisdiction was without bounds; that it may impeach for any cause, and there is no appeal from its judgment." A third (John A. Logan) said much the same as Bingham. And it was argued by Butler that when the words "high crimes and misdemeanors" were used, "they are without signification and intended

merely to give solemnity to the charge." Under these interpretations "everything this tribunal may deem impeachable becomes so at once." Said Groesbeck, pursuing the issue of attainder:

"To sustain this extraordinary view of the character of this tribunal we have been referred to English precedents, and especially to early English precedents, when, according to my recollection, impeachment and attainder and bills of pains and penalties labored together in the work of murder and confiscation."

The Constitution, Groesbeck declared, placed limitations on the executive and judicial departments, and he had supposed the legislative was also limited. But according to the argument made in this trial, it was otherwise. The Senate "has in its service and at its command an institution [impeachment] that is above all law and acknowledges no restraint; an institution worse than a court martial, in that it has a broader and more dangerous jurisdiction."

The question of attainder was sharpened by a vitriolic attack on Johnson by Thaddeus Stevens, who asserted that the Senate had rendered final judgment against Johnson even before the House impeached him. It did so, he declared, in a resolution adopted on February 21 (three days before the House acted) declaring that the President had no power to remove Stanton. By that vote, Stevens maintained, the senators were committed to find him guilty. Exclaimed the fiery Radical Republican leader:

"And now this offspring of assassination turns upon the Senate... and bids them defiance. How can he escape the just vengeance of the law? Wretched man, standing at bay, surrounded by a cordon of living men, each with the ax of an executioner uplifted for his just punishment!"

Defense counsel Evarts seized on this as one more proof that the Managers were seeking to pass a bill of attainder. If, said he, judgment was rendered in that vote of February 21, "then you are here standing about the scaffold of execution." If so, of what service was the constitutional prohibition of bills of attainder? He asked, as had a fellow counsel:

"What is a bill of attainder; what is a bill of pains and penalties?... It is a proceeding by the legislature as a legislature to enact crime, sentence, punishment all in one.... [If you follow the Stevens rule] you are enacting a bill of pains and penalties upon the simple form that a majority of the House and two thirds of the Senate must concur, and the Constitution and the wisdom of our ancestors all pass for naught."

To emphasize the element of attainder, Evarts quoted the admission of House Manager Buchanan in the case of Judge Peck that to convict the judge of impeachable official misbehavior, "we are bound to prove that the respondent has violated the Constitution or some known law of the land." He endorsed the argument of his colleague Curtis, "upon the strict constitutional necessity, under the clause prohibiting *ex post facto* laws, and under the clause prohibiting bills of attainder," that articles of impeachment be confined to "what is crime against the Constitution and crime against the law."

Here was the clearest statement that to go beyond crimes against the laws and Constitution and give sanction to general ideas of misbehavior was to convert impeachment into both a bill of attainder and an *ex post facto* law. If the case of Warren Hastings was to be used as a guide, Evarts declared, the standard of impeachable misconduct must meet the specifications laid down by Edmund Burke as manager of the Hastings trial. He quoted Burke's opening address to the House of Lords:

"We know, as we are to be served by men, that the persons who serve us must be tried as men, and with a very large allowance indeed to human infirmity and human error. This, my lords, we knew, and we weighed before we came before you. But the crimes which we charge in these articles are not lapses, defects, errors of common human frailty, which, as we know, and feel, we can allow for. We charge this offender with no crimes that have not arisen from passions which it is criminal to harbor; with no offenses that have not their root in avarice, rapacity, pride, insolence, ferocity, treachery, cruelty, malignity of temper; in short, in nothing that does not argue a total extinction of all moral principle, that does not manifest an inveterate blackness, dyed ingrain with malice, vitiated, corrupted, gangrened to the very core."

Evarts could have carried his case further. For at the close of that seven years' trial the Lords, passing on Burke's catalog of heinous accusations, found Hastings not guilty. They found that his conduct consisted, not of crimes in office, but of errors of judgment in performance of his duties as governor general of India. For these he could not properly be impeached. Thus prosecution and defense, in combination, narrowed the grounds of impeachment permissible under British precedents. Both sides cast aside the Tudor-Stuart concept of impeachment. The British reform went further: Public opinion in and out of Parliament discarded the entire institution of impeachment. Except for one trivial case a few years later, no impeachment has taken place in Great Britain from 1786 to the present. But members of Congress claim that the framers, without saying so, embodied British concepts of impeachment in the Constitution, and cite as their only evidence the fact that the Constitution was written during the Hastings impeachment—which put an end to the British system.

Evarts's quotation from Burke brought to a climax the fundamental defense of President Johnson: that the articles of impeachment brought against him constituted a bill of attainder. The argument was answered by total silence. Not once was the word "attainder" spoken by any House Manager, nor did any touch on the concept of attainder. Any attempt at rebuttal would have brought the issue fully before the Senate, and the weakness of the Managers' denials would have given their arguments a hollow ring. Even the admission that grounds of argument on attainder existed might have given a new aspect to the trial, producing in some senatorial minds an unwillingness to cast a vote for an unconstitutional conviction. Indeed, the one-sided discussion had that tendency, reducing the case against Johnson to two narrowly technical points— denial by the Managers that when the President removed Secretary Stanton, he intended to test the constitutionality of the Tenure of Office Act, and the question of criminal libel in Johnson's criticism of Congress.

The defense met the first of these arguments by putting General William Tecumseh Sherman on the stand. He testified that when the post of Secretary of War was being offered to him, the President said: "If we can bring the case to the courts it would not stand half an hour." Pursuing that line, defense counsel Nelson argued that the Tenure of Office Act was unconstitutional, but that in any case impeachment was unwarranted because "the President acted from laudable and honest motives, and is not, therefor[e] guilty of any crime or misdemeanor."

Manager Bingham brought the case against President Johnson to a close by defining freedom of speech in terms of the Sedition Act of 1798. This he linked with an 1806 set of Army regulations by Congress in which military officers and soldiers were made subject to court-martial for using "contemptuous or disrespectful words" against the President, Vice President, or Congress. If those two laws are constitutional, declared Bingham, seditious utterances "are indictable as misdemeanors, whether made by the President or anybody else, and especially in an official charged with the execution of the laws." Indeed, he continued, seditious utterances by an executive officer always were indictable at common law:

"But, say counsel, this is his guaranteed right under the Constitution. The freedom of speech, says the gentleman, is not to be restricted by a law of Congress. How is that answered by this act of 1806, which subjects every soldier in your Army and every officer in your Army to court-martial for using disrespectful words of the President or of the Congress or of his superior officers? The freedom of speech guaranteed by the Constitution to all the people of the United States, is that freedom of speech which respects, first, the right of the nation itself, which respects the supremacy of the nation's laws, and which finally respects the rights of every citizen of the Republic."

Thus an unconstitutional Sedition Act (so pronounced by the Supreme Court more than a century after it expired), and a military regulation laid down to maintain discipline in the Army, were to measure the right of the President of the United States to criticize Congress. What this meant was that the First Amendment was worthless without the enforcing strength of the Supreme Court. On the constitutional level, impeachment trials throughout American history have been prosecuted on the legal plane occupied by the Sedition Act of 1798. In every instance where the drive for impeachment has been politically motivated—the prosecutions of Judge Pickering, Justice Chase, and President Johnson, and the abortive moves against Justices Field and Douglas—the same passions that produced the Sedition Act of 1798 have inflamed and degraded the driving forces in Congress.

The ordeal of President Andrew Johnson ended on May 16, 1868, when, after a two-month trial, the Senate voted on the eleven articles of impeachment. The vote was the same on each: guilty, 35; not guilty, 19—only one short of the needed two thirds. Before the balloting began, Senator Lyman Trumbull of Illinois presented a written opinion in which he said:

"In view of the consequences likely to flow from this day's proceedings, should they result in conviction on what my judgment tells me are insufficient charges and proofs, I tremble for the future of my country."

The ferocity of the prosecution and closeness of the verdict combined to establish the Johnson impeachment as a menacing portent of the future. The failure of this case to serve as a permanent warning against perversion of the Constitution is more ominous still. Nevertheless, if the cogent and powerful arguments of the defense influenced a single senator—and they probably converted several—they prevented the deepest tragedy in American political history.

NO

Harold M. Hyman

HOW TO SET THE LAW IN MOTION

The Tenure law [Tenure of Office Act] provided that persons appointed by the President and confirmed by the Senate should not be removed without Senate concurrence. The President could suspend an official if the Senate was not in session, but must report the suspension to the Senate on its reassembly and ask its consent. Republican congressmen differed on the question of whether the Tenure bill embraced Lincoln holdovers such as War Secretary [Edwin M.] Stanton in Johnson's cabinet. But enough sentiment obtained to lock Stanton in to comfort those in and out of the Army who feared the quality of a Johnson-appointed successor, a pleasure increased by provisions in the Army Appropriations Act requiring Congress's assent to transfer orders directed to the commanding general from the President.

In unhappy chronological conjunction, ambitions and events transformed efforts during March 1867 at stability into nervous near crisis. All through spring and summer, the President and Attorney General Henry Stanbery interpreted the Reconstruction statutes to hamstring commanding generals. A central issue was a general's authority to remove from office provisional state civil officials who failed to enforce state and local laws when blacks and Unionists were the victims of illegality and violence. In late April, Mississippi resorted to the Supreme Court for a permanent injunction directed against the President and the Army commander in that state, to forbid enforcement there of the allegedly unconstitutional Reconstruction statute. But even Johnson and his Attorney General acknowledged that Mississippi's request was unprecedented and outrageous; no court could enjoin a President. Congress had required the President to execute a law constitutionally enacted with respect to procedure, Stanbery told the court. The Mississippi petition, without legal or historical merit, received no support in the Court.

Almost simultaneously, Georgia sought injunctions against enforcement of the Reconstruction statute in the state, naming the Secretary of War and generals from Grant down. Georgia's counsel stressed Congress's alleged obliteration of the state. Responding for the defendants, Stanbery insisted that the Court's jurisdiction ended at political matters, and the Congress's decision

From Harold M. Hyman, *A More Perfect Union: The Impact of the Civil War and Reconstruction on the Constitution* (Alfred A. Knopf, 1973). Copyright © 1973 by Harold M. Hyman. Reprinted by permission of Alfred A. Knopf, Inc. Notes omitted.

concerning Georgia's status was political. Accepting Stanbery's argument on May 13, 1867, the Supreme Court dismissed both petitions.

By denying the Georgia and Mississippi petitions, the Court avoided for its own convenience direct confrontation with Congress concerning the Reconstruction law's constitutionality. The jurists' grounds were historical and jurisprudentially proper; plaintiffs' counsel had misfired.

Congress's Reconstruction authorizations to the Army appeared to have passed all foreseeable constitutional and political obstacles that the provisional southern states and the President could raise and the Supreme Court would entertain. Despite partisan contrary assertion, no judicial decision yet issued questioned directly the Reconstruction law or the Army's derivative policies in the South. In substantial confidence and good humor, therefore, on July 19 Congress passed over Johnson's veto another supplement to the Reconstruction law. Directly contradicting the Attorney General's hamstringing efforts, it authorized Army commanders to follow Grant's precedent instructions and to remove provisional state and local officials who failed equally to enforce their states' civil and criminal statues. Retrospectively, along with the McCardle case and the impeachment, this amendment forms the context in which Reconstruction's beginning ended and in which Reconstruction's end began.

Under Congress's authorization and Grant's orders most Reconstruction commanders became involved in numerous details of life and labor including criminal-law enforcement, professional licensing, municipal police, and debt collections, without which more decent political action, racially defined, was impossible, according to General [Daniel] Sickles in South Carolina. Sickles suspended execution of debt-collection judgments and debt-imprisonment sentences issuing from all courts, including national tribunals. He explained to Grant that under the 1789 Judiciary Act federal courts were required to employ the procedures of forum state courts. But it was precisely to reform state procedures that Congress had ordered the Army to Reconstruction duty. Therefore Sickles had suspended existing state laws and derivative judgments that in his view were unfair to citizens. But it was all fruitless if national courts, employing state procedures, substantively reinforced that state's unjust processes and results. Federal courts obeyed Congress's 1789 order to use state procedures. Should not national judges obey also Congress's 1867 laws that the southern states' constitutions, laws, and procedures become at least as decent as those of other states?

Though Grant and Stanton sustained Sickles and other generals, it was clear that Reconstruction matters had gone awry. Even [Supreme Court Chief Justice Salmon P.] Chase felt that however worthy the goals, Congress had given the Army too much latitude and had upset both power separation and national-state relationships. Whether Chase objected more to Sickles's intrusions into state and local commercial tax, debt, labor, and criminal matters, or into inferior national court procedures, is not known. But he believed fervently in the maintenance of state governments as the base of the federal union. Chase revered the national judiciary as the pacific links for Union, and he saw nothing amiss in the tradition that national judges use applicable state pleadings and procedures. The Army as servants for Congress and the national courts was one matter; the Army as master of federal court procedures was quite another.

Conservatives sniffed the shifting wind and discerned opportunity in the Army's intrusion into property and judicial matters. Lawyers and southern politicos picked up the theme that Reconstruction laws were unconstitutional not only as infringements on civil liberties but also as deprivations of property rights. "The [South's] only gleam of hope for the Constitution then was in the Supreme Court," recalled Alabama's conservative constitutionalist, Hilary Herbert.

But appropriate litigation in the sense of dramatic, politically compelling qualities did not come up every day. A Louisiana suit remained obscure in state courts even though it challenged the Army's power to set aside interest payments on a municipality's debt and despite plaintiff's argument that the suspension deprived good-faith bondholders of property in a manner the national Supreme Court had declared unconstitutional in the Gelpcke v. Dubuque decision.

Nationwide political attention turned instead to William McCardle's suit. He was a Vicksburg newspaper publisher whose editorials encouraged violent resistance to racial-equality provisions of the Reconstruction statutes. Arrested and awaiting a military commission trial, McCardle sought release by means of a habeas corpus writ from the United States Circuit Court. Its judge denied his petition and remanded him to Army jurisdiction.

Responding sensitively to growing civil-law concerns among lawyers, Jeremiah Black and David Dudley Field, McCardle's counsel, without abandoning the basic theme of the Reconstruction law's unconstitutionality, played down civil-military aspects. In order to get the case to the Supreme Court the appellants had to overcome the Vallandigham and Milligan precedents, which, taken together, suggested that no Supreme Court jurisdiction existed in appeals from military authority and that only wartime executive extensions of Army courts over civilians were unjustifiable. Instead McCardle's counsel seized on Congress's 1867 Habeas Corpus law and insisted that it gave adequate jurisdiction to the Supreme Court to protect McCardle.

Many elements made McCardle's case dramatic. Although the Attorney General had appeared very recently on behalf of the government and its officers in the Georgia and Mississippi injunction litigation, he refused to appear against McCardle. Grant obtained for the Army the services of Senators Lyman Trumbull and Matthew Carpenter. Only a week after denying itself competency to issue Georgia the requested injunction against the Reconstruction law, the Supreme Court accepted jurisdiction of McCardle's appeal. A decision was possible adverse to the congressional statutes now being militarily enforced. Further, events determined that judgment in McCardle's case must issue in the superheated politics of the nation's first impeachment, which in its unique way was also testing issues implicit in McCardle's case.

In short, McCardle kept the Supreme Court in the most exposed salient of Reconstruction politics. As Henry Dutton noted, McCardle's case involved the fates of the South's states and Negroes, of the President of the United States, and of the Army. Unique among the world's courts, the United States Supreme Court was to determine national policy, the destiny of races, and the quality and direction of a great society.

Aware of context and implications, the government's counsel chose to fight McCardle's appeal on his selected battlefield. Carpenter boasted confidently that in his brief he had "avoided all talk of the rights of conquest, a theme that is very unpalatable to that [Supreme] court... & placed [Congress's] right to pass the [Reconstruction] law upon entirely peace powers of the [national] government. This foundation is as solid as a rock, & if that Court decides the case upon judicial, not political, points, we have a sure thing."

Congress made a surer thing of it. Over somnambulistic Democratic resistance and a tepid presidential veto—the impeachment was under way, after all—on March 27 Congress repealed the provisions of the February 1867 law that provided it appellate jurisdiction in McCardle's case. In April the Court acquiesced and dropped consideration of McCardle's appeal.

But it dropped only that litigation. Accepting Congress's jurisdiction limitation, Chase stipulated carefully that "Counsel [for McCardle] seems to have supposed, if effect be given to the repealing act... that the whole appellate power of the court in cases in *habeas corpus* is denied. But this is an error." Instead McCardle meant only that quite constitutionally, Congress determined the Court's jurisdiction, which it elected now partially to excise.

While McCardle's appeal made its way to Washington, the President asserted his alleged right to independent control over the Army, i.e., to issue orders contrary to Congress's Reconstruction purposes. In August 1867, complying with the Tenure law, he suspended Stanton and named Grant ad interim successor. The President relieved from command Sickles and other generals who had actively enforced Congress's Reconstruction statutes. Wearing two hats as commanding general and temporary War Secretary, Grant saw to it that the Army kept in motion Congress's basic Reconstruction directives involving redistricting, voter registration, and new state constitutional conventions. In December when Congress reassembled, as the Tenure law required, the President reported Stanton's suspension to the Senate. It refused approval. The President refused in turn to readmit Stanton to the Cabinet. Grant turned the War Office keys back to Stanton, who occupied the Secretaryship in defiance of the President.

Unable to reverse Reconstruction through appeals to voters, to standpat and retrograde congressmen, or to courts, the President, defying a national law, reached out for control over one of Reconstruction's two essential instruments, the Army. Therefore, despite the clear political hazards and ambiguities involved in the unprecedented move, the Republican center decided for impeachment, a wholly constitutional procedure.

Johnson's obstructive replacements of Reconstruction generals and rejection of Stanton were last straws calling impeachment into action.... Laws on confiscation, test oaths, Freedmen's Bureau courts, Civil Rights, and Military Reconstruction had suffered Johnson's nonenforcements, malforming interpretations, or outright obstructions. Yet his piecemeal impediments had kept impeachment only a minority dream. Fall elections in 1867 and a worrisome business recession had disposed many Republicans against further political unsettlements and made impeachment the more unlikely despite the President's now-open appointments of conservative generals to commands in the South. Nevertheless, in early 1868 Johnson managed to transform the Republicans' search for stability into an impeachment consensus.

It was easier to decide on the need for the act than to know confidently how to proceed or to anticipate the consequences of success. Since 1789 impeachments had been whistled up sporadically for Presidents, but never came to action. A very small number of lesser official fry had been impeached.

The Republican decision to impeach Johnson was hardly an expression of partisan contempt for the Presidency, as distinguished from the incumbent. M. L. Benedict, author of the best inquiry into the subject, concludes that the impeachment grew from Republicans' incapacity to be legislative despots or to conceive of Military Reconstruction without the Army's Commander-in-Chief commanding. In Benedict's judgment, "Historians should view the... impeachment for what it was,... one of the great legal cases of history in which American politicians demonstrated the strength of the nation's... institutions by attempting to... give a political officer a full and fair trial in a time of political crisis."

This moral victory would have been impossible had the Constitution's sparse impeachment clause failed to work. Impeachment became another instance in the Civil War and Reconstruction when politicians and legal scholars reviewed history in order for the first time actually to apply a dormant part of the Constitution.

Fortunately for congressmen a useful literature was available by early 1868 as a result of abortive efforts at impeachment in 1867. In this literature, attitudes about the law and politics of impeachment—and impeachment mixed characteristics of a trial at law and of a political contest—were sharply variant. A narrow view, insisted on throughout the trial by Democrats and conservative Republicans, was that English and American precedents applied which allowed impeachment of an official only if he had committed an indictable criminal act. The broad view, taken up by Republicans, insisted that English precedents were not wholly applicable. There the House of Lords could punish as well as try any offender, including officials. Here Congress could only remove officials. Therefore American precedents failed to sustain a need for indictable crime as a reason for removal.

History leans strongly toward the broad Republican position. "That an impeached official can be tried in a criminal court after his trial on impeachment does not imply [that] only those who can be tried in a criminal court can be impeached," Benedict concluded. "It means, rather, that where an officer is impeached for an indictable offense, the impeachment does not preclude a later indictment." The Constitution's framers and ratifiers had themselves carefully sidestepped their own double-jeopardy, jury-trial, and pardon provisions when dealing with impeachments, envisaging instead a special political process set to lawlike procedures.

Perhaps any strictly legalistic analyses would have assumed the Constitution's creators. As John Norton Pomeroy noted just before the Johnson impeachment got under way, the men of 1787 aimed actually to check unpredictable future power abuses at the highest political level, where discretion had to exist, else free government could not live. Therefore the framers wrote into the Constitution a brooding impeachment threat rather than a precise weapon.

Impeachment's adversary features gave the President's counsel ample scope to develop the narrow tradition that an indictable offense was necessary for conviction, that the Tenure law did not cover Stanton, that the President had equal right with Congress to determine if a law was unconstitutional, and that by violating the disputed law the President aimed at a court test. These lawyerlike arguments-in-the-alternative well suited the substantively political yet procedurally legal contours of the impeachment proceeding. Concerning Stanton's amenability to the Tenure law, Benedict's careful analysis convinces that by the final vote on its passage congressmen had "concluded [that] the bill protected Stanton after all," and that Johnson's retention of Stanton in the Cabinet "was... a virtual reappointment" acquiring tenured status. On the matter of the President testing a law he thinks is unconstitutional by violating it, no evidence exists that Johnson actually tried for a court test. Benedict properly raises the derivative query, what if after violation a court or the Congress finds the law constitutional? As a defense, the President's argument raised endless abysses for the survival potential of American government.

This evaluation of the President's scattergun points suggests a need to reevaluate also the Republicans' omnibus accusations against him. They too were equivalents to a lawyer's arguments-in-the-alternative aimed to sweep as wide horizons as possible. In terms of Republican intraparty factionalism in the House the impeachment articles sought to accommodate conservative and centrist waverers whose goals were won with the President's mark-time response to impeachment, and who therefore felt little or no compulsion to proceed on the unmarked road to conviction.

Mixtures of politics and law featured also the Senate's maneuvers in committee and on the floor concerning rules of procedure for the impeachment trial. If the Senate proclaimed itself a court then the presiding officer stipulated in the Constitution, the Chief Justice of the United States, could "vote" as well as interpret points of evidence and law. But if the Senate retained its noncourt character, the Chief Justice could not claim a vote. Deciding that the Senate was not a court, senators determined also that they had the power to overturn Chase's rulings on disputed questions of law and evidence.

But senators' efforts not to be bound by Chase's unpredictable rulings on law collapsed in the trial's first days. As Chase administered oaths to senators to do impartial justice, Democrats insisted that Ben Wade should not sit, since he would succeed Johnson if the President were removed. Chase ruled that Wade should sit, since the Senate was a court and his status as president of the Senate was irrelevant. The Chief Justice implicitly resolved in his own favor the matter of his right to vote. It all meant that the trial would proceed far more slowly than Republicans wished. The conservatives won time for reaction to set in.

In constitutional terms, Edward S. Corwin concluded, "the impeachers had the better of the argument for all but the most urgent situations." And there was the heart of the matter. For conviction of Johnson involved the nation's most urgent situations, ranging from the unhappy prospects of Wade as President supporting agrarian monetary and tariff heresies, of continuing racial instability southward, of Negro suffrage issues in northern states, and of political corruption everywhere. Republican centrists impeached the President for refusing to execute their statutes. If the impeachment swerved his course, conviction became unnecessary.

While the trial was on Johnson made clear his intention to name a moderate general to be Secretary of War; forwarded to the Senate the Reconstruction constitutions of Arkansas and South Carolina, created by terms of Congress's Reconstruction laws which he said were unconstitutional, including ratification of the detested Fourteenth Amendment and provisions for blacks' voting; and ceased obstructing the progress of congressional Reconstruction in other provisional states by devious interpretations of the laws or other overt means. Politically, the seven recusant Republican senators who voted not to convict Johnson merely affirmed impeachment's victory. Little wonder that contrary to tradition, they did not suffer disastrously at the hands of their constituents or party. Little wonder also that history is redressing opinion concerning the senators who voted finally and unavailingly to convict. They were, Benedict concludes, "motivated by the same desire for impartial justice [or lack of it] that historians and partisans ascribed only to the recusants."

Between die-hard Democrats convinced of the need to acquit the President and Radical Republicans determined to convict him, senators in the center wrestled to come to decision on ambiguous technical points. Days, weeks, and months passed in complex skirmishes on the admissibility of evidence and on such technical legal points as estoppel and the President's independent power of removal. An over-all review sustains Benedict's judgment: "After the events leading to impeachment... it is difficult to understand how anyone could have accepted at face value the moderate and reasonable interpretation Johnson's lawyers put on his activities." But because evidential disproofs of the President's inner intentions were impossible to evoke, because Republican senators wished to retain existing constitutional configurations, and because all senators wished to prevent the "Mexicanization" of the Presidency, Johnson benefited. He received the one vote needed to secure nonconviction; in mid-May the impeachment ended.

A kind of quiet returned to the Potomac. The President, smarting from his one-vote escape and his inability to win the Democratic party's 1868 nomination for a whole term, contented himself with giving a "little lecture on constitutional law" to such captive visitors as youthful political reporter Henry Adams. But the scholarly pose failed to conceal the stubborn activist. Immediately after the Senate vote, Johnson considered sliding in the detested [William] Seward as War Secretary, but, fortunately dissuaded, named conservative General John Schofield. The Senate consented "inasmuch as... Stanton has relinquished his place." Mutual ill-humor aside, the President's belated acquiescence in the impeachment's verdict indicated that at last he had learned the lesson which Republican congressmen had been trying for two years to teach him. Now Reconstruction would proceed as Congress had prescribed.

A profound psychological release, the impeachment was another of the proofs accumulating since early 1861 concerning the Constitution's tough workability. In terms of early 1868, it allowed a procedurally pacific. institutional readjustment between the nation's governing branches, badly skewed in favor of the White House by reason of the War, another item in the South's debits. It was an article of Republican faith that Reconstruction of the South also involved improved equilibrium between the nation's branches, which helps to explain Congress's devotion to increasing the federal courts' jurisdictions and powers.

Contemporaries saw impeachment's nonviolent course and constructive outcome as proof of Reconstruction's terminal phase. From 1866–68 Congress had embodied in legislation the War's "logical results," according to publicist Samuel Bowles. Insuring the protection of these results without the second civil war which reasonable men feared, the impeachment began a two-year-long wrapping-up of the War's residuals. By 1870 Ignatius Donnelly believed that "not a single issue of the many which agitated us in the past remains alive today—slavery—reconstruction—rebellion—impartial suffrage—have all perished." However coarse, his perception required a view of impeachment as a constitutional process accompanied by enormous political hazards that had rasped the nation's tight nerves. Pressures increased on politicians to close off Reconstruction. These pressures played essential roles in determining impeachment's hair-breadth outcome, the 1868 presidential elections, the Fourteenth and Fifteenth Amendments' ratifications and enforcements, and the nature of certain Supreme Court judgments.

POSTSCRIPT

Was It Wrong to Impeach Andrew Johnson?

Authority for the impeachment and potential removal from office of federal officials is established in Article 1, Sections 2 and 3 of the Constitution of the United States, which delegate sole power to impeach to the House of Representatives and the power to try all impeachments to the Senate. This power, however, has been invoked only 16 times in 200 years and only twice —in the cases of Andrew Johnson and Bill Clinton—against a president of the United States. The other cases involved a U.S. senator (William Blount, 1798), a Supreme Court justice (Samuel Chase, 1804), a Cabinet officer (William Belknap, 1876), and 11 federal judges. Less than half of the cases have resulted in conviction and removal from office.

In *Federalist,* No. 65, Alexander Hamilton noted that impeachment was an instrument to be used when individuals engaged in misconduct that abused the public trust. Recognizing the political nature of such offenses, he warned,

> The prosecution of them . . . will seldom fail to agitate the passions of the whole community, and to divide it into parties more or less friendly or inimical to the accused. In many cases it will connect itself with the pre-existing factions, and will enlist all their animosities, partialities, influence, and interest on one side or on the other; and in such cases there will always be the greatest danger that the decision will be regulated more by the comparative strength of parties, than by the real demonstrations of innocence or guilt.

Such was undoubtedly true in the case of Andrew Johnson.

For historical studies of Johnson's impeachment, see Michael Les Benedict, *The Impeachment and Trial of Andrew Johnson* (W. W. Norton, 1973) and Hans L. Trefousse, *Impeachment of a President: Andrew Johnson, the Blacks, and Reconstruction* (University of Tennessee Press, 1975). Johnson's biographers also devote attention to the impeachment. See Albert Castel, *The Presidency of Andrew Johnson* (Regents Press of Kansas, 1979); James E. Sefton, *Andrew Johnson and the Uses of Constitutional Power* (Little, Brown, 1980); and Hans L. Trefousse, *Andrew Johnson: A Biography* (W. W. Norton, 1989).

For more general studies of impeachment, see William H. Rehnquist, *Grand Inquests: The Historic Impeachments of Justice Samuel Chase and President Andrew Johnson* (William Morrow, 1992) and Michael J. Gerhardt, *The Federal Impeachment Process: A Constitutional and Historical Analysis* (Princeton University Press, 1996).

CONTRIBUTORS
TO THIS VOLUME

EDITORS

LARRY MADARAS is a professor of history and political science at Howard Community College in Columbia, Maryland. He received a B.A. from the College of the Holy Cross in 1959 and an M.A. and a Ph.D. from New York University in 1961 and 1964, respectively. He has also taught at Spring Hill College, the University of South Alabama, and the University of Maryland at College Park. He has been a Fulbright Fellow and has held two fellowships from the National Endowment for the Humanities. He is the author of dozens of journal articles and book reviews.

JAMES M. SoRELLE is chair and a professor of history at Baylor University in Waco, Texas. He received a B.A. and an M.A. from the University of Houston in 1972 and 1974, respectively, and a Ph.D. from Kent State University in 1980. In addition to introductory courses in American history, he teaches upper-level sections in African American, urban, and late-nineteenth- and twentieth-century U.S. history. His scholarly articles have appeared in *Houston Review, Southwestern Historical Quarterly,* and *Black Dixie: Essays in Afro-Texan History and Culture in Houston* (Texas A&M University Press, 1992), edited by Howard Beeth and Cary D. Wintz. He has also contributed entries to *The Handbook of Texas, The Oxford Companion to Politics of the World,* and *Encyclopedia of the Confederacy.*

STAFF

Theodore Knight   List Manager
David Brackley   Senior Developmental Editor
Juliana Poggio   Associate Developmental Editor
Rose Gleich   Administrative Assistant
Brenda S. Filley   Production Manager
Juliana Arbo   Typesetting Supervisor
Diane Barker   Proofreader
Lara Johnson   Design/Advertising Coordinator
Richard Tietjen   Publishing Systems Manager

AUTHORS

RODOLFO ACUÑA is a professor of Chicano studies at California State University, Northridge. He is credited with being active in the efforts to establish Chicano studies curricula at several universities.

BARRY J. BALLECK is an assistant professor of political science at the Georgia Southern University Center for International Studies.

IRVING H. BARTLETT is the John F. Kennedy Professor Emeritus of American Civilization at the University of Massachusetts, Boston, and the author of *The American Mind in the Mid-Nineteenth Century* (Harlan Davidson, 1982).

JOHN B. BOLES is the Allyn and Gladys Cline Professor of History at Rice University in Houston, Texas, and managing editor of *The Journal of Southern History.* His publications include *Black Southerners, 1619–1869* (University of Kentucky Press, 1983) and *The Irony of Southern Religion* (Peter Lang Publishing, 1995).

PATRICIA U. BONOMI is a professor in the Department of History at New York University in New York City. She is the author of *Colonial Dutch Studies: An Interdisciplinary Approach* (New York University Press, 1988).

IRVING BRANT was an editorial writer for several major newspapers, including the *St. Louis Star-Times* and the *Chicago Sun.* He is the author of over a dozen books, including the six-volume biography *James Madison* (Bobbs-Merrill, 1941–1961) and *The Bill of Rights: Its Origin and Meaning* (Bobbs-Merrill, 1965).

JON BUTLER is the William Robertson Coe Professor of American History at Yale University in New Haven, Connecticut. He is the author of *Awash in a Sea of Faith: Christianizing the American People* (Harvard University Press, 1990).

LOIS GREEN CARR is an adjunct professor at the University of Maryland at College Park, and she is also associated with St. Mary's City Historic Commission. She is the author of *County Government in Maryland, 1689–1709* (Garland Publishing, 1987).

DAVID A. CARSON is an associate professor of history at Buffalo State College in Buffalo, New York.

ALBERT CASTEL is a retired professor and Civil War historian. He is the author of *Decision in the West: The Atlanta Campaign of 1864* (University Press of Kansas, 1992) and *William Clarke Quantrill: His Life and Times* (General's Books, 1992).

AVERY CRAVEN is a noted historian who served as chairman of the history department at the University of Chicago. He is the author of *Repressible Conflict, 1830–1861* (AMS Press, 1989) and *Civil War in the Making, 1815–1860* (Louisiana State University Press, 1968).

RICHARD N. CURRENT is the University Distinguished Professor Emeritus at the University of North Carolina at Greensboro. He has edited and authored numerous books and articles on the Civil War and Reconstruction periods. A classic work is *The Lincoln Nobody Knows* (Greenwood Publishing Group, 1980).

CARL N. DEGLER is the Margaret Byrne Professor Emeritus of American History at Stanford University in Stanford, California. He is a member of the editorial board for the Plantation Society as well as a member and former president of the American History Society and the Organization of American Historians. His book *Neither Black Nor White: Slavery and Race Relations in Brazil and the United States* (University of Wisconsin Press, 1972) won the 1972 Pulitzer Prize for history. He is also the author of *In Search of Human Nature: The Decline and Revival of Darwinism in American Social Thought* (Oxford University Press, 1992).

JOHN MACK FARAGHER is the Arthur Unobskey Professor of American History at Yale University. He is the editor of *The American Heritage Encyclopedia of American History* (Henry Holt & Company, 1998) and the author of *Women and Men on the Overland Trail* (Yale University Press, 1980), which won the Frederick Jackson Turner Award of the Organization of American Historians.

NORMAN A. GRAEBNER is the Randolph P. Compton Professor Emeritus of History at the University of Virginia in Charlottesville, Virginia. He has held a number of other academic appointments and has received distinguished teacher awards at every campus at which he has taught. He has edited and written numerous books, articles, and texts on American history, including *Foundations of American Foreign Policy: A Realist Appraisal from Franklin to McKinley* (Scholarly Resources Press, 1985) and *Empire on the Pacific: A Study in American Continental Expansion,* 2d ed. (Regina Books, 1983).

MARY F. HANDLIN is coauthor of several books with Oscar Handlin, including *The American College and Culture: So-cialization as a Function of Higher Education* (McGraw-Hill, 1970) and *The Wealth of the American People: A History of American Affluence* (McGraw-Hill, 1975).

OSCAR HANDLIN is the Carl M. Loeb Professor of History at Harvard University in Cambridge, Massachusetts, where he has been teaching since 1941. A Pulitzer Prize–winning historian, he has written or edited more than 100 books, including *Liberty in Expansion* (Harper & Row, 1989), which he coauthored with Lilian Handlin, and *The Distortion of America,* 2d ed. (Transaction Publishers, 1996).

VINCENT HARDING is a professor of religion and social transformation at the Iliff School of Theology and has long been involved in domestic and international movements for peace and justice. He is the author of *There Is a River: The Black Struggle for Freedom in America* (Harcourt Brace, 1993) and *Hope and History: Why We Must Share the Story of the Movement* (Orbis Books, 1990).

MICHAEL F. HOLT is the Langbourne M. Williams Professor of American History at the University of Virginia in Charlottesville, Virginia. He has written a text-book called *The Political Crisis of the 1850s* (John Wiley & Sons, 1978), and he has published a collection of his many journal articles, *Political Parties and American Political Development from the Age of Jackson to the Age of Lincoln* (Louisiana State University Press, 1992).

HAROLD M. HYMAN was the William P. Hobby Professor of History at Rice University from 1968 to 1996. He has also taught at Arizona State University, the University of California, and the University of Illinois. His scholarly concerns center on U.S. constitutional and legal history and on the U.S. Civil War and Reconstruction. He is the author of many books, including *To Try Men's Souls: Loyalty Tests in American History*, which won the Sidney Hillman Award in 1960, and *A History of the Vinson and Elkins Law Firm of Houston, 1917–1997* (University of Georgia Press, 1998).

SEYMOUR MARTIN LIPSET is the Hazel Professor of Public Policy at George Mason University in Fairfax, Virginia. He is the author of *The Radical Right: A Problem for American Democracy* (Irvington, 1993).

JAMES M. McPHERSON is the Edwards Professor of American History at Princeton University in Princeton, New Jersey. His publications include *Abraham Lincoln and the Second American Revolution* (Oxford University Press, 1990) and *The Atlas of the Civil War* (Macmillan, 1994).

SANDRA L. MYERS (1933–1991), a specialist in western history and women's history, was a professor at the University of Texas at Arlington.

MARY BETH NORTON is the Mary Donlon Alger Professor of American History at Cornell University. She is the author of *Founding Mothers and Fathers: Gendered Power and the Forming of American Society* (Alfred A. Knopf, 1996) and *Liberty's Daughters: The Revolutionary Experience of American Women, 1750–1800* (Cornell University Press, 1996).

ALBERT J. RABOTEAU is the Henry W. Putnam Professor of Religion and director of the Stewart Seminars in Religion at Princeton University in Princeton, New Jersey, where he is also dean of the graduate school. His publications include *Slave Religion: The Invisible Institution in the Antebellum South* (Oxford University Press, 1978).

ROBERT V. REMINI won the D. B. Hardeman Prize for *Daniel Webster: The Man and His Time* (W. W. Norton, 1997). He has written biographies on Andrew Jackson, Henry Clay, and Martin Van Buren.

JOHN P. ROCHE (1923–1993) was the Olin Distinguished Professor of American Civilization and Foreign Affairs at the Fletcher School of Law and Diplomacy in Medford, Massachusetts, and director of the Fletcher Media Institute.

ROBERT ROYAL is the vice president and Olin Fellow in Religion and Society at the Ethics and Public Policy Center in Washington, D.C. He is the author of *1492 and All That: Political Manipulations of History* (Ethics and Public Policy Center, 1992).

KIRKPATRICK SALE is a contributing editor to *The Nation* and the author of *Rebels Against the Future: The Luddites and Their War on the Industrial Revolution: Lessons for the Computer Age* (Perseus Press, 1996).

JOEL H. SILBEY is the President White Professor of History at Cornell University in Ithaca, New York. He has written several books and many important articles on the political parties during the Civil War. He has published two major collections of articles, *The Partisan Imperative* (Oxford University Press, 1985) and *The American Political Nation, 1838–1893* (Stanford University Press, 1991).

KENNETH M. STAMPP is the Morrison Professor Emeritus of History at the University of California, Berkeley. He has written numerous books on southern history, slavery, and the Civil War, including *And the War Came: The North and the Secession Crisis, 1860–1861* (Louisiana

University Press, 1970), *The Peculiar Institution: Slavery in the Ante-Bellum South* (Vintage Books, 1989), and *America in 1857: A Nation on the Brink* (Oxford University Press, 1990). He is also the general editor of *Records of Ante-Bellum Southern Plantations from the Revolution Through the Civil War* (University Publications of America, 1985).

IAN TYRRELL is a professor of history at the University of New South Wales in Sydney, Australia.

ANTHONY F. C. WALLACE is an anthropologist whose published works include *King of the Delawares; Teedyuscung, 1700–1763* (Syracuse University Press, 1990) and *St. Clair: A Nineteenth-Century Coal Town's Experience With a Disaster-Prone Industry* (Cornell University Press, 1988).

LORENA S. WALSH is a fellow with the Colonial Williamsburg Foundation and the author of several key articles on seventeenth-century Maryland.

ALFRED F. YOUNG was a professor at Northern Illinois University in De Kalb, Illinois, before retiring. He is the author of *Dissent: Explorations in the History of American Radicalism* (Northern Illinois University Press, 1992) and coeditor, with Lawrence W. Towner and Robert W. Karrow, of *Past Imperfect: Essays on History, Libraries, and the Humanities* (University of Chicago Press, 1993).

INDEX